D1108277

THE MEDIEVAL HERITAGE
OF ELIZABETHAN TRAGEDY

THE ORIGIN OF TRAGEDY:
ADAM AND EVE ENTER THE WORLD OF SUFFERING AND DEATH

From *Boccace des Nobles Malheureux* [1506?]

The Medieval Heritage of Elizabethan Tragedy

By Willard Farnham

✛ O WORMES MEATE: O FROATH: ✛
O VANITIE: WHY ART THOV
SO INSOLENT?

BARNES & NOBLE, Inc.   •   NEW YORK
Publishers • Booksellers • Since 1874

©
FIRST PUBLISHED 1936
REPRINTED WITH CORRECTIONS 1956

Printed in Great Britain by
Lowe and Brydone (Printers) Limited, London, N.W.10
and bound at the Kemp Hall Bindery

CONTENTS

LIST OF ILLUSTRATIONS

PAGE

Preface

TRAGEDY has always taken the form of drama when it has been able to reach its fullest expression and its eminently rightful manner. A preliminary word of explanation is demanded for a book entitled *The Medieval Heritage of Elizabethan Tragedy* which offers through something like half the number of its pages a discussion of matter that has nothing directly to do with the stage.

In the ensuing chapters I have sought to follow a consistently developing tragic spirit as it found more than one specialized form of artistic and critical approach to the mystery of man's suffering on earth. The record begins, after an introduction, with an account of tragic expression apart from the stage in the medieval Europe of established Gothic art, where Gothic form of presentation for tragedy commanded almost no benefit from the examples of classic form left by the Greco-Roman culture; and it ends with an account of tragic expression on the stage in Elizabethan England—the sixteenth-century stage, except for brief consideration of mature Shakespearean tragedy—where Gothic form commanded much of that benefit, but where the Gothic spirit retained in large measure its integrity. Here and in later connections I use the term Gothic, much as we use it when we speak of Gothic architecture, to describe something that took distinctive character from the medieval creative impulse. The English stage under Elizabeth was notable among the national stages of Europe in its time by being the particular, and on the whole unapologetic, heir of the medieval stage.

It is only fitting that tragedy upon the Elizabethan stage should have accepted with the same particularity and in the same spirit a medieval heritage which was wider than the dramatic and should thus have provided the culmination of the development which I have attempted to present.

Much of that development took place within the form of story which was created by Boccaccio in his *De Casibus Virorum Illustrium* and which was carried through a long succession of transmutations over more than two centuries. Thus part of my undertaking is a critical analysis of the nondramatic tragedies written by Boccaccio and his followers. I hope that it is somewhat corrective of a common type of scorn visited upon these writers because of their moralizing and their medieval "misconception" of tragedy, and yet that it does not disregard their frequent literary failings. To consider *De Casibus* narrative as tragedy and do so unapologetically is, of course, to follow not only medieval but also Elizabethan usage, for narrative in the *De Casibus* tradition had a vested right to the name and the dignity of tragedy even so late as the seventeenth century. But it has certainly not been my intent to discuss anything and everything that was called tragedy by medieval or Elizabethan custom. It has not been part of my main purpose to discuss what is no more than sad story, or even to discuss epic story containing tragic event. As I have already intimated, I have been guided by a conception that tragic expression is a special artistic and critical approach to the mystery of man's suffering on earth; particularly I have sought to follow the critical impulse as it led to what may loosely be called choral comment upon the meaning of the tragic fact. *De Casibus* narrative receives a large share of attention in the discussion because it consciously segregates matter which is proper to tragedy, takes special shape around it, and almost invariably provides choral comment upon the nature of the world and upon destiny. Much that it does in these ways is significant preparation for tragedy on the Elizabethan stage.

What appears in this book as Chapter III is in large part what was delivered as the Charles Mills Gayley Lecture for 1933–1934 at the University of California. For permission to incorporate in Chapters X and XI a few passages from matter already published, my thanks are due to the editors of *Modern Philology* and the editors of the *University of California Publications in English*.

It is a pleasure to acknowledge the major contributions of aid and kindness which have helped to make my work possible. To Professor G. L. Kittredge, of Harvard University, I owe an inestimable debt of gratitude for learned guidance in studies basic to this study. It is a debt of long standing which has grown with the years. Professors J. S. P. Tatlock, Benjamin P. Kurtz, and Rudolph Altrocchi, of the University of California, and Mr. Cyril Bailey, Fellow of Balliol College, Oxford, have given advice wisely and generously out of their special knowledge. If I have not always been able to benefit by this advice, it is my fault assuredly, not theirs. From Professor Lily B. Campbell, of the University of California at Los Angeles, I have received much kindness; our interests in the study of Elizabethan nondramatic tragedy have been in many respects parallel. From the authorities of the British Museum, the Henry E. Huntington Library, the University of California Library, and the University of California Press I have received aid given with the truest of courtesy. And from my wife I have received an aid which has left its mark on all that I have written in these pages. w. f.

The University of California
September 29, 1935

Chapter I

GRECO-ROMAN SURRENDER
OF THE WORLD

IN A WORLD where every human effort must pass through
suffering and must wind itself into the knot of death,
all narrative and dramatic imitation of life has tragic
potentialities; but this is not to say that every narrative or
dramatic art of high cultivation must eventually segregate
and develop them. The Chinese and Sanskrit cultures, despite their wealth of artistry and despite their very real
achievements in drama especially, have never so far as we
know produced what men of the European tradition would
call full-formed tragedy. In the classic Nō drama of Japan
is an art of severely refined technique which at times can
move us as does our own tragedy and which uses certain
of the Greek methods to a highly remarkable degree, apparently by independent discovery, but even here we are apt
to find the tragic note ill sustained.[1]*

It is not sufficient for the attainment of tragic art upon
the stage that a people should dramatize worshipfully the
passions of Osiris, of Dionysus, or of Jesus; or that they
should imitate this suffering in religious ritual with the aim
of procuring material and spiritual benefits. It may be that
unsophisticated man seeks such benefits in a kind of sympathetic magic, which represents the intense dramatic struggle in nature between the abstract forces of death and life,
winter and summer, fruitfulness and barrenness, and which

---

* Superior figures refer to notes which will be found at the back of the book.

is intended thereby to aid the cyclic rebirth of the world. Again it may be that he seeks them in a dramatic dance before the tombs of his heroes, mourning the dead and by a representation of their sufferings hoping to please their souls and get protection and aid. These matters are much in dispute.[2] But however the passion-play or the tragic ritual begins, consciously artistic tragedy upon the stage does not begin until man in all seriousness brings intellectual curiosity, critical ability, and, what is paradoxical and most important, even creative pleasure to the dramatic imitation of life's destructive forces. Despite Aristotle's magnificent attempt at definition, this pleasure is mysterious and for the most part indefinable, since to take pleasure in the contemplation of pain may seem either perverse or morbid, and yet is actually neither when the contemplation is of the most profound tragedy. We may say, then, that fully developed tragedy is possible only where keen desire and high ability to understand human suffering unite with noble capacity for taking pleasure in its artistic representation. To say why the union does not more generally exist were as difficult as to anatomize the soul.

Many peoples, certainly those of China and India, have had the will and the ability to meet human suffering with the achievement of religious or philosophical wisdom, but, to our European perception, only two peoples have also purged human suffering by the creation of tragedy in the grand style. These two are, of course, the Greek and the Christian European. Through the intermediate Roman imitation of the Greek, the two great tragic arts may be joined into one art, begun with Aeschylus, in large measure forgotten in the "Dark Ages," and consciously revived with the New Learning. So we often do join them in a post-Renaissance world accustomed to make Greece our fountainhead of nobility and beauty. Yet in paying generously our debt to Greece and Rome there is real danger that we shall rob ourselves of what is rightfully ours. The European tragic genius which Shakespeare absorbed and dominated had a style and a creative afflatus of its own.

II

To record the growth before Shakespeare of a tragic temper and a manner of tragic expression in medieval Europe and Elizabethan England as I endeavor to record it in the following chapters is to be constantly reminded that the early Christian temper which later metamorphosed itself into a tragic temper was quite largely a heritage from Greece through Rome, but that the heritage was in many ways an unpromising gift from a classic world devitalized. It was frequently a heavy hand of the dead laid upon the living. Before Christian Europe could produce Shakespeare it needed to evolve slowly its own Gothic sense of tragic form and content. Before it could discover during the Renaissance that the classic culture had an inspiring tragic art which it might study with profit, it needed to experience something of the same vision out of which the earlier classic world had produced tragedy. Aid to that vision northern Christianity could not find in its cultural heritage from Rome. The gift was paid in coinage which had passed through many hands since those of Periclean Athens, which had gradually worn thin and suffered debasement, and which had become only metal of indistinct worth by the end of its Roman appropriation. At this time Greek tragedy as a creative force was dead because the vision which had brought it into being had vanished. In order to understand how this had happened we must know that tragedy, like any other art of mankind, can live and grow only so long as men have hope of making it say something new about the significance of the world—in other words, so long as they can range the matter of life in new forms that will have some understandable meaning. At the end of its domination by Rome, classic culture had in very large measure lost the idea that the immediate world of flesh and blood, whatever one might say of a transcendent otherworld, had any inherent meaning or order which men could grasp. Greek thought through centuries of creative vitality had built a chaotic world into an ordered structure, and then through centuries of decaying vitality it had grown more and more skeptical of what it had done. At last the main philosophies in the Greek tradition surrendered the world. They tended to find it a welter of unexplainable evil, and in various ways they discovered the good, the true, and the beautiful elsewhere, in realms which tragedy could not touch.

That critical spirit which, as extreme skepticism, killed Greek tragedy had in the beginning, as fruitful questioning, created it. When the tighter bonds between drama and conservative religion were broken, Greek tragic drama began its artistic development. Ritualistic or religiously commemorative drama, as we can see it among other races than the Greek, is too reverent of tradition to make creative changes in the essential matter of a story handed down from the immemorial past. It has the embryo art of the passion-play, which is often associated with some particular group of folk actors and repeated from year to year in the conservative and uncritical manner of other folk custom. It does not even know its author or authors, for its composition has been "communal" in whatever sense that much discussed word may apply to folk ballads. Lacking the individuality of sophisticated authorship, it also lacks that critical comment upon life which appears in art with the individualized artist and, though it records passion and suffering, has no more to say about them than does the ballad. At most it elaborates the record with a naïve realism. For further development a Thespis must take it away from the community or shrine to which it has hitherto been sacred and must teach it to be less conservative of ritual tradition. In Gothic Europe we have a fairly complete record of that development which took the drama from communal tradition and anonymity to individualized artistry. In Greece the record before Aeschylus has been in large part lost, but the signs of development are plain enough.

The tragic artist who appropriates the folk drama selects and arranges the matter of life, even changes radically the traditional dramatic content, in order to impress upon it his vision of significance. He, the single and separate man, is daring to shape an order in the world. The primitive tragic ritual may still be preserved uncritically among the simple folk, but the tragic artist has departed from their time-honored ways to brood and create. He may at first be reverent toward the gods and the old religion, but he has embarked upon the perilous course of reason, which looks

before and after in the divine manner of the gods themselves, and he has begun to challenge the rightness of things
as they are. His work is now a point of implication between
religion and philosophy, and in the growing secularity of
its subject-matter it may even be regarded as an early form
of biography, commemorating critically the heroic life of
suffering wherever it may be found in the racial tradition.'

When an artistic Thespis defends himself by saying that
there is no harm in speaking "lies" and acting thus "for
sport," he can expect a religiously conservative Solon to strike
the ground with his staff and answer, "If we go on praising
and honouring this kind of sport, we shall soon find it at
work in the serious affairs of life." The tragic artist is as
honestly concerned with the mystery of human suffering
as are the folk, but instead of accepting that mystery with
simple reverence he soon begins to assault it with insistent
questions "How?" and "Why?" In order to do this it is not
necessary that he introduce a chorus to comment upon the
fate of his characters nor that he make his characters comment upon their own fate, though he often does both. It is
sufficient if the creator shapes the order of events—as, indeed, his artistry will not let him escape from doing. Such
things as inevitability or irony do not lie exposed in the raw
stuff of life. They are exposed through the artist's perception and are only made plain to us when his hand has so
molded life as to bring their lines into high relief. Hence
the plot of an artistic tragedy is itself a philosophy of life
provided by the maker.

Behind and around the tragic artist lies a philosophy of
life which his people are shaping by other means of expres-

sion than art. They, too, are raising the eternal questions "How?" and "Why?" that their forefathers through fear of the gods did not dare to raise, or through faith in the gods did not need to raise. Tragedy and philosophy are both, then, plots for that stream of events which carries man and so often engulfs him. Both try to chart the currents in the stream, the one concretely and poetically, the other abstractly and rationally. Both draw vitality from a hope that their attacks upon the mystery may produce an ordered answer, may make life, including all its evil, more glorious with poetic penetration or more tolerable with understanding. For a time at least, both have a growing courage and a daring unchecked by any canker of thought that, because the mystery is infinite, man's attacks upon it are puny.

We know that the beauty which Aeschylus and Sophocles discovered in man's earnest gropings through the world's evils and the truth which Socrates and Plato sifted from falsity were esteemed by these men as more than worth their effort, yet were recognized by them as pitifully fragmentary. Paradoxically, such minds heighten our realization of life's mystery whenever their genius most searchingly exposes the meaning of some part of it. It is the greatness of these seers that they enlighten us and firmly lead us into more mighty darkness at one and the same time, that they never pretend to bound that darkness and nevertheless continue to push forward with supreme courage. They were brought forth at the high tide of vitality in Greek wisdom.

But this vitality, this full-nerved courage, so stimulating to us even after intervening centuries as we abandon ourselves to its presentation, was all too short-lived. With growing complexity came tunnels of doubt subtly undermining the old assumption that life in this world was something that man could surround and support and handle effectively, even though he could perhaps never understand it completely. Intellectual and emotional despair began to show itself. Eventually there came to the thought and art of the later classic world what Professor Gilbert Murray calls the "failure of nerve."[5] Though fearless critical temper had at first seemed not to check but actually to encourage a faith that life was essentially rational and ultimately just in its divine order, no matter how much man might have to criticize the gods or abandon some of the old religious beliefs in the questing career of his spirit, criticism had reached a point where it had become poison instead of stimulant. It had become poison not only to the old vital conviction that the world was somehow conquerable and malleable under man's hand and spirit, but poison also to the old myths used by the poet so far as they might have concrete and essential rather than abstract and decorative appeal to the souls of men, and poison finally to criticism itself, because so many of the old beliefs open to criticism had gradually been done to death.

When tragedy becomes pessimistic about the worth and meaning of man's activity in this world, there is quite obviously a limit beyond which it cannot go and still be tragedy, if we agree that tragedy should have dramatic quality even though it may depart from the form of stage presentation. The pessimistic tragic poet reaches that limit when he represents life as never justifying hope, yet ironically producing the momentary will to live and some consequent struggle. Deeper pessimism can only produce apathy which nullifies all struggle and consequently all dramatic quality, since drama without struggle is no true drama at all. Thus tragedy which goes to the extremes of pessimism tends to be merely diatribe against life and against apparently meaningless forces which overpower man. If it is still cast in the form of stage presentation, it becomes declamation by characters who do little but talk, and even the talk moves nowhere. It becomes a shell in which the seed of action has shriveled and no longer possesses creative virtue.

Though so many of the plays have been lost, Greek tragedy gives every indication of having come to its death in such futile declamation concerning the puny will of man and the hopeless evil of the world, just as Greek philosophy reached a fatal impasse by its surrender of the world as inherently and irrationally evil. Even before the death of Euripides, Greek tragedy looks toward the later age and falls away from the heroic faith of Aeschylus.

In holding the scales between humanity and destiny Aeschylus gives mankind all the validity which tragedy permits. Not many men, he would have us perceive, may overbalance destiny, but the exceptional soul may do so, even though such a one must retain ineradicable marks of agony. Orestes seems doomed by the curse which lies upon the blood of his house, a curse conceived originally in sin. This is the weight which Orestes must overbalance or be overbalanced by. It predisposes him to sin, and for this predisposition he is not responsible, but it is barely possible for him to escape the consequences of sin by a purity of motive for which he is responsible. The Orestean trilogy is there-

fore, to change the figure, a record of many attempts by the
members of a family to swim against a powerful tide of sin.
Thyestes, Atreus, Agamemnon, Aegisthus, and Clytemnestra are not pure in motive. They all turn and go with the
tide instead of breasting it, and they all add to its increasing
force by acting, in part at least, with selfish motives. Only
Orestes sins without adhesion to any but the unselfish motive, setting himself against the current instead of going
with it. With him the curse eventually loses all its power.
Thus the force of this greatest of the Aeschylean creations
lies in its affirmation of the strength of man's will. We do
not know, of course, what the poet did with the lost Prometheus plays, but we suspect that he saw here a god tri-
umphing through rebellion and suffering, as Orestes the
man had done through sin and suffering, by steadfastness
in purity of motives. It is the greatness of Aeschylus that he
has no inclination to free an Orestes easily by minimizing
the sinfulness of his action. Men like Orestes are not to be
heroic in ascetic goodness, which strives to get beyond evil
or to retire from it, but are to sin actually and fully and then
nullify the act by an unconquerable will to nobility. This
transmutation by Aeschylus of worldly evil into good is
poles apart from the surrender of the world which is later
dominant in classic thought. It is supreme evidence of the
faith which Aeschylus had in the ultimate goodness of life.

Sophocles, to whom the critical spirit has given a more
seeing eye for essential humanity and less concern with any
human ability to rise through suffering to titanic or demi-
godlike heights, never quite gives us the sense of validity in
heroic endeavor which Aeschylus conveys in the Orestean

trilogy. Oedipus and Antigone, his noblest heroic figures, yield tragedy that is much more painfully ironic than that yielded by Orestes. It is chiefly because we feel a subtle irony and an overpowering completeness in their enmeshment that we are accustomed to call Sophocles the master of plot in Greek tragedy.

When Euripides holds the balance between man and destiny, he gives man a dead weight to lift and much frailer humanity with which to lift it, though the vitality of his questioning spirit and of his faith that questions are worth posing save him from anything like despair. Hippolytus is ruined by the jealous whim of an Aphrodite to whom the larger concepts of justice are wholly foreign. His "sin" against her is chastity, which, in refusing to reproduce the flesh, may truly be what Shakespeare might call the sin against kind; but to say that Euripides based his tragedy seriously upon such a conception is to make a sophisticated skeptic into a naïve worshiper of the life force. In this world of Euripides the thing called virtue, which he pulls so low that he can represent it in a weakly sentimental Hippolytus harping on his chastity, has gone awry and can ironically crush the practicer. Medea and Jason are more willful and more active entities, but they are placed in no better position. They are caught in the necessity of hurting each other for the most selfish of motives, and they do so with hopeless inevitability. Euripides deserted the heroic for the all-too-human level of tragedy, but if he preferred to see human frailty rather than heroic sin, he saw that frailty, it must be said, with an eye of genius which his Roman emulator Seneca never possessed. He was accepted even by his contemporaries as the herald of a new and revolutionary order in tragedy who, if comment in the *Frogs* of Aristophanes is to be believed, made the sonorous grandeur of Aeschylus seem old-fashioned and who brought tragedy down to earth to be democratic, realistic, sentimental, and too often super-ficially clever. Just as we should expect, Euripides was the most popular of the old tragic writers in the later classic world.

In this later world, tragedy continued to have life on the Greek or Greco-Roman stage until well into the Christian era, but less and less was that life creative. Original trag-edies were the principal feature of the City Dionysia at Athens down to the beginning of the Christian era, and new tragedies appeared at certain other Greek cities for a century more. After A.D. 100, original creation seems almost wholly to have ceased, and for the remaining period of Greek culture under Roman political rule the old plays were revived or imitated. Thus Greek tragedy became moribund among men who first lost the genius to create it anew at their festivals in the old nobility of spirit, who then realized and confessed their failing genius as they turned more and more to revivals of their tragic masters, and who finally made classic tragedy a literature of their schools with only occasional production on the stage, as we do now with Shakespeare.

Early Roman writers such as Ennius (*ca.* 200 B.C.) and his successor Accius produced free imitations of Greek tragedy on the stage and sometimes dealt patriotically with Roman themes. It is difficult to judge their success, but there seems to have been a degree of the old vitality in their work. Later, when men like Seneca imitated the ancient art at Rome, the imitation was done with much rhetorical brilliance and little spiritual insight. Also, it was a literary exercise probably not intended for the stage and was obviously for connoisseurs, not for a general populace. In the Senecan plays, chiefly imitations of Euripides, we may see the decadent tragic art resulting logically from an extension of Euripidean irony and skepticism. Here tragedy is at the point where denial of validity in human effort kills dramatic action and leaves diatribe in its place. The lengthy speeches are fit for declaiming rather than for acting on a stage. Everywhere is a monotonous excess of talk, directed against blind chance or against gods who are utterly unreal except as they represent vague malign forces irresistibly overpowering mankind.

As classic tragedy was more and more confined to the schools its place among the populace was partly taken by pantomime. In this cheapest degradation of the tragic spirit the heroic myths were presented as spectacles before the gaping mob.[6] Tragic poetry for the actors, with its urge to the criticism and exploration of tragic forces, was an unnecessary accompaniment. Apparently before it dissolved into pantomime Greek tragedy had exhausted all the profounder variants of truth which it was capable of discovering, and had surrendered a world of mystery in which there was no more enticement for either the intellect or the spirit. By all the signs which remain to us, it had finally come to an emotional and intellectual conclusion beyond which it could say nothing new—the conclusion that man is blown hither and thither in an evil world by the winds of chance which cannot be charted, and that his choice contributes nothing significant to the outcome.

III

Three outstanding systems of Greco-Roman philosophy show the progress made in later classic thought toward this conviction that the world of the flesh, with all the striving of men therein, is a welter of unexplainable evil. They are Stoicism, revived Platonism, and Gnosticism. Hellenistic and Roman philosophy abounded in a paradoxical complexity which resists simplification, but some simplification is nevertheless necessary, for we are here concerned with a dominant temper and with a composite picture of evil which Christianity borrowed. During the centuries between the death of Christ and the triumph of Christianity, "revived Platonism was the only serious rival to Stoicism as a philosophy for religious men within the sphere of Greek culture." To these two systems of thought must be added Gnosticism if we are to have a completely logical development of the Hellenistic idea of evil, though Gnosticism was too extreme to be dominant, even in the very latest period. It was chiefly from Stoicism, Neo-Platonism, and Gnosticism (or related philosophies like Manicheism) that early Christianity acquired ready-made descriptions of the world as irrational and evil disorder. It was from their conceptions of evil combined and modified by early Christian thought that medieval tragedy and Elizabethan tragedy had to escape in order to achieve Shakespeare's profound analysis of the lines of tragedy in responsible human action.

In Stoicism the evil of the world is to be met by a good

soldier's faith that all is for the best, no matter what the captain may command, and by a philosopher's faith that evil can be reasoned away. Stoicism may be called a materialistic pantheism which refuses to separate matter and spirit and which makes the physical world, regarded as spirit-matter, into something benevolently divine, instinct with providence. Thus it provides a basis for reasoning evil out of existence. For if a benevolent God is immanent in the world, no part of it *can* be truly evil, however desperately men may view things as evil. Moreover, though God's providence may bring upon any man, for mysterious reasons, that which the world calls evil fortune, the man must remember that since he is part of the whole and hence has the divine spark, he has the same providential direction over his inner self that God has over the world, and he is free at least to control his reaction to the event. Therefore the distinction of good and evil is something which we have somehow created by our vain imaginings, and evil actually does not exist except in human opinion or *dogma*. Man is capable by his will of abolishing evil and living secure in his inner self, no matter what storms from the external world may assail his retreat. And thus paradoxically man has freedom of action. He has freedom to act wisely in accepting with good grace the truth that he has no freedom to control his worldly fortune.

In one breath Epictetus can speak of his unconstrained will (meaning his moral purpose) and of his absolute acceptance of God's will (meaning God's determination of all worldly fortune): "For my own part I would wish death to overtake me occupied with nothing but the care of my will, trying to make it calm, unhindered, unconstrained, free. I would fain be found so employed, that I may be able to say to God, 'Did I transgress Thy commands? Did I use the faculties Thou gavest me to wrong purpose? Did I ever accuse Thee? Did I ever find fault with Thy ordinance? I fell sick, when it was Thy will: so did others, but I rebelled not. I became poor when Thou didst will it; but I rejoiced in my poverty...'."[8] The Stoic was free to rebel against or accept the evils of the world. He believed that happiness lay only in accepting them, but whether he accepted or rejected, one thing was sure: they went on happening and the choice had no effect on them. Seek not, urges Epictetus in effect, to have things happen as you would choose them, but rather choose that they should happen as they do.[9]

Evil, against which the Stoic preached as an unreality, was in truth so real a thing to him that he was forever talking about it. He was so sensitive to it that he had to surround it and work a metamorphosis in it if he was to have any peace of mind. He closed his hand lovingly upon the nettles of the world and thanked God for their sting, dwelling upon his hurts in fascination. Marcus Aurelius uses strong and even revolting terms to characterize the miseries of life, and Epictetus, for all his staunchly optimistic faith that all is good, gives much the same dark picture of everything worldly. There is a witty condensation of the whole paradox which has often been quoted and which is worthy of perpetuation: "For the Stoic this is the best of all possible worlds, and everything in it is a necessary evil."

It is plain enough, then, that the Stoic was in a practical sense "conquering" the mortal world by giving it up as both

FORTUNE AND HER WHEEL

From Lydgate's *The Siege of Troy*, MS Royal 18 D ii, *ca.* 1450.

evil and unmanageable, however nobly he may have sustained himself by a belief that the scheme of things was somehow good. He was retreating into the citadel of his spirit, pulling up the drawbridge against the world of so-called hard fact, and magnificently daring that world to harm him. In conquering the world by such tactics he was giving up hope that it could be worked upon and to some extent directed by man.

Nor did all Stoics have the staunch faith of the slave Epictetus. The emperor Marcus Aurelius had his moments when he looked into the bottomless pit. One may find him saying: "Either all things spring from a single source possessed of mind, and combine and fit together as for a single body, and in that case the part has no right to quarrel with the good of the whole: or else, it is a concourse of atoms, a welter ending in dispersion. Why then perturb yourself?"[10] Even at its most optimistic reaches Stoic thought hardly spoke of a purpose in the universe, but rather of a plan, a plan run over and over again like an eternal phonograph record, an impersonal thing to the laws of which God himself was subject. This plan provided for cosmic cycles, each of which should go through the same essential development as the one before, even repeating the lives of individual men like Socrates and Plato, and each of which should end in a general conflagration. "Those of the gods who are not subject to destruction, having observed the course of one period, know from this everything which is going to happen in all subsequent periods. For there will never be any new thing other than that which has been before, but everything is repeated down to the minutest detail."[11]

The logical aim of Stoic doctrine is complete resignation in man so far as the active life is concerned. In tragedy the only struggle which a Stoic hero could consistently make would be the effort to know that evil did not exist, that he ought to remain calm because his misfortunes were in no sense true misfortunes—in short, that the tragedy in which he was participating was no tragedy at all. Nor would there seem to be any call for a good Stoic to spend his time dramatizing and making real in tragic art what he regarded as absolutely unreal. One wonders why Seneca imitates Greek tragedy and especially why he never loses the chance to elaborate with loving care the horrors and the gory details of the stories he inherits. Where Euripides makes Medea in a refinement of cruelty refuse the bodies of her slain sons to Jason, Seneca knows a better way. He has her toss the corpses from the housetop to the feet of Jason below like so much meat. And so on through numberless examples, many of them worse. But one wonders at this only until one remembers that it is again the Stoic paradox. Seneca is in fact obsessed by the evils of life and compelled to talk of them constantly just as Marcus Aurelius is, though his manner conveys far less sincerity of purpose. He succeeds in making the whole business cheap, meretricious, melodramatic. In him morbidity replaces the earlier Greek virility, which opposes suffering with noble action and with less rhetoric.

Seneca is reasonably consistent in dwelling upon the uselessness of ambitious willing and doing. He says in his *De Providentia* that it is a great consolation to be swept away together with the entire universe, and that whatever law is laid upon us, thus we must live and thus we must die. For "the creator and ruler of the universe himself, though he has given laws to the fates, yet is guided by them; he always obeys, he only once commanded." But one may well ask, "Why was God so unjust in His distribution of fate as to assign poverty, wounds, and untimely deaths to good men?" The answer is simply that "the workman cannot alter his materials: this is their nature." Anyhow, unmerited misfortune is good for any man. "Fire tries gold, misfortune tries brave men."[12] In the Senecan tragedies over and over again comes emphasis in some form upon the folly of all ambitious effort. Seneca is a fountainhead of much ready-phrased thought for Christian Europe; and one stream of it, not the least, eddies around the general idea that high place draws misfortune just because it is high. The lightning strikes the highest trees, cold blasts smite most keenly the highest mountains, tallest buildings are most easily shaken from their foundations, storms toss mariners who venture farthest from shore; the variations are endless, but the moral always is essentially as Seneca makes the chorus state it in his *Agamemnon:* "Modest estate has longer life; then happy he whoe'er, content with the common lot, with safe breeze hugs the shore, and fearing to trust his skiff to the wider sea, with unambitious oar keeps close to land."[13] In England the age of Marlowe and his *Tamburlaine,* compact of infinite ambition, frequently found strong appeal in such philosophy; this paradox will require consideration in due time.

Thus to nullification the Stoic philosophy brings tragic struggle, and thus it perverts the classic ideal of the golden

mean. Hug the shore, erect no mighty structures, practice
the golden mean by living meanly. If your head is never
raised above the heads of your fellows, Fate will be less able
to find you with her bludgeon. It is pointless to say that the
greatest Greek tragedy knew at moments something like
this. It knew the thing only by mood, as one of the various-
seeming sides of life, and its ideal of moderation actually
did aim at moderation, not nullification, of human action.
Prometheus in Aeschylus wanting to be happy through
hugging the shore of life would outrage us. Seneca himself,
of course, was inconsistent enough to acquire the highest
and wealthiest position in Rome, as tutor to Nero when
Nero's immaturity allowed the tutor to be in effect emperor. He justified the action by holding himself ready to
give up his winnings without murmur when Fate should
command. Fate finally did command in the person of a
jealous Nero, and Seneca acted in accordance with the last
Stoic paradox, namely, that suicide was justifiable in a
world where all was good. Whatever nobility of fortitude
Stoicism fostered, it could not foster nobility of action
against tragic odds. It preached a fine scorn for materialistic struggle in the world, but only at the expense of preaching by implication against all struggle in the world, even
such heroic ethical struggle for the good in life as Aeschylus
allotted to Orestes.

In pursuing further the development of Hellenistic philosophy for its bearing upon tragedy, we must look at the
steps by which the Stoic reached his position and the steps
by which other thinkers were to go beyond him in the renunciation of the mortal world. "Socrates," says Mr. Paul

Elmer More, "would overcome the evils of existence by strength of character and by trust in the ultimate justice of the gods; the Cynic makes the power of endurance an active principle of life, and attains security from fear of suffering by his contempt of hardship as a force inferior to his own energy, and so in a way regards evil as a matter of opinion or self-estimation; the Stoic will go a step further and will assert that there actually is no evil in the world except as our opinion, or judgment, imagines it to be."[14] The Cynic was in many ways simply a Stoic without religious faith, meeting the world's misfortunes by inner strength but not identifying that inner strength with God or the Universal Reason. He belittled the world of affairs. Antisthenes, Diogenes, and other Cynics even made knowledge impossible, since they would not hear of abstract qualities and would hold to nothing but particular things which could be seen and felt. They maintained that external goods were useless, that marriage and a home were encumbrances, and that the man who was wise and reasonable wandered the earth a homeless beggar, blessed with his virtue. Like many Stoics, they delighted in telling themselves constantly that wine was only a little decomposed grape juice, that man's body was subject to disgusting putrefaction while dead and to disgusting natural processes while alive. Whether true or not, the story that Diogenes performed in public those bodily acts which are usually held private is in keeping with Cynic doctrine. The world was vile and man needed to be shown and often reminded that it was. Certainly one Cynic virtue was hate of hypocrisy.[15]

Diogenes died in 323 B.C., on the same day, tradition iron-

ically says, as Alexander the Great, whose worldly glory he
had made no secret of despising. Zeno, the founder of Stoicism, died about 264 B.C. So soon after Socrates, who died
in 399, and Plato, who died in 347, had a large part of Greek
philosophy come to feel that the world's evils were desperate and that they must be met with desperate measures.
These desperate measures commonly involved retreat, and
the refuge sought in retreating from the world was unas-
sailable individualism. Epicurus, who died in 270 B.C., and
who believed that wisdom could teach man to live for the
highest pleasure in this world, idealized the pleasures of the
mind removed from the world and showed the common
desperate individualism of his age by trying to free mankind from any belief that the gods or Fate would interfere
in its affairs. The gods, granted that they existed, were living utterly to themselves, not giving either pleasure or pain
to mankind. Aristotle, of course, had refused to give the
world up to opinion, had claimed it for science, and had
labored to organize it.

A step onward from Stoicism in the renunciation of
the mortal world was taken in the revival of Platonism.
Something of the Neo-Platonic tendency was apparent in
Stoicism itself. Beginning as a proud consciousness of individual liberty based upon refusal to identify oneself with
anything worldly or finite and transitory, Stoicism found
that the individual subject could not be identified with
divine reason except by a process of sinking his individuality willingly in God and therefore "losing" it. A natural
development of later Stoicism was therefore a spirit the
reverse of its earlier spirit, a sort of self-despair instead of

self-confidence, and through this self-despair a yearning to
lose and find oneself in God."[16] This spirit was never dominant in Stoicism because Stoicism really deserves the accusation that it was materialistic. It still kept a hand upon the
world's activities and supplied a way for man to gather
wealth and position, yet at the same time to despise such
things and yearn for unmaterial reality. Because its God was
immanent in the material world it was an ideal manner of
thought for the practical Roman who wished to live a life
of luxury and yet be religious. But Neo-Platonism recoiled
from any process of finding God in a world which it could
see sinking faster and faster into iniquity. God was not in
the world. He was transcendent. His realm was utterly removed from this world, and man's energies should all be
bent toward absolute escape from the mortal coil and toward the ineffable sinking of himself in God. The logical
life for the Neo-Platonist was one of asceticism, monasticism, secluded meditation, mystic ecstasy, anything but
immersion in the world's affairs. He sought to give the lie
direct to the Stoic contention that man can live in the world
(after a fashion) and in God also: "It is not possible, my
son, to attach yourself both to things mortal and to things
divine. There are two sorts of things, the corporeal and the
incorporeal; that which is mortal is of the one sort, and that
which is divine is of the other sort."[17]

Here we encounter another paradox of later classical philosophy. The Neo-Platonist, as represented by Plotinus, who
died about A.D. 270, both renounced the world and did not
renounce it. In tortured exposition which stretched his philosophy upon the rack, Plotinus sought to prove that the

One, which is also the Good, is the source of this world, and yet that the material world is opposed to the divine, and that the one aim of the moral and religious life is to escape from it.

Plotinus was brought to this pass by the Gnostics, who took finally and completely the step which Plotinus took equivocally. In them a part of later Greek philosophy, largely tinged with Orientalism, utterly renounced the bright world beloved of the earlier Greek and maintained that it was created by an evil *Demiurgus,* an evil Jehovah, a Satan, who was forever separate from God. Man, they said, so long as he was in this world was subject to a pollution by evil which could never be twisted into good. The only way he could escape to the divine world was by means of secret knowledge possessed by the Gnostic sect and by means of a Redeemer who could descend from the divine world to the world of evil and lead man's soul up the heavenly path beyond Change and Fate to its ultimate peace. Plotinus and other Neo-Platonists could not accept such crude and absolute dualism. They were after all still under the aegis of Plato and, with his example, had a lingering hope that an aspiring idealism seeking to free the intelligence from the fetters of sense could be perfectly poised against an artistic feeling which could find in the sensible a foreshadowing of the ideal. Plotinus looked into the abyss of Gnosticism, to which his own philosophy had brought him, and then turned in abhorrence from the idea that the material world was essentially and eternally evil. He countered by saying that the world was undoubtedly evil, but that it was only evil accidentally.

Both Neo-Platonist and Gnostic, in turning away from a hopeless world, turned to God for comfort, but that comfort was infinitely far away, infinitely difficult to reach. Only the purest in heart or the wisest could reach it. Despite the warmth of mystic ecstasy in which the elect could mingle with God, this comfort of God must have seemed to the ordinary man cold and abstract. How was one to get hold of such a God? He had no form, nothing finite about him. The descriptions of him were all paradoxical. He was everything and he was nothing. Gone was all the sustaining nearness and solid anthropomorphic reality of Zeus, Apollo, Athene, who after all did things for men, even though at times they seemed to act against men unjustly. It is indeed true that "the mystic who finds everything in God seems to speak the same language as the agnostic who finds nothing in him."[18] Plotinus could not admit that God was in any way finite; so in the court of last resort he denied to him even the abstract terms "Good" and "One" as being too concrete.[19] Since God was too great to characterize, he was also nothing —that is, no thing. Greek philosophy, beginning with its courageous effort to unify the objective or not-self, had by the critical spirit been driven back into the self, and had finally been driven beyond the self to find a unity transcending the opposition of self and not-self. But that unity was not of this world.

IV

With God, Purpose, Good, Scientific Order, or whatever one wishes to call a power of sweet reasonableness in the universe, robbed of practical immediacy or relegated to a transcendent other world, little but irrational necessity remained whereby one might explain human misfortune. If a man was a Stoic, he sought virtue to endure tragedy without making any attempt to question and understand misfortune. If he was a Neo-Platonist or a Gnostic, he believed that he knew the way to a better world. If he was just an ordinary member of the non-Christian multitude, he must often have felt hopeless indeed. Whichever a man he was, he was likely to be convinced that the material circumstances to which humanity is subjected are in no way influenced by men's choosing. To twist the words of Shakespeare, he was likely to feel that

> The fault, dear Brutus, is not in ourselves,
> But in our stars, that we are underlings.

In fact, the fault that lies in our stars was an obsession with the later classic world. It was an age when faith in astrology filtered everywhere. Emperors from Augustus to Alexander Severus turned zealously to Chaldean astrology; the common people grasped at the belief as they could; Stoics, Neo-Platonists, and Gnostics propagated it with conviction. The Epicureans, however, who had abolished the gods as interferers in human destiny, refused to substitute the stars.

In almost all the religious systems of later antiquity the seven planets were dominating and terrifying forces operating upon man.[20] For the Gnostics especially, man's struggle to escape from the evil earth involved the use of secret charms by which his soul might get itself past the seven successive spheres of influence ruled by the malevolent planets around the earth and issue at last into the realm of freedom and perfect peace. The earth lay at the center of the evil system, then came the sphere of the moon, then that of the sun, and so on through the seven spheres. The planets were the Kosmokratores, rulers of the universe, and above these was an eighth region, the home of the ultimate God, whose being was before the Kosmos, and whose being was the true home of man in his union with God. Saturn, the chief of the evil planets, was the most malignant; sometimes he was Jaldabaoth, the lion-headed God, the evil Jehovah.[21] As man's soul, or as his Redeemer, descended from divinity through these spheres of evil influence, he sank farther and farther into prison. Finally he sank beneath the moon, the ruling planet closest to earth, whose essential quality made for changeableness, illogicality, disorder. Beneath the moon man was the sport of pure chance or fortune. All changeable mortal things, which grow and die and vary, were under its sway. Above the moon there was no chance, but there was necessity under the other six rulers. There was no freedom until the eighth region, that of God, was attained.

"Beneath the moon" was for a large part of the later classic world the inscription of despair over the portals of life. Man was born into illogical trouble. Plutarch, in the first century of our era, deemed a lack of unified goodness to be natural in "the world on this side of the moon, which has become irregular and various, and such as to undergo all manner of change."[22]

In the fourth century, just before Christianity was finally to triumph, Julian the Apostate sought to propagate in his empire a tolerant synthesis of the beliefs which he regarded as more beautiful than those of harsh Christianity, with its emphasis upon sin. His beloved associate and counselor Sal-

lustius, evidently under his inspiration, produced a simple
and authoritative summary of the later pagan beliefs, a sort
of creed "Concerning the Gods and the Universe," in which
all good pagans could join, even the Epicureans.[23] The gods
whom it recognizes care for humanity merely by existing,
as the sun gives heat, not by any act of will or labor. Sallustius knows that he must gather into the fold, not only the
simple people, but also the intellectuals who regard all
myths as superstition. His system is very abstract, impersonal, nonanthropomorphic. One realizes as one reads him
why the world he aims at was so soon to embrace the warm
reality of the man-God Jesus as preached by the Christians.
Sallustius urges firmly that all is for man's good, and he has
a clinging faith that man does will certain things. As he
says, to attribute our acts of injustice and lust to Fate is
to make ourselves good and the gods bad; what faith he
has left rebels at that. But human beings, especially in their
material constitution, are ordered by celestial bodies. And
beneath the moon there is Fortune, which makes things
happen contrary to expectation. "Fortune's power rests in
the moon, since above the moon nothing whatsoever could
happen because of her."[24] One wonders just how much freedom of will Sallustius actually believed in for man.

And so we come to Fortune, which, beneath the moon, as
Sallustius says, was worshiped at this time as a goddess, and
especially by cities—fittingly enough, "for every city consists of elements which are not uniform."[25] The figure of
Fortune which Sallustius allows to rule the things in life
that "are not uniform" had grown in importance for the
classic world as it gave up its gods and despaired of unity

in life; by the medieval world it was to be inherited and
developed until it should become the vividly concrete expression of fickleness in mortal affairs. Poets, theologians,
and all manner of men in the Middle Ages were to picture
Fortune's feminine whimsicality, revile her ways, dispute
with her as they would dispute with the inexplicability of
life itself. They were to create the image of Fortune's wheel
and imagine Fortune as governing the round of worldly
routine, elevating men to the "sweet fruition of an earthly
crown" and casting them down into ruin, all without reason. They were to make her a convenient image of all those
ways of God which were past finding out.[26]

Gradually they penetrated her realm and took much of
it away, transferring what they had won from her rule to
the rule of justice. The history of Fortune in the Gothic
world includes the history of her enfeeblement by a new
order of philosophic unity, a new acceptance and explanation of the world.

Concurrently as Fortune was deposed from her autocratic
rule of sublunary events, the Gothic spirit discovered that
heroic misfortunes were not to be merely bewailed as inexplicable falls from high to low degree, but were to be plotted
with the subtlety of tragic poesy. Yet it continued to pay lip
service to Fortune, even as it learned to cast off her yoke.
We shall see by what process Fortune was subdued before
the Shakespearean tragedy which issues out of human character could be created—subdued, it must be said, not entirely
overthrown. For the writers of Elizabethan tragedy were
often poets in so true a sense that they did not pretend to
abolish the mystery which they penetrated.[27]

Chapter II

GOTHIC ESPOUSAL AND CONTEMPT
OF THE WORLD

GOTHIC TRAGEDY had its origin in a clash of other-worldliness and worldliness that came with the Renaissance. It does not owe its being merely to the Italian revival of learning, which produced widespread imitation of classic tragedy. It began as a result of a more general European Renaissance, a rebirth of creative vitality which had clearly manifested itself in various forms long before Christian Europe came to the point of imitating classic drama effectively. It is increasingly plain that "with each attempt to draw a sharp line of demarcation between the Middle Ages and the Renaissance, this border line has receded further and further backward." The Italian Renaissance was not so decisive as has often been supposed. Contrast with what had gone before was far less sharp than it seemed to the humanists and their followers, since "within the Middle Ages there were intellectual revivals whose effect was not lost to succeeding times, and which partook of the same character as the better known movement of the fifteenth century."

Customarily, we dwell upon the otherworldliness of medieval Christianity. Its physical world, we say, was an unreal or imperfect place and its Heaven was a very real and perfect place. Since it believed that man's true home was Heaven and that his highest aim should be to attain felicity after death, it saw only folly in any man who would attach himself to this world or probe for its meaning. For this world had no meaning except as a vestibule to Heaven. In the Middle Ages, we hear, "human nature had gone bankrupt; and for centuries it needed to be administered ... in receivership,"[3] the receiver being a Catholic Church. All this has enough truth behind it to be pardonable for the broader purposes of emphasis, but it lacks the subtlety which would explain the appearance of a Renaissance in the midst of these very Middle Ages.

From its inception Christianity offered not merely a hope of Heaven, but also a way of life in this world. The new theology crystallized around the worshiped personality of a God-man, Jesus, and Jesus preached the fullness of mortal life as well as the Kingdom of Heaven. His recorded ideas were often perverted through the influence of Greco-Roman philosophies which denied the world, and Christians were often impelled to overemphasize the unworldly side of Christlike character, but the Church could not abandon the core of hope for the world which lay in its new dispensation. The advantage which this core of hope gave to Christianity was incalculable, even though the Church did not realize it as we may realize it. Christianity could offer the comfort of a new anthropomorphism to a world which by intellectual criticism had banished the Homeric gods into an abstract realm of vague forces or had thought them out of existence altogether. It could offer something comparable to a conviction that the gods of Olympus had returned to earth to walk among men in warm reality. Jesus by being the son of God *was* God, but he was also man in all points tempted like as we are. Those who imitated his meeting of temptations were to have hope of participating both in the divine life after death and in the good life on this earth. In this unique personality the transcendent and formless God had mysteriously been given form with full accompaniment of flesh and blood, and the Church, pulled as it might be toward ascetism, always faced the necessity of recognizing that life in the flesh could be good. One life in the flesh, and no hermit's life either, had been perfect or divine. Thus simply by Christianity was the Christian Church saved for other than negative influence upon men's lives. The two teachings, negative and positive, reached beautiful balance in the consciousness of Jesus. He had burning faith in self-realization through self-sacrifice, and he read divine goodness in mortal life even in the face of fiercest evil. Man was to give up self and to give up the material view of worldly life that he might find a fuller self and a fuller life here and now. He was not to pray like the Gnostics that he might escape from the evil earth to Heaven, but that God's kingdom might come and God's will be done on earth as it was in Heaven.[4]

In consequence, one history of Christian thought is the history of its secularization. Often against its conscious will, which would gladly have contemplated Heaven, it was driven by inward force to gather various beauties and actualities of life and to use them. Its destiny was creative activity, not passivity. If in the Renaissance it eventually overbalanced itself on the worldly side and embraced what may fairly be termed corruption, neither its earlier nor its later secularization was essentially corruption, but a continuous vital attempt to comprehend a worthwhile world.

REGULUS TORTURED BY THE CARTHAGINIANS
From Laurent de Premierfait's translation of Boccaccio's *De Casibus*,
MS Royal 14 E v, late fifteenth century.

The best early example of such secularization is seen in the violent struggle of the Church to free itself from negative Greco-Roman philosophy, or at least to engulf that philosophy and make it harmless for the active work of redemption which the Church was to do. The Church was sorely beset by Gnosticism. There was much in Gnostic asceticism, with its reasoned contempt for the body, which was attractive to the early Christian severity of conscience, and the Gnostic Redeemer descending from the divine world to the mortal was strangely like Christ. But the Gnostic held that part of creation was the work of an evil Jehovah, and the Church clung to the belief that the whole creation was of God and somehow good, no matter how bad the world might seem. Gnostic theology was therefore, after a struggle, cast from the body of the Church as heretical. A more subtle influence was Neo-Platonism, not so crudely dualistic as Gnosticism, and attractive to nobler minds. As time went on, the early Church gave up its hope of an immediate millennial regeneration of the world through the second coming of the Christ, and its figure of Jesus tended to recede farther from earthly affairs into a distant Heaven. There can be no doubt that Neo-Platonism, with its emphasis upon the transcendence and formlessness of God, widened the gulf between Jesus the God and Jesus the man. It took strong hold upon St. Clement and upon Origen, for example, and later, by its effect upon St. Augustine in the fourth and fifth centuries, gave Christianity a pronounced ascetic bias. The Church at times almost gave up the world in theory, but even during the darkest of the "Dark Ages" saved itself by declaring the logical last step

D

to be heresy. It was heresy to make Jesus all God and no man, and it was heresy to deny that realization of the life of Jesus in other men was possible, though Augustinian Christianity commonly deferred this realization to another world, for which our world was merely a preparation with qualities that by themselves were to be despised. The early Church was not ready to embrace life fully. Instinctively it seems to have felt that it yet had no intellectual scheme into which it could put the fullness of life.

Christianity had even to conquer an ascetic heresy that aimed to make an end of the human race. Those Christians who tended to magnify an antagonism of flesh and spirit naturally saw monasticism as the way of life most accept-able to God. Giving up the world meant most specifically giving up sexual reproduction of the flesh with its sensual delights. Hermits and holy ascetics like St. Simeon Stylites flourished. In the third century, austerities in Christian life began to be mentioned as blessed, and the Church quickly had to deal with parts of itself which with fiery conviction sought to make all Christian life an abstention from sexual life, even from matrimony. The Church instinctively would have none of this denial of life which aimed to quell the very fount of life. It is a marvel of true catholicity to see how it crushed the movement toward universal monasti-cism as a heresy, and how it yet provided holy and exalted place for men and women genuinely called to monasticism. But the struggle was a long one. As late as the twelfth cen-tury there were traces of the extreme Manichean doctrine which condemned marriage and which had at one time attracted St. Augustine. A twelfth-century story is recorded which to the modern mind, according to its temper, is quaint or pitiful. A clerk of the Archbishop of Rheims encountered a comely maiden near that city and in courtly fashion asked her to be his mistress. With gentle gravity she said that this would mean eternal damnation of the soul, and from the way her refusal was expressed the clerk knew that she was a member of a "most impious sect" condemning all sexual relationships which was being dealt with at that time in France and England. He disputed with her theologically and then was the means of getting her burned at the stake "to the admiration of many who marked how she uttered no sighs, no tears, no laments, but bore with constancy and cheerfulness all torments of the consuming flames, even as the martyrs of Christ (yet for how different a cause!)."[5]

Also in other ways than the conquering of ascetic heresies Christianity soon reached out for the world of concrete reality. Neo-Platonism might succeed somewhat in separating the God and the man in Jesus, but the need for finding the divine in the human drove Christians to create new godlike intermediaries closer to human frailty. The cult of the Virgin and the cult of the saints grew steadily in the early Middle Ages and beyond all bounds in the later.[6] Images and pictures which for Origen about A.D. 240 were unnecessary to Christianity, and were products of an art which dragged down the eyes of the soul from God to earth, were argued for five centuries later by Pope Gregory II and many others in the iconoclastic controversy.[7] The Church was finding the world and using it, fortunately for all who know beauty in Gothic art and thought.

It is commonly accepted that one sure sign of the Renaissance was a revived interest in classic learning. This was
bound to come eventually in Christian Europe as intellectual and artistic consciousness grew. The first manifestation
of the new reverence for ancient thought occurred in the
ninth century and has been called the Carolingian Renaissance. Weak as it was, if we compare it with what happened
later, this Renaissance under Charlemagne was real and
left its mark. "Its scribes saved to the modern world the
Latin classics, nearly all of which have come down to us,
directly or indirectly, through Carolingian copies."[8] The
spirit of that movement revisited men with increasing force
through what has been called the Ottonian Renaissance
of the tenth century in Germany, the Renaissance of the
eleventh century in France and Italy, and the wider European Renaissance of the twelfth century and later.[9]

II

By the twelfth century, the tide of new life and new learning was flowing strongly in Gothic Europe, breaking bar-
riers, entering arid spaces. This is the century which saw the
culmination of Romanesque art and the rise of Gothic art,
the emergence of vernacular literature, the rapid creation
of European universities, and the discovery of much Greek-
Arabic thought. It vibrated with new power and with a
creative spirit which could shape the world into new forms.
Let us regard the motion as continuous, though of varied
speed, until the seventeenth century. Not until then did the
tide cease to meet resistance and settle calmly over the Europe which it had covered.

Resistance was natural. The first stirrings of new vitality had apparently brought an access of fear that humanity might be overwhelmed by the sins of the active life, and before the twelfth century a period of ascendancy for the "penitential books" had indicated a peculiarly conscience-stricken character in Christian Europe. From the twelfth century onward, men were being impelled with breathless rapidity by some mysterious inner force to compass beauty and create intellectual order in this world which they had hitherto shrunk from comprehending and had often thought inherently dangerous to their hopes of Heaven. It was something to give all good Christians pause. A great many of them did pause—even when they were most busily in the midst of the new activity—to write literature and create art *de contemptu mundi*. There was a sudden increase of need and willingness to contemplate the sufferings of this life and its inevitable snuffing out in death.

It is just the universal ardor of this new contemplation of mortal evils in all their grisly reality that constitutes its real distinction from the older Christian austerity. Warnings against the delights of life and injunctions to think of death had been made by the Fathers and ecclesiastics from the beginnings of the Church, but there was now a remarkable acceptance of the theme by the world in general.[10] Nor did the early patristic writings show the violent realism of the medieval writings or artistic representations. They cannot be made to give a completely satisfactory explanation of the later fashions in horror any more than can passages in *Job*, *Ecclesiasticus*, the *Wisdom of Solomon*, and other books of the Bible. The newly earnest vilification of the body may have begun slightly before the year 1000 in such writings as the Old English *Address of the Lost Soul to the Body*, with its revolting picture of the greedy coffin-worm.[11] By the fifteenth century it was universal.[12] Everywhere, with participation by all classes of men, there was then a swelling chorus of *memento mori,* remember death and despise mundane life. But there was no question here of an actual surrender of mundane life by the common man, as there was in Manicheism, which the Church fought so ruthlessly. The chorus had a quality which we are tempted to call hypocrisy, or "false taste,"[13] or other hard names. For, as I shall try to make plain, the new scorn of the world frequently accompanied, even in one and the same man, a very lively and fruitful love of the world. *Contemptus mundi* in the medieval sense represents the alter ego of many a man who contributed significant worldly activity to the Renaissance, whether he lived in the twelfth or the sixteenth century.

From one point of view it is perversely contradictory for a man thus to enjoy vilification of life in art and literature and then enjoy actively the very life which he has despised theoretically. It seems, indeed, like the grossest sentimentality, the most flagrant divorce of what one says from what one does. It would be more understandable to the modern world if this were a manifestation of occasional morbid moods, of occasional failure in nerve. But medieval nerve seems often to have been good, even when death and mortal corruption were contemplated in what would be for us a morbid fashion. A classic illustration is the juxtaposition of life and death in the churchyard of the Holy Innocents in Paris. Of their own free will and with the best stomach in the world the rank and file of fifteenth-century Parisians made it a daily lounge and rendezvous. Here they came in great numbers not only for spiritual meditation but also to walk and talk about the business of life. At the same time they viewed the gruesome pictures and read the stanzas of the Death Dance on the walls of the cloisters, watched the burials and exhumations that were always going on in this most popular burial ground, and gave their custom to the shops established near the charnel houses, where exhumed skulls and bones by thousands were heaped in public view to make room for the newly dead.[14] St. Paul's in London also exhibited a Death Dance and was a popular rendezvous of somewhat similar sort. In their homes, too, healthy people were writing *memento mori* and picturing the death's head over their fireplaces, on articles of daily use, wherever they would be likely to look while they were most immersed in the business of living.[15]

But if this is incongruous, then tragedy itself is incongruous. One of the knottiest problems the critic of tragedy has ever sought to solve is the paradoxical pleasure which a healthy and vitally creative people can find in a dramatic art emphasizing suffering, death, and mortal defeat for men. Aristotle attempted the solution as successfully as anyone, but his discovery of "purgation" for the emotions of pity and fear makes us rather respect the profundity of the problem than rejoice in its final answer. Medieval Contempt of the World never had the subtlety of great dramatic tragedy. Outright crudity characterizes the Dance of Death or the death's-head *memento mori,* for example. Yet these things and others like them looked forward to and were echoed in Elizabethan tragedy—not by any means only in Hamlet's meditation over Yorick's exhumed skull. Contempt of the World was for a time closely bound up with ascetic religious practice, but in the growing secularity of its appeal we have something which must be considered even as the paradoxical appeal of tragedy is considered. It began to be not only an ascetic duty to scorn the world, but also a pleasure, a truly artistic pleasure, a kind of tragic pleasure. It was emotional balance. Indeed it seems in the mysterious tragic fashion to have purged the complex emotions of the Renaissance and both to have expressed and to have calmed the uneasiness of an age which was impulsively shifting its realm of values from Heaven to earth.

Contempt of the World in literature and art took at least three distinct conventional forms which are of first importance in a discussion of the new tragic view of life. During the Renaissance from the twelfth to the seventeenth centuries these forms came into existence one after another and finally flourished all together. They decayed in the seventeenth century, when the Renaissance had been accomplished past all possibility of counteraction and when with the growing secularity of the age the tragic emotion had found more subtle and effective expression in the drama. The earlier dramatic tragedy we shall find absorbing and transmuting many conventions of this contempt, though it did not pretend to serve any purpose of religious contemplation. Contempt of the World as a common exercise died in the seventeenth century because man by this time had killed his lingering fears (except for revivals by puritan or ascetic sects) and for good or ill had elected to concern him-

self in art and science with the so-called "realities" of mortal
life. His faith in the utter reality of hard facts began to be as
worshipful, sometimes as "naïve," as his former faith in the
utter reality of Heaven.

The first major form in which contempt for the new life
was conventionally expressed was the set disquisition on the
vileness of the world and the death or corruption of the
flesh, which often got the title *De Contemptu Mundi* and
has so given us a name for the emotional reaction under discussion. It appeared in the twelfth century under professional religious inspiration, but was later adopted by many
secular men of letters and was popular in England even
in the time of Elizabeth. The classics in this form are, of
course, the *De Contemptu Mundi* by Bernard of Morlaix,
written at the beginning of the twelfth century, and that
by Innocent III, written at its close. The second form was
the medieval tragical narrative. Boccaccio created it in the
middle of the fourteenth century with his *De Casibus Virorum Illustrium,* and for more than two centuries Europe
found fascination in this and similar collections of moralized stories concerning the falls of princes and great ones
from their high estates into misery and death. The third
form was the artistic representation of death in all the gross
horrors which imagination could contrive. It was popular
in a number of varieties; there were, for example, the Dance
of Death and many ingenious *memento mori* devices. The
preparation for this art is to be found in literature of the
eleventh, twelfth, and thirteenth centuries,[16] but the actual
picturing and carving of Death as a skeleton, a death's-head,
or a decaying corpse preyed upon by worms came into sud-

den popularity at the end of the fourteenth century and the beginning of the fifteenth.[17] The age of *memento mori* was the fifteenth, sixteenth, and seventeenth centuries, and its popularity had a climax in the designs of the sixteenth century. Its devices appeared everywhere, in paintings and prints, on sepulchral monuments, as architectural ornaments, on many kinds of jewelry, in books of emblems, books of hours, and other devotional books, on rosary beads, and on medals.[18] Contempt of the World found expression in a multitude of forms related to those just given—for example, in *Ubi Sunt* poems and in ubiquitous popular treatises on the art of dying—but the three may be fairly regarded as preëminent.

It is clear that these forms of scorn for the world flourished during the general European Renaissance, and that they united closely in the quality of their reaction to that Renaissance. Also, it is clear that this reaction became less and less mere preaching by the Church, and more and more something springing from the souls of the people. It was when such expression began to leave the rule of the Church and to find extensive secular sponsorship that it sounded most promisingly the tragic note. The analogy between this process and what happened to Gothic drama is inescapable. Just as drama began in religious practice, was secularized, and found new artistic values without benefit of clergy, so did formal Contempt of the World.

III

The peculiar qualities by which Contempt of the World could be avowedly inimical to the new vitality of the Renaissance and yet come to exist upon friendly terms with it will be clearer if we now look at ways in which scorn was expressed, inconsistently, side by side with love of the world by one and the same man. The Renaissance inconsistencies which were wrestled with in the tragical narratives of Boccaccio and his imitators must in the main be left to the ensuing chapter. For the moment it will be to the purpose to consider contradictions of more general implication.

In two men of extraordinary genius Renaissance espousal of mundane life and scorn of mundane life are so sharply contradictory that ingenious attempts to minimize that side of their natures which expressed Contempt of the World have been made by modern admirers of their able worldliness. These two representative men are Giovanni Lothario Conti, of the late twelfth and early thirteenth centuries, who became Pope Innocent III, and Geoffrey Chaucer, of the fourteenth century.

Innocent wrote his *De Contemptu Mundi* before he became pope. Here with learned reference to Holy Writ and to the writings of the Fathers, and with apparent zeal, the author demonstrates the worthlessness of this world as a field of activity. In lively fashion he traces the misery of man from the corruption of birth to the corruption of death. But later as pope this classic scorner of the world showed such surpassing ability to organize it and dominate it that under him the papacy reached its peak of temporal power, making, subjugating, and deposing kings. It is not surprising that men looking back at him with a modern sense of values sometimes conclude that the contemptuous treatise was "a scholar's exercise, a display of technique" composed for professional recognition in the Church, and that "it reveals his abilities, not his opinions."[19] In short, this may seem to be a plain case of ecclesiastical hypocrisy. Further possibilities, if one is resolute in the conviction that Innocent cannot have been of two minds at once, are either that as an ambitious young ecclesiastic he scorned worldly power only to compensate psychologically for his lack of it, or that as a fanatically religious youth he honestly thought one way but in wise maturity honestly thought the other.

The case of Chaucer is different, for he is a poet. On one side of his character, especially in his maturity, he has a passport to our affection because of his ready eye for the glories of living and his flexible play of intellectual curiosity over the things of this world. On the other, he participates in Contempt of the World. The creator of the Wife of Bath wrote the *Monkes Tale*—and a dreary assembly of tragical stories it is, drearier than Boccaccio's. Also, though we do not have the work, Chaucer says himself that he translated Innocent's *De Contemptu Mundi*—a part of it at least. He engaged in other moral and devotional writing. One cannot explain this contradiction as arising from ecclesiastical hypocrisy, and one can hardly lay it to unsatisfied worldly ambition. But perhaps the "false taste" of Contempt was an artistic sin of his youth, and perhaps he outgrew it?

There is no trustworthy sign that he did so. We know that he matured in tolerant worldly wisdom, but he seems never to have accepted the good things of the flesh quite so whole-heartedly as he might. The most judicial critics believe that Chaucer, for all his light-heartedness, was a truly devout man to the day of his death and that his retractation following the *Persones Tale* is genuine and honest.[20] Devotion there consists in abasement of himself for his "endytinges of worldly vanitees." He rests his salvation on his religious and moral writings. It is in the revised Prologue to the *Legend of Good Women,* probably written in 1394,[21] when his life was nearly done, that he mentions his translation of Innocent's *De Contemptu Mundi.* He thought well enough of it to add it to the list of works philosophical and devotional given in the first version of the Prologue, probably eight years earlier. Nor can we call the *Monkes Tale* merely immature work of Chaucer's. Some part of the collection was written not earlier than 1386.[22] As for the possibility that Chaucer incorporated his collection of tragedies in the *Canterbury Tales* with the purpose of satirizing a "false taste,"[23] it is true that the Knight does not like the monotonous relation of the Monk and stops it, and that Harry Bailly makes fun of it. But Chaucer was that rare sort of humorist who can honestly laugh at many kinds of taste without condemning them, including his own. Moreover, it will not do to make the Knight exclusively represent Chaucer's opinions nor to take Harry the innkeeper too seriously as a literary critic.

We should perceive, I think, that in its religious aspects Contempt of the World was true devotion, practiced quite naturally by many intelligent medieval men who found it good at times and bad if indulged in fanatically. One who was not a sincerely ascetic monk was probably very realistic about the matter. He knew full well that he had to spend much of his life pursuing the things of this world, but he believed more firmly than we do now that thereby he jeop-

ardized his soul, and he balanced his sense of values by a
form of meditation which reviled his ordinary pursuits. He
did not spend all his time praying; neither did he spend
all his time in such meditation. If this is so, it is gratuitous
on our part to "defend" Innocent III and Chaucer in this
connection by seeking to find in them an ideal consistency.

Even in such a leader of humanistic emancipation as
Erasmus, a century later than Chaucer, we do not find any
pronounced turning against the general taste for Contempt
of the World. Here we have what we do not have for either
Innocent or Chaucer, namely, direct criticism recorded in
his maturity upon a *De Contemptu Mundi* written in his
youth. The comment is apologetic, but not for the reasons
which we might expect. Erasmus says that he wrote the
book when he was scantly twenty years of age at the in-
stance of a certain man who was urging his nephew to the
solitary religious life. People are passing it around and
threatening to print it. Hence he will guide it into print
himself, though he hates to because, as Thomas Paynel
translates his words (1533), it was one of the foolish trifles
"compiled when I was yonge, not for that entent: that they
shuld be redde in this tyme whiche hath dyvers men of excellent lernynge and great vnderstandynge; ... nor also to
I was not than enstructed in redynge of good auctours." This
sounds more like an apology for youthful failings in scholarly background and in Latin style than an apology for out-
grown ideas.[24] It is true that Erasmus had lost his vocation
for strict monastic life, and that so far as this early disquisition upon the dangers and insecurities of the world actually
aimed at proving monastic life best, he had modified it by

his later addition of a chapter on monastic corruption. But he saw nothing strange in the fact that people should still want to read a book that would justify scorn of the world. Neither did Thomas Paynel when he translated the book for English readers and called it eminently salutary in an age that was rapidly deserting the good religion of the older time.[25]

To find contemporary realization that the Renaissance soul as it was impelled to reach for the glory of worldly life was also impelled to check such activity by Contempt of the World, we may turn to Petrarch. While many other intelligent men faced the struggle uncritically, Petrarch analyzed it by searching the depths of his nature. If his sensitive perception of irreconcilable forces in his make-up foreshadows our own awareness of Renaissance contradictions, then indeed he is the "first modern man of letters."

Revelation of Petrarch's spiritual struggle is to be found in the series of dialogues which he calls the *Secretum,* though the Latin edition probably of 1475 adds *De Contemptu Mundi* to the title and so gives the work its more popular name. It was written, apparently without view to publication, about 1342 or 1343, when Petrarch was thirty-eight or thirty-nine years old. When it was published after his death, the book was hailed as another godly disprizal of this world. But along with its conventional disprizal of mundane affairs goes staunchly unrepentant revolt against the argument that absolutely all earthly things are essentially valueless and that another world of bliss is all that is worth striving for. The work is in reality a debate between Petrarch's two selves. On one side stands the active Petrarch rejoicing in his intellectual effort, in the fame and glory which he gains thereby from the world, and in an idealized love for Laura which he can see only as beautiful and uplifting to his soul, never as a snare and a delusion. But on the shoulder of this first Petrarch the second Petrarch lays his restraining hand. This second self is Petrarch the ascetic, a very real Petrarch and one to be reckoned with. This is the Petrarch who loved solitude and who could say in his *De Vita Solitaria* that he admired in the Brahmans "their contempt of the world, which cannot be too great in a right-minded man";[26] who could bewail lapses of love which had brought his illegitimate son and daughter into the world; who could argue that woman as a mate is man's confusion; who could feel thankful to God that as he approached his fortieth year he had banished physical love for woman entirely from his thought and his remembrance.

Petrarch offers his *Secret* in the form of a discussion between himself and St. Augustine. The saint who in life and works was so ardent a supporter of asceticism that he was tempted at one time toward heretical exaggeration of ascetic virtue is made by Petrarch into a wise father confessor. He may be taken as the concrete embodiment of that part of Petrarch's nature which cried caution to the more worldly part. At the beginning of the book Truth appears to Petrarch in a vision and with her St. Augustine. They agree that Petrarch is sick of soul and needs instruction. Petrarch reveres both and gladly accepts counsel. Then follow three dialogues between St. Augustine and Petrarch. The first two reveal a highly reverent listener in Petrarch. He admits that he is in a parlous state, and St. Augustine urges that to escape he has only to desire relief from his miseries strongly enough. Petrarch is surprised. Has he not shed tears and desired greatly? Yes, says St. Augustine, but not with negative as well as with positive spirit. To desire the noble and good is not enough. One must also detest the ugly and evil. Much that follows is St. Augustine's elaboration of the snares which the world spreads for mankind. Contempt of the World is offered as the spiritual exercise which Petrarch is neglecting. For, says St. Augustine, "what I had set out to do with you was to make clear that the first step in avoiding the distresses of this mortal life and raising the soul to higher things is to practice meditation on death and on man's misery; and that the second is to have a vehement desire and purpose to rise."[27]

Petrarch accepts with good grace this injunction to practice contemplation of death and misery for his soul's good, but reverence for his preceptor does not stop independent thought. And in the third dialogue he comes forth as definitely, though politely, rebellious.

"I do not think my way of looking at it is so unreasonable as you imagine," he says. "My principle is that, as concerning the glory which we may hope for here below, it is right for us to seek while we are here below. One may expect to enjoy other more radiant glory in heaven, when we shall have there arrived, and when one will have no more care or wish for the glory of earth. Therefore, as I think, it is in the true order that mortal men should first care for mortal things; and that to things transitory things eternal should succeed."[28]

Here is Renaissance espousal of life in all its frightful temerity, actually contemplating "glory" on earth and de-

E

ferring the contemplation of heavenly glory. It arouses good St. Augustine mightily: "O man, little in yourself, and of little wisdom! . . . that delusion has betrayed thousands of men thousands of times, and has sunk into hell a countless host of souls. Thinking to have one foot on earth and one in heaven, they could neither stand here below nor mount on high. Therefore they fell miserably and the moving breeze swept them suddenly away."[29]

Thus speaks the fear of the Renaissance that spoke in many a man who found attraction in its activity. Petrarch is impressed, but not wholly convinced. After all, he is living in a vital world calling for the exercise of his intellect and has his work to do. Here is an eminently practical question: Shall he put his studies to one side and renounce every ambition?

At this point St. Augustine, who before was so directly and simply condemnatory, cannot bring himself to kill the new learning. He throws off his historic character and stands revealed as a Renaissance, instead of an early Christian, contemner of the world. For, says he in effect, one may truly give oneself to the work of the world and yet scorn it duly. He advises Petrarch not to live without ambition, but always to put virtue before ambition. Glory will naturally follow virtue if virtue is regarded first. Petrarch has already declared firmly but with all due respect to his teacher that there are two worldly things which he can never give up and will not admit to be utterly evil: first, his love for Laura, which spiritualizes the physical beauty of his world, and, second, his love for study and even for the fame and glory which he gains in the world by it. Now

that St. Augustine has shown him the way to hold fast
to learning by putting virtue before it, Petrarch ends the
dialogue in fitting Renaissance fashion. After meditation
under his teacher's guidance upon the hollow nature of
the world's affairs, he hastens back to those worldly affairs
which are calling him.

It would be wrong-headed to hail such a work, arresting
as it is at times for its modern acceptance of the world, as a
triumph of the new order over the old. Petrarch here has
not freed himself from Contempt of the World. He has
merely made clear why love of the world and scorn of the
world were fated for a long time after his death to play com-
plementary and counterpoising rôles in the thought of the
Renaissance.

Small wonder that in his *De Remediis Utriusque For-
tunae* Petrarch dwells upon the disagreeing of the mind as
one of the miseries to which flesh is heir. To quote his words
in an Elizabethan translation: "There is no warre woorse
then this, no not civile warre: For that is betweene factions
of citizens in the streetes of the cities, but this is fought
within the minde, betweene the partes of the soule."[30] The
Renaissance increasingly felt stresses and strains between
the parts of its soul, but it had to wait for Shakespeare
to achieve profound tragedy based upon inner struggle or
spiritual civil war.

The *De Remediis* is Petrarch's contribution *de contemptu
mundi* in the less subtle manner which so many of his contemporaries followed. The man who in the *Secretum* could
balance worldly evil against worldly good is here putting
his literary ability to the single task of proving that the

world is in no wise to be trusted. He betrays none of the
doubts that are in the other work. The *De Remediis* is an odd
mingling of Petrarch's literary sophistication with a humor-
less determination to prove the case at all costs which in
the modern world so often goes by the name of "medieval
naïvety." But here the "naïvety" is as old as Roman Stoicism.
Behind Petrarch is a work ascribed to Seneca, the *De Remediis Fortuitorum,*[31] where in dialogue form Stoic answers
are returned to the various ills of life. Petrarch's is a more
ambitious effort in exactly the same dialogue manner, using
much of the Stoic philosophy for Christian purposes, yet
manifesting an originality which we must respect. It makes
better reading than many another set disquisition upon the
vileness of the world. When we are not forced to smile, we
can find in it a certain real wisdom.

The work sets out to show how man must meet the fortunes of the world if he would save his soul. He must know
that the world is to be despised, not only when it sends bad
fortune, but also when it sends good; indeed, good fortune
is the harder for man to meet wisely. The first book, dealing
with good fortune, is a discussion between Joy and Reason
with some concluding argument between Hope and Reason. The second book turns to bad fortune, and in the same
schematic manner there are discussions between Sorrow
and Reason and between Fear and Reason. The capacity
of Reason to checkmate the good and the bad in life is dev-
astating. It can expose as hollow not only the more frivol-
ous and more sensual delights, but also all that we might
call the higher joys, even the best of human relationships
and the finest of artistic beauties. Reason is the perfect Chris-

tian Stoic dissecting mortal joys and mortal miseries to kill
all man's attachment to the things of the world.

Joy gives briefly the things in which it delights. Reason
is never at a loss. Does Joy delight in a nimble horse? "A
most fierce and vnquiet beast," says Reason, "which sleepeth
not, and is never satisfied." But, insists Joy, "I am desirous
to ryde horses." Reason counters, "It is not muche more
daungerous to sayle vppon the raging sea, then to ride vpon
a fierce prauncer."[32] Joy may find pleasure in something less
physical than horsemanship: "I am delighted in synging
and instruments." And Reason, coldly: "Ah, how muche
better were it in teares and syghinges? It were better to
come to ioy by weeping, then by ioying to teares."[33] Or
Joy may find worthiness in marriage and dwell at length
upon its beauties, concluding, in all happiness, "I have met
with a noble, chast, gentle, humble, obedient, vertuous, and
faythfull wyfe." "Humph!" comments Reason, "Thou art
a notable fouler, thou hast founde a whyte crowe: and yet
there is no man that thynketh he hath founde a blacke
one."[34] Thus the first book proceeds through a heterogeneous
list of subjects, which receive Elizabethan headings such
as: Flourishing Yeeres, The Goodly Beautie of the Body,
Freedome, Daunsing, Playing at Dice and Lottes, Precious
Stones and Pearles, The Abundance of Freendes, Treasure
Layde up in Store, and Sundry Spectacles and Shewes.

For the concerns of Sorrow the answers of Reason are no
less ready. Our miseries are not nearly so bad as they might
be; nay, they are blessings in disguise to expose the world
as it is and to fix our minds on higher things. If you lose
your mother by death, know that she has only gone the way

of all flesh and that a harsher mother still remains to take
your own body. If you lose your wife by death, you get
peace; only fools love their fetters, even though they are of
gold. Meet all sorrows with such wisdom: Deformitie of
the Bodye, Shamefull Byrth, Thynne Fare, An Unchaste
Wyfe, Blyndnesse, The Gout, or Payne of the Guttes.

This meanest of tribulations, Payne of the Guttes, for
example, is far from lacking in lessons of the highest worth
to the soul of the sufferer. *"Sorowe.* I suffer the payne of
the guttes. *Reason.* Begyn to hope, for there can happen
now nothing more greevous vnto thee. . . . *Sorowe.* I am tormented with the Iliacke passion. *Reason.* It is, I confesse,
an hard kynde of comfort, that a man can suffer nothing
more bitter . . . *Sorowe.* I am martyred with the payne in
the guttes. *Reason.* Whyle thou lyvest learne to dye, and
that which must be done but once, assay thou to do often . . .
The payne in the guttes is much lyke vnto death, saving that
death is shorter and easier, so that he that can beare that
payne valiantly, vnlesse some other feare come betweene
and alter the case, shal much more valiantly endure death.
Sorowe. I am torne in peeces by the iliacke passion. *Reason.*
The vehemencie of the payne promiseth an ende: for there
is no man long a dying."[35]

Let no reader rashly assume that Petrarch (or his Elizabethan translator) is here driving Contempt of the World
to a logical extremity with intent to satirize a "false taste"
of the Middle Ages.

IV

There is striking appearance of incongruity when Contempt of the World is found mingled with Renaissance

vitality in the ardently adventurous England of Elizabeth. Elizabethan Contempt was not indulged in by Puritans alone as an expression of their desire to return to an earlier, severer, and, as they thought, less contaminated Christianity. The taste for Contempt was general among the Elizabethans and called forth numberless works in the medieval tradition, both translations and more or less original productions. These were often put forth by men who were otherwise worldly enough in all conscience. Thomas Twyne, who provided the English translation of Petrarch's *De Remediis* which has just been laid under contribution, was apparently of this sort. The conflicting tastes of the age are rather neatly indicated by the fact that three years before he translated Petrarch's guide to the scorn of the world he compiled a guide to the lighter enjoyment of the world. He called this effort *The Schoolemaster or Teacher of Table Phylosophie* (1576). It is a concoction of good cheer concerning meats, drinks, sauces, and other such things, ending with a choice collection of jests, many of them bawdy, to be related at table.

Throughout the gallantly creative period of the Tudor and Jacobean reigns England produced literature contemning the world. In 1547, the year of Surrey's death, William Baldwin, who was later to make himself the chief of those responsible for the *Mirror for Magistrates,* published a book of classified sentences from the ancient philosophers. He called it *A Treatise of Morall Phylosophie.* Contempt of the World has more than due place in the collection. At the close of each chapter Baldwin offered a bit of indifferent versification serving as summary and unification of the ideas there recorded. That for Chapter IV of Book II has the familiar burden:

> The worlde is a region dyvers & variable,
> Of God created in the begyunyng
> To contayne his creatures of kynde innumerable.
> Where in eche one shoulde lyve by his winnyng.
> Whose many pleasures are cause of gret sīning
> Wherefore al that gladly, as vayne do thē hate,
> Shal after this worlde, have permanent estate.

Expression of this philosophy of life is by no means limited to that particular chapter.

Also in 1547, Robert Whyttynton translated the *De Remediis Fortuitorum,* which has already been mentioned in connection with Petrarch. In his dedication Whyttynton says that Aristotle is a prince of philosophers in ethics, but that none can compare with Seneca for practical benefit.

In 1556 came a Tudor translation of the *De Consolatione Philosophiae* of Boethius. It was done by George Colvile, or Coldewel, who dedicated it to Queen Mary with the pious hope that it would make men take their eyes off the world and fix them on Heaven. Though Boethius met adversity with an eclectic Hellenistic philosophy rather than with Christian doctrine, he was still a vital influence and still readily adaptable to the Christian scheme. On the title page of Colvile's translation it is said that the arguments of Boethius show the diversity of the life active and "the lyfe contemplatyue, that alwayes dyspyseth the worlde, and all thinges therin." Another translation of Boethius, by "I. T.," was published in 1609.

The year 1576 saw the publication of Innocent's famous

De Contemptu Mundi in two separate translations. One is by Humphrey Kerton, called *The Mirror of Mans Lyfe*. Kerton's epistle dedicatory is an excellent piece of prose for so early a work, and his translation is vivid, well-knit English. Kerton praises the book which he puts into English and agrees that man at his entrance into the world meets three capital enemies, namely, pain, care, and sorrow. It is no life to love here on earth. He praises but does not name the author, contenting himself with saying that he translates a work written "above three hūdred and threscore yeeres past, entituled The miscrie of man." Perhaps this was in deference to a Protestant England unlikely to see good in a pope, even when a pope wrote so praiseworthily. Kerton's work was popular. A second edition appeared even in the year of publication, a third in the next year, and a fourth in 1586. The other translation is by that facile participator in profane life and letters, George Gascoigne. Called "The View of Worldly Vanities," it makes the first part of his *The Droomme of Doomes Day,* a collection of weighty moral documents which Gascoigne himself says he assembled and translated in an attempt to balance his past sins. In his dedication to the Earl of Bedford he confesses with sadness "much time mispent, & of greater curiositie then was convenient, in penning and endightyng sundrie toyes and trifles." Gascoigne may have suffered, for the moment at least, a sort of religious conversion, or he may not. He says, again in his dedication, that he was pricked and much moved by the grave words of a friend, who, when hearing his (Gascoigne's) thriftless poesies undeservedly commended, remarked that he liked well the smell of these posies but would like the gardener better if he would employ his spade in the ground of divinity or moral philosophy. This critic may have been an honest friend calling Gascoigne to the life that is not transitory; then again, he may have been only a publisher urging a new and profitable kind of scribbling upon a man ready to take such advice. Like Kerton, perhaps again for a discreet purpose, Gascoigne does not name Pope Innocent. He simply says that he got his material from an old torn pamphlet imperfect in beginning and end, and that he does not know the author.

Three years later, under the same date that is borne by Twyne's translation of Petrarch's *De Remediis* (1579), Haly Heron's *A Newe Discourse of Morall Philosophie* was published. It was dedicated and given as a New Year's gift to John Kay the younger, Gentleman, by his "governour." Heron covers well-known ground. He begins with a chapter "Of Humilitie," showing how evil the world is and how foolish man is to prize it, and proceeds from the miserable calamities of this world to the inestimable joys of Heaven. His book is advertized on the title page as "not so pleasant as profitable for younge courtiours."

In 1584, one year after Paynell's translation of Erasmus' *De Contemptu Mundi,* there appeared a translation of a work in scorn of the world by Diego de Estrella, *The Contempte of the World and the Vanitie Thereof.* With familiar argument it declares that man can have no spiritual delight unless he despises the world and its pleasures, including the beauty of the body. This translation is notable because it is apparently a Catholic book.

A work showing strong Protestant bias on the part of both author and translator is *A Discourse of Life and Death Written in French by Ph. Mornay ... done in English by the Countesse of Pembroke* (1592). Philippe de Mornay, Seigneur du Plessis-Marly (1549–1623), was a Huguenot religious and political leader, the temper of whose thought appealed both to the Countess of Pembroke and to her brother Sir Philip Sidney. Sir Philip began a translation of another work by Mornay. It was finished by Arthur Golding and published as *A Woorke concerning the trewnesse of the Christian Religion, written in French: Against Atheists, Epicures, Paynims, Iewes, Mahumetists, and other Infidels* (1587). The *Discourse of Life and Death* was published by the Countess of Pembroke in a volume also containing her translation of Garnier's tragedy *Marc Antoine,* and this linking shows clearly the affinity which formal Contempt of the World and dramatic tragedy had for each other in the mind of at least one intellectual Elizabethan. As the two translations are arranged in the countess' little book, the *Discourse* is obviously regarded as introduction, in the way of moral philosophy, to the profound matters of life and death around which the tragedy takes its shape. Garnier's lengthy Senecan moralizings are well supported by its argument. Mornay's *Discourse,* despite its Protestant authorship, is but the time-tried Contempt developed by Catholic Christianity. Life, it maintains, is a series of vanities where one wins, at the cost of great struggle, a progress through the ages of man: Childhood, a foolish simplicity; Youth, a vain heat; Manhood, a painful carefulness; Old Age, a noisome languishing. Death is the one thing certain in life. It is the issue out of our miseries and the entrance into that haven where we shall ride in safety from all winds. Man is from Heaven. Heaven is his country and his air. When he is in his body, he suffers exile and confinement. But suicide is cowardly and in no wise allowed.

The formal disquisition contemning the world in medieval fashion quickly lost general popularity in the England of the seventeenth century. In 1613 there was published *The Golden Meane,* probably by Antony Stafford. It dwells upon the chief misfortunes which can happen to men of "honour and nobilitie," such as neglect, banishment, imprisonment, death. The philosophy is far more classical than Christian. Heaven is not the end toward which man should strive so much as the Golden Mean "aunciently commended," the possession of oneself in resolution and moderation. However, George Strode's *The Anatomie of Mortalitie* (1618) offers comfort to pious Christians by closing with a chapter on "The Glorious Estate of the Saints after this Life." Strode is described as "Vtter-barister of the middle temple."[36] Likewise religious in the older manner, John Moore's *A Mappe of Mans Mortalitie* (1617), which preaches at length that this transitory world is a dungeon of ill favors, is the work of a minister and is buttressed with Biblical texts.

During the years of the sixteenth and seventeenth centuries which called forth these works of moral philosophy scorning the world and which at the same time produced manifold worldly activity, the Elizabethan taste in poetry was divided between serious contemplation of the world's vanities and happy, often delicate, realization of its beauties.

If the more gallant mood survives as overwhelmingly dominant in our own anthologies of Elizabethan poetry, it is not
because the dominance had been so clearly established in
Elizabethan times. The two most popular anthologies for
Elizabethan readers, Tottel's *Miscellany* (1557) and *The
Paradise of Dainty Devices* (1576), may stand for the division of taste. The first sets the lighter tone. The second sets
a tone of seriousness in the best manner of Contempt, be
ginning with a "translation of the blessed Saint Barnard's
verses, conteynyng the vnstable felicitie of this wayfaring
worlde" and living up to its beginning. In later editions the
Paradise becomes even more sedate.[37] If popularity is to be
judged by frequent republication, then the *Paradise* with
its ten editions from 1576 to 1606 actually had the best of
Tottel's *Miscellany,* with its eight editions from 1557 to 1587.
With the exception of Tottel's, no other miscellany reached
a popularity anything like that of the *Paradise.*[38] The *Mirror
for Magistrates* was enormously prolific in editions and imitations until 1610, but it was no true miscellany. Its popularity is partly to be accounted for, however, by the fact that
it offered the same kind of doleful moralizing that was
offered by the *Paradise.*

v

The access of interest in human suffering which accompanied the development of Contempt of the World could
only become the foundation for a great tragic art by changing ascetic scorn for the active life that produced suffering
into sympathy and understanding. The change was made
gradually and surely, though conventional ascetic scorn
continued even so late as the sixteenth century to find such

frequent expression as has been indicated. The tide was bearing men from otherworldliness to thisworldliness, and the movement involved a general shift from the ascetic view of the substance of tragedy toward the artistic or poetic view.

The otherworldly and ascetic temper in the Middle Ages was content to regard the suffering and evil of mortal life merely as a dark foil against which the beauties of Heaven could be made to glisten with greater splendor. It seems to have had a feeling that God in his infinite wisdom had permitted this world to become a trackless forest of unexplainable evil dominated by an utterly fickle spirit of Fortune so that we should yearn more strongly for the perfection of Heaven and strive more earnestly to reach it after death. Medieval vilification of the world of flesh in order to detach man's desires from it may be paralleled in Buddhism—for the ways of asceticism are peculiar to no creed. Buddhism has its positive contemplations upon the illimitable sublime moods, but for aspirants who are overly susceptible to the blandishments of the world it has a negative meditation "On Foul Things."[39] If the aspirant loves the body, he may meditate on it part by part, beginning, "For as the body when dead is repulsive, so is it also when alive." He points out to himself that it is a prey to vermin and the seat of disease, that through its nine apertures it is always discharging matter "like a ripe boil."[40] He may walk in a charnel field to find some fit object for meditation; such as the decaying body of a once beautiful woman. Or he may fix before his mind the idea of a skeleton.[41] These devices differ from the medieval treatise *de contemptu mundi* and kindred products of Christian asceticism in only one way. They are aids to an elevation of spirit which has no ultimate need for anything like a Christian Heaven. A wholly logical accessory to the picture of the evil world in any treatise *de contemptu mundi* is a picture of Heaven. The second picture follows as naturally in George Strode's *Anatomie of Mortalitie*—a work published as late as 1618—as in the twelfth-century *De Contemptu Mundi* of Bernard of Morlaix, which has produced our hymn *Jerusalem the Golden.*[42] Where the second picture was not presented by the author, men's faith was equal to the task of supplying it. Otherworldly Christianity in the Middle Ages argued the vanity of mortal affairs with eclectic appeal to later classic philosophy. It took much help from Stoicism, but where the ascetic Stoic sought to outface mundane vanity by possessing his soul here and now, the ascetic Christian sought rather to flee mundane vanity and possess his soul hereafter. In that respect he was closer to the Neo-Platonist. He reminds us, for example, of Maximus of Tyre (second century of our era), who thought of the blissful soul after death as "like one who from a land of barbarians has come amongst Greeks, from a city lawless, despot-ridden, torn by faction, has come to a city where law prevails, where the ruler is a king, where all is peace."[43]

Medieval otherworldliness *per se* was thus as unfavorable to a beginning artistic development of Gothic tragedy as the later classic philosophy which surrendered the world was unfavorable to a continued artistic development of Greek tragedy. It, too, pictured the suffering of this world as lacking in any inherent order and saw no heroism in tragic struggle; the man who strove and suffered under the yoke of the world it thought a fool. It sought to realize Heaven without realizing earth, and its approach to the misfortunes of mortality was the opposite of poetic. For the business of the poet is to realize life here and now and thereby to realize a life of the spirit, if he will; it is the special business of the tragic poet to realize the meaning of suffering in terms given by earthly life. Not by reference to a future life and by that reference alone can he make human agony have significance. It is his privilege to take our mortal senses under his spell and somehow make them subscribe to an immortal truth in his vision.

Nevertheless, the Contempt of the World in which medieval otherworldliness found one of its most satisfying means of expression was not brought into being in the same way as later classic scorn for the world, since it was a reaction against growing vitality instead of an expression of dying vitality. And for reasons growing out of this difference it contributed powerfully to the development of Gothic tragedy. As it acquired secular appeal it assumed, as we have seen, a rudimentary tragic function, however incompatible with tragedy it might be in ascetic purpose. And with tireless iteration it beckoned attention to the matter upon which a tragic art could exercise itself. The spirit of the Renaissance which worked for man's espousal of the world was not slow to accept the challenge.

Certainly as early as the fourteenth century an approach to human suffering which may be called tragic in the artistic sense was in definite process of revelation for Gothic Europe. A new willingness was being shown to search the suffering of mortality for some primary and inherent meaning. This was manifested with great clearness, for example, in a religious cult of Christ's Passion accompanied by an expressive religious art. The Christian scorn of the world which viewed the fortunes of mankind as inherently meaningless really made the agonies of Jesus, by logical implication, just as meaningless in their mundane setting, since it could not escape the Christian doctrine that Jesus, though he was God, was likewise completely man and had suffered as men do. But granted a development of artistic and humane potentialities, Christianity had perforce to know eventually that through artistic representation the Passion of its Christ could be made to speak of mortal fortunes in a tone far different from that of scorn or contempt, and could be made to discover a bond of pity and love for the souls of men.

By the fourteenth century such representation was assured, and through the fifteenth and sixteenth centuries it proliferated in a great variety of forms. Chiefly, of course, it had to do with Christ's figure on the cross. There was complete contrast between the later Gothic figure of Christ crucified and that of early Christianity. In the course of ten centuries restraints had been withdrawn one by one. Artistic realization of the crucifixion had proceeded from merely symbolic representation to actual representation in which the figure of Christ appeared, then from representation of a robed figure to that of a disrobed figure, then from representation of a living figure to that of a dead figure and concurrently from representation of Christ's calm triumph over death to that of his torture by death." At the same time that other religious art had turned from allegory and symbol

F

toward realism—in other words, turned from hinting at inexpressible beauty in shadows toward capturing express-ible beauty in firm material—the art of the crucifixion had brought Christ down from a spiritual calm which men could only guess at to a mortal agony which men could feel and understand.

By the fifteenth century a nude Christ was represented upon the cross with a full showing of emaciated flesh and of sinews racked by torture.[45] Where the thirteenth century had delighted in picturing the teaching of Christ, this cen-tury delighted in picturing the blood from his wounds as itself a teaching. The head of the crucified figure now sagged in a swoon of pain or in death, and the nailed hands, instead of being stretched horizontally, were elevated to bear the full weight of the body. The head was not bare, as formerly, but thorn-crowned; sometimes blood trickled over the hair and beard. From all that we know we must judge that this picture would have been repulsive to primi-tive Christians.

The art of the later Middle Ages—from the beginning of the fourteenth century—occupied itself also with other aspects of Christ's suffering. It represented him as bound and awaiting crucifixion, or as laboring to carry the cross.[46] A cult of the precious sacrificial blood produced such curi-ous traditions in art as the Fountain of Life and the Mystic Wine-Press, the first representing the blood from the cruci-fied Christ as pouring into a basin in which humanity may bathe, and the second representing it as expressed from his body under the screws of a wine-press and gathered into vats and casks by industrious seekers after salvation.[47] By

extension, the Passion of Christ created the Passion of Mary
the Mother and the Passion of God the Father, each with
various imaginative realizations of the suffering surrounding the crucifixion.[48]

With Professor Émile Mâle, the learned and sympathetic
historian of medieval religious art, one must pose the question why "in the fourteenth century Christians wished to
see their God suffer and die." As he says, it explains nothing
except popular familiarity with details of the crucifixion
if we appeal to the mystery plays. The taste for realistic representation of the crucifixion in drama must also have had
its origin in the desire which we seek to explain.[49] We may
turn back to St. Francis of Assisi, who had a revelation of
the Passion as he contemplated the crucified Christ and was
the great rediscoverer of pity for Christianity.[50] But even
so, whence came St. Francis and whence came the mood in
other Christians which accepted his discovery with such
fervor? It is preferable perhaps to leave the explanation implicit in a general development of the Gothic spirit: interest
in suffering for its inherent meaning was part of the growing interest in the world.

Tragic preoccupation with the details of suffering and
death as something other than a contrast to the glories
of Heaven even crept into the traditional expressions of
Contempt of the World. The artistic temper inconsistently
existed side by side with the ascetic temper, sometimes doing its best to make Contempt no contempt at all, but an
evidence of emotional absorption in the world. Artistic
espousal of the world is never very obvious in the formal
treatise *de contemptu mundi*. But when one studies the

realism of the Death Dance, of the representations of death on funeral monuments, of the miniatures illustrating in profusely gory detail the falls of princes, one must realize that here was a growingly affectionate absorption of the artist in human misfortune for its inner self. It came at the same time as absorption in the suffering and death of Jesus, and was similar in so many ways that it must be referred to the same moving spirit. It has been said that the plague in Europe in the later Middle Ages brought men to face death with new realization. That it helped men to realize the inevitability of death is certain, but to advance it as first cause for the access of interest in the frailty of mortal life would be shortsighted indeed.

Thus that vital desire of the Renaissance to study and to realize the world of men, which Contempt of the World was meant to countervail, grew so vigorously that it found matter for study even in the life pictured by Contempt of the World as enforcement of its arguments. Nowhere is this fact plainer than in the tragical stories of the falls of princes which are now to be discussed. Here the tragic inner meaning of life was pursued philosophically in the very midst of counterargument that mortal struggle was utterly without inherent meaning. Again we shall see that in the Renaissance one and the same man could both scorn the world and espouse it.

Chapter III

FALLS OF PRINCES: BOCCACCIO

IN 1362 an obscure man, who is mentioned as a Carthusian monk named Ciani, sought out Boccaccio at Florence and conveyed to him an apocalyptic warning. Boccaccio's death was imminent, and his damnation in Hell was certain unless he should repent of his sins. This had been seen in a vision by one Pietro Petroni, whose blessed religious life and whose death in the odor of sanctity gave authority to the revelation. Boccaccio was profoundly shaken. He wrote to Petrarch, proposing to give up his pursuit of profane literature, sell his treasured library, and go into an ascetic retirement where he would devote what remained of his life to religious contemplation. Though Petrarch had something of asceticism in his own character, his humanism was stronger. He knew the virtue which lay in abjuring the world's vanities, but he could not be persuaded that learning was vain. Surely God rejoiced at the perfection of man's soul through learning! Petrarch gave his friend sympathetic but prudent counsel. Boccaccio kept his books and did not retire into contemplative inactivity.[1]

Here is more than the passing aberration of an impressionable and rather unstable temperament. The incident does not inaugurate a change in Boccaccio's character, but it does reveal the extent of a change which had already taken place. For almost ten years Boccaccio had been undergoing religious and artistic conversion from what he considered his youthful follies, and the news of Petroni's vision simply came at the right time to fan the fires of repentance already burning briskly. Soon after his completion of the *Decameron,* when he was forty years of age, Boccaccio began to feel that life and letters were not to be taken with gay zest, but with the utmost seriousness.[2] What was only indulgent raillery against women in the *Decameron* turned to bitter invective and moralizing in the *Corbaccio,* and through personal resentment aroused by one woman approached monkish scorn of womankind. Finally, somewhat as Tolstoy did late in life, Boccaccio abandoned a creative art which had been highly successful in the capture of life's color and flavor, and, embracing asceticism at least as an ideal, he devoted his gifts to a moral and humanistic purpose. It was an ideal of scholarly as well as moral asceticism that he struggled to hold before himself. He decided to abandon writing in Italian, the vulgar tongue of worldly activity, and to write in Latin, the enduring tongue of wise antiquity and of learned posterity, as Petrarch had taught him to believe. His new writing was to be based upon scholarly researches into books more than upon observation and experience of life. But the genius of Boccaccio was not dead. He still possessed an ability to seize unerringly upon the primary emotional concerns of his age and make them articulate in new literary forms.

The first of Boccaccio's Latin works produced under the impulse of a new moral and humanistic fervor was the *De Casibus Virorum Illustrium.* It was also the greatest in its power to take hold upon men's imaginations and to compel translation into, or imitation in, Italian, French, Spanish, German, and English. This culling from history and tradition of eminent men and women who had suffered notable falls from prosperity into misfortune had the vitality of varied appeal. On its ascetic side it was an earnest and effective contribution to the literature *de contemptu mundi*. On its humanistic side it was a learned and eminently useful compilation from universal history. Finally, on its artistic side it was a true innovation in that it gave for the first time a definite form to the vague medieval conception of tragedy, which, according to its most famous definition, found in Dante's epistle to Can Grande, was that "tragedy in its beginning is admirable and quiet, in its ending or catastrophe foul and horrible."

The story of a fall from felicity into misfortune cast in the form which Boccaccio devised bore the name of tragedy down through the Middle Ages and even later. In Elizabethan England it bore the name without apology along with the newly born dramatic tragedy, and there is small evidence of anybody's critical concern that it should not do so. Its extremely popular method of approaching tragic material could not fail to affect the Elizabethan dramatist, and we shall see in due time how much he was under its influence. Long before Gothic popular drama came to the point of analyzing misfortune in the way of tragedy, the Boccacesque *De Casibus* story was attempting the process.

In fact, for the Middle Ages the *De Casibus* was Boccaccio's greatest book, greater even than the *Decameron*. The first version of the *De Casibus* was probably finished about 1360 and given to the world about 1363–1364; a revised version was finished sometime before the death of Petrarch, that is, before October, 1374. The *Decameron* had probably

been completed as early as 1353.ª Yet in France and Spain
the *De Casibus* was the first by some few years to be translated, and in England the first by more than a century.
More strangely still, the international reputation which
Boccaccio acquired was at its beginning frequently unac-
companied even by general knowledge of the *Decameron*
among the reading public. This was apparently true in
England as late as the sixteenth century.ᵃ Of course, Latin
was an international language and Italian was not. But we
today, delighting as we do to honor the *Decameron* for its
joie de vivre and accustomed as we are to decry and neglect
the *De Casibus* for its monotonous asceticism or its "commonplace"⁵ moralizing, must make the effort to realize that
the *De Casibus* in its time had power to speak to men's souls
of human destiny as the *Decameron* never could. It had
high seriousness, at least for its own age.

Boccaccio himself repudiated his *Decameron* as not only
light-minded but also pernicious, and he apparently suffered
sincere agonies of contrition for it. Mainardo dei Cavalcanti, the very same friend to whom he offered the *De Casibus* with an affectionate dedication, was willing to let the
women of the Cavalcanti household read the *Decameron,*
and innocently thought to compliment Boccaccio by telling
him so. The compliment provoked a letter from Boccaccio
written in a vein of highly emotional and rhetorical penitence. Most certainly, Boccaccio replied, he would not commend Mainardo for exposing the noble ladies in his family
to the vulgar jests of the *Decameron:* "Rather indeed I be-
seech you in the name of your moral beliefs not to do this.
You know how many things are therein which are indecent

and inimical to chastity, how many unfortunate goadings
to lust, how many incitements to crime even if breasts are
sheathed in iron, because of which though noble ladies are
not impelled to unchaste deeds—especially when sacred
shame sits enthroned on their brows—alluring temptations
steal in with stealthy step."[16] This conviction that the book
was sinful was shown at other times and not only to Mainardo. How much it led Boccaccio to hinder the circulation of the *Decameron* in manuscript, we can only guess. It
must have had something of that effect.[7]

These two collections of stories, the *Decameron* and the
De Casibus, so largely antithetical in temper, show again ♭
the close juxtaposition in the Renaissance of espousal and
contempt of worldly life. In Boccaccio one attitude tended
to supplant and exclude the other. Mainardo perhaps was
a more normal man of his time, able to enjoy both and to
let even the ladies of his household enjoy both, remaining
content that the two attitudes should alternate and balance
each other. But we may guess that even Mainardo found
the *De Casibus* a more profound and greater work than the
Decameron.

II

The *De Casibus* is a series of prose stories in a vision framework. Boccaccio pictures himself besieged by a regiment
of unhappy ghosts who know of his intent to write a book
concerning the misfortunes of illustrious men and women,
and who beg with all degrees of mute or loquacious insistence to have their stories told. Usually they come weeping
or lamenting. From this procession of misery, Boccaccio,
as he sits in his study writing, chooses those whose misfor-

tunes seem to him important enough to be recorded at length. The rest he passes in review, sometimes naming this one or that one and bestowing perhaps brief words of description upon their ills. Frequently between stories we find the troop of perturbed ghosts returning to beg for pitiful recognition in that mortal world which they have left so unhappily. Boccaccio is harassed by the numbers and hurries on, though not unkindly. The method is monotonous, yet artistically effective in its dramatic implication that the weight of misfortune in the world is incalculable and that its line of victims will stretch out to the crack of doom. Sometimes it is even more dramatic, as, for example, where the long story of Queen Brunhilde is told entirely as a spirited debate between Boccaccio and the queen herself concerning the degree of her guilt. Usually Boccaccio tells a story instead of letting the subject tell it. The author leaves himself free to break the procession of incident wherever he wishes to indulge in moral comment or personal digression. Through nine books he thus records the most notable tragedies of all races and ages, with an attempt at chronological order. Naturally, the tragedy of Adam and Eve comes first. That of King John of France, who was defeated and captured by the British at Poitiers in 1356, comes last.

There is true originality in Boccaccio's conception.[8] The pitiful desire of the damned in Dante's *Inferno* to tell their calamities and to be remembered on earth has obvious similarity to the desire of Boccaccio's ghosts for recognition of their tragedies, but Boccaccio's concern with misfortune is quite different from Dante's in essential quality. Nor is the essential quality possessed by the *De Casibus* to be found

in any previous formal collection of the lives of illustrious
men. It is difficult to see how the plan of the book could
have come from the *Fables* of Hyginus, as has been suggested,⁹ though Boccaccio certainly used Hyginus in the
De Claris Mulieribus for the stories of Argia, Hypsipyle,
and Hypermnestra.¹⁰ The impelling purpose of Hyginus is
utterly different from that of Boccaccio in the *De Casibus*.
Hyginus collects notable gods or human beings of myth
and legend with no framework in which to place them
and with no moral or artistic purpose. He is the scholar
simply and solely, giving a brief summary and partial classification of antique lore. When he deals with famous unfortunates, he is often pedantic in a way that Boccaccio never
is. For example, he laboriously assembles unadorned information concerning fathers who have killed their daughters,
mothers who have killed their sons, wives who have killed
their husbands, husbands who have killed their wives, persons who have killed themselves, or those who have been
torn to pieces and eaten by dogs. In no way are such classified summaries tragedies in the Boccacesque sense, though
there is material here out of which tragedies could be made.
Hyginus was a freedman of the Roman emperor Augustus
and superintendent of the Palatine library. It may be that
his book of fables is not now as he left it, but we may judge
his instincts to have been wholly those of the scholarly
librarian, the maker of reference books.

As a source of Boccaccio's inspiration a more promising
collection of human misfortunes would be the *De Mortibus
Persecutorum* of Lactantius, written at the beginning of the
fourth century. Boccaccio, as we should expect, knew Lac-

tantius.[11] The *De Mortibus* unquestionably has primary concern with the falls of princes from high place into misery and death, though it has nothing of the ghostly machinery which Boccaccio gave the *De Casibus*. It looks on misfortune from a Christian moral viewpoint, details torture and suffering with righteous realism, and at times sounds notes similar to those produced in the medieval chorus contemning the world. It plays more than a minor part in the history of the Christian idea of divine justice and the application of that idea to tragedy. But it shows very little of the artistic tragic sense which gives to particular misfortune a certain universal significance. Lactantius is not dealing with princes in general, and he is not dealing by choice with the humanity of princes. As he sees them, his sufferers are mostly villains, monsters who have cast themselves off from humanity and can never for a moment elicit sympathy, at least from a Christian. His book is one long ecclesiastical lawyer's brief attempting to prove that the Roman emperors and officials who persecuted Christians were so smitten by the hand of an angry God that they died in terrible and repulsive fashion. It is in the main purely partisan theology, attempting not so much to justify the ways of God to man in general as to justify the ways of a tribal god to men of an enemy tribe worshiping other gods. This is not tragedy, not even the naïve tragedy showing a general and absolute poetic justice. Boccaccio now and then can show the same theological spirit, but his guiding philosophy is of quite another kind.

On the fringes of Lactantius' pageant of emperors and hirelings smitten by God we occasionally find less villainous sufferers far enough removed from the theological argument to be near tragedy, at least in the medieval sense. Galerius is one of the most vicious of the persecutors, a ferocious wild beast who deserves the most exquisite form of punishment and gets it. He dies corrupted and devoured by worms. He is nothing more than a typical villain whose case history the author uses for his argument. Lactantius dwells with zest upon the foul odor of his corrupted flesh, his terror at his living dissolution, and his last-minute useless attempt to placate the Christians and their God. But Galerius leaves a wife Valeria, who is later drawn into the general destruction along with her mother Prisca, and toward these women Lactantius is less cruelly righteous, perhaps because he cannot quell an admiration for Valeria's chaste refusal to marry again. Daia, the adopted son of Galerius, offers to put away his own wife to marry Valeria, but she indignantly rejects him. Daia seizes all her possessions, tortures her eunuchs to death, and banishes her. For fifteen months she wanders in mean garb from province to province. At length she is discovered in Thessalonica and apprehended with her mother. Says Lactantius: "Both the ladies were conducted to execution; a fall from grandeur which moved the pity of the multitude of beholders that the strange sight had gathered together. They were beheaded and their bodies cast into the sea. Thus the chaste demeanour of Valeria, and the high rank of her and her mother proved fatal to both of them."[12]

Some part of this story has the right medieval sound: the fall from grandeur of one who had been a princess, the pity of beholders, the high rank which proved fatal to its holder.

It would be but a step for Lactantius to moralize it all by referring to the fickleness of Fortune and the folly of trusting in the world. He prepares for the moral almost as well as Boccaccio might have done, yet does not finish with medieval logic. The truth is, of course, that Lactantius was preoccupied with the struggle of Christianity for a place in the world and not with its struggle to keep love of the world from killing its faith in Heaven. That other struggle became intense only with the Renaissance, as we have already seen.

But the informing spirit of the *De Casibus* had existed before Boccaccio, though not in any ambitious collection of stories. Boccaccio's presupposition or working hypothesis amounts in its simplest terms only to this: All the notable tragedies which a diligent man can collect from literature, tradition, and observation show without exception that the mortal world (as distinct from Heaven) is ruled by Fortune, the irrational spirit of chance. The fact that the power of Fortune is really the power of God, when considered rightly, since all things proceed from God, does not make Fortune any the less irrational. God simply has different methods of procedure in Heaven, which is perfect, and on earth, which is imperfect. On earth, because of imperfection and because of Fortune's dominance, there is no perceptible order of cause and effect such as would permit an ambitious man to avoid material misfortune by forethought, by wise judgment and action, or even, strange to say, by the most perfect allegiance to God and the Christian religion. In other words, no man, no matter how great or powerful—and the falls of the great ones are best proofs of the argument—has any control whatever over his mortal fate. The moral is plain enough: Trust not at all in this world, but in the next world; the one mortal event certain for all men is death; embark upon no ambitious worldly action, covet nothing that the world can give you, busy yourself with nothing in this world except spiritual preparation for Heaven. Manifestly, the idea stated thus baldly, and, it must be admitted, with some unfairness to certain subtleties in the *De Casibus,* is only a specially developed branch of the old argument for Contempt of the World.

Yet if Boccaccio had done no more than pursue without subtlety a plan based on this presupposition, he would deserve credit for giving literary body to what other men had only hinted at. He would have shown that truly original aspect of genius which either revives the old and transmutes it or develops the old into a new fullness, instinctively at just the time when the world needs and will gladly welcome the new creation.

Long before Boccaccio, the possibilities of exploiting the *De Contemptu Mundi* theme in tragical storytelling were quite obvious. Earlier writers whose concern was the proper scorn of the world frequently enforced their arguments by casual mention of a sheaf of great men who had suffered indignity at the hands of Fortune. In classic literature we need look no farther than Seneca for an example of the method which would appeal to the Middle Ages. In his dialogue *De Consolatione* addressed to Marcia upon the death of a son, Seneca asks: "Why need I remind you of the deaths of the other Caesars, whom fortune appears to me some times to have outraged in order that even by their deaths they might be useful to mankind, by proving that not even they, although they were styled 'sons of gods' and 'fathers of gods to come', could exercise the same power over their own fortunes which they did over those of others?"[13] For the particular benefit of Marcia, Seneca reviews briefly the misfortunes of Augustus and Tiberius Caesar, who suffered the loss of children or grandchildren. Seneca's Stoic scorn of the world magnified self-possession and did not turn the eyes Heavenward as did Christian contempt, but the Senecan picture of Fortune, "capricious in her rewards and punishments as a fickle, whimsical, and careless mistress is with those of her slaves,"[14] was easily taken over into the Christian magnification of Heaven. The argument of Seneca that imperial misfortunes show how little any man may control the world, and his mention of specific examples, are by the same token a Christian *De Casibus* in the germ.

Boethius also, in his *De Consolatione Philosophiae,* which became a Christian classic though it offers no truly Christian consolation, shows all the possibilities of a *De Casibus*. Philosophy puts the question to Boethius: "Can kingdoms or the familiarity of princes make a man mighty?" And Boethius replies in the simplicity of a heart still unconverted from worldliness, "How can it be otherwise, since their felicity doth always endure?" Philosophy is firm with such gross delusion. "Mistake not," she says, "for both antiquity and the present times abound with examples of kings and potentates who have been forced to change an happy for a calamitous estate. And then we may justly cry out, how great and glorious a thing is Power, which is not of ability to preserve even itself?"[15] Had Boccaccio been looking for a text, these words of Philosophy would have served neatly. And in Boethius, too, names are named to make such tragedy concrete. Down through the Middle Ages this fashion of casually naming mighty unfortunates in discussions of Fortune was inordinately popular. Jean de Meung helped to establish its popularity in a passage of that thirteenth-century classic, the *Roman de la Rose*.[16] Here Reason strives to turn the Lover from his infatuation by arguing that Fortune deals as capriciously and unkindly with lovers as with princes and other great men of the world. Nero is cited as a preëminent victim of Fortune. When Chaucer imitated Boccaccio's *De Casibus* in his *Monkes Tale,* he laid this passage under contribution.

In *Ubi Sunt* lyrical poetry there is many a *De Casibus* in little. Again there are the lists of great names, but it is not the conqueror Fortune that is sung; it is the conqueror worm. Still, the moral is much the same: Think not that power lasts. The *Ubi Sunt* verses of St. Bernard—if they are indeed his—are not the fountainhead of it all, for behind them is one of the meters of Boethius quite in the manner, and behind that is much similar melancholy meditation in later classical authors.[17] Christian Contempt of the World usually betrays its debt to Hellenistic despair of the world. But like Boccaccio for his *De Casibus*, St. Bernard—or someone else—for his *Ubi Sunt* poem must be credited with the genius able to put into a memorable developed form what before had been casual. The twelfth century, discovering anew the temptations of power, was ready for his verses, and his instinct filled a need. The meter of Boethius is mild in spirit by comparison with such stanzas as

G

these, taken from the Elizabethan translation of "the blessed Saint Barnards verses" in *The Paradise of Dainty Devices:*

> Where is the sacred king, that Salomon the wyse?
> Whose wysdome, former time, of duetie did commend:
> Where is that Samson strong, that monstrous man in syze?
> Whose forced arme, dyd cause the mighty pillers bend.
> Where is the peareles Prince, the freendly Ionathas?
> Or Absolon, whose shape and fauour did surpasse.
>
> Where is that Caesar nowe, whose hygh renowmed fame,
> Of sundry conquestes wonne, throughout the world did sound?
> Or *Diues* riche in store, and rich in richely name,
> Whose chest with gold and dishe, with daynties did abound.
> Where is the passing grace, of *Tullies* pleding skill?
> Or *Aristotles* vayne, whose penne had witte and wyll.
>
> O foode of filthy woorme, oh lumpe of lothsome clay,
> O life full like the deawe, which mornyng sunne dooth waste:
> O shadowe vayne, whose shape with sunne dooth shrinke away,
> Why gloryest thou so much, in honour to be plaste?
> Sith that no certayne houre, of life thou dost enioy,
> Most fyt it were, thy tyme in goodnesse to employ.[18]

Had Boccaccio, then, done no more than elaborate the suggested tragic material in previous moralizings upon Fortune and in *Ubi Sunt* poetry, he would have raised a self-sufficient literary form where none such had existed before. He would have realized the dramatic potentialities of the vision setting for tragical stories and have made a pageant of what before had been rather lifeless cataloguing. He did more than this, very decidedly. In the *De Casibus,* Boccaccio obviously sets out to write one more piece of testimony to the utterly fickle ways of Fortune and the need of scorning the world. But as he proceeds, immersing himself in the details of his stories, asking himself why this man fell and why that, he lets himself make or imply answers which cannot be fitted into the orthodox scheme of a *De Contemptu Mundi*. Sometimes he attempts to reconcile contradictions. Again he allows them to stand, giving no sign that he realizes them as we do. He is constantly held by his *De Contemptu Mundi* scheme, yet is constantly urged to break it with the fullness of life which he pours into it. The *De Casibus* is more than the literary curiosity, the dry museum piece, which modern criticism often makes it. Its author has something of the artistic subtlety possessed by the poet who subjects himself to the norm of iambic pentameter, yet strains beyond the norm toward other rhythms. The variation is the mark of vitality. The *De Casibus* is full of personal vitality which cannot easily be cabined and confined.

What the vitality of Boccaccio does is at times to reach forth for tragedy that is more than "medieval" in the commonly accepted meaning of the term. Where ascetic Contempt of the World would despise the activity of life, Boccaccio can let himself deal with life fondly and sympathetically. Where Contempt would postulate that calamity is brought to pass by irrational Fortune and cannot be plotted, Boccaccio can let himself suggest a plot for it. And where Contempt would nullify ambition and the desire for fame, Boccaccio can let himself defend ambition in other men and, like Petrarch in the *Secretum,* stoutly assert his own hope of fame. After his conversion the will to asceticism is in Boccaccio, but the flesh is weak.

III

At the very beginning of the *De Casibus,* Boccaccio faces the problem of what causes misfortune. He makes his entry confidently as a moralist and theologian, and only hesitantly as a tragic artist. He says that as he was pondering some means by which he could make his studies of profit to the world, he thought of noble and illustrious characters and wondered at their misadventures. As he was blaming their follies and marveling at the patience of a benign God, the idea which he sought occurred to him. He would tell the stories of great unfortunates in such a way as to show truly "the power which God, or (according to their own manner of speaking) Fortune, has over those in high place."[19] He would review the misfortunes of the great of all times and both sexes in order not to tax any special time or either sex. And so when great rulers should read of princes old and broken, shattered in their falls, they would realize the power of God, their own weakness, and the small surety which lies in Fortune. They would use moderation and discretion when affairs went well with them, and they would profit by the example of others. To break the monotony of this succession of stories he would interject from time to time attacks upon vice and incitements to virtue. All this Boccaccio vowed to do by the sufferance of God and to the glory of God.

It is a pious and ambitious but not wholly clear beginning. Boccaccio wishes great men to profit by the examples which he will give them, but he is somewhat vague about the form of profit. He does not say that by gaining in-

centives to the use of moderation and discretion they may
escape the misfortunes exemplified; yet he seems to hint at
this very benefit. His central theme as he tells the stories
is not to be man's rational power either over himself or
over circumstances, but man's powerlessness in an irrational
world. Seemingly, the only lesson which Boccaccio can teach
is humility, and the only profit to be expected from the lesson is the inheritance of Heaven. Such a lesson would be in
strict accordance with the *De Contemptu* tradition. Yet even
in his announcement of intention Boccaccio betrays a tendency in conflict with the *De Contemptu* preachments. As
for his assertion that the power of Fortune is in reality the
power of God and his following statement of intention to
make his stories show both the power of God and the small
surety which lies in Fortune, we shall see later the meaning of this apparent confusion and the manner in which
Boccaccio inherited it from Christian thought. Boccaccio
is glorifying the omnipotence and rational justice of God,
yet clinging to Fortune as the expression of a fickle chance
which operates in the world.

The power of Fortune came into being because of Adam's
and Eve's disobedience to God, as Boccaccio explains in his
first story. This first Fall of Man made possible the later
falls of princes. Through that first Fall all miseries entered
this world of ours, all misfortunes, all those things by which
men post along the road toward inescapable death: in a
word, all the "mockery of Fortune."[20]

This, then, was the origin of tragedy. It subjected the
world to irrational evil forces and made possible sudden
reversals of Fortune such as Lydgate describes in the *Fall*

of Princes when he seizes the opportunity to expand Boccaccio's argument at this point:

> Sodeyn departyng out of felicite
> Into miserie and mortal hevynesse,
> Vnwar depryvyng of our prosperite,
> Chaung off gladnesse into wrechchidnesse.[21]

The moral, as Boccaccio gives it, is that we should keep
God's commandments and endure the sacred yoke of obedi-
ence so that, though this world is transitory and evil, we
may inherit after death a world which is eternal and good,
the world which Adam and Eve lost for us. The mortal
world, it seems, is by nature given over to tragedy which it
is useless to struggle against or strive to understand.

By the beginning of his third book we find Boccaccio
stopping to ponder the matter further. It is the place at
which he tells the famous story of the combat between Poverty and Fortune. He raises the philosophical problem of
the measure of responsibility in the individual man for his
own misfortunes, and here, we may think, is a step on the
way toward subtle artistic plotting of tragedy. But if it is
the artist and the thinker in Boccaccio who proposes the
question, it is the ascetic who answers it. As we shall see,
he pulls himself back to Contempt of the World.

After achieving so much of a lengthy journey through
the misfortunes of great men, he must stop to rest like any
other traveler, says Boccaccio, and consider what he is doing. At last it seems to him (if his judgment is to be trusted)
that these people who have fallen into misery have provoked their own misfortunes. He remembers and finds true
a fable which he heard in his youth. He was studying astrol-

ogy at Naples in a class under a certain Andalò di Negro.
They happened upon the words, "One must not accuse
the stars when one is himself the cause of his misfortune."
Andalò smiled and said that this saying was illustrated by
an old story. The teacher was affable and easily led by his
students. He was prevailed upon to stop and tell the story.

The story goes that Poverty, dressed in rags, was once
seated by the side of the road when Fortune passed by. Fortune taunted her with scornful words. Poverty with like
scorn taunted Fortune and laid claim to a power of her own
which Fortune could not touch. "I do not fear you," said
Poverty, in effect. "I have renounced everything of yours.
I have nothing. I want nothing. I am utterly liberated from
slavery to you." Fortune was so much angered that she con-
descended from supercilious argument to physical combat.
The end came quickly. Lean and sinewy Poverty easily
downed luxurious Fortune and with a knee upon her breast
made her acknowledge defeat. As reward of valor Poverty demanded only one thing, although, as she said, she
had thought of breaking Fortune's wheel, stripping her of
power over men, and retiring her to private life. The one
thing was a promise. Fortune must chain Misfortune to a
stake in some public place so that he might attach himself
to no man unless that man should be foolish enough to
break the chains and thus of his own free will expose himself to what might happen. But Good Fortune might go
anywhere. This promise fickle Fortune, who had never
held faith before, actually kept.

This is the personal responsibility for misfortune which
Boccaccio discovers after his pondering! So far as can be

seen, he does not in the least imply the delicate operation of a tragic flaw in character. What he does imply plainly is that men who do not strive for anything in the way of worldly reward are not subject to Fortune and that those who embark upon the life of action are fairly asking for misfortune. Boccaccio points the moral as he returns to his storytelling, called back, as he says, by the clamors of those who have unbound Misfortune from his stake. The victims exacting his immediate attention are Romans. For, he explains, the Romans came to know misfortune through worldliness. At one time they were a rude people troubling themselves little to acquire the goods and honors of the world, but as quickly as the desire came to them to conquer their neighbors and spread their empire, they had violent changes of kingship and all manner of misfortunes which they had not known before.

Thus tragedy is merely life itself in the world of daring; we create it for ourselves the moment we embrace that world. This explanation of personal responsibility for tragedy leaves the chain of events in the life of tragic action as irrationally linked as before. Boccaccio has tantalized us by facing toward the larger truth with a questing desire to see it and then flatly refusing to see it, though in all fairness we should remember that his age and environment made such perception difficult.

But let us see how consistently Boccaccio subscribes to this philosophy in the practice of his storytelling. Grant that all the figures with whom he deals have embraced life actively (indeed, he would not have found them celebrated in history unless they had) and that to that degree they have

THE FORTUNES OF PORTIA, WIFE OF BRUTUS
She dies by swallowing live coals.

From Boccaccio's *De Mulieribus Claris,* 1473.

brought tragedy upon themselves. The question is whether Boccaccio ever goes farther in the fixing of personal responsibility, plotting human activity in order to discover the issuance of tragedy out of character and event after the life of action has been decisively embraced.

For Contempt of the World the theoretically right story of misfortune is that of a great and good man overwhelmed through absolutely no fault of his own, always excepting the initial fault of choosing the active life. The greater and better the man the righter the story, since the aim is to show that neither eminent power nor eminent virtue can achieve security here below nor make this evil world into a good world, and if those cannot, what can ? This may be regarded as the normal sort of tale in the *De Casibus,* the central pur-

pose of the book being what it is. Boccaccio tells it with
gusto. We need not look here for the issuance of tragedy out
of character and event.

An outstanding example is the story of Agamemnon.
Agamemnon, says Boccaccio, was descended from Tantalus
and Pelops, and by royal right was born to honor. That somber background of vice and crime, the curse upon the royal
house, in which the *Agamemnon* of Aeschylus and the
Agamemnon of Seneca both take their rise, Boccaccio does
not give. Agamemnon, he says, was brave, and for a time
fickle Fortune favored him in everything. By his marriage
to Clytemnestra he greatly increased his royal power. He
was chosen to lead the Greeks against Troy because he was
the very flower of militant Greece. Truly, says Boccaccio, if
one considers the kings and princes and nations whom he
led in this long war, it is not easy to find another man who
had such high honor, such high place, such high commission. Finally, Troy taken and his army enriched with booty,
Fortune gave him glory almost immortal.

But this was the point of reversal.[22] As he was returning from Troy, a terrible storm scattered his fleet. Almost
alone he won safely to his kingdom. And then came the
irony of a miserable end which had been preparing for him
while he was so gloriously compassing the end of Priam
and of Troy. While he was expecting to be fêted and ban-
queted, his wife brought him a robe without any opening for his head, and as he attempted to don it, struggling
blindly in its folds, her paramour Aegisthus slew him. So
Agamemnon, who by his prowess had mastered kings, with
the nations of the world for his field of action, was van-

quished by his lustful wife at home. So great, concludes Boccaccio, is the power of treachery over virtue.

Grave failings of the heroic Agamemnon, such as Aeschylus with high tragic art shows adding their forces to the evil curse upon Agamemnon's house and helping to cause his downfall, Boccaccio either does not know or minimizes. He says nothing of Agamemnon's sacrificing of his own daughter and his raising of implacable enmity in Clytemnestra thereby. He does say that Clytemnestra was perhaps angered because her husband took Cassandra as concubine, but he does not pretend to know, and he makes nothing of the incident in plotting the story. Agamemnon was a great man, none greater; yet a storm at sea shattered his army, and he made the most tawdry of exits from life, tangled and muffled in that tricky robe of Clytemnestra's. In all this there is no shred of reason or justice or decorum that Boccaccio can find, and no cause that was contributed by Agamemnon to his tragedy. If the end was totally unheroic and even ludicrous, so much the better, he would imply, because the hollowness of great achievement and its insecurity are thereby shown the more plainly. He makes sure of the moral by writing a chapter "In Praise of Poverty" to follow the story. Poverty here, as in the story of the combat between Poverty and Fortune, means more than lack of riches. It means, as Boccaccio says directly, a general lack of all concern with the activity of the world, its striving for honor, its voyaging hither and thither, and its making of wars. If Agamemnon had only lived in such lowly content, his tragedy would not have happened.

Boccaccio applies the same formula over and over. All the

grandeur and virtue of King Arthur of Britain was snuffed out by a traitorous and wicked son. Men with eyes may see what that means. Nothing is durable in this world except humility. Priam fell most miserably through no fault of his own. Dido was so virtuous and guiltless that Fortune in bringing her to misery did her the gravest outrage. (Boccaccio does not tell the story of Dido and Aeneas, but a more ancient story: Dido killed herself in memory of her dead husband when a king of Mauretania sought to force her into remarriage. Boccaccio has ardent admiration for her lack of libidinousness, which he finds highly unusual in woman.) Darius fell simply through Fortune's whims. And even Samson fell guiltlessly, for Boccaccio is so much concerned to vilify Delilah and women in general that he makes nothing of any failing in Samson.

But the story of Pompey follows this formula and does something more. Boccaccio tells it at great length, with lavish attention to moral implication, and in order to emphasize the mighty fall which was Pompey's he builds up the greatness of his hero step by step and balances him precariously upon the apex of a pyramid. He creates a dramatic point of suspense, making Fortune hesitate whether to save or desert her darling Pompey. Finally she smiled upon Caesar at Pharsalia, and Pompey fled to Ptolemy in Egypt, whom he had placed upon the throne and from whom he rightfully expected aid. He was treacherously murdered as soon as he disembarked, and Boccaccio makes the most of the mutilation and indignity which was visited upon this flesh that was once proud Pompey's. His head was impaled upon a spear to be exposed to the street mobs of Alexandria, and his body was left at the seaside. A loyal follower buried it there by stealth. What a change was here—all Pompey's mortal glory at last hidden in six feet of Egyptian sand!

Then Boccaccio becomes lyrical with emotion. Why go on with his writing? What more can he say to prove the instability of this world and of Fortune? Quite obviously he admires Pompey, as he does not, for example, admire Agamemnon, and he is deeply shocked at the indecorum of Pompey's fall, as he is not with Agamemnon's. The result is that this story is not supplied with comment that is coolly and unsympathetically exultant over the insecurity of mortal effort, as consistently ascetic scorn of mortality must needs be. It has something of that sympathetic espousal of life and of the hero's action which makes a good tragedy profound art instead of shallow case history. Boccaccio even uses those magic words of Aristotle, "pity" and "fear," which describe surely but simply the binary emotion aroused by any tragedy worth the name; and for whatever reason he does it, Boccaccio uses them legitimately. "If such greatness," he says, "suffered a fall, what may we suppose might happen to us? We ought certainly to pity Pompey; but we ought much more certainly to fear for ourselves."[23]

Thus Boccaccio deals with Pompey in such a way as to develop the tragic emotion, which is incompatible with purely ascetic Contempt of the World. Contempt, strictly speaking, fears not for itself in that world of action which it has abjured, and it supremely lacks pity for the foolish men who persist in mortal struggle. Before the matter with which it deals could ever be used poetically for tragedy, this advance in emotionalization which Boccaccio attempts had

first to be made. We must not forget that it is attempted only
exceptionally in the *De Casibus*. In moralizing his stories,
Boccaccio usually shows the sign manual of ascetic Contempt with which we are familiar. And he has interchapters
which are not only in praise of poverty and against riches,
but against women (pay your debt to posterity and then
avoid them as evil), against beauty (remember the beautiful young man who freed himself from beauty's snares by
slashing his face with a knife), and against true pity for the
miserable condition of mankind in general.

But though Boccaccio in the sort of story just described
makes much of virtue causelessly brought to grief, he tells
a second sort of story which reminds us that evil men as well
as good men have fallen from high place. It was not at all
necessary here that he should think of punishment justly
meted out to vice. Frequently, as we have seen, writers *de
contemptu mundi* say or imply that good men and vicious
men both fall when Fortune takes the notion to turn her
wheel; she makes no distinctions. The vicious man is punished in after life, of course, but in this life he thrives or
perishes exactly as the good man does—more proof that the
world is not worth our time and effort. But in proportion as
the Christian moralist hated vice and dwelt upon its consequences it was hard for him to follow any theory that those
consequences were never of this world.[24] After all, the Hebrew God of righteous wrath, who destroyed Sodom, was
close at hand in Scripture. Also, as the Renaissance accepted
the world and studied it for a general order in its events, the
moralist was stimulated to find a mundane order of justice,
even while he talked of Fortune.

Thus, for those men whom he counts truly vicious, Boccaccio often, though not always, attempts to make misfortune a matter of tragic justice. In some sense this may be said to be a motion toward plotting the effect of character upon event and relieving the tragical story from the ascetic conception of a whimsical Fortune. But it is sometimes not easy to decide whether Boccaccio is emphasizing the direct judgment of an angry God, discovering laws of cause and effect in the world of action, or merely implying that one of Fortune's methods as she whimsically turns against a great man is to make him first sin and then fall. Certainly Boccaccio does not always cease to talk of Fortune when he carries vice to a fall. It is possible that he sometimes holds Fortune responsible for elevating the man, but the man himself responsible for embracing sin—pride, for example—and through that sin allowing Fortune more easily to impel him to his ruin. Others in Boccaccio's age had that idea.[25]

Boccaccio shows the direct divine punishment of wickedness in the stories of Nimrod and Julian the Apostate. Both men raised themselves up against God, exhausted divine patience, and finally were crushed. Nimrod sinned in pride, built the tower of Babel which challenged the heavens, considered himself a god, and finally saw his tower and his grandeur crash to earth. God has countless ways to punish the evil, remarks Boccaccio. Instead of arrogance, embrace humility, he advises—the humility against which Fortune has no power. The story of Julian is more dramatic. At first Julian was a monk and served God. Then the devil tempted him; and he fell into perfidy, yielded to a desire for power, and gave himself to the sin of magical incantation. God finally turned upon him and brought him to a miserable death at the hands of a Persian soldier (according to one story). He recognized the power of God as he died, crying, "You have conquered, O Galilean."

The stories which seem to involve the workings of more abstract laws of retribution are pointed variously. Boccaccio despises Antony from the beginning as cruel, sensual, even mad. Cleopatra was lascivious, but that was only to be expected in a woman. She did not corrupt Antony, who was excessively corrupt already, but only helped him to his degradation. Joan, the legendary woman who became pope and then showed the further effrontery to have a child, was vile. What will not women attempt? Brunhilde, Queen of France, whose shade engages in lengthy argument with Boccaccio, attempts to cover up her guilt as she tells her misfortunes and to make herself an example of Fortune's insecure favor. Boccaccio will not have it so. He says plainly and heartlessly as she tells of the sordid plots and counterplots, the ambition, murder, and vengeance which made up her life, that her misfortune was caused by her own viciousness and perfidy. It was easy for Boccaccio to see retribution for vice when the subject was a woman.

Constructed with more plot are the stories of Prusias, King of Bithynia, and Antiochus the Great. The first is unusual in telling of the operation of a curse put upon his betrayer Prusias by Hannibal. The curse drove Prusias further into perfidy and hence to his destruction. So severe was Fortune, whatever that may mean in such a connection. Antiochus was dissatisfied with the grandeur which he already possessed and set out to capture certain Greek cities ruled

POMPEY BEHEADED

From Laurent de Premierfait's translation of Boccaccio's *De Casibus*,
MS Royal 14 E v, late fifteenth century.

by the Romans. After some success the ambitious king fell into sloth and debauchery, and thus became an easy prey to the Romans.

The stories so far mentioned as plotting retribution all lack that tragic realization which can arouse pity or fear in us. They make some advance in connecting misfortune with character, but they do not even get so far toward the deeper concerns of tragedy as the story of Pompey, which makes misfortune purely a result of chance, yet evinces emotional unification of author and subject. They are all of men and women so villainous to Boccaccio's eyes as to need scorn and vituperation rather than understanding.

Boccaccio could do better than this. Because they add sympathetic realization to some measure of plot bonding character with event, the stories of Hannibal and Alcibiades are, in all the *De Casibus,* the closest to profound dramatic tragedy. Both of these men, as Boccaccio sees them, are admirably heroic and in no sense vicious; they are not even sinners in the moralist's sense of the term. They are great souls with failings to make them human, and their failings become tragic only because of the positions in which their ability has placed them. But it is to be remembered that even for them Boccaccio makes much of Fortune and her irrational changes, apparently oblivious of the fact that he is here touching tragedy unlike that in the stories of Agamemnon and Pompey.

The career of Hannibal is plotted with greater skill than the career of Alcibiades. We hear that from childhood he was dedicated to the destruction of Rome and dominated by one ambition. Through many hardships he reached suc-

H

cess after success. Fortune, says Boccaccio, was with him up
to the time when he gained his victory over Quintus Fabius
and the Consul Varro, when the field was thick with Roman
dead and when he sent back to Carthage three bushels of
finger rings taken as spoils of war. This was his fourth victory in an ascending scale of triumphs. Now came a change
in Fortune and a descent from the summit which he had
gained. "All that he did hereafter tended either to the over-
turn of his acquired prosperity or to his decline."[26] He had
Rome completely at his mercy and had only to press forward to destroy it and to attain that ambition to which
his life was sworn, but a fatal inability to close his fingers
upon what they surrounded now manifested itself. Mar-
habal gave him the right advice. Hannibal did not take it.
He was too sure of ultimate victory. He wintered at Capua
and let his soldiers fall into idleness and corrupt living.
Their valor was softened. When he was ready to move
again, he sent for aid to his brother Hasdrubal in Spain.
Hasdrubal died. This was a shrewd stroke of Fortune. Hannibal had to return to Carthage. The Romans sought his
life, and he fled, taking refuge with Prusias, King of Bithynia. Prusias betrayed him. Hannibal cursed his betrayer
(see the story of Prusias mentioned above) and took poison.
Behold in this great man's ruin, concludes Boccaccio, the
instability of Fortune and the nature of all things mortal.

Though Hannibal has the finer tragic presentation, Alcibiades has more wholehearted admiration from Boccaccio.
Alcibiades was blessed from the beginning with beauty,
noble lineage, valor, and wisdom. His career was one of ups
and downs. Here was no steady rise toward a single desired

aim, as with Hannibal. At last, though, he reached a pin-
nacle of honor with the Athenians which was almost divine,
and he thought that he had made Fortune stable. But a vast
alteration was at hand. He led an army into Asia and because of his feeling of security became a careless general.
He permitted himself to be ambushed by King Cyrus, and
almost all of his disordered army to be slaughtered. He was
exiled from Athens and finally was burned to death in his
bed by Athenians who still feared him and would not let
him live in peace.

IV

One thing at once to be noted after an examination of narrative craftsmanship in the *De Casibus* is that Boccaccio at
his best evolves a pyramidal structure foreshadowing the
rise and fall of much tragic action in Shakespeare. Granted,
it is only the flimsiest shadow of the later full-bodied structure; yet this does not make the similarity less important to
recognize. Hannibal, driven up the long incline toward
Rome by the single desire for revenge and then, with Rome
powerless at his feet, fatally hesitant to press forward to
consummation, is vaguely a Hamlet unwilling to kill the
praying king, a simple Hamlet, if such can be imagined.
Like Hamlet's, his decline toward ruin at the hands of an
opponent let slip begins at this point, and the downward
slope of the pyramidal action tends to balance the upward
in length. Here, then, is the sketch of a Shakespearean Hannibal, merely waiting for the finer lines of character to be
filled in. This story of Boccaccio's is highly exceptional, and
some of its resemblances to the great Shakespearean tragedy of revenge are fortuitously attained, but its attainment

of tragic effect through pyramidal structure is not fortuitous. We have seen Boccaccio working toward that structure elsewhere, not only in the story of Alcibiades, where
likewise failure of character at the apex of the hero's achievement contributes to the fall, but also in the stories of Agamemnon and Pompey, with their long inclines leading up
to the climax of Fortune's favor. The pyramid of balanced
rise and fall seems so natural a development of *De Casibus*
storytelling, and its advantages of vivid detailed contrast
between felicity and misery are so obvious that Boccaccio
surprises us by not making more consistent and effective use
of it than he does.

That picture of climbing human ambition and bound-
less aspiration which the Elizabethans loved with all their
hearts to see presented on the stage was already for Boccaccio a thing of fascination. It was confusion to his ascetic
preachments upon Contempt of the World. Nothing in the
De Casibus is more amusing and engaging than the author's
long "Defense of Alcibiades" following that hero's story.
Here the ascetic Boccaccio sinks in the wave of Renaissance
admiration for heroic action—not without a struggle, but
only a weak and formal struggle. He does not deny that
Alcibiades brought misfortune on himself by choosing a
life of ambitious action and thereby unbinding evil from
its stake; but what would you? This man Alcibiades was
of noble proportions in all ways and by no means to be imprisoned. The human mind is a divine gift. "It has a fiery
vigor, a celestial origin, and an insatiable desire for glory."[27]
Alcibiades launched forth to attain the whole world and
the stars besides. Events went contrary to his daring hopes.

What of that? In the inactive life body and mind go soft. Much more famous is Ulysses hounded by Fortune in daring adventure than the slothful Aegisthus staying safely at home. Thus, too, Alcibiades, though he was thrown low after mounting high, has kept his illustrious name down to our own day. It might be Marlowe saying these things, except for the apologetic attitude. The high astounding terms and the emotion of the rhetoric are worthy of him.

Boccaccio shows the same Renaissance ability to turn from scorn to espousal of the world in his lively description of the apparition of Fortune at the beginning of the sixth book. After argument with Fortune concerning her fickle and untrustworthy nature, he has the effrontery to beg for help in the completion of the *De Casibus,* that his name may be eternally famous. Fortune sees the delicious irony: the ascetic moralist embracing ambitious activity and craving glory, unbinding misfortune from the stake and subjecting himself to Fortune's whims in order to finish a book urging men not to subject themselves to Fortune. Of course Boccaccio appreciates the irony, too. His ability here to laugh at himself is Chaucerian.

Thus his inextinguishable love of the world of action and his curiosity concerning its patterns of cause and effect give to the plotting of certain stories in the *De Casibus* more than what usually passes as "medieval" tragic art. But Boccaccio never succeeds by rational means in reconciling these things with his asceticism. The very last words of his book are incompatible with whatever scorn of the world he has previously expressed. The moral of what he has written, he says, is that one must love God, follow wisdom, and seek

after the virtues. Also "seek honor, praise, and fame." (He
lets that injunction stand without even a hint that he recognizes an inconsistency with his preachment *de contemptu
mundi*.) If you do all these things you will show yourself
worthy of the elevation which you achieve. "And if it should
befall you to be hurled from your height, it would not appear to be because of your fault but rather because of the
wantonness of Fortune, who is ever changing."[28]

Here, without that equivocation to which he descends in
the story of Fortune and Poverty, Boccaccio is finally con-
strained to recognize for tragedy a certain measure of human responsibility which he has actually discovered in his
stories. At least, he says that there can seem to be a fault in
character contributing to misfortune; and if this is not full
declaration of belief, it is guarded admission of the idea
into his philosophy.

v

Though Boccaccio never draws his scattered comments
upon the causes of misfortune into a definitive and consistent philosophy, and though to the end of the *De Casibus* his ideas are obviously in a formative and sometimes
contradictory state, his meditations upon the spectacle of
human greatness fallen into ruin have true historical importance. The causes of misfortune which he admits to
discussion, according to various circumstances, are Fortune,
the stars, God, and the tragic protagonist himself. Thus
he brings into the scope of consideration for Gothic tragedy all those commonly distinguishable controlling forces
which the Elizabethan tragic poets recognize, with whatever degree of seriousness. We need go no farther afield

than to the following characters of Shakespeare for examples of Elizabethan reference to the fateful powers acknowledged by Boccaccio:

Richard II.

> Thoughts tending to content flatter themselves
> That they are not the first of fortune's slaves,
> Nor shall not be the last; like silly beggars
> Who sitting in the stocks refuge their shame,
> That many have and others must sit there.
>
> (*Richard II*, V, v, 23–27.)

Romeo.   My mind misgives

> Some consequence yet hanging in the stars
> Shall bitterly begin his fearful date
> With this night's revels, and expire the term
> Of a despised life clos'd in my breast
> By some vile forfeit of untimely death.
>
> (*Romeo and Juliet*, I, iv, 107–112.)

Hamlet.

> There's a divinity that shapes our ends,
> Rough-hew them how we will.
>
> (*Hamlet*, V, ii, 10–11.)

Cassius.

> Men at some time are masters of their fates:
> The fault, dear Brutus, is not in our stars,
> But in ourselves, that we are underlings.
>
> (*Julius Caesar*, I, ii, 138–140.)

Doubtless when Boccaccio takes into account the various
aspects of man's relation to destiny, he often assumes some
reconciliation of apparent contradictions as having already
been made and generally accepted. An Elizabethan dramatist can make the same assumption. Shakespeare, for example, allows Romeo in the lines given above to speak of a

tragic consequence yet hanging in his stars, and then with his very next breath to say:

> But He, that hath the steerage of my course
> Direct my sail!

Romeo can be made to believe without question both in astrology and in the guiding hand of God.

Boccaccio, even though the figure of Fortune is continuously before his eyes and her name constantly on his lips, can say in so many words that her control of men is really referable to God, no matter what the men themselves may think—"the power which God, or (according to their own manner of speaking) Fortune, has over those in high place."[29] He can also imply—as he does in his story of the struggle between Fortune and Poverty—that the power of Fortune is somehow equivalent to the power of the stars; for the text which Andalò discusses is one urging men not to accuse the stars of calamity, and he illustrates it to Boccaccio's great satisfaction by a story showing why men should not accuse Fortune after they have willingly put themselves under her sway. Logically, these two passages in the *De Casibus* when fitted together maintain the very real existence of a certain power in mortal affairs which it is excusable to call rather indiscriminately Fortune or the stars, but which it is not excusable to separate from the all-embracing and guiding intelligence of God. This is probably very nearly what Boccaccio himself would have said if he had been asked to state the conclusion of his scattered observations upon Fortune, the stars, and God. It agrees substantially with thought widely accepted in his time. Let us retrace the steps by which that thought was formed, omitting for the moment a consideration of the fourth source of tragedy, man himself.

Before Christianity began of its own accord to reconcile these three aspects of fate, the ancient world had made a natural association between the power of Fortune and the power of the stars. Fortune began to take prominent place as a deity at the same time that acceptance of Chaldean astrology spread through all ranks of men under Greco-Roman culture. Both the belief in Fortune and the belief in the stars as supreme rulers of human destiny were products of fatalistic despair in a civilization which no longer had easy faith that the world was ruled by some divine intelligence benevolently interested in the affairs of men. Both represented fate as in large part or entirely a matter of chance, one embodying chance in a whimsical feminine form, a Fortuna Panthea or universal goddess who had gradually absorbed the powers or even the insignia of the earlier and more rational deities,[30] and the other wrapping it up in the influence of heavenly bodies, which in their eternal round turned up good or bad fortune for mankind —with no more plan than is apparent in the spinning of a roulette wheel.

Merging of the chances that lay in Fortune and the stars took place most specifically in a close association between Fortune and the moon. Of all the stars the moon was the nearest to earth and had the strongest of the influences working for mundane variability and mutability, showing its power most obviously in such matters of essential mortality as generation and corruption. Connection of the moon with the instability and changeableness of physical nature was affirmed by the classic world[31] and reaffirmed by that Arabian science which entered Europe through Spain and which stimulated medieval thinking in its first attempts to solve the problems of the universe. For example, Albumazar, the most famous of Arabian astrologers who were translated for medieval use, held that the fixed stars exercised a general rule over the stable or gradually changing affairs on earth, that the planets, wandering with rapid and diverse motions through the heavens, ruled the more rapidly changing affairs below, and that the moon, moving more swiftly than any other planet, was the most powerful as a bringer of change into mundane affairs.[32]

The prime importance of the moon in relation to earthly events was recognized by the Middle Ages in countless treatises upon astrology and in a constant practical application of astrological doctrine to daily life. Not only for professional astrologers was the moon the ruling queen of variability in man's destiny; for the unlearned and practical man of affairs she was the very center and head of all astral influence, the one body in the night sky whose changes he could observe easily without professional help and by which he could guide the critical actions of his life. For his especial benefit there came into being the *lunarium,* a sort of almanac listing under all the days of the month the chances, lucky or unlucky, which the moon conferred upon common undertakings. From perhaps as early as the ninth century through the sixteenth century such moon books were common.[33] They told people which days gave good and which bad chance to a child's birth, or to such adventures as bloodletting, buying and selling, setting of houses, journeying, fleeing from enemies, and dreaming.[34] Books of this kind are, of course, not unknown today.

It was not illogical, then, that Fortune should be allied with the moon, and through the moon with the other planets of diverse motion making for instability on earth, since Fortune was the personification of earthly instability. Plutarch, as early as the first century after Christ, was convinced that even if the whole cosmos is not subjected to a force making for instability (he seems to have had his doubts about that), at least the world on this side of the moon "has become irregular and various and such as to undergo all manner of change."[35] Sallustius, in that abstract of what he conceived to be orthodox pagan belief which he made for Julian the Apostate in the fourth century, says that Fortune has power beneath the moon—and he can even be interpreted as saying that Fortune's power rests in the moon—since above the moon nothing whatsoever could happen because of her.[36] In the Middle Ages, association between Fortune and the moon was of such ready occurrence to men's minds that Fortune was continuously compared with the moon in attempts to elucidate her changeableness. Like the moon she waxed and waned, like the moon she raised the tide of our happiness and lowered it. Like the moon, indeed, was her famous wheel, upon which men who attached themselves to worldly ambition never ceased from rising and falling.[37] Such things were inevitable figures of speech, but they probably aided the spreading of a general idea, expressed by many medieval authors, that Fortune's gifts, after all, came from the stars, and that Fortune and

the stars, one or both indiscriminately, might be blamed
for human sufferings.[38]

Thus the common medieval picture of man's slavery to
the forces of mutability had strong similarity to that evolved
by the Gnostics at the end of the classic civilization. Sinking into the world of matter from Heaven, which was his
home, man was subjected to a scale of increasingly variable
influences from the stars, beginning with the farthest fixed
stars and ending with the nearest "planet," the moon. Under
the moon were all those irrational happenings which characterized the world as distinct from Heaven, all those things
which made tragedy possible, and it was against this sublunary world, so proper to be hated as the antithesis of
Heaven, that medieval contempt was directed. The world,
says a fourteenth-century poet once thought to be Richard
Rolle, is like these four things: the sea, which ebbs and
flows, casts a man up to riches and honor, then down to
tribulation; a wilderness full of wild beasts; a forest full
of thieves and outlaws which rob man of all he has; and a
field of battle, since the world fights against man with two
hands, the right hand of wealth and the left of sorrow and
poverty.[39] Peculiar to the world, he adds, is Fortune, or the
spirit of chance:

> Bot with the world comes dam fortone,
> That ayther hand may chaung sone;
> For sho turnes about ay hir whele,
> Up and doune, als many may fele;
> . . . .
> The whilk thir clerkes noght elles calles,
> Bot happe or chaunce, that sodanli falles.[40]

With very few exceptions, and those of dubious meaning, medieval writers quite definitely restricted the power of Fortune to the province of the mortal world, just as this poet did. Her gifts were primarily honor, fame, glory, and riches; and these she could, of course, take away according to her whim.⁴¹ In short, she regulated the striving of mankind after purely mundane rewards, and as Boiardo says, ruled "all things under the moon."⁴² Her power over man ended with man's death, for blind chance was the ruling power of the mortal world, not of the immortal. As Chaucer (following Boethius) makes Fortune say in answer to man's complaint against her:

> The hevene hath propretee of sikernesse,
> This world hath ever resteles travayle;
> Thy laste day is ende of myn intresse:
> In general, this reule may not fayle.⁴³

Hence, as the Gnostic might have expressed it, man should strive to escape beyond the moon and Fortune, beyond the planets causing less violent perturbations, to the realm of heavenly security.

But though Fortune and the stars could thus be easily conceived as working their effects upon mankind in a sort of peaceful alliance, aiding and abetting each other or even merging their operations, the reconcilement of a Christian God with such powers as these was a far more difficult matter. As we have already found, Fortune and the stars in the Greco-Roman world were commonly thought of as forces which did good to men on earth only by chance, not according to an intelligible plan for the human scene. Indeed, such happiness as they gave in this casual manner only increased men's sense of the predominant evil in life when by chance again that happiness was swept away. Where intelligent guiding divinity still had existence in religious minds, it was often one which was far removed from, or did not deign to concern itself with, the earthly welter, and which beckoned man to a like state of happy desertion. But the Christian God could not be thought of as like this and remain Christian, no matter how great might be the attraction of Gnostic or Neo-Platonic thought for ascetic followers of Christ. Christianity could not escape its inner genius for the remaking of the world, the genius of Jesus himself, and it was eventually compelled to espouse the world and build there an earthly City of God. In like manner it could not escape the God preached by Jesus, the God of infinite loving forethought for the minutest details of life on earth, numbering the hairs of a man's head and noting the sparrow's fall. Even when it was most tempted to be hopeless of the world and was most under the influence of classic philosophies of despair, Christianity was compelled to make some theoretic provision for that God's power over mortal affairs.

From earliest times, the Church had members who made war upon pagan Fortune and pagan astrology. But the truth was that though Christianity possessed faith in a rational personal God, yet so long as it had not developed strong faith in a rational world it was not ready to relinquish Fortune and the stars of the astrologers. They were familiar conceptions and quite suitable to indicate fateful ways of God which were past finding out. Church Fathers early and late—among others, Lactantius, St. Augustine, St. Jerome, and St. Thomas Aquinas—might condemn For-

tune practically out of existence,[44] and St. Augustine, for-
mulating for the Western Church its condemnation of
divination, might attack astrology with such vehemence
that for many centuries after his day it apparently played no
vital part in the life of Christian Europe;[45] yet the growing
philosophic and poetic genius of Gothic Europe insisted
upon recognizing with a new creative fervor both Fortune
and the stars as influencing human destiny, and upon elab-
orating a Christian scheme in which to put them.

Basis for such a scheme was to be found in the *De Consolatione Philosophiae* of Boethius (early sixth century).
The foundation of that comfort which Philosophy offers to
Boethius after his imprisonment and tragic fall from high
place is faith in a wholly personal God—not the Christian
God of pity sacrificing his son for mankind, but nonetheless
a benevolent and directly ruling intelligence. In conceiving of God in this way Boethius has gone to the Neo-
Platonists for inspiration, but in the course of his reasoning
he emerges with a result which attacks the Neo-Platonic
thinkers at a cardinal point. Like them he talks of an all-
seeing Providence, and under it places Fate with its manifold agencies for executing the providential decrees; but
where the Neo-Platonists construct a complicated hierarchy
from the one omnipotent essence, far too holy and abstract
even to name, down through Providence and Fate to that
evil substance, matter, Boethius names divinity "God" in
concrete anthropomorphic fashion and shortens the bridge
of abstractions between God and the world.[46] The effect is
most decidedly to raise hope of order for the world and to
lighten the pall of gloom cast over it by those pagan philos-

ophies which pictured it as lost to evil or as so far removed from God as to feel the divine touch but faintly. God is no longer ineffably transcendent, but capable of wrapping all creation in the famous "bond of love" over which Boethius makes Philosophy grow lyrical. One thing is always certain: nothing can exist separate from this guiding love, and therefore our faith should always remind us that all fortune must be good, no matter how it may seem to man with his merely mortal powers of perception. Religious men of the Middle Ages found in the *Consolation of Philosophy* a courageous metaphysical justification of confidence in universal purposiveness, and quite properly they reverenced it as Christian, even though the book never once makes mention of Christ.

Thus the way was open for the placing of Fortune and the stars—if men should persist in talking about their power— under God as ministers of his will. Boethius makes Philosophy explicit in declaration that the stars and all other aspects of Fate, without any exception whatsoever, are taken under the care of Providence: "For as a workman conceiving the form of anything in his mind taketh his work in hand, and executeth by order of time that which he had simply and in a moment foreseen, so God by His Providence disposeth whatsoever is to be done with simplicity and stability, and by Fate effecteth by manifold ways and in the order of time those very things which He disposeth. Wherefore, whether Fate be exercised by the subordination of certain Divine spirits to Providence, or this fatal web be woven by a soul or by the service of all nature, or by the heavenly motions of the stars, by angelical virtue, or by dia-

THE DEATHS OF ANTONY AND CLEOPATRA
From Laurent de Premierfait's translation of Boccaccio's *De Casibus*,
MS Royal 14 E v, late fifteenth century.

bolical industry, or by some or all of these, that certainly is manifest that Providence is an immoveable and simple form of those things which are to be done, and Fate a moveable connexion and temporal order of those things which the Divine simplicity hath disposed to be done. So that all that is under Fate is also subject to Providence, to which also Fate itself obeyeth."[47]

It is to be noticed that, in this analysis of Fate as working under Providence, Boethius does not mention Fortune, but certainly this is not because he has any thought that chance could operate in the world independently of God's forethought. It is a curious fact that though Boethius did as much as anyone to make the whimsical feminine Fortune and her wheel a familiar figure to the Middle Ages (his is the first clear reference to the wheel as we know it in medieval literature),[48] yet he did not at the last resort allow her any reality as causeless chance. He makes Philosophy offer consolation by easy stages; and like a priest who knows that at one stage of development humanity must have images for its gods and its demons, she imagines for Boethius in Book II a colloquy with Fortune. She takes him through all the Stoic remedies against Fortune, including the deflation of joys and evils and the meditation upon the hollowness of fame and glory. But she makes no secret of what she is doing. This is only one of her "lighter remedies" for Boethius, who is not yet strong enough to digest the truth, and she promises that later he shall have the whole truth. She keeps faith and administers that truth in the last book of the *Consolation*. At the very outset of this concluding flight to the higher realms of reason, Philosophy denies the

I

existence of any kind of fortune in the world which might
be called whimsical chance: "If any shall define chance to
be an event produced by a confused motion, and without
connexion of causes, I affirm that there is no such thing, and
that chance is only an empty voice that hath beneath it no
real signification. For what place can confusion have, since
God disposeth all things in due order?" Even when things
seem most to happen by fortunate accident, they always
have causes "descending from the fountain of Providence."[49]
Indeed, after the discussion at the beginning of the *Consolation,* Philosophy has had very little to say about whimsical
Fortune and, as we see, is now happy to be rid of her.

Nevertheless, Dante and many other writers of the Middle Ages gave Fortune an actual existence among those
manifold executors of Fate which Boethius subjects to
God.[50] In Dante's vision of cosmic order the stars exert their
influence as instruments of God's will,[51] and Fortune is appointed by God to rule over the world as

> general minister, which at due time
> May change the empty vantages of life
> From race to race, from one to other's blood,
> Beyond prevention of man's wisest care.[52]

She knows what she is doing; but man never does, and
therefore cannot even by utmost wisdom prevail against her.
She is the personification of mundane mutability, which
must remain to us irrational, though it is perfectly rational
to God. In other words, Dante comes very close to poetical
statement of a paradox which the Middle Ages seem commonly to have assumed: the world in metaphysical truth is
a part of God's beautiful eternal order, but in practical truth

it is ugly disorder, and God surely desires that we should despise it as such for the good of our souls. Disorder somehow serves the purposes of God's order and is made part of it, just as evil serves the purposes of God's goodness and exists practically, though not metaphysically, under its universal sway. Thus, by heaping execrations on Fortune and the stars, who are ministers of God, men do not succumb to Job's temptation and curse God's decrees, but actually acquire grace by cursing that which is divinely appointed to be cursed. At most, one could say that such men do not see far enough to praise Fortune for the lesson of worldly vanity which she has taught them. As Dante ennobles her:

> This is she,
> So execrated e'en by those, whose debt
> To her is rather praise; they wrongfully
> With blame requite her, and with evil word;
> But she is blessèd, and for that recks not.[53]

But even in this gallantly poetic provision for Fortune in a rational Christian universe, the necessary magnification of God's hidden order was subtle preparation for the deposing of Fortune as a serious conception. With further increase of faith in universal purposiveness, man was more and more willing to admit that the world beneath the moon was a direct expression of God's laws, not merely an indirect expression such as one would have in legalized disorder. The ancient irrational figure of Fortune could hold recognition only so long as men still wished to say by her poetically that the world was evil and that God had never intended us to understand it. A rational doubt often existed side by side with the poetic recognition. Much as they wrote

about Fortune in the practice of literature, both Boccaccio and Petrarch found occasion to deny her when they
were pressed into coldly critical comment or theological
debate.[54] She whom men had been taught to think of as
proof against understanding was fated to be ultimately denied in a world of new scientific confidence, which defined
chance as an order only temporarily hidden from man's intellectual grasp and capable at any time of being exposed
by some triumphant discoverer of its laws.

In like manner the stars lost power over men's minds in
the later Renaissance, though they continued to serve as a
poetic expression of fate after belief in practical astrology
had been for the most part abandoned.[55]

VI

The survey that has so far been made of the common aspects under which the Middle Ages saw Fate is sufficient to
demonstrate that there was good reason why Boccaccio in
the *De Casibus* should proceed upon a rather unsettled assumption of relationship between God, Fortune, and the
stars. At the very beginning of its theological debate with
paganism, Christianity had declared faith in its ability to
prove the equation: Fate equals an intelligent God. In Boccaccio's day it was still in the somewhat unsure process of
canceling out certain pagan factors of Fate in order to establish this theorem, and Boccaccio was no more unsure than
most of his contemporaries. Like them, he wrote with the
guiding desire to glorify the power of God.

But, as we have found, Boccaccio suggested that another
force than external Fate might sometimes help to create

misfortune, namely, the power of human character. Thereby in an age whose strongest instinct was still to glorify God
by belittling man—an instinct which Boccaccio himself
often followed—he gave a share of glorification to man.
However, the fact that he sometimes gave human individuality a worth which the ordinary writer *de contemptu
mundi* would not give did not place him so much at variance with his religion as might at first appear. We may say
that Boccaccio did this partly because he had observed life
with something of the secular scientific spirit born of the
Renaissance, but we must add that he had some measure
of support in a newer Christian metaphysics coming into
acceptance in his day.

Some two centuries before Boccaccio, Christianity began
to find itself confronted anew with the ancient problem of
free will. In order to meet the world that was turning toward discovery of Greek and Arabian science it was forced
to extend its philosophical provision for man's individual
freedom and responsibility in the face of God's unquali-
fiable omnipotence. This mystery of free will is one of the
darkest matters in Christian theology—or in any theology—
and one cannot thread all its mazes casually. It will perhaps
be sufficient to indicate briefly that the greater recognition of human individuality allowed by scholastic philosophy was a logical outcome, on the theological side, of the
movement in Christianity to espouse the world for its meaning, and that it had import for the development of tragedy.

Early Christianity had held to its faith in man's free will
with the greatest tenacity, though its theology had placed
that faith in the greatest difficulties. Pagan fatalism had fre-

quently found the gods careless of man, malicious toward man, or nonexistent in a universe abandoned to evil mechanical necessity or chance. The early Fathers saw this fact with entire clearness and bent themselves to quell pagan fatalism at all costs by magnifying the all-wise disposing power of God. Christianity immediately found itself substituting divine determinism for pagan fatalism. So far as man's free will and validity were concerned, there was little to choose, theoretically speaking, between the old fatalism and the new determinism. It made no difference whether a mechanical necessity, without rationality, or God, with rationality, forced man at all points to be what he was. Whichever it was, logically the result either way was destruction of man's value as an individual. The Christian belief in predestination ought theoretically to have produced the same despair of a final order of justice as pagan fatalism. Needless to say, it did not. As we know from our experience with the Calvinistic revival of predestination at its sternest, those who hold this belief are capable of a most lively sense that sin suffers justly. It was so in the early Church. The newer civilization of which the Church was a part felt the promise of its basic vitality and knew by common sense, whatever impasse it may have reached through logic, that achievement came to man partly through his own choice and responsibility. Only a dying civilization like the pagan, whose work was done, could afford to believe otherwise.

The task of discovering philosophical justification for its faith in free will Christianity found at first the more difficult because it lacked impulse to recognize inherent good in a mortal world of multiplicity and variation—in other words, a world which can produce creatures and men who are valid individuals. It is the instinct of Augustinian Neo-Platonic Christianity to regard passage from unity into multiplicity as a lapse from the perfection of being and therefore from goodness. Unity is the goodness of God; difference and division are the evil of the world. If one says further, as St. Augustine and many after him do, that evil is only absence of good and therefore has no reality and no active cause, one saves God from responsibility for evil, but at the peril of abolishing any definable responsibility for evil whatever, even in man. All that man truly is comes from God, nay, is God, if one carries this argument to its logical conclusion, and what, then, remains in man to let him do evil and suffer? His "free" will? That, so far as it is an actuality, is derived from God and is therefore a divine principle which could not choose evil. The basis of evil must, therefore, lie in an aberration of the will, a metaphysical imperfection which is nothing, where the will is something, and which therefore has no more existence than evil has. Thus, the mortal world of multiplicity in which men show individual characters and embark upon various courses of action is evil; not an evil *thing,* however, but an evil *no-thing,* since evil by definition lacks reality.

The first important scholastic philosopher, Johannes Scotus Erigena (ninth century), was also the last great name in the Augustinian otherworldly tradition. His mysticism had warmth where St. Augustine's tended to chilly severity; he had the power to gather followers among later mystics, and he takes honorable place as a precursor of the Renaissance Platonists. But Christianity very soon after his time felt a need to philosophize, in a measure at least, the world of individual reality, and it had small use for his services. With increasing vigor, in the centuries that ensued, the guiding spirit of the Church was to discountenance mysticism whenever the mystical temper went beyond beatific contemplation and declared in forthright philosophy that all living things flow out from and return to the divine heart in cosmic systole and diastole, and that all are ever one being in God, "separateness" being merely illusion. Thus Erigena, despite his spiritual kinship with St. Augustine and his indebtedness to that greatest of early Fathers, was looked at askance. It was certainly not in accord with the destiny of scholasticism to maintain, as Erigena did, that the essence of all things is nothing but the knowledge of them in the mind of God; that the numberless differences between men are accidents of the form, which do not belong to the original creation, but to the corruptible qualities of generated nature; that if the Divinity is one and undivided, then humanity, as made in the image of Divinity, must be one and undivided also; that the creature which is thus one with the Creator will pass into the Creator according to the law of ebb and flow in the universe, not by a destruction of substance, but by a wonderful and ineffable reversion to its first state lost by the Fall.[56] Those men who followed Erigena were persecuted, and some even died at the stake. Giordano Bruno was burned so late as the year 1600 for a mysticism which perhaps owed something to Erigena indirectly.

In St. Thomas Aquinas (d. 1274) the new sense that the world of individualities was not merely illusion obtained the definitive philosophical justification which it had been seeking. Here, as in so many other matters, the indomitable genius of St. Thomas was able to bridge the threatening chasm between the old and the new, and to build a structure upon which Christianity might rely.

The situation which was encountered by St. Thomas had become acute through the introduction to the Western world of the ideas held by the last important Arabian philosopher, Averroës (1126-1198). Averroës recognized the principle of individuality, but held that that principle lay within mutable matter, and denied that man had in himself any rationality other than a "material understanding," similar to the understanding of other animals, though higher in degree. The principle of truly rational comprehension was of another order, never obtained by man's own efforts, but shed upon him from a universal Intelligence, as the sun's light is shed upon earth. A natural consequence of this thinking was the denial of individual immortality to man and the allowance of immortality only to a world soul. Man died, but the soul of his race lived on. A second consequence was the negation of man's free will.[57] Especially in the decade from 1260 to 1270 these doctrines fomented trouble at the University of Paris.

Thomism eventually conquered both the idealistic otherworldliness of Neo-Platonic Christianity and the naturalistic worldliness of Averroism, the one as it tended to lose man's individuality in God, the other as it tended to rob man's individuality of validity. Fundamental to the teaching of St. Thomas is the argument that difference and division are not merely an aspect of the world's material mutability nor are they in any sense whatever a lapse from God's perfection. It is impossible, says St. Thomas stoutly, that the perfection of the universe, which consists of the diversity of things, can be a thing of chance. "Hence we must say that the distinction and multitude of things come from the intention of the first agent, who is God. For He brought things into being in order that His goodness might be communicated to creatures, and be represented by them; and because His goodness could not be adequately represented by one creature alone, He produced many and diverse creatures, that what was wanting to one in the representation of the divine goodness might be supplied by another. For goodness, which in God is simple and uniform, in creatures is manifold and divided; and hence the whole universe together participates the divine goodness more perfectly, and represents it better than any single creature whatever."[58]

Here, even while many Christians are contemning the world with a new fervor, St. Thomas rejects the early ascetic idea that goodness lies only in the other world. Goodness of one sort lies there, with God, but goodness of another sort can lie in this world, and God intended that it should be so.

This is not to say, however, that this world is not defective, and it is not to say that God is responsible for the defects of mankind. "The evil which consists in the defect of action," maintains St. Thomas, "is always caused by the defect of the agent. But in God there is no defect, but the highest perfection, as was shown above. Hence, the evil which consists in defect of action, or which is caused by defect of the agent, is not reduced to God as to its cause. . . ."

Now, the order of the universe requires, as was said above, that there should be some things that can, and do sometimes, fail. And thus God, by causing in things the good of the order of the universe, consequently and as it were by accident, causes the corruptions of things. . . . Nevertheless the order of justice belongs to the order of the universe; and this requires that penalty should be dealt out to sinners. And so God is the author of the evil which is penalty, but not of the evil which is fault, by reason of what is said above."[59]

St. Thomas knows that in order to give man this responsibility for his defects of action the theologian must also give him a power of choice and a power of reason to guide that choice which shall be stamped with human individuality. He teaches that rational individuality arises through an indissoluble union of soul and material form, where individual shape is given by the perishable body to the rational divine breath which enters into it. The process has been aptly compared with the casting of a bronze statue, in which form is printed by a fragile structure of clay upon enduring metal.[60] Thus man's power of choice is his own at the same time that it owes itself to God, and thus St. Thomas stands sponsor for a practical dualism of matter and spirit which works toward good.

Whether one may or may not think that there is philosophical sufficiency in St. Thomas' reasoning, one must admit that it is an unequivocal fixing of fault upon humanity for human failure in action, and that it is heroic in its effort at justification of evil and pain. Certainly it does not hold with thoroughgoing Contempt of the World or with any belief that the struggle of mortal life is inherently evil, since it allows that "many good things would be taken away if God permitted no evil to exist; for fire would not be generated if air was not corrupted, nor would the life of a lion be preserved unless the ass were killed."[81] Its sturdy insistence upon a meaning always lying behind the order of life, and upon the power of divine reason even to make good out of evil, is akin to the vital faith of Greek philosophy at its best, a faith which St. Thomas was able to appreciate in Aristotle. It is far from the later Hellenistic surrender of the world of human suffering and very near indeed to the Aeschylean acceptance of that world as caught up into a universal scheme of justice. We must remember that here, as elsewhere in cultural borrowing, when the new takes truly fruitful inspiration from the old, it does so because it has developed creative power in its own right and finds something in the old which it is already struggling to be or say. The borrowing from Aristotle by Christian scholasticism must be called fruitful in that sense.

This deliberate shift in the thirteenth century from an Augustinian Neo-Platonism to a Thomistic Aristotelianism as the basis of theology meant philosophical recognition of a nascent interest in the material universe as law and order; in a very real sense it meant recognition of certain principles of science by that same Church orthodoxy which was later to be despised by secular science as its greatest enemy. It encouraged men to use their intellects and discover reason in life, instead of contemning the world as unworthy or incapable of rational interpretation, and it fostered a belief that intellect would justify faith and add a new glory to God. St. Thomas is explicit on that matter: "Nothing may be asserted as true that is opposed to the truth of faith, to revealed dogma. But it is neither permissible to take whatever we hold to be true, and present it as an article of faith. For the truth of our faith becomes a matter of ridicule among the infidels, if any Catholic not gifted with the necessary scientific learning, presents as a dogma what scientific scrutiny shows to be false."[62]

By recognizing a material reality in the universe as well as the immaterial reality of God, St. Thomas bargained for much more than he knew. He, of course, had no realization that the jinni of scientific reason which he had conjured up to his service could eventually grow beyond proportions controllable by his own or other ecclesiastical power. The "tough-minded" intellectual principle in man may demand its unifying philosophy, its conception of the universe as one basic reality, no less than the "tender-minded" mystical principle. On one side, an extremity of mystic or intuitional experience may demand that all existence be realized as spirit; on the other, an extremity of intellectual experience may demand that it be realized as soulless matter. One can force the conclusion that the real is God, and good; the other that the real is not-God, and evil, or at best indifferent. Between these two extremities lies a realm of precarious balance where spirit and matter, or good and evil, are always threatening to destroy each other and can be kept from doing so only by a philosophy which seems to the true idealist or the true materialist an utterly unsatisfactory patchwork. Thus, Thomistic Christianity in abandoning the ascetic integrity of Augustinian Neo-Platonism was deserting a secure fortress to fight in dangerous open country. It was exposing itself to, even using the methods of, a force which was fated to grow stronger, to cause desertion from the religious ranks, and eventually to find its own logical integrity in materialistic monism.

However precarious the position may be for lack of integrated philosophic fortification, it would seem to be here upon the open ground between the two extremes that the tragic mind is most nobly creative. Here may be developed a morality balancing good and evil in the world of material action and generating force by polarity, a morality which sees man participating with an invigorating spirit of adventure in a real battle of opposites, adding his ponderable weight to one side or the other, and finding the fight worth while. A world of such ethical struggle, where good is good and evil evil, yet where their opposition makes man heroically creative rather than hopelessly nihilistic, and where there may be momentary poetic vision of transcendent good in the struggle itself, is the true world of tragedy for Shakespeare no less than for Aeschylus and Sophocles. It is not a world easily circumscribed. Practically it is very simply dualistic, but poetically it can take us close to mystic quietism when it purges the violent emotions aroused by suffering and brings calm apprehension. It is thus one distinction of St. Thomas Aquinas to have prepared a part of the way for Shakespearean tragedy.

Also it is one distinction of Boccaccio, living under Thomistic Christianity, to have compassed, however unsurely, that artistic realization of dignity in mortal action and of individual effectiveness in human character upon which the best dramatic tragedy of a later age was built. Granted more assurance of effective worth for man's decisions, his conception of tragedy reached at the conclusion of the *De Casibus* would be one to which the greatest tragedians might subscribe. He there counsels you to seek honor and fame in worldly affairs—but to seek wisely and virtuously. Then if it befalls you to be hurled from your height, it will not appear to be because of your fault but rather because of the wantonness of Fortune, who is ever changing.[63] In his *Comento sopra Dante,* where his judgment is more coolly critical and where he is not hampered by the ascetic thesis of the *De Casibus,* Boccaccio shows even greater tolerance of the idea that humanity has some individual responsibility for its mortal destiny. Men are under the powerful sway of the stars, he says, but reason and free will permit them to act counter to the influences of the heavens. This action rarely happens, however, in the choice of a career.[64] Many medieval thinkers admit the same influence of the stars over the corporeal make-up of men, and at the same time declare the power of intellect and will to go counter to the fateful impulsion.[65] How much this power has definitely come to be thought of as an ability to control physical event and how much it is still thought of as an ability to master the passions and give up the physical world, we are not always sure. As early as Plotinus the Neo-Platonic tradition gives man free will to liberate himself from the stars by renouncing the sensible world which they control.[66] But certainly Boccaccio, along with St. Thomas, has some thought of a power to change physical event.

Thus Boccaccio momentarily sees tragedy in the grand manner: for a tragic character there are lines of cause and effect having to do with individual choice and its lawful result, which can be plotted and brought to the light of our understanding; mingling with these and stretching dimly beyond them are lines of destiny, which we may refer to Fortune, the stars, divine purpose, or some other fateful force, but which are to us inexplicable.

Chapter IV

FALLS OF PRINCES: CHAUCER
AND LYDGATE

THE EXAMPLE of tragical narrative which was set by Boccaccio in the *De Casibus* was followed by two English poets of greatly unequal merit but, during the fifteenth and sixteenth centuries, of not incomparable popularity and influence. In Chaucer, Boccaccio found an imitator and appreciator who had the capacity of true genius. In Lydgate, Boccaccio found a translator and redactor whose humble industry was incapable of working any great poetic transformation in borrowed matter, though his extensions, interpretations, and gratuitous comments often showed a simple, manly independence.

But the finer genius of Chaucer had little share in his writing of that obvious imitation of the *De Casibus,* the *Monkes Tale.* The Monk says to the Canterbury company that he has a hundred tragical stories in his cell and that he will give a scattered selection. Chaucer may be making the Monk, in the Monk's own character, use "hundred" as a number without particular meaning—"any amount of such stories"; or, through the Monk, Chaucer may be telling us that he himself had at one time planned a sort of *Decameron* in the *De Casibus* manner, a sheaf of one hundred tales which should reveal the insecurity of mundane achievement. Needless to say, he could have fixed upon the round number one hundred without knowledge of the *Decameron,* a knowledge which it is extremely doubtful that Chaucer had, even though in the *Canterbury Tales* he gives us versions of certain stories to be found in the *Decameron*. Grant that Chaucer had begun a long and rather ambitious collection of tragical narratives which were to have been independent of any such fiction as the Canterbury pilgrimage, since it seems entirely probable that he had entered upon such an undertaking; whatever length may have been schemed for the *Monkes Tale* apart from the *Canterbury Tales,* and whatever may have been its original framework, we need not mourn that Chaucer actually gave us no more than the seventeen stories which the Knight allows the Monk to tell. We should agree, perhaps, that if we had to choose one of Chaucer's incomplete works whose end we could best go without, we should have to choose this.

The reason is not that the *Monkes Tale* represents a "false taste" of the Middle Ages in which we have no call to take interest; nor is it that Chaucer was out of sympathy with the taste; it is, I think, that this particular expression of that taste was ill suited to Chaucer's temper and that its opportunities, as he quickly learned, did not provide sufficient challenge or inspiration to keep up his enthusiasm. He had it in him, as we shall see, to write in *Troilus and Criseyde* a lengthy contribution to the tragic literature of fallen princes, but the *Troilus* is not at all in the bald style of the Monk's storytelling. Chaucer seems to have been peculiarly unfitted to write an encyclopedic *De Casibus*. His best narrative art is of the expansive and intimately personal sort, the sort that in Fielding and Sterne established the classic tradition of the English novel. The *Monkes Tale,* as we have it, shows a most sterile confinement of Chaucer's spirit, and shows it even more plainly than does the encyclopedic and also unfinished *Legend of Good Women.*

II

In the seventeen stories told by the Monk, Chaucer adds nothing important to Boccaccio's conception of tragedy, and in many respects falls behind his guide. He makes some use of those lines in Jean de Meung's part of the *Roman de la Rose* which deal with miscellaneous victims of Fortune (ll. 5839 ff.), but these are no aid to improvement upon Boccaccio in narrative method or philosophy. The Monk's stories have no vision framework, and they fail of having strictly chronological order, though such order was probably intended by Chaucer for any complete collection which he had planned, and though the Monk opens at what is conceived to be the beginning of things, as Boccaccio does. That beginning, however, is not with Adam, but with Lucifer; and here the Monk confesses apologetically that he is somewhat illogical. His business is with the falls of illustrious men, and Lucifer was an angel, not a man. Nevertheless, says he, "at him I wol beginne," for his fall was great. The choice of the stories which follow is in no sense dictated by Boccaccio. Adam, Samson, Zenobia, Nero, and Croesus are dealt with at full chapter length in the *De Casibus* and these also appear in the *Monkes Tale.* Chaucer evidently draws upon the *De Casibus* here and there. But the Monk tells stories that are not in Boccaccio, or that are sketched only briefly in those interchapters of the *De Casibus* which pass a host of unfortunates rapidly in review. A notable addition is the tragedy of Bernabò, which is based upon events that happened as late as 1385. It may be said to have been made out of the day's news.

The Monk need not have been so apologetic at beginning with Lucifer. He might have justified himself fully had he been given the realization that the story of the fall of Lucifer from Heaven is a right prelude to the theme of man fallen from Paradise into the world of tragedy. But for some reason Chaucer neither gives the Monk the larger perception which would save him from pedantic concern over the fact that Lucifer was not a man nor gives him the desire to tell the story at any but the briefest length. Where Boccaccio relishes the fall of Adam and Eve, and tells of it carefully as the cause of all the worldly ills to which Adam's seed are subjected, Chaucer's Monk sees nothing particularly dramatic in either Lucifer or Adam and is surprisingly silent on the significance for mankind that lies in their tragedies. To each he gives a bare eight lines of verse, as little as he gives to Bernabò or Pedro of Cyprus—modern instances both—and far less than he gives to most of his tragic figures. The question arises whether the stories of Lucifer and Adam may not have been among late additions to the collection and even have been hastily written as a formal opening for the worthy but literal-minded Monk (somewhat changed since his appearance in the general Prologue), by whom Chaucer perhaps indicated a continued respect for the moral tone of tragedies already written but an amused boredom with their lack of imaginative variety.

But at least the Monk's pedantry makes it clear that he has a true perception of the *De Casibus* as an intended contribution to the literature *de contemptu mundi* and that

he is accepting its central theory that tragedy is a manifestation of man's powerlessness in an irrational world. He
says of Lucifer:

> For, thogh fortune may non angel dere,
> From heigh degree yet fel he for his sinne
> Doun in-to helle, wher he yet is inne.
>
> (B, 3191–3193)

Fortune, of course, could not harm an angel, because she
had no power in the region above the moon, and it is only
with the operations of whimsical Fortune in her realm of
mortality that we should be concerned. The punishment of
Lucifer for his sin was therefore to the Monk not strictly
tragic, but extratragic.

The Monk remains in his way true to this theory of tragedy; he is much truer to the formula than Boccaccio and
consequently much less capable of Boccaccio's inspired violations. In no one of his stories do we find anything comparable to Boccaccio's emotional defense of worldly activity
for Alcibiades, or Boccaccio's sympathetic and detailed plotting of the rise and fall of Hannibal showing the hero's own
contribution to his misfortune through a subtle weakness
peculiarly tragic in one so truly great. Most of the Monk's
efforts are open-and-shut tragedies showing how Fortune
at her pleasure overthrows the innocent and the wicked
alike. It is true that Adam fell through misconduct, Samson
erred fatally in telling his secret to a woman, and others,
especially Antiochus, fell both through the operations of
Fortune and through pride, the sin to which fortunate people are most prone and which God, to show man's weakness, particularly allows Fortune to chasten. But Hercules,

Zenobia, Pedro of Spain, Pedro of Cyprus, Bernabò of Lombardy, Ugolino of Pisa, Alexander the Great, and Julius Caesar were entirely free from tragic sin or fault and fell through no cause but Fortune's aversion of her face. Nero, even while he was most wicked, had Fortune's favor for a while and fell merely because she changed, though she did offer his vicious character as an excuse for her turning against him.

Thus the Monk at times indicates some connection between men's failings and their falls, but never very sharply or wholeheartedly, certainly not so noticeably as Boccaccio. One has the feeling that he is never getting far away from his teaching that misfortunes have no rational causes and are to be expected simply because the world is a vale of tears. The very brief moral at the end of the tragedy of Hercules, who was innocent of any specified sin, represents as much philosophic effort as he makes in the direction of fixing human responsibility for tragedy:

> Lo, who may truste on fortune any throwe?
> For him that folweth al this world of prees,
> Er he be war, is ofte y-leyd ful lowe.
> Ful wys is he that can him-selven knowe.
>
> (B, 3326–3329)

This has the implications of those ascetic conclusions of Boccaccio's which are supported by the tale of Fortune's battle with Poverty, and like them is nothing more than equivocation as an explanation of tragedy by personal fault. The active man is responsible for any disaster that comes to him, but only because he chooses in the first place to enter the world of endeavor. Thereafter, his voluntary actions would seem to have little bearing upon his mortal fate. He has subjected himself to Fortune and she abases him at her pleasure—or she does not abase him, if the whim suits her. The only sure course is to give up, and to hold in scorn, the world of ambition.

The Monk makes sure that we understand the unique eminence of many of his subjects because thereby he makes sure of the moral that even the greatest mundane power can guarantee itself no security. He says with tiresome iteration that there was never such another as Samson; there was never anybody since the world began who slew so many monsters as did Hercules; there was nobody who excelled Zenobia in boldness, lineage, or "gentilesse"; there was no one in this wide world while Nero was emperor who was not subject to his power; there was never such another as Antiochus; there was never another conqueror who might be compared with Alexander. Such men and women, as we have already found, are the theoretically right subjects for a tragic writer turning scorn upon the unstable world, though less eminent sufferers may also contribute to the general picture of insecurity, as, for example, does Ugolino of Pisa for the Monk.

The Monk, whose definition of tragedy includes the bewailing of misfortunes, lets himself show sympathy for many victims, but most lyrically and most movingly for Ugolino and his children. In a sense, then, their story is the best which the Monk tells. But its sympathy is of a sort to make it little better than merely sentimental tragedy. The Monk does not present Ugolino as an actively heroic figure; and though he gives him much sympathetic appreciation, it

is an appreciation which neglects to seek tragic faults in the man and to understand his fall dramatically. Dante's Ugolino[1] is infinitely more tragic, even though Dante is not concerned, as the great writers of dramatic tragedy are, to bound the issues of action with death and achieve tragic effect in the world of the flesh. Dante's Ugolino, a man outrageously tortured but not entirely innocent, whose somewhat excusable inability to forgive the wrong to his innocent children binds him eternally to prey upon their persecutor like a very beast, is not merely a pitiful but also a fearful figure. The Monk's scheme of narration, of course, forbids his taking a sufferer into the next world, and it is not to be expected that he would follow Dante's account of Ugolino in Hell, but it is to be expected that, unless he had good reason not to do so, he would follow Dante's suggestion that Ugolino sinned when he betrayed the city of Pisa. The Monk apparently had his good reason. By leaving Ugolino innocent he shapes the story to fit his main thesis that the world is a realm of causeless misfortune.

It is plain, then, that the Monk, in spite of the fact that he mentions sin, is impelled to face personal responsibility for tragedy less squarely than Boccaccio, that he does not show Boccaccio's depth and subtlety of philosophical interest in tragedy, and that for the development of later tragedy he is less fruitful than Boccaccio. The Monk adheres to the ascetic formula more pedantically and in his violations of it does not show so much vitality. I say that the Monk does so, not Chaucer, because I feel that here we must give Chaucer full leeway in what he is undoubtedly to some degree engaged upon—the dramatic presentation of character.[2]

III

With *Troilus and Criseyde* we are upon more certain ground. Here is the most ambitious work which Chaucer brought to completion. It was conceived in his maturity, though not at the very height of his power, and it manifests, obviously in his own person, a vital interest in tragedy. And here Chaucer achieves what his Monk does not achieve, an inspired glorification of Boccaccio's conception of tragedy.

The originality of the *Troilus* is multifarious, and the work can be appreciated critically from widely different angles of observation. But viewed as a tragedy in the tradition set by Boccaccio's *De Casibus* its originality chiefly consists in its discovery that a story of serious misfortune gains enormously in force of tragic impact when it is plotted at greater length than that of any story in the *De Casibus* or the *Monkes Tale* and with more leisurely attention to the details of setting, dialogue, and action. In the *Troilus*, Chaucer discards that part of the *De Casibus* method which makes the force of tragedy depend mainly upon a cumulation of many tragic figures not necessarily related except through the common solution of didactic purpose and moral comment in which they are suspended. Thus Chaucer simply writes a *De Casu* instead of a *De Casibus,* but he expends upon it an amount of care and effort which might have produced a collection of stories like Boccaccio's. If the change sounds too simple and obvious to be original, let it be remembered that the artistic unity and capacity of the single tragedy were not obvious to the Greeks until long after many tragic heroes had been known to them in epic

and other collections of stories. As Aristotle fully appreciated, the artistic discovery made when the tragic story was
given its own self-sufficient wholeness as drama was one of
a high order, because it was productive of a form needing
more rigorous unification than the epic. Chaucer's *Troilus*
is of a new high order for the Middle Ages in presentation
of tragedy as narrative.

The manner of the *Troilus* is essentially that of unhur-
ried narrative, though we may be tempted to find in the
poem a dramatic quality. To compare it with a psychological novel is on the whole quite just. But it is nevertheless
true that Chaucer, with his bent for sharply characteristic
dialogue and vivid setting, and with his tendency to let the
story fall into a succession of well-marked separate scenes,
constantly reminds us of drama.[3]

The use made by Chaucer of the varied matter which he
borrowed for his *Troilus* and the place which his work occupies in the development and adaptation of the Trojan legend
by Christian Europe have been studied with recurrent interest.[4] Much that has been learned, though of high value for
the general understanding of Chaucer's mind, is not pertinent to the present discussion. But the fact that Chaucer
deliberately and consistently altered Boccaccio's *Filostrato*,
his principal source, to make it into a tragedy according to
his understanding of the term, calls for close attention. To
what has already been said on that score something may
well be added.[5]

In order that we may have no doubt of the general intention, Chaucer addresses his book in conclusion as "litel myn
tragedie," and in order that we may know what kind of

tragedy he has in mind, he makes Troilus mourn the change
of his fortune in this wise:

> O Troilus, what may men now thee calle
> But wrecche of wrecches, out of honour falle
> In-to miserie, in which I wol biwayle
> Criseyde, allas! til that the breeth me fayle?
>   (IV, 270–273)

Quite apparently, there is here a reminder of the much-
quoted words by which the Monk in the Prologue to his
tale defines a tragedy as a story

> Of him that stood in greet prosperitee
> And is y-fallen out of heigh degree
> Into miserie, and endeth wrecchedly,
>   (B, 3165–3167)

and of the very first words of his tale proper:

> I wol biwayle in maner of Tragedie
> The harm of hem that stode in heigh degree.[6]
>   (B, 3181–3182)

Boccaccio neither refers to the *Filostrato* as a tragedy nor
has an equivalent for the words of Troilus echoing the
Monk. On his own responsibility, then, Chaucer regards the
famous story of Troilus as fit for a Monk's Tale,[7] and that
means as a tragedy to which can be given the structure and
spirit of a story in the *De Casibus*. Let us see what changes
he is thus led to make in the *Filostrato* by this combination
of inspiration from Boccaccio the youthful writer of love
romance and Boccaccio the repentant and ascetic writer of
narrative tragedy. Let us see incidentally how much Chaucer is able to improve the tragic effect of a *De Casibus* story
with the advantage of leisure for its unfoldment which he
permits himself.

Boccaccio tells the adventures of Troilus in the *Filostrato* with a very personal aim. Here is a delicate romance of courtly love, and the poet offers the clever confection to his mistress, Maria d' Aquino, daughter of the Countess d' Aquino and probably of King Robert of Naples illegitimately,[8] whose favors he has not yet completely enjoyed. She is absent from Naples, and he is impelled to express his own sorrow by telling the sorrows of Troilus in love. Chaucer is freer than Boccaccio to find general interest in the tale, and says so at the outset with whatever mixture of seriousness and lightness there may be in the asseveration, often repeated elsewhere in his poetry, that he himself does not dare to love because of his "unlyklinesse." Before he has done with Troilus he proves that the business of courtly love, to which Boccaccio is attached so unquestioningly and ardently as a noble and beautiful thing, has its aspect of sad vanity which can be viewed with truly detached spirit.[9] Boccaccio begins the story with recognition that it is one of sorrow at separation, sorrow like his own. Before the sorrow of Troilus there comes the joy of Troilus—which, of course, might just possibly suggest to Maria the granting of complete joy to himself, though he is delicately careful in hinting so. The only reason for his dwelling upon Troilus' joy, he hastens to add, is that by contrast with joy we understand how great is the misery which follows after. This is a curious forecast of the effective method of decrying the search for insecure worldly joy that he was to use in many stories of the *De Casibus,* though he cannot here be suspected of being moved by an ascetic spirit. Chaucer begins by making a simple outline of a tragic structure, a structure which is like the plot of the Hannibal story in the *De Casibus* except that it has to do with love rather than affairs of state. He says he is to tell how Troilus, the son of a king, adventured upward from woe to joy and then fell from joy to woe. We are led to expect a dramatic pyramid of rising and descending action.

It is not long before Chaucer in the first book of his *Troilus* lets us feel that the tale is planned to have a far more serious overtone of worldly insecurity than Boccaccio gives to it, and that it is to tell not merely the amorous misadventure of a courtly young man, but also the fall of a prince who was proud and confident, yet who could not change the fateful way of the world. At this point Chaucer takes a suggestion from Boccaccio, but markedly changes and elaborates the borrowed matter. Boccaccio says that before Troilus sees Cressida he boasts to his loitering companions that he is free from love's snares and glad of it. Not that he has not known the sweet pangs of love and its very real courtly benefits. But now he is out of love and he will take care to remain out, laughing at those who are foolish enough to serve inconstant women. Then Boccaccio makes the brief choral comment: "O blindness of mundane minds! How often follow effects all contrary to our intentions! Troilus now raileth at the weaknesses and anxious loves of other people without a thought of what heaven hasteneth to bring upon him, whom love transfixed more than any other before he left the temple."[10] In Chaucer's hands this becomes something only externally similar.

Chaucer's Troilus likewise boasts that he is free from the folly of love, but with the difference that apparently he has never yet known what love is. He has "heard told" how lovers suffer and he has no intention of following such fools. It is a light touch, but it is a sure one, changing a sophisticated Troilus into an innocent one, to whom disillusion and the knowledge of a fate that allows man no surety of temporal happiness can come with the unique force of first experience. Now Chaucer catches up the choral comment and spins it into three stanzas for Boccaccio's one. He begins:

> O blinde world, O blinde entencioun!
> How ofte falleth al th' effect contraire
> Of surquidrye and foul presumpcioun;
> For caught is proud, and caught is debonaire.
> This Troilus is clomben on the staire,
> And litel weneth that he moot descenden.
> But al-day fayleth thing that foles wenden.
>
> (I, 211–217)

Troilus, continues Chaucer, is a proud Bayard feeling his oats, but when a Bayard feels also the lash, he settles into his traces and knows that he is only a horse after all, and must suffer under horses' law.

> So ferde it by this fers and proude knight;
> Though he a worthy kinges sone were,
> And wende no-thing hadde had swiche might
> Ayens his wil that sholde his herte stere.
>
> (I, 225–228)

The change again is subtle but sure. Boccaccio makes nothing of Troilus' being a king's son, and Chaucer makes much. In a tone with which we are familiar in the *De Casibus* stories Chaucer draws a pointed moral that kingliness and pride may think themselves less held to the way of all flesh, but in their presumption they fall, and then they realize that all men, high or low, are driven in the world's traces and put under the lash of mortality. It is true that by this homely figure Chaucer means nothing more obvious immediately than that the pride of Troilus cannot keep him from a fall into love; it is also true that at this point in his story Chaucer does not disprize profane love—nay, even goes on to say that since all men are subject to it, one had better surrender and acquire whatever benefits it can yield; but we know from the beginning of the poem the more serious fall that is in store for Troilus, and now we may guess that his pride in princely rank and his ignorance of the world's power over all mankind will soften that fall no more than this.

So Troilus falls into his first woe and proceeds out of it to his greatest joy. Like many of the more carefully plotted stories in the *De Casibus,* Chaucer's *Troilus* has a peak of good fortune very near the middle of the action, marked with moralizing upon Fortune's mutability. Here, in some degree, Chaucer follows the *Filostrato,* which, even though it was not written especially to expose and anatomize the mutability of the world, yet as a love poem could rail at Fortune with plenty of precedent. At the end of the third book of his romance Boccaccio has a single stanza saying that the joy of Troilus with Cressida, of which he has just finished a description, lasted all too short a time, thanks to envious Fortune, always unstable in this world. She turned her bitter face upon Troilus and changed his happy love into woeful mourning. With no more ado Boccaccio proceeds with the story. This stanza Chaucer finds much too casual for his purpose and expands into a *prohemium* for his fourth book accusing Fortune of her faults, declaring that now she is to cast Troilus off her wheel and set up Diomede in his place, pitying Cressida for her weakness, and invoking Mars and the Furies to aid in the telling of Troilus' loss of both love and life. Thus Chaucer gives to the passage more emphatic position and more tragic implication.

Very soon after Fortune has turned the bitter aspect of her countenance toward Chaucer's Troilus, we come to his famous Boethian soliloquy upon fate and man's free will.[11] Pandarus finds his friend convinced that God has foreknown and predestined his loss of Cressida from the very beginning of things and that nothing which he himself or anyone else can do can make any difference in the result. Troilus has arrived at consideration of the question which lies at the heart of any tragedy that goes beyond the simplest stages of presentation: whether a man's suffering is caused by external influence, by himself, or by both. In the *Filostrato* there is nothing of the sort. Nor was there in the first draft of *Troilus and Criseyde*.[12] Chaucer evidently put the passage into his poem thoughtfully and with no idle purpose, whatever we may think of the result.

One effect, at least, is that of preparation for Chaucer's disparagement of profane love and his ascetic advice to young people *de contemptu mundi* given at the end of his poem. This conclusion is completely at variance with any feeling that it is better to have loved and lost than never to have loved at all, which may be the ruling sentiment of a romantic *Filostrato,* or even of a romantic tragedy, but never of a *De Casibus* tragedy running true to type. By the time Chaucer added Troilus' meditation upon destiny to his poem, he had seen to what conclusion the story had led,

THE SLAYING OF TROILUS BY ACHILLES
From Lydgate's *The Siege of Troy*, MS Royal 18 D ii, *ca.* 1450.

and he gave to Troilus such thoughts of destiny as befitted a prince beginning to learn the *De Casibus* lesson, the lesson that no man has the power by will, by action, or even by merit, to secure himself in any worldly possession, and that therefore such a possession is worthless from the beginning. For it must always be remembered that though Chaucer's Cressida is no mere lay figure in most respects, yet as a participant in a *De Casibus* tragedy, she is simply a worldly possession of Troilus. Like wealth or a crown she takes wings and leaves him. Chaucer is notoriously lenient with her. For one thing, no doubt, he deals gently with her because a tolerant nature usually restrains him from harsh condemnation of human frailty. But also, so far as *Troilus and Criseyde* is the tragedy of a prince who puts too much faith in an unstable world, it would be out of place for its author to show spleen over the fact that Cressida—or the world—actually does turn out to be untrustworthy. That surely is only to be expected, and Chaucer finds in false Cressida hardly more of voluntary and reprehensible faithlessness than he would find in a false inanimate object like worldly riches. In her, as Professor Root says truly, "he sees the type of mutability, of the transitoriness and fallacy of earthly happiness."[13] It is not unwarranted, then, that even so early, with Cressida haled away from Troy by a combination of forces beyond control, Troilus should be made to meditate hopelessly upon a destiny which can give a worldly joy and take it utterly away.

The Christian Fathers held that though there is predestination of human affairs, yet there is human free will nevertheless.[14] Chaucer has deliberately given Troilus the arguments of Boethius which represent the shortsighted opinions of a sufferer blinded by his misfortune, and he has omitted the answer of Philosophy to the erring Boethius which triumphantly provides for free will. But too much can be made of the omission.[15] After all, Troilus is a man sunk in all the blind error of unphilosophical attachment to the temporal world, and it is just as fitting for him to embrace heresy momentarily as for the unconverted Boethius. The argument of Philosophy which proves the existence of free will to Boethius by an appeal to a world where time does not exist and where the future is the present, could be expected to have for the lovesick Troilus no force whatever. What Chaucer himself would have said about free will in a serious confession of faith we do not really know, though we are sure that the intricate problem was full of interest for him and that the paradoxes of the clerks who tried to solve it could arouse his humor.[16]

Moreover, no matter how shockingly heretical the words of Troilus might be literally,—

> And this suffyseth right y-now, certeyn,
> For to destroye our free chois every del,—
>   (IV, 1058–1059)

the spirit of what he says would be the opposite of revolutionary. The only freedom in which he is really interested is freedom to win and keep Cressida; and this sort of freedom the most conservative Augustinian Christianity of the Middle Ages certainly had as little desire to argue for as it had conviction that the fleshly world, in which men possessed and lost mistresses, was the real world. Denial of the soul's freedom to do good or evil and then to receive merited

reward or punishment in an eternal world was very real
heresy, but Troilus shows no true concern with these eternal
issues. In effect, it is for the body rather than the soul that
he visions fate; and even the Philosophy who proves to
Boethius that man has spiritual freedom would gladly admit that in bodily love for Cressida Troilus had enslaved
himself. As she says: "The minds of men must needs be
more free when they conserve themselves in the contemplation of God, and less when they come to their bodies,
and yet less when they are bound with earthly fetters."[17]
The bodily principle itself has no freedom whatever, but
can only put the soul's freedom in bondage, as many leaders
of the Church were fond of saying. Thus the fatalistic philosophy of Troilus really amounts to that of many a writer
de contemptu mundi. Its burden is that *worldly* delight
always comes to a man and goes from him through nothing
else than external necessity.

When Chaucer's Troilus has sounded the extent of his
misery yet farther, his sister Cassandra offers him a practical application of this philosophy, but he does not find her
conclusions more palatable because he has already specu-
lated upon the necessity of his suffering. Perhaps it is only
according to human nature that the finished statement by
another person of the thing that he already knows, yet illogi-
cally hopes to find untrue, should arouse his anger. The use
which Chaucer makes of Cassandra is completely different
in spirit from that which Boccaccio makes of her, and the
difference is almost all in the direction of changing an
atmosphere of romance into an atmosphere of tragedy.
Furthermore, the tragic aura which Chaucer permits the

prophetess to see surrounding her brother has very definitely the colors of the orthodox *De Casibus* tradition.

In the *Filostrato* the dejected Troilus is visited by a party of ladies who are to raise his spirits by filling his chamber with music, song, and gayety.[18] Cassandra is among them, and she pays her attentions to Troilus in a way that no one would expect to be cheering. The truth is that Cassandra is thoroughly a shrew and thoroughly a snob. She takes the chance to tell Troilus that, granted he had to fall sick of love, he might at least have loved a lady of respectable social position, not the daughter of a wicked priest, a man of no importance. Troilus lies manfully, as a courtly lover should, to protect his lady's reputation. He swears that Cressida has never granted him her favors. Then he gives himself away, as a completely smitten lover would, when he has a chance to talk about his lady. Suppose Cressida *has* given him her love, he says; kind hearts are more than coronets—and Cressida is a marvel among women. Finally, he dismisses Cassandra from his house under a shower of hard names. It is a light scene, more comedy of manners than tragedy.

In contrast, Chaucer creates a Cassandra who is dignified instead of petty and who is a true prophetess instead of a snooping gossip. Chaucer's instinct has led him to make use of her in such a way that she adds to the pall of destiny which already hangs over Troilus; and, though she does not presage her own fate, she approaches in some small degree the tragic character of the Cassandra in Aeschylus' *Agamemnon*. Chaucer lets Troilus send for her and ask interpretation of his dream that a wild boar has had possession of Cressida (where Boccaccio lets Troilus interpret

a similar dream for himself). Cassandra smiles—whether
ïronically or tenderly we are left to guess—and says that
first her brother

> most a fewe of olde stories here,
> To purpos, how that fortune over-throwe
> Hath lordes olde.   (V, 1459–1461)

And she composes a brief *De Casibus* (derived from Sta-
tius) of the rises and falls in that line of princes from which
Diomede is descended,[19] beginning with Meleager, who
slew the famous boar sent by Diana to ravage the fields of
Calydon. The boar in Troilus' dream thus betokens Diomede, and the meaning of the dream in general is that once
more, touching the line of Diomede, Fortune has sent a
change which is tragedy for one man and joy for another:

> Weep if thou wolt, or leef; for, out of doute,
> This Diomede is inne, and thou art oute.
>   (V, 1518–1519)

Chaucer's Troilus is as angry with Cassandra as Boccaccio's, but his rage has a different psychological depth. The
poor man swears that Cressida is as true as Alcestis, just to
smother that inner self which knows the truth. Here and
elsewhere in the *Troilus,* Chaucer does something which
no hurried collector of worldly transmutations would be
able to do: he refines the telling of *De Casibus* tragedy by
showing at length the pitiful grasp which a man can keep
upon his world of illusion even after convincing demonstration of its vanity has been given him.

At this point we are reminded that the *Troilus* does not
merely tell the tragic fall of a princely lover, making the
course of one man's joy and sorrow a complete mirror of

the world's transmutations. An opportunity given to Chaucer by the leisurely method of his poem is that of setting his hero's fall within and against one of those mightier mutations of Fortune which bring to us a deeper sense of mortal insecurity than the fall of even the highest single potentate can bring. Chaucer seizes the opportunity with full appreciation and great skill. Over and over again the poet lets us know that Troilus and Cressida, no matter how keenly we may feel the personal force of their tragedy, are only particles suspended in the stream of Trojan doom. As Professor Kittredge says with the customary wisdom of his criticism in *Chaucer and His Poetry:* "This is no mere rhetorical analogue—no trick of symbolism. Their drama is an integral part of the great Trojan tragedy. They are caught in the wheels of that resistless mechanism which the gods have set in motion for the ruin of the Trojan race."[20] In order to give us this impression with especial force, Chaucer introduces a stanza of choral comment in his own person immediately after Cassandra has departed from Troilus. The effect is to draw us back from consideration of the shorter waves of mutation which Cassandra has shown us in the falls of princes—though it is true that she has alluded to the destruction of Thebes—and make us feel the ground swell of *De Casibus* tragedy in the falls of races:

> Fortune, whiche that permutacioun
> Of thinges hath, as it is hir committed
> Through purveyaunce and disposicioun
> Of heighe Jove, as regnes shal ben flitted
> Fro folk in folk, or whan they shal ben smitted,
> Gan pulle awey the fetheres brighte of Troye
> Fro day to day, til they ben bare of joye.
>
> (V, 1541–1547)

If we were looking for one stanza in the poem which should express essentially both the conventional nature of the tragic philosophy in the *Troilus* and the unique spirit with which Chaucer surrounds that philosophy, giving it a setting like nothing in Boccaccio's *De Casibus* or any other book of his time, this stanza might well be the one to choose. It begins in stately terms with a picture of the conventional *De Casibus* figure of Fortune, behind whom stands the omniscient and omnipotent divinity of Boethius and, more particularly, of Dante,²¹ delegating to her care the mysterious flux of worldly change which somehow serves his purpose. But it concludes with a couplet which is Chaucer and Chaucer alone—the elfish Chaucer, the ironically detached Chaucer, the wisely balanced Chaucer, the Arnoldian Chaucer lacking in sustained high seriousness, whichever we elect to call him. Into this picture of Fate in all its epic grandeur the poet casts the figure of Troy being plucked of its gay feathers like any barnyard fowl. Here is that well-known instinct of Chaucer to discount his own heroics whenever he finds himself getting caught by them, an instinct, however, which is never so light-minded as completely to destroy profound emotions previously aroused. Probably nothing in small compass could better represent the almost indescribable mingling of sad sooth and smiling irony, of heroic elevation and homely shrewdness, which is the seriocomic spirit of the *Troilus*.

The climax of the changes that Chaucer has made throughout the story in order to accomplish its shading as *De Casibus* tragedy is an out-and-out *De Contemptu Mundi* moral offered by Chaucer himself after the death of Troilus.

Boccaccio, too, concludes the story with a moral, but his is a very worldly one. To young men he gives the sage advice that not all women are to be trusted, especially young women, who are apt to take delight in many lovers without any regard for virtue or reason. Do not be in haste to choose, but if you find the apparently perfect lady, cleave to her—and pray that you may love so wisely as not to die in the end of feminine faithlessness.

Chaucer shifts the major implication of the story's conclusion from this world to the next, and he does so first by following the soul of Troilus in a flight which reaches above the realm of mortal change to a realm where the hitherto deluded lover can look down upon all mortality with understanding, can hear the music of the spheres, and can at last despise "this wrecched world" in which he has suffered. Troilus laughs at those who weep for his death, and condemns

> al our werk that folweth so
> The blinde lust, the which that may not laste,
> And sholden al our herte on hevene caste.
>
> (V, 1823–1825)

Ultimately, the ideas connected with the flight of Troilus' soul come from Cicero's *Somnium Scipionis,* which, in addition to describing the spheres surrounding the earth, inculcates aspiration toward the eternal abode of the human soul and a Hellenistic, but potentially Christian, contempt for the insecure rewards and pleasures of the corporeal life. Incidentally, it is hardly fair criticism to say that this Troilus who has concerned himself with the gratification of the wretched world's appetites is now most unjustly "rewarded with perfect felicity in heaven," and that Chaucer's disposition of his soul is as false to tragedy as would have been the singing of Hamlet's spirit to its eternal rest by flights of angels.[22] Chaucer does not say that Troilus inherited eternal bliss. He quite definitely thinks of the final judging of Troilus' soul as happening beyond a threshold over which he will not follow. For a moment Troilus is granted the boon of unhampered vision in that high sphere, but his merited dwelling-place is elsewhere—unspecified:

> And forth he wente, shortly for to telle,
> Ther as Mercurie sorted him to dwelle.
> (V, 1826 1827)

What is specifically granted to Troilus is apparently no more than a quiet period of backward-looking immediately after death, a period when his soul can rapidly survey the whole course of events in its life just past and with the advantage of detached perspective consolidate the lesson which they have given. We may know from the vision of Er described by Plato at the end of the *Republic* that, according to ancient tradition, such a place as the one from which Troilus views the spheres and understands their meaning can be separate from what could properly be called Heaven. In the vision of Er those souls, some from Heaven and some from earth, who are to choose their destinies for new incarnations are assembled at a point where they look upon the spheres, hear their harmony, and see the bond of Necessity. Thus, though Troilus laughs, it is for satisfaction that the scales have fallen from his eyes and for scorn of those who persist in his own previous delusions, but not for heavenly happiness.

After Troilus has learned his lesson, Chaucer drives it home for all who need it. Boccaccio's counsel to young men about town subject to love becomes in Chaucer the famous counsel to "yonge fresshe folkes, he or she," to repair home from worldly vanity, to substitute sacred love for profane love, and to remember that this world is only a Vanity Fair. For here in Troilus, Chaucer says, we may see the end of a life given to the service of worldly appetites and to the cursed ways of paganism.

Before he comes to this unmistakably ascetic moral, Chaucer does not draw from the story the fully conventional lesson *de contemptu mundi*. To many modern readers the end is so unexpected that it seems indefensible as comment upon what has gone before. It must be admitted that many of Chaucer's alterations in the Troilus story have nothing to do with that framing of a conventional *De Casibus* tragedy which we have followed in selected detail. It is unnecessary to bring into discussion the innumerable evidences in the *Troilus* of Chaucer's warm worldly understanding and his sympathetic delight in the palpable business of living which have been appreciated and praised by readers and critics. Undeniably, Chaucer commonly gives us the impression that he is far from scorning what he relates. Through a great proportion of his lines he writes a heart-felt tale of love in worldly fashion. Hence there is a very large measure of contradiction when, as Professor Tatlock says, "the heart-felt worldly tale is interpreted in an unworldly sense,"[23] and it is contradiction which still must be allowed to stand even after we take note that Chaucer has frequently indicated that he is writing *De Casibus* tragedy, a variety of tragedy fathered by Contempt of the World.

This contradiction is much the same as that which we have found in Boccaccio's own *De Casibus*. It is a result of that curiously paradoxical partnership between scorn of the world and espousal of the world which we have found natural to the Renaissance. Boccaccio's earnest condemnation of all ambitious worldly activity in the *De Casibus,* surrounding and apparently nullifying such things as his spirited defense of the active worldly life for Alcibiades, and likewise Petrarch's monkish Contempt of the World in the *Secretum,* inextricably mingled with his instinctive defense of worldly activity and the rewards of fame, have the same emotional origin as Chaucer's asceticism in the *Troilus*. They rise from a need deeper than any need for logical consistency. The new love of active life has its creative hold upon these men, but part of their instinct is still to fear it, still to check it. So in the *Troilus* Chaucer takes hold of worldly life in no gingerly fashion, realizes it, sympathizes with it, in general makes us feel that his genius is for worldly life, and yet, with no more apology than some of the greatest of his contemporaries might offer under the same circumstances, tells us flatly that worldly life is vanity.

But Chaucer's contradiction, though it is the same in kind as Boccaccio's, goes farther than the contradiction within the *De Casibus*. Chaucer gives to the *Troilus* a circumstantial development of psychologic detail, implying cause and effect in deliberate human action, which Boccaccio, even if he would, could not give in the space of his briefer tragedies. Therefore Chaucer's espousal of life for inherent meaning is in that way much stronger. At the same time, in comments upon the causes of tragedy, he supports a philosophy of events as determined by God-through-Fortune, and not by human choice, more consistently and far less questioningly than does Boccaccio. Often these comments are his own, and where they are his own he never raises the slightest doubt that the hand of external fate presses upon men to determine all that happens to them in active life. He does not even argue plainly, as Boccaccio does, for the measure of personal freedom which lies in man's ability to abjure the world of activity in the first place, though that argument is implicit in the ascetic advice to young people that concludes the poem. The most glaring inconsistency of which Chaucer is guilty in his own comment is between this final admonition not to love in the way of the world and his earlier admonition, when Troilus first sees Cressida, not to scorn love, since the worthiest of mankind have been and always will be conquered and ennobled by it.[24] In this earlier admonition the philosophy has a strong cast of fatalism, for Chaucer adds that Love will strike you anyhow, if he will, and a staff is better when it bends than when it breaks. On the whole, then, Chaucer is more reactionary and unworldly than Boccaccio in tragic theory even though he is more worldly in the actual development of tragedy as issuing dramatically from human character.

To put the matter another way, Chaucer makes the philosophy of the *Troilus* very thoroughly deterministic, so far as events in this world are concerned, and quite possibly he does so in accordance with his own well-considered theory of life; but when he comes to distill his actual experience of life into this long poem, he makes his creatures act vitally, that is, purposefully and hopefully. It would seem that we are here face to face with the truth of the Johnsonian dictum that no matter how successfully theory may place itself against freedom of the will, experience is always for it. Chaucer makes Troilus and Cressida do many things which give us the impression that human deliberation and choice have their material effects.[25] Fate or chance plays its part in impelling Cressida toward Troilus, but we see much more than this impulsion in Cressida's actions. After Chaucer has skillfully guided us behind the scenes, we are convinced that she is far more the very woman choosing to be overcome and to yield than she is a puppet of the gods or of her scheming uncle. The more alive Troilus and Cressida are, the more they act as though not wholly enchained by an external necessity. Hence, praise of the *Troilus* as vitally dramatic is well founded. Yet it would be even better founded if Chaucer had permitted his keen observation of human character and its effects to alter his deterministic philosophy of tragic causes and his deterministic tragic paraphernalia. He might have let us see, like Boccaccio, that his age was just beginning to give recognition in philosophy as well as in literary practice to the conception that tragic event is the product both of fate for which the individual is not responsible and of characteristic deed for which he is. One of Chaucer's contemporaries in England, John Gower, may be found attributing so much responsibility to human character that he seems to reduce external fate to nothing. When he does so, his philosophy, postulating absolute

tragic justice, is as much unfitted to be the basis of great
tragedy as the contrary absolutism attributing all misfortune to chance or predestination:

> The man is overal
> His owne cause of wel and wo.
> That we Fortune clepe so
> Out of the man himself it groweth;
> And who that other wise troweth,
> Behold the poeple of Israel
> For evere whil they deden wel,
> Fortune was hem debonaire,
> And whan thei deden the contraire,
> Fortune was contrariende.[28]

But Gower at least serves to demonstrate that personal responsibility for tragedy was far from being an unheard-of
conception in the poetry of Chaucer's own society.

For another and more capital reason, *Troilus and Criseyde* never reaches the stature of the greatest tragedies in
the Greek or Christian European traditions. Chaucer finds
his fable in a love story told with all the myopic attention
to the details of tender individualized emotion that romance
demands. He sees its narrowness. He does much to widen
the story by making us feel the tragic fate of this one man
and this one woman as part of the tragic fate of Troy.
But still the events of the fable insist upon eddying far too
closely about the absorbing interest that Troilus has merely
for Cressida and that Cressida has merely for Troilus. It
is not for nothing that Aristophanes in the *Frogs* makes
Aeschylus say with fine scorn that he has had an eye for
the tragedies of heroes, not of lovers, and that he doubts
whether in all his dramas he has ever exhibited a woman

in love. The reply of Euripides, that Aeschylus was too stern and too stupid to understand matters of love, is an amusing *argumentum ad hominem,* but nothing more. Less stern Euripides certainly is,—and not stupid,—but he often opens himself to the well-deserved accusation of triviality. The romance that came to Chaucer in the *Filostrato* was packed with things that were trivial in tragic import, and some of the triviality was bound to remain when Chaucer conceived his own work as hybrid romance-tragedy, so close to Boccaccio's work as to be almost translation. To change the figure, no matter what interlining of tragedy his genius might give to the picture, the original lines would be perceptible and confusing. Entirely fresh drafting was necessary. As Chaucer's work stands, Troilus can be freed from the imputation of being merely a lovesick boy, but only by an effort in our concentration. His place as a hero in the counsels of Troy and on its windy plains of battle we perceive in only a few very briefly narrated or unemphatically dramatized scenes.

A still further widening of the fable to give it participation in a universal drama of struggling forces, in a drama pitting right against wrong, or duty against desire, or one good against another good, is neither attempted nor hinted at by Chaucer. When Troilus debates free will, the argument does not reach to the larger issues; and all through the poem we feel the influence of that courtly love code which is inherited from the *Filostrato* and which excludes itself from any ethical consideration except the loyalty of lover to beloved. In the *Troilus,* as in his other mature work, Chaucer often shows the final authority of genius in search-

ing the springs of human action, but that searching of his
which rouses our highest admiration is in the direction of
Shakespearean comedy rather than of Shakespearean tragedy. Perhaps the ethical depths reached by the greater tragic
poets were waters which Chaucer would have had neither
inclination nor ability to sound, even if models of their kind
of tragedy had been available to him.

IV

In medieval English tragedy the passage from Chaucer to
John Lydgate was not in all ways the recession that Lydgate's poetic inferiority or his monkish predilections might
lead us to expect. Viewed historically, Lydgate had something of importance to contribute to the idea of tragedy
conceived by Boccaccio. He was to serve as a link between
medieval and Elizabethan tragedy not merely because he
translated the *De Casibus* into English and made it available to Elizabethan readers, but also because as he translated the work he changed it.

Lydgate's *Fall of Princes* is only in the loosest sense a
translation of the *De Casibus,* and the modern reader who
depends upon the English work alone, even if he allows
for free rendering, is often much farther removed from
Boccaccio than he suspects. Lydgate used a French version
of the *De Casibus* made by Laurent de Premierfait. Laurent
worked from Boccaccio's first (unrevised) issue of his book
and made two versions, the first in 1400, a reasonably close
translation, and the second in 1409, so much extended with
learned and moral interpolation that it is really a new book
built around Boccaccio. It was this second and more elab-

OEDIPUS BLINDED BY HIMSELF
From Lydgate's *Fall of Princes*, MS Harley 1766, *ca.* 1450.

orate version by Laurent that Lydgate in turn made over into the *Fall of Princes* during the decade 1430–1440.[27] Furthermore, Lydgate was more independent in thought than Laurent, who, with all his elaboration, kept his second version of the *Des Cas des Nobles Hommes et Femmes* fairly close to the *De Casibus* in spirit.[28]

In both Boccaccio and Chaucer we have observed certain impulses toward the freeing of tragedy from those ascetic conceptions which allowed no inherent rational order to the world of the flesh. Without such freedom, tragedy could not have become drama presenting that interaction of character and event for which Shakespeare developed infinite shades of perception. Chaucer, though he was certainly no less ascetic in ostensible philosophy than Boccaccio, and though his genius may be more properly called seriocomic than tragic, nevertheless by an artistic love of life and an instinctive discernment for the details of action and reaction in the human scene, did much in *Troilus and Criseyde* to advance medieval narrative tragedy toward Elizabethan dramatic tragedy. Lydgate was a good and simple monk incapable of following his master Chaucer in any such way as this, even if he had elected to write a *De Casu* instead of translate the *De Casibus*. Yet he was far from having an asceticism wholly inimical to a worldly realization of tragedy. He even had qualities of tolerant sympathy rather surprising in a man of his kidney—one of them a gallant fair-mindedness in the defense of women from the sweeping condemnations of monastic convention. But where Lydgate's attachment to this world had most meaning for the development of tragedy it was not the attachment of the

sympathetic lover of life. It was that of the impatient moralist ardently desiring, and finding, retribution for sinners
here and now rather than in the hereafter, a worldliness
separate from the worldliness of sensuous attachment, yet
worldliness nevertheless. In this way Lydgate did make
contribution to the progress of medieval tragedy away from
thoroughgoing Contempt of the World. That his crude
moral didacticism, using examples of tragic justice for its
transparent ends, could of itself never have produced great
tragedy, is of course no less true.

When Lydgate, turning the pages of Laurent's book,
comes upon a story which strikes his fancy as a means of
demonstrating that tragedy is punishment for vice, we may
often see his ardor carry him beyond Boccaccio. He is much
more prone than Boccaccio (and Laurent) to make sin the
whole apparent cause of a tragedy, and to dwell with the
unlovely pleasure of narrow righteousness upon horrible
details of retribution. Let us see, for example, what he does
with the story of Antiochus the Great. In his telling of this
tragedy he consistently makes more of lechery and sensuality than does Boccaccio, and in an envoy wholly his own
he lists all the sins, deadly or not, of which he finds the king
guilty, including pride, sloth, gluttony, riot, cruelty, and all
manner of excess. The moral that he then draws takes its
stand upon the most absolute principles of poetic justice:

> Noble Princis, of prudence ful famous,
> In al your grettest roial mageste
> Remembreth pleynli, yif ye be vertuous,
> Ye shal perseuere in long prosperitie,
> Where the contrarie causeth aduersitie,
> As this stori afforn doth specifie.   (V, 1614–1619)

Be good, then, and you will always be happy, not in the Christian hope of Heaven, not in the Stoic sufficiency of inner virtue, but in crassly materialistic "long prosperitie" and in the retention of your worldly power if you are a prince! Contrariwise, if you are evil you can always expect material punishment. Boccaccio has nothing so flat-footed as this. Nor does Boccaccio so far forget the cardinal faith of otherworldly Christianity that worldly pomp is a hollow reward for virtue, if it ever is a reward, and that worldly adversity is a spiritual blessing in disguise, for both the good man and the bad. Thus Lydgate is capable of the same simple morality as Gower, and in abandoning the extreme of asceticism, which dwarfs tragedy by denying that we may see any finite meaning in adversity, can fall into the opposite extreme, which dwarfs tragedy just as effectively by assuming that we may see all the meaning of adversity immediately and schematically.

Lydgate's satisfaction over the smiting of the wicked rises to its height when the sinner is an enemy of the Christian faith. Julian the Apostate is his *bête noire.* Throughout the chapter dealing with this man, who was such a horrible contrast to Constantine, the defender of the Faith, Lydgate is far less charitable than Boccaccio or Laurent. Perhaps it is partly because mention is made that Julian was at first a monk, and because the English monk felt here particularly that there are limits beyond which we cannot take human dereliction calmly.[29] This "cursid Iulian" had a "gynyng cursid" and a "cursid fyn." His false gods could not save him from death. His body was flayed, and his skin was tanned with greatest care at the order of the Persian King

Sapor and nailed on Sapor's palace gate. Lydgate declares that Julian came to his bad end through many vices, but most of all through blasphemy against the true God, the blessed Galilean. Boccaccio despises Julian, and calls him hard names, but does not show so much excited animosity. Though he, too, flays the perfidious carcass, he does not do so with the same transparent pleasure.

Mohammed also is for Lydgate an archsinner as a foe of Christianity and thereby the cause of his own inglorious death, in which men of the true religion may find comfort. Boccaccio at the beginning of his ninth book gives only two sentences to the founder of Islam, leaving him among those beggars for recognition to whom he cannot grant full attention. In those two sentences he condemns him with all severity as a seducer of mankind, a usurper of the name of prophet, and a licentious man in general. He says nothing about Mohammed's death or its causes. Laurent, as he so often does, expands a hurried reference into a story, and Lydgate follows him fairly closely except in his conclusion. Laurent gives Mohammed a comparatively mild death after a sickness. Lydgate cannot be content with such an end for so terrible a blasphemer and finds something more to his liking. He says that Mohammed commanded his followers to drink only water, but himself was accustomed to drink good wine to excess. One day, while he was stupefied with drink, he fell into a mud puddle, and there he was devoured by swine. For the complete irony in such poetic justice—Mohammed destroyed not only by wine but also by pork, the objects of his two famous prohibitions—Lydgate has no comment.

Heresy produces the same quick and sure retribution, as Lydgate views its results. Heraclius and Constantine, his son, both given only a word or two by Boccaccio without any allusion to their sins, have fully developed tragedies in Laurent and in Lydgate. Following Laurent, Lydgate talks much of the lapse into error which Heraclius suffered. By divine grace he had great success of arms until he embraced froward beliefs.

> But whan he gan susteene heresie,
> God took from hym, withynne a litel space,
> His hap, his weelfare, his fortune & his grace.
> (IX, 558–560)

Constantine also became a mortal enemy of the Faith, acting as chief supporter of evil heresy, and was slain through the conspiracy of his own knights while he was all naked in a bath. Boccaccio has the death in the bath, but only in barest outline. His details do not give us the sense of peculiar indignity which the details in Lydgate contrive to give.

Thus Lydgate shows a stronger taste for schematic retribution than Boccaccio or Chaucer, and a morality more fanatic than theirs at the same time that it is far less perceptive of life's complexity. His temptation to embrace the simplest and most materialistic formula of tragic justice becomes manifest even as we scan the headings in the *Fall of Princes*. Not at all inaccurate as indications of general spirit in the designated stories are summaries like the following: "How Amazias in India kyng for pride and presumpcioun was venquysshed in bataile & aftir slayn"; "How the proude tirant Aman was honged and the Innocent preserved"; "How the proude tiraunt Domytyan Emperour of

Rome and many other Emperours & nobles for ther out-
rages & wrecchidnesse mischeuesly ended"; "How pope
Iohn the xij^the for lechery & vicious lif was put doun"; "How
Iocelyne prince of Rage for pride slouthe & lecherie died in
pouert"; "How Duk Gualtere of Florence for his tyrannye
Lecherye and couetise ended in mischef."[30]

Yet despite this aggressive morality and this frequent
indulgence of a desire to see evil suffer in the immediate
world through an unnaturally complete tragic justice, Lydgate can often blame calamity upon irrational Fortune quite
emphatically. At such times he has obvious relish for the
De Contemptu lesson that tragedy occurs for reasons which
men may not see and that this evil world below is naturally
a realm of disorder.

In some stories Lydgate, when he makes much of Fortune, is simply following Boccaccio. The tragedy of Pompey, which in the De Casibus is made to support a lyric
outburst against the delusion of human desire for high
place in the world, he accepts for all the meaning that Boccaccio gives it and, further, for its meaning as a stimulus
to think of Heaven, where the Blind Lady is powerless. He
makes a gratuitous pun on the name of the protagonist:

> Geyn worldli pompe mak Pompeie your merour.
> (VI, 2519)

King Arthur, Boccaccio would have us perceive, was an
example of virtuous greatness which in this imperfect world
could not assure itself against a wicked scheming traitor.
Lydgate accepts the lesson. In his envoy he makes the most
of it, by saying that no one was ever braver and more famous
than Arthur; yet "Fate and Fortune" destroyed him.[31]

In other stories Lydgate makes even more of Fortune than Boccaccio does. Under the inspiration of Laurent he tells of Darius at much greater length and adds platitudinous comment upon Fortune's ways; in an envoy of his own he berates Fortune. In telling of Hannibal, whose tragedy in the *De Casibus* has arresting suggestion of a contributory flaw in the hero's purpose and will, Lydgate talks of Hannibal's decline in moral fiber, but is not able or willing to separate this from the decline in fortune. Certainly Hannibal should have proceeded to the taking of Rome after his greatest victory, Lydgate grants, only to add sagely:

> But I suppose Fortune list not assente.
> (V, 2025)

He reveals even less ability to concentrate upon Hannibal's tragic failings when he comes to write the envoy. There he says that the tragedy makes his heart bleed because Hannibal committed the horrible sin of self-murder after his fall from greatness, and he draws no other lesson. Dramatically, his moralizing is completely impertinent. Another of Boccaccio's more subtle tragedies, that of Alcibiades, is in Lydgate a wholly unsubtle example of the folly which lies in trusting Fortune. As he tells the story he curses Fortune at great length and with much vigor, and in the moral which he appends he will have nothing to do with Boccaccio's dramatically sympathetic defense of Alcibiades' worldly activity, which is accepted and translated by Laurent.[32] Lydgate sees nothing whatever in Alcibiades to excuse him. He was a good man, yes, and Fortune struck him down at the height of his prosperity. Well, we knew beforehand that the Fatal Sisters can slay the worthy and spare the wretches, that Hector dies while Thersites lives. Anyone who is guilty of pursuing hollow worldly possessions calls tragedy down upon himself.

It is plain that Lydgate, whether he is attributing calamity to forces of justice working themselves out in a world of perceptible order or blaming it upon the feminine irrationality of Fortune in a world of rank disorder, usually has honest intent to make a good job of the matter. If it is human fault that we are to see, then the fault must be dressed in black, it must have features that all of us can recognize instantly, and it must be given the stage a good part to itself. If it is Fortune that we are to see, then she must be Fortune in the most orthodox tradition, and she must be given the stage a good part to herself. If Boccaccio has cursed Fortune, then it will do no harm to add a few more curses and ring a few more changes on the theme. Boccaccio and Chaucer often have praiseworthy perception for the subtleties of tragedy, but Lydgate is almost always incapable of a view of tragedy which gives suffering some traceable cause in human character without making the cause a simple sin easily classified, or which mingles and balances traceable cause with impenetrable fate. His story of Prusias, King of Bithynia and betrayer of Hannibal, is highly exceptional in the quality of its moral comment. Lydgate declares that in the events of this story there are two things of which we must take good heed: the sudden mischance to Prusias, and the vengeance of Hannibal's curse falling upon him for his hateful treason. For once, at least, Lydgate has a glimpse, however fleeting, of chance and characteristic deed working in common to the tragic issue.

Even those vistas of plain tragic justice which open for Lydgate as he writes his book, now in the story of this sinner and now in the story of that, have a peculiarly fleeting quality. The memory of them seems to be utterly lost by the time he comes to the end of his work and feels called upon to compose a few words of essential comment upon the whole. He is then no more than a monk who sees the world as a flux of unmitigated disorder and who believes that it should be abandoned by all right-thinking men. He seems to imply that everything mundane without exception is determined by irrational Fortune, and that struggle in the world is vain. Boccaccio, in a valedictory injunction, urges all who would profit by these tragedies to seek honor, praise, and fame at the same time that they live in the honest love of virtue; but not Lydgate. Lydgate praises virtue, of course, but he says nothing such as Boccaccio says about avoiding through virtue the appearance of having caused your disaster, should Fortune turn against you. Some people are vicious, he remarks, and some people shine with virtue, but this makes no difference so far as tragedy is concerned. Without any consideration of goodness and badness Fortune rules them all; that is to say:

> In a breeff somme this book to comprehende:
> Fortunis wheel bi reuolucioun
> Doth oon clymbe up, another to discende.
>
> (IX, 3300–3302)

We have found an unresolved discord in the tragic philosophy of both Boccaccio and Chaucer, but not so harsh a discord as this. If we were to read this conclusion of Lydgate's alone,[33] we might think that what he did in the *Fall of Princes* was once more to give tragedy utterly to Fortune. On the contrary, no medieval narrator of tragedy did so much as Lydgate to make tragedy show retribution for sin.

v

Tragedy as a critical term was a wide and capacious net in the Middle Ages. What we have found in Boccaccio, Chaucer, Laurent de Premierfait, and Lydgate is a literature deserving to be called a body of tragedy far more truly than any other medieval literature to which the label of tragedy was affixed by its own age. It shows a special power of organic growth and a special concern with heroic subject-matters and ethical problems which were destined to have attraction for a new tragic stage.

Medieval critical theory held in general to an idea that tragedy must have a certain nobility of character, though the term *tragoedia* was sometimes applied to literature of the most curiously unworthy sort. Johannes Anglicus (*ca.* 1260), telling a story of fatal rivalry between two washerwomen who had divided between themselves the love of sixty soldiers in a beleaguered city, could prove that the tale was properly tragic by appealing to a common opinion held by his age that tragedy was narrative in elevated style beginning in joy and ending in tears, while comedy was its opposite.[34] No more than Dante does he say that tragedy must deal with kings and nobles, though that opinion, too, was often held.[35] The *Magnae Derivationes* of Uguccione da Pisa (d. 1210), the very Latin dictionary from which Dante seems to have derived the definitions of *comoedia* and *tragoedia* used in his letter to Can Grande, makes kings and magnates the proper heroes of tragedy: "Differunt *tragedia* et *comedia,* quia *comedia* privatorum hominum continet acta, *tragedia* regum et magnatum."[36]

The Boccacesque tragical story quickly gained the name of tragedy, and under the sponsorship of Chaucer and Lydgate it bore the name with increasing assurance. However, we must remember that Boccaccio did not write his stories of the falls of princes in order to illustrate any learned medieval theory of tragedy. His purpose is never so stated, and his desire to follow his moral idea, let the form of his stories be what they may and let men call them what they may, is quite obvious. Chaucer is sure that such narratives are to be justified theoretically as tragedies and, in his *Monkes Tale,* goes to the trouble of defining the proper tragic matter as a reversal from good to bad fortune suffered by a man of high degree. In support of this conception of tragedy the words of Boethius in a passage which had often interested translators and commentators could be cited.[37] As for Lydgate, he never forgets that he is writing tragedy in the *Fall of Princes,* and besprinkles his pages with that appellation for his work, especially in his envoys. Seneca too wrote tragedies, as Lydgate often reminds us.[38] An even more forthright association of Boccaccio's tragical stories with Seneca's tragedies was made by the Spanish poet Iñigo Lopez de Mendoza, Marquis of Santillana, in 1444.[39] If one is considering spirit and not form, one must grant that there is something to commend in this association of Boccaccio and Seneca.

It is fatally enticing to patronize the Middle Ages for not possessing the benefits of intellect with which we count ourselves blessed and to imply that darkened critical knowledge of classic tragedy kept them from producing full-formed tragedy of their own. It is tempting to think that classic models of tragic drama were to be had at the cost of a little well-directed research, that a new tragic drama was to be had at the cost of intelligent adaptation or transformation of these models, as the next age was quickly to prove, and that the manifold spiritual virtues of the Middle Ages cannot be made to excuse their deadly sin of mental sloth in this matter of tragedy and in other matters. If we yield to the temptation, our pride of intellect, whatever justification it may or may not have in the face of certain very real intellectual achievements in the Middle Ages, has the better of our understanding, and we incline to view tragedy as an art which a people may foster at any time simply by taking thought. True discovery of classic tragedy came duly in Christian Europe when the power to perceive the tragic in life had had a slow and natural growth, of which Boccacesque tragical story is one of the most faithful records.

Chapter V

TRAGEDY AND THE ENGLISH MORAL
PLAY: FIFTEENTH CENTURY

ROM ITS BEGINNINGS, by the very nature of its origin
in the representation of incidents connected with the
sacrificial death and the resurrection of Jesus, the
drama of Christian Europe had tragic potentiality. Yet development of that potentiality was not a progress toward
the profoundest realization of tragedy in the Passion of the
God-man Jesus and through that toward the profoundest
realization of tragedy in the suffering and death of man.
Sophisticated Latin plays such as *Christus Xylonicus*
(printed in 1529), written by Nicolas Barthélemy in France,
and *Christus Redivivus* (printed in 1543), written by Nich-
olas Grimald in England, came into being, but they were
merely academic by-products of dramatic evolution, without any vital influence whatever upon the course of dramatic history.[1]

The mystery plays, as they lengthened their chain of dramatic incidents, came finally to the presentation of Jewish
and Christian sacred history in much detail and in one epic
sweep toward the fulfillment in Jesus of God's purpose for
the redemption of man. But though the life and crucifixion
of Jesus received increasing elaboration, and though Biblical
narrative was drawn upon for other matter highly capable
of tragic structure and highly capable of bearing choral
comment upon the meaning of mundane suffering, the
tragic spirit must be said to have remained rudimentary

among the writers of mysteries. Those of their plays which arouse in us something of tragic pity or fear do so with little more than the unstudied simplicity and the casual art of the folk ballad. Obviously the guiding purpose here, as elsewhere in the Biblical pageant of the mysteries, is the purpose of a commemorative folk drama intent merely upon vivifying each story as it is inherited from sacred writ or sacred tradition, though there is a constant drift toward an epic unification of the several stories by reason of the natural absorption of all Christian thought in the heroic figure of its Christ.

It must not be forgotten, however, that the elaboration of detail in plays of the crucifixion—such elaboration, for example, as the realistic nailing of Jesus to the cross by a taunting Roman soldiery—probably had repercussions in, and was in turn encouraged by, the cult of the Passion. We have seen that in the later Middle Ages the cult of the Passion produced highly conscious forms of meditation upon the wounds of Jesus, upon his agony, and upon his death; and that all this was reflected in Gothic pictorial art and in a changed crucifix representing an emaciated, nerve-wracked, and thorn-crowned Christ, with the eyes closed, and the head fallen limply in death. We have seen also that such things had their connection with an increased sensibility among the people to suffering and death in general. A growing fascination with the ruder aspects of death was shown markedly in the popularity of the Dance of Death.

There need be no wonderment that the figure of Jesus suffering for mankind did not eventually become tragedy as great as the Aeschylean tragedy of Prometheus. In the first place, one must consider the faith in the perfection of Jesus which was a cardinal principle of Christianity. He was not merely a god in human form, but very God in human form, and thus possessed all divine finality. Behind him and exterior to him Christianity could not conceive a higher operation of fate such as Aeschylus could conceive for Prometheus and even for Zeus, whose destiny included the threat of an overthrow similar to the overthrow of his father Cronus. Prometheus and Zeus were above man's fate, but not above all fate. They were also above man's imperfection of character, but not above all imperfection of character. It was entirely possible for them to possess the flaws that lead to tragedy. But in order to represent Jesus in any such failure to embody true perfection, Christianity would have had to pass through a radical change in substance toward which, at the time, it was in no way disposed. The tendencies manifested in the Arian heresy had long ago been conquered. Hence the crucifixion could at the most be made to arouse a tragic pity for perfect goodness suffering ironically at the hands of lost creatures whom it had come to save; it could not be made to arouse the tragic terror that comes with the view of a hero helping to seal his own doom through imperfections recognizably like our own. A further consideration, if we seek a reason for the failure of the Christian stage to embody the Christ in a Christian tragedy *par excellence,* must be the fact that the miraculous resurrection of Jesus and his divine victory over suffering and death, conceived as the true climax of his drama, went far toward nullifying the tragedy of pity in his crucifixion. His mortal agony could thus yield but little meaning in terms of this world such as great tragedy has always set itself to discover.

Somewhat similar religious conceptions worked against the development of tragedy in the miracle plays. Here, too, we find that the dominant interest is not the inexorable fate and the inexorable laws of an essentially tragic world, but the exorable necessities of a world in which the possibilities for miraculous nullification of tragedy are infinite. The saint who is represented in a miracle play as suffering for his faith the crudest and cruelest of physical tortures at the hands of gross humanity is a spiritual hero who has approached perfection of being; he is hardly a human hero. Very properly he reminds us of the crucified Christ. In lesser fashion he has the power to make physical suffering naught, to rise above it into a world where it does not exist. He can, for example, attract miraculous power to heal his wounds and to restore the skin of which his torturers have denuded him. His persecutors are naïvely chagrined at their failure to make the natural laws of suffering effective for him. Those miracle plays in which not saints but ordinary human beings—sometimes innocent, sometimes guilty— are subjected to suffering and are relieved by the miraculous intervention of God or the Virgin, plays of which many examples have been preserved for France, often come nearer to tragedy. However, the guiding spirit of a *miracle de Notre Dame* was always opposed to the tragic. That which kept the extremely popular medieval saint's legend and miracle legend from reaching tragedy as the *De Casibus* story reached tragedy also operated to keep the miracle play from reaching tragedy.

But in the latest of the major forms evolved by medieval religious drama, namely, the moral play or morality, we may find a tragic spirit definitely developing. Apparently from its very beginnings the morality essayed a longer step than had before been taken in drama beyond the simple unquestioning presentation of those matters which are of gravest import for man and which make for tragedy. Indeed, its form was created for the express purpose of what may with justice be called choral comment upon human destiny. Here the dramatist did not vivify a Scriptural or traditional story, but shaped a story more or less of his own and gave it meaning, thereby providing implicit comment upon life. Didactic as he was, he also, of course, offered explicit comment generously. Where other religious drama might try to realize the facts of sacred history, the moral drama enforced the doctrine preached from the pulpit and made the preacher, in whatever guise, its chorus. Thus we may say that "one received its first development in connection with the antiphonal elements of the Mass; the other was the direct outgrowth of the ensuing homily."[2] If in one way the allegory and the abstract characters to which the morality was in large measure committed represent an unfortunate retreat from the concrete immediacy of the mysteries and miracles, yet in another way they represent a true advance for the drama in architectonic and critical power. Furthermore, the logical protagonist of the moral drama was man—never spiritually perfect or saintly man, but simply man—placed in that moral world of stresses and strains between good and evil where humanity by reason of its freedom of choice shapes character. Man in his pil-

N

grimage through life, balancing over the pit of evil, often falling into the pit as deviltry undermines his footing on the edge, can yield much comedy, and the morality made increasing discovery of its comic possibilities. But it was not for this reason false to its tragic possibilities, of which it likewise made increasing discovery.

The process by which this discovery was made in the English morality we shall now undertake to follow. It must be said at once that the morality as morality, strictly speaking, made no discovery in the way of tragic form comparable with the classic. But if a careful student of French drama may be led to waive that consideration and to say, "Il me paraît en effet incontestable que c'est la Moralité, autant et plus que le Mystère, qui a ouvert les voies à la tragédie classique,"[3] then certainly the student of English drama should make the matter of form no barrier to his realization that the English morality was essential preparation for Elizabethan tragedy. It may be added that Thomas Sebillet, who was an observer of the French morality at first hand and was also a translator of Euripides, seems to have waived technical consideration of form without compunction when in 1548 he made the assertion: "La Moralité Françoise represente en quelque chose la Tragédie Gréque et Latine, singuliérement en ce qu'elle traitte fais graves et Principaus. Et si le François s'estoit rengé a ce que la fin de la Moralité fut toujours triste et doloreuse, la Moralité seroit Tragédie."[4] It is plain from the context that he is talking of the moral plays in which secularization has led away from allegory and abstraction toward concreteness. If one grants that this observation of Sebillet's is more than a patriotic and rhetorical flourish—as the general character of his *Art Poétique Françoys,* in which it appears, would indicate— then one must call it a noteworthy recognition, in the morality's own age, of the morality's tragic potentiality.[5] What Sebillet says of the French morality is equally applicable to the English.

II

About the year 1522, Sir Thomas More undertook a treatise in English upon *The Four Last Things,* which he never finished. It is a lay sermon, written with the mixture of bright wit and wise earnestness of which he was peculiarly capable, upon a famous text from *Ecclesiasticus:* "Memorare novissima, & in eternum non peccabis." The introduction reveals its intent:

The phisicion sendeth his bill to the poticary, & therin writeth sommetime a costlye receite of many straunge herbes and rootes, fet out of far countreis, long lien drugges, al the strength worn out, & some none such to be goten. But thys phisicion sendeth his bil to thy selfe, no strange thing therin, nothing costly to bie, nothing farre to fet, but to be gathered al times of the yere in the gardein of thyne owne soule.

Let us heare than what wholesom receit this is. Remember (saith this byll) thy last thinges, and thou shalte neuer sin in this world. Here is first a short medicine, conteinying onely foure herbes, comen and well knowen, that is to wit, deth, dome, pain, and ioy.

This shorte medicine is of a marueylous force, able to kepe vs al our life fro sin.... But yet this medicyne thoughe thou make a sowre face at it, is not so bytter as thou makeste for. For well thou wottest, he byddeth thee not take neyther deathe, nor dome, nor payne, but onelye to remember them, and yet the ioye of heauen therewith to temper them with all.[6]

Such a treatise as this of More's, upon the Four Last Things which had become a conventional focus of medieval moralizing, may serve as an introduction to the spirit in which the moral drama was written at its heyday. A book on the same subject had been published by Caxton in 1479 under the title of *Cordyal,* "translated out of frenshe into our maternal tongue by the noble and vertuouse lord Anthoine Erle Ryuieres, Lord Scales & of the Isle of Wight." Behind this lies the *Cordiale Quattuor Novissimorum* of Gerardus de Vliederhoven (fourteenth century). The Four Last Things dilated upon by More and his predecessors in this kind of preaching are the primary realities of man's destiny as the earlier moral dramatists saw them: bodily death, the day of judgment which death brings to man's soul, the pain which his soul suffers in Purgatory if not in Hell, and the heavenly joy which his soul may win if he will only remember the first three things and thereby refrain from or repent of sin while he makes his pilgrimage through the world. And of the things to be remembered, says More, death is "farre the least," but an examination of the power which lies in remembrance of death will show all the better "what maruellous effect may grow by the diligent remembraunce of all fower, towarde thauoiding of al the traines, dartes, sleightes, entisinges, and assaultes, of the three mortall enemies, the deuil, the worlde and our owne fleshe."[8] His examination never got beyond an analysis of the Seven Deadly Sins and the power which remembrance of death can maintain over them. Remembrance of death, of course, involves Contempt of the World and its well-known accompaniments: "Therfore let euery manne . . . enforce himself . . . to conceiue a delite and pleasure in such spiritual exercise, and thereby to ryse in the loue of our lord,

with an hope of heauen, contempt of the world, and long-
ing to be with God."[9] The deepest meditation upon death
is thus not a slackening of man's spirit, a giving of it to
nerveless fear, but an uplifting of it. "For nothyng is there
that maye more effectuallye withdrawe the soule fro the
wretched affections of the body, than may the remembrance of death, yf we do not remember it houerly [i.e.,
hoverly, inattentively], as one heareth a worde, and let it
passe by hys eare, without any recciuing of the sentence
into his heart. But if we not onely here this word death,
but also let sink into our heartes, the very fantasye and depe
imaginacion therof, we shall parceiue therby, that we wer
neuer so gretly moued by the beholding of the dance of
death pictured in Poules, as we shall fele our self stered and
altered, by the feling of that imaginacion in our hertes."[10]
In the moral drama also death may be "farrc the least" of
the remembrances, yet a potent matter. It was apparently
least common as matter for central elaboration, but it was
usually present, in the background if not in the foreground.
Certain changes in the dramatic conception of death must
be part of our consideration in following the development
of English tragedy.

As it happens, the first extant English morality, a fragmentary play known as *The Pride of Life* (*ca.* 1400), has
the coming of Death as its dominant theme. Though Death
does not actually appear in the opening part of the drama,
which is preserved to us, we know that he did appear in the
complete drama, because a summary of the action is given
in the prologue. At the opening of that action we find the
King of Life living "in pride and likinge." In the suffi-

ciency of his power he takes boasting delight. His faithful supporters and companions are his knights, Strength and Health, and his messenger, Mirth. He also has for Queen a beautiful lady. With her beauty the Queen unites wisdom, and she warns him that he must think upon his ending, must live well in order to die well, for Death will surely come to him. Death spares neither knight, nor kaiser, nor king. Let him leave pleasure, she pleads, and save his soul. He calls all this an old wives' tale. The Queen sends for the Bishop, who adds preaching to wifely petition. Bishops should preach in church, says the King; and he sends his messenger, Mirth, to proclaim that he dare fight with anyone, even Death. (At this point the fragment ends, and we must complete the story by means of the prologue.) Death in turn sends his messenger to the King of Life to say that he will come to try his might. Death does strive with the King of Life and deals him a deep death-wound. Then, when the King's soul leaves his body, it knows great sorrow and is caught by the fiends. But Our Lady will pray to her son for the soul's release.

It is plain that *The Pride of Life* takes the same tone and has the same essential meaning as the Dance of Death. Upon the cloister walls of the Church of the Holy Innocents at Paris the most famous of all the Dances of Death was painted in 1424–1425.[11] Of paintings in this kind there is none older upon record, but we know that the ideas involved had a previous artistic history. We are not sure why the Dance of Death at Paris was called *La Danse Macabré*. (*Macabre* was so accented until the seventeenth century, rhyming with *degré*.)[12] The pictures were apparently of some thirty human beings of all ranks of life, from the highest to the lowest, each escorted from life toward death by a gruesome decaying cadaver. Accompanying each pair of dead and living were short dramatic verses. For example, in the verses which Lydgate says that he translated from this Dance of Death at Paris in order that proud men "as in a mirrour" might see their ugly ending, the Pope, highest in rank, and hence first addressed by the representative of Death, admits that it behoves him to lead the way in a dance to which all men are called.[13] He is followed by Emperor, Cardinal, and King; and the rout of lesser folk trail after. In *The Pride of Life* it is somewhat as though the figures of the King and of Death in the Paris Dance of Death, or in the similar painting at St. Paul's in London, had been given dramatic life and an elaborated story to suit the conception of dramatic opposition.

A question inevitably arises about the Dance of Death. As we know it in paintings scattered over the length and breadth of Europe,[14] and in manuscripts or printed works capitalizing the popularity of the paintings, was this Dance itself originally a simple drama? The arguments that it was are highly plausible. Behind the versions of the Dance in the vulgar tongues there is a Latin poem which may be dated as of about the beginning of the fourteenth century. This introduces twelve figures, from Pope to Pauper, each speaking two lines of sad farewell to life pointed with the words "Vado mori," which have given a title to the poem. The King, for example, is given the distich:

> Vado mori rex sum quid honor quid gloria regum
> Est via mors hominis regia vado mori.[15]

In a probably later development of this mortal processional, dialogue structure appears, and some interlocutor, who is apparently not Death, speaks a companion couplet beginning "Vive Deo." That such poems were peculiarly fitted for dramatic representation as vivid aids to sermonizing upon the inevitability of death is beyond question. It is possible that a homilist into whose exhortation the pageant was inserted was to speak the *Vive Deo* as he commented upon each passing figure from his pulpit. "On such a theory," as Miss Eleanor P. Hammond says, "the Dance Macabre, in its rudimentary or its developed form, would have its fountainhead even where the medieval drama rose. Such a presentation, after it began to use the visible figure of Death, which at first did not appear, could manage with one Death, who met and seized each personage as he entered from the 'wings' and convoyed him across in front of the congregation."[16] There are signs that when a figure was first introduced to represent death he was not Death in the abstract but a dead man or woman, a counterpart of the living figure with whom he was linked and a mirror of the state into which that figure was going.[17] If so, there would be rather close analogy between the Dance of Death and the popular legend of the Three Living and the Three Dead, in which three men of high rank and lusty attachment to the world meet three corpses and are warned by them that a like state of mortal decay must soon be their own portion.[18]

In the fully developed Dance of Death the Preacher is a well-marked and an important chorus. Paintings and poems often represent him as addressing comments upon the procession to a group of auditors. At the end of Lydgate's poem is a set of verses by "Machabre the doctour" which draw the moral that man's life is transitory as the wind. Sometimes the Dance is preceded not only by the picture of the Preacher in his pulpit, but also by a tableau of Adam and Eve tempted by the serpent and bringing death into the world.[19] The essential lesson which the Dance could aid a pulpit orator to drive home was, of course, the lesson of the most truly religious moral dramas, namely, that one must not wait until tomorrow to eschew vice and follow virtue, for Death may see to it that a tomorow will never come. In the Church of Notre Dame at Kermaria, in Brittany, fifteenth-century mural decorations representing the virtues to which man should devote himself are placed near pictures of the Three Living and the Three Dead (the Three Living being pictured here as kings) and of the Dance of Death.[20] Likenesses in character between the Dance of Death and the medieval drama, particularly the moral or preaching drama, are thus abundant. Also, a dramatic origin for the pictorial Dance of Death appears extremely probable, though it has not been demonstrated to every scholar's satisfaction.[21] Professor Émile Mâle, at least, is sure of the matter, and would here again find relationship between medieval drama and the decorative art of the churches: "Jouée dans l'église au xive siècle, la danse macabre fut peinte au xve. Ici encore le drame a précédé l'œuvre d'art."[22]

If the Dance of Death did not originate as drama, it was quickly made into drama. Among records of performances in the fifteenth century there is one for the year 1449 of a "certain jeu, histoire et moralité sur le fait de la danse macabre" given at Bruges in the presence of Philip the Good.[23] How much of the processional quality this may have had is open to question; perhaps it had no more, or even less, than the Spanish *Farsa llamada Danza de la Muerte* of Juan de Pedraza (printed in 1551), in which three characters are overcome by Death and carried away protesting.[24]

In drama such as *The Pride of Life* the processional quality of the Dance vanishes before a specialization which focuses attention upon a single exponent of proud living. Though this exponent is a king, he is not so much the abstract of all kings as he is the abstract of all men so far as they take regal pride in their physical powers of health and strength. Thus he becomes "everyman" in the procession toward death. He is at once an evidence of the advance in medieval drama toward compactness in form and meaning, and of a sacrifice in concreteness which it was therein temporarily forced to undergo.[25]

Somewhat less obvious than the alliance of *The Pride of Life* with the Dance of Death is its alliance with *De Casibus* story. The protagonist of the play is a king, even though only figuratively. There is much the same erection of mortal achievement into "nonesuch" position as we have found in Chaucer's *Monkes Tale,* in order to make the fall, in a world that the Queen characterizes as "bot ffantasye & fful of trechurye," the more significant. The King boasts:

> On erth in brede ne leynth
> Ne was nere ȝet my make.[26]

In its general teaching the Dance of Death, or related drama, must quite naturally support and be supported by

the *De Casibus* and *Ubi Sunt* tradition. Even as early as
Seneca, a combination of something like *De Casibus, Ubi
Sunt,* and Dance of Death moralizing may be found. Where
are the great cities of the past, asks Seneca, naming well-
tried examples? "It would be tedious to recount all the ways
by which fate may come; but this one thing I know: all the
works of mortal men have been doomed to mortality, and
in the midst of things which have been destined to die, we
live. . . . You should not estimate our worth by our funeral
mounds or by these monuments of unequal size which line
the road; their ashes level all men! We are unequal at birth,
but are equal in death. What I say about cities I say also
about their inhabitants."[27] All this, he adds, comes from
Fortune, who controls the earthly round. There is but one
essential difference between the Stoic teaching here embodied and the Christian teaching which owes so much to
it. Seneca concludes that men should confront death and
its implications with philosophic fortitude. But the medieval Christian, as long as he still believed that the world was
unreal and irrational, had for logical conclusion such words
as those inscribed on a bit of jewelry, a pendant shaped like
a coffin, preserved in the British Museum: "COGITA MORI VT
VIVAS."[28] Let a man think upon his own death—and by all
means, too, upon the deaths of princes and of cities—in
order that he may not suffer death in his immortal soul.

Though the Dance of Death, drama such as *The Pride of
Life,* and ascetic *De Casibus* story were thus otherworldly
in their aim, and though they very obviously sought to present suffering and death in terms other than those of this
world which tragedy must employ, a growing shadow of

tragedy had fallen upon them all. They were produced by a century which succeeded in fixing the eye upon spiritual life as the conqueror of worldly death less surely than the preceding century. We see this change of temper in funerary art, as well as in arts which have already been discussed. In the funerary art of the thirteenth century sculptured figures may be found with hands joined in peace, eyes open, faces seemingly transfigured by the soul's participation in eternal joy. But at the end of the fourteenth century, the age with which we are now concerned, funerary sculpture tends to represent the physical horror of death and to make note of it realistically, embodying a new spirit entirely. Here the dead man may take the form of the desiccated cadaver, exposed in his nudity as a warning to the fleshly pride of the onlooker.[29] It is the same kind of warning that is conveyed by the cadaver in the Dance of Death. Death and mortal suffering have here been made a more stubborn reality, more potent, less yielding to the alchemy of spiritual faith.

III

The second of the extant English moralities, *The Castle of Perseverance* (*ca.* 1425), undertakes to present upon a much wider stage the adventures of mankind among those ills to which human flesh is condemned. The coming of death is here but an incident in the whole, though no less inescapable and worthy of constant forethought. The story seeks to embrace nothing less than the entire pilgrimage of the life of man; and *The Castle of Perseverance* is perhaps the most effective example of the so-called "full-scope" moralities.

The action opens with the World, the Flesh, and the

Devil boasting of their power and scheming evil for man
as they sit upon their scaffolds. The World has gained possession of all lands and nations through the aid of Sir Covetousness, and he tells them over with high satisfaction.
Belial, the Devil, grips men in a sure grasp and ruins them.
Three of the Seven Deadly Sins—Pride, Wrath, and Envy—
are subject kings to him. Flesh lives in great ease and joy,
aided in his desire to debase humanity by Gluttony, Lechery, and Sloth. Into this den of iniquitous powers we see
Mankind introduced at birth, naked, faint, and feeble, lamenting that he must come, as he full well knows, to woe
and weeping. He takes his first, unsure steps between two
angels, a good and an evil, who have been assigned to him.

What happens next is calculated to show that mortal life
by its very nature is an insidious blindness and a heady
drunkenness to the ordinary human soul, no matter how
clear his vision may be before he wraps himself in flesh. Yet
man must for some reason go through with it, and must
always be allowed free will to choose the evil that seems
to him, in his blindness, good. As Mankind enters the mortal scene he is praying to Christ that he may always follow
the guidance of Good Angel. The play has not progressed
more than eighty lines before he has allowed Bad Angel
to capture his confidence. "Come back!" cries his Good
Angel; "think on your ending day!" But Mankind accepts
as the most profound wisdom his Bad Angel's comment
that there is time enough for that when he is sixty winters
old and his fleshly fires burn low.

Spiritually, Mankind descends posthaste. Materially, he
ascends with equal rapidity. He is led to the World and

avidly takes all that the World can give him. He wants to be a lord, to rule over lands and towers, to be famous, to have a lovely lady paramour. His every desire is gratified and the World sees to it that Pleasure and Folly dress and serve him. Covetousness gives him money, and the others of the Seven Sins get from him willing promises to follow their ways. At the apex of his material grandeur comes clearness of vision, as sudden as his blindness. His Good Angel and Confession confront him, and Penance pierces his heart with the lance of sorrow. Suffering now comes upon him, but it is in no sense physical calamity brought about by his acts; it is in no sense the effect of causes in terms of mundane law; it is purely the spiritual suffering of contrition. His regeneration follows.

Mankind, clear-sighted once more, purified through confession and absolution, feels the need of greater protection than his own strength can give him, and is glad to accept haven with the Seven Virtues in the Castle of Perseverance. The advance of the legions of sin to besiege the fortress and to engage fruitlessly in a mighty battle with the virtues is one of the famous passages in English medieval drama. Craft wins for the powers of evil where force does not. Covetousness obtains a parley with Mankind and argues that in Mankind's old age (he now has graying hair) money will be his best friend. The film again descends over Mankind's eyes; he agrees that this argument is good, and leaves the Castle. "Lock him up!" cries his Good Angel as Mankind descends to Covetousness, but Meekness reminds the forces of good that man's will must be left unfettered. Mankind espouses again the evil ways of the world, and gives himself insatiably and unscrupulously to the hoarding of money, the peculiar sin of old age.

And then, in the midst of his new access of sinning, Death enters to claim him. Here, too, Death is that same leveling and abasing force which we find in the Dance of Death and in so many *De Casibus* tragedies. He is not at all retribution for sin, but only the means whereby a sudden and unexpected period is put to sinning and the pride of life. He proclaims that he is "drery Dethe" with the surest of power over all the dukes, lords, kings, and knights of the world; and he strikes Mankind with his dart. Wracked with pain, Mankind expires, reproaching the World and Covetousness for their desertion of him and discovering sadly that the precious treasure for which he has jeopardized his soul will not even go to his wife and children as he has willed it, but to a stranger. He dies with one of the Deadly Sins full upon him, bound for Hell, but in his last words he cries upon God for mercy.

We are still far from the end of the play, for the action is carried on into the otherworld of souls, in which a law of retributive justice must finally make its claims, though it has not been given tragic validity in the mundane world and though it may be given only minor validity even in the next world. Mankind's soul appears (from beneath his sickbed) and reproaches his body for brewing it a "byttyr bale." The Bad Angel claims the soul as his due, and the Good Angel admits that Mankind must go to Hell with Covetousness *unless* he receives help from Mercy, upon whom he has called with his last breath. Mercy does give help, and there follows the trial of Mankind before God,

developed by the dramatist as a version of that popular
medieval allegory known as The Four Daughters of God,
which was founded upon *Psalms,* 84:11: "Misericordia et
Veritas obviaverunt sibi; Justitia et Pax osculatae sunt."[30] In
the play the Four Daughters are the attorneys at Mankind's
trial. Mercy and Peace are advocates for the accused, pleading that Mankind should be shown mercy in spite of his
very real sin. Righteousness and Truth prosecute the offender, pleading that men who commit mortal sin to the
end of their lives must suffer in Hell, and that the law
must be fulfilled. Peace makes the final, and successful,
plea—that the four sisters should kiss each other and return
Mankind to the Heavenly joy that was God's ordinance.
The Father, seated upon his throne, gives judgment. He
declares that he thinks upon peace, not upon affliction, and
that he will not damn Mankind according to Mankind's
deserts. For a dominant part of his divinity is mercy:

> I menge with my most myth,
> Alle pes, sum treuthe, & sum Ryth,
> & most of my mercy.[31]

So Mankind is taken up to God's scaffold and seated upon
the Father's right hand, where he is told that divine mercy
quenches sin as the sea might quench a spark of fire. The
concluding lines of the play are a brief sermon having the
burden of Sir Thomas More's *The Four Last Things* (so
much of it as he completed): O men, think ever of death
and what follows.

> To saue ȝou fro synnynge,
> Evyr at the begynnynge
> Thynke on ȝoure last endynge![32]

This merciful denouement of *The Castle of Perseverance* introduces us to a matter of the largest importance in any consideration of the moral play for its tragic potentialities. So long as the moral dramatist and his audience conceive that a universal law of justice, under which man lives and engages himself with his destiny, is dominated by the force of mercy, their recognition of tragedy must necessarily be small. The grip of tragic forces is allowed to be formed in this world only to be broken either in this world or the next; and the sense of irreparable loss—partial if not total—and of inevitable suffering by which the greatest tragedies move men to a peculiar pity and fear must remain thwarted. Merciful intervention by divinity in Greek tragedy is decidedly of a different order and a different magnitude. Throughout the fifteenth century, and even into the sixteenth, the English moralities show a preoccupation with mercy which stands in the way of tragedy, but it is a decreasing preoccupation. In fact, no ensuing English morality has quite the intense preoccupation with mercy that we find in *The Castle of Perseverance*. Finally, as we shall see, the balance tips from the side of mercy to the side of justice, justice having come more and more to be conceived of as a mundane principle. This shift in balance has as much bearing upon the development of tragedy as the shift from Fortune to retribution in *De Casibus* narrative.

The predominantly merciful morality, however, shows in its defeating of tragedy nothing remotely comparable to the spirit of tragicomedy. It is in no sense a kind of sacred Fletcherian drama of dalliance with danger. The merciful morality avoids a final catastrophe though coming near it,

O

and it may even narrowly avoid a mundane catastrophe instead of the supramundane threatened in *The Castle of Perseverance*. But the avoidance is accomplished by no sophisticated and skillfully theatric subterfuge, as it is in Fletcher and in those who follow him. Instead of being an amiable emasculation of tragedy, the merciful morality represents an incompleteness of tragedy in an age which has not yet fully developed the tragic view of life.

Our understanding of this fact may be helped by consideration of a sermon placed in the mouth of St. John the Baptist in the so-called *Ludus Coventriae*, that cycle of mystery plays which so often falls into the tones and attitudes of the moralities.[33] The path to salvation, says St. John, lies exactly centered between two emotional forces. Upon the right you must understand hope, which springs from our knowledge of God's mercy; upon the left you must understand dread, which springs from our knowledge of God's justice. A swerving to the right is a swerving toward hope without dread, which is presumption; to the left, toward dread without hope, which is desperation. Thus presumption and desperation jeopardize man's soul equally. In those English moral dramas which retain serious concern with the fortune of man's soul as it adventures through the world we find constant emphasis laid upon the sin of presumption, as when man delays his repentance in order first to have his fill from the fleshpots, and likewise constant emphasis laid upon the sin of desperation, as when, after having so delayed, man concludes that his case is hopeless and that the one thing remaining to him is the last and most sinful act of despair, suicide.

But when St. John the Baptist would have his hearers swerve no more toward hope than toward dread and centers the path to salvation between them, he urges an ideal balance most difficult, if not strictly impossible, of attainment. It is questionable that man can ever steer a course, or that any religious practice can ever steer a course, which does not bear more or less to one side or other of the line. The benignity and the malignity, the humanity and the inhumanity, the loving mercy and the harsh justice, of gods or God would seem to be a stubborn dualism like good and evil which religion can neither escape nor rationally reconcile. They would seem to be aspects of divinity, contradictory to mortal eyes, upon one of which more than the other a religion must fix its attention if it is to be effective in a world that has only partial vision for truth. The Christianity which is reflected in the early moralities saw God as strongly preëminent mercy. Even in the *Ludus Coventriae* sermon of St. John the Baptist, with its ideal of balance, mercy is placed upon the right hand of man's path as though it should have a traditional place of honor. And in *The Castle of Perseverance,* as we have found, God's power is analyzed to yield far more of peace and mercy than of truth and justice. This medieval Christianity which could never forget the Fall of Man and the infinite baseness of his "natural" quality, which would not willingly forget Hell and the infinite torture of the damned, was so paradoxical in its "gloominess" that it could gladly neglect to dwell upon the horror of punishment for sin because of a strong desire to represent the beauty of mercy. It was so paradoxical in its distrust of human nature that it could gladly trust human-

ity to view an easy defeat of justice by mercy as the ending
of a miracle or moral play, apparently without serious uneasiness over the possibility that men might thereby get out
of hand. Nothing could show more clearly the essential
benignity in medieval Christianity, and nothing could show
more clearly that the moral plays were not merely bludg-
eons of fear held over the laity by the clergy.

The two English moralities a generation or so later than
The Castle of Perseverance which have been commonly
associated with it under the name of Macro Moralities, because the three were part of the collection of the antiquary
Cox Macro, turn from denouement in the next world to
denouement in this world. Never again in the English
morality do we find an otherworldly conclusion to the human drama like that given to *The Castle of Perseverance*
and indicated for *The Pride of Life*.[34] But the later two of
the Macro Moralities—*Wisdom, Who Is Christ*, or *Mind,
Will, and Understanding* (*ca.* 1460); and *Mankind* (*ca.*
1470)—are nevertheless otherworldly in preachment and
benign in temper. Though they do not go so far as to show
the human soul supported by infinite mercy after it has left
the body in deadly sin, they both magnify the mercy which
is available to the repentant soul before death.

Mind, Will, and Understanding is in many ways less
worldly than *Mankind*, perhaps because the audience at
which it was aimed was monastic.[35] The play is remarkable,
even among the moralities, for the space given to theological doctrine. It has a notable disputation concerning the
relative excellences of the contemplative, the active, and
the "mixed" ways of life; the tempting done by Lucifer is

partly by means of an insidious argument (to a monastic congregation) that Jesus himself led the mixed life and that absolute retirement from mundane activity is contrary to his example.[36] The drama opens with lengthy instruction given to the Soul, Anima, by Everlasting Wisdom, who represents the second person of the Trinity. The Soul is thought of as divided into two parts, Reason and Sensuality, the one pure white and the other black, as indicated in Anima's habiliments of white covered by a black mantle. Attendant upon Anima are three mights, Mind, Will, and Understanding. In their goodness the mights respectively know God, the Holy Ghost, and Christ, and produce faith, charity, and hope. By corruption they may be led respectively into pride, lechery, and covetousness, which are given as the core of the Seven Deadly Sins. Above all else, Anima has free will to choose either good or evil. Lucifer, of course, succeeds in the corruption of the three mights that was so much to be feared. Redemption is made possible when Wisdom calls Mind to remember that death is certain for every creature and when, by Wisdom's aid, the mights are filled with disgust, sorrow, and repentance. Anima calls upon divine mercy and compassion with complete success, "Magna est misericordia tua!" The play is warm in praise of mercy at the expense of justice, but otherwise it is cold in abstraction, beyond the usual measure of its kind.

In *Mankind* coldness of abstraction is often dissipated by a lively warmth of action, and there is a less ponderously disputatious atmosphere. Here the world as a theater of man's daily labor and delight is put before us in much more homely detail, and broad humor is more generously admixed, than in any previous morality. But the central other-worldly teaching is still secure: man fell originally through disobedience; now in his baseness of inherited evil he must turn to the mercy of God for redemption. He can rejoice that the divine mercy is to be had for the asking. The dramatist has even made Mercy the single character in the play representative of the forces of good. At the outset we encounter Mercy as the ghostly father to whom Mankind turns for instruction as he enters upon the tribulation of a life in which the soul must ever be at variance with "that stynkyng dunge-hyll" the flesh. Mankind has clarity of spiritual vision after Mercy has counseled him; he is resolved to labor honestly, fight like a lusty soldier against the body, do all things by measure, and, in short, spend life well. As he delves with his spade and earns subsistence by the sweat of his brow, he is at first even able to repulse the minor forces of evil, a set of precious roisterers named New Guise, Nought, and Nowadays, who jeer at his honest toil. He belabors them with his tool. But he is no match for the roaring devil Titivillus, who goes cannily to work, buries a board in the soil to make its tilling difficult, and insinuates into Mankind's slothful slumber a dream to the effect that Mercy has stolen a horse and been hanged. Titivillus soon has Mankind so infirm of purpose that he is ready to go to a tavern with the roisterers, to take a wench, to have a good time. Mercy reënters to expostulate with Mankind, who now refuses to listen to him, and Mercy in his grief prays to the Virgin: "Lett Mercy excede Justice, dere Mother!"[37]

Finally, mercy does exceed justice and Mankind is reclaimed, to rejoice in God's grace, but not before he has tried to hang himself in the desperation of his dread without hope, and in his agony of conviction that sin has made him unworthy of the gentle persistent Mercy. The play ends with a short sermon *de contemptu mundi:* Remember that the world, by its diverse transmutation, proves itself nought but vanity; think upon God's mercy and upon Heaven.

IV

A much more essential sort of worldliness than that appearing in *Mankind* pervades the play *Nature,* written by Henry Medwall, chaplain to Cardinal Morton, probably in the very last years of the fifteenth century. Here a view of life is revealed in which material order and reality are rapidly taking honorable places beside spiritual order and reality without too much apology for so doing. The play is well named, for it makes Nature the beneficent sponsor of mankind. From Nature, in a long disquisition, Man receives his guiding instructions at the start of his journey through life. Lady Nature, as she explains for herself, has been granted marvelous powers by God and has been made, as one may say, a worldly goddess, responsible for the perpetuation of creatures and the effects of things natural. Let anyone who wishes to know of such things read Aristotle, whom Nature calls "my phylosopher electe." We are led to understand that God and Nature together (much as St. Thomas Aquinas would say) are the makers of humanity. As Nature releases the protagonist of the play into the theater of the world, he is accompanied by Reason and Innocency. Sensuality makes claim to be recognized as a proper companion of Man also, and Nature does not deny this claim, but she specifies that Reason must ever be preferred as the true guide and that Innocency must be Man's tender nurse. Thus the natural senses, which are an utterly evil side of man in *Mind, Will, and Understanding,* receive a certain cachet of respectability in *Nature.* They change character in accord with the growing idea of the time that the things of the world have goodness when rightly controlled.

Yet life in the flesh brings upon Man something of the blindness by now so familiar in the moral drama. With full understanding he praises God and Nature, secures himself in his good resolutions, steps forth from Nature, and immediately sinks deep under the spell of Worldly Affection and the forces of evil. Under the guidance of Sensuality he follows the "new guise," frequents taverns, and goes wenching. Only as his hair turns gray and his desires grow cold does he listen to Reason and turn to reform, becoming through Repentance and Confession the child of salvation.

Once more, then, mercy prevails over justice, but only after a sinister note has been sounded. Man says, when at last he turns to Reason, that he is deserving of nothing by his repentance, for he is eschewing sin only in old age when it has lost its savor. Reason then instructs him that his first step must be the conquering of all manner of despair. And Meekness, who succeeds Reason as teacher, reminds Man that Lucifer fell from his angelic position according to rightful justice, that Adam fell from Paradise likewise rightfully, and that in justice all men would be lost were it not for God's mercy. So far, there is no doctrine that makes the drama less merciful in spirit than previous moralities. But as Reason awaits Man's return from confession, he moralizes the matter of the play for the audience with more than a touch of severity. The gist of his comment is that the sinner is *sometimes* suffered by God to have a long life in honor and great prosperity simply because God is always hoping, in his mercy, that the man will forsake his evil ways and be reclaimed. In other words, this is a play in which the sinner escapes, but we *might* have seen his footsteps dogged by retribution. Distinctly, the implication of Reason is that when sin goes unpunished during mortal life, we are not to say in the manner of certain disquisitions *de contemptu mundi* that this is because the world is naturally irrational or disorderly and because justice comes only after death; for when God so chooses, a law of retribution operates in this world. Thus *Nature,* which in so many other ways discovers the natural world as something not to be contemned, briefly touches upon, though it does not rest upon, an order of mundane, and even tragic, justice.

The tragic aspect of death as retribution—not merely retribution in general for the sin of Adam, but also retribution in particular for the sin which descendants of Adam may add to the general account—is turned toward us for an even longer moment in *Everyman*. This best known of all the English moralities may also be dated as from the close of the fifteenth century. The play is English by thorough adoption, as is shown by the four extant English editions, which all appeared soon after 1500, even if it is a translation of the Dutch play *Elckerlijk*. (There are those who believe the Dutch text to be a translation of the English.[3]) The God who starts the train of action, which the prologue calls "the somonynge of Eueryman," is no longer the God of *The*

Castle of Perseverance, delighting to let mercy overcome justice. He perceives that all his human creatures are blind of ghostly sight, sunken in worldly prosperity, and living more and more shamelessly each year in mortal sin without any dread of the sharp rod of his justice. He has offered his people mercy in great store, but few have asked it heartily. Now he must do justice on every man living. Where is his mighty messenger, Death? Death enters and receives the command to bring Everyman to a sure reckoning. Following the spirit in which God has spoken, Death announces:

> Lorde, I wyll in the worlde go renne ouer all,
> And cruelly out-serche bothe grete and small.
> Euery man wyll I beset that lyueth beestly
> Out of Goddes lawes, and dredeth not foly.
> He that loueth rychesse I wyll stryke with my darte,
> His syght to blynde, and fro heuen to departe—
> Excepte that almes be his good frende—
> In hell for to dwell, worlde without ende.[39]

This is quite different from the spirit of the Dance of Death, and of *The Pride of Life,* so far as the spirit is apparent in the surviving fragment of that first and only other English morality centered in the coming of Death. But a retributive Death certainly does not walk the English religious stage for the first time in *Everyman.* In the *Ludus Coventriae* Death comes to strike Herod and his knights after the massacre of the innocents and reveals that he is commissioned as an agent of God to punish particular evil:

> I am deth goddys mesangere.
> All myghty god hath sent me here
> 3on lordeyn to sle with-owtyn dwere
> ffor his wykkyd werkynge.[40]

An audience before which *Everyman* was presented probably had only a somewhat blurred apprehension of Death
as any such selective agent of retribution as we find punishing Herod. Who is this Everyman about whom the play is
written and whose summoning by Death is to provide the
moral lesson? Was the audience to infer that Death eventually comes to every man living, rich and poor, good and
bad? It is one of the certainties of life that Death does do
so. The Dance of Death, which was in the immediate consciousness of both dramatist and audience, dwelt upon that
certainty and doubtless cast a shade of meaning over Everyman's name. Yet Death gives his hearers to understand that,
in the present dramatic action at least, he is to be particularly the Nemesis of sinners as he comes to Everyman.
Nevertheless, by the very nature of his abstraction Everyman cannot be a sinning Herod attracting an individual
punishment by Death. At best he can only be an essential
representative of the common run of humanity, which has
become more sinful than it used to be, as God declares in
his opening words, and is to be chastised by some extraordinary visitation of death such as a plague. A morality adher-
ing to the earliest fashion of abstracting all mankind in one
character could go no farther than this toward the conceiving of tragic retribution.

As a matter of fact, *Everyman,* despite the threatened
severity of its beginning, ends as a merciful morality. While
Everyman is walking in all the blindness of his worldly life,
Death accosts him. He must die and go to the reckoning
for which he is all unready. Says Death, "I gyue the no res-
pyte." But Death does give respite, though it is not respite

until the morrow, as Everyman begs; Death leaves Everyman to the making of that brief and anxiously hurried
preparation which gives the play distinctive and effective
quality. Protesting to the last that he is pitiless, Death has
allowed Everyman to entertain the desperate hope that
some companionship and support for the journey may be
found. There is no reason why Everyman should not be
smitten at once and die in hopeless agony as a horrible example to thoughtless mankind, except that the dramatist
really has another lesson to teach. Later moral dramatists
are often not so neglectful of such an opportunity. Everyman, of course, finds that all worldly companionship and
support, no matter what easy first promises are made, fall
away from him as he descends into the dark shadow of
fleshly dissolution. And without the brief respite which
Death has given him even his Good Deeds would have
proved too weak to go the journey with him. The precious
stay of execution permits him to strengthen Good Deeds
by confession and repentance in such wise that when he
finally enters into the grave he has one faithful companion
and advocate who will bespeak that mercy of God without
which he can in no way be saved. We are assured by angelic
pronouncement that he obtains the heavenly forgiveness
which he has been so narrowly in danger of missing.

In the moralities which have been considered hitherto
there has been suggestion that mundane retribution was
possible, but it is a most noteworthy fact that there has been
no dramatic employment of physical suffering to show the
wages of sin or folly in terms of the material world. Of
spiritual suffering in the way of remorse and shame there

has been an abundance, but we have not found mankind, in any of his guises, encountering disease, loss of goods, bereavement of loved ones, loss of high position, or death as part of a tragic chain of cause and effect. Even in *Everyman,* where Death at first assumes the character of retribution, we are hardly conscious, if at all, that as the protagonist draws closer and closer to the grave he is in any way dreeing his own peculiar weird, and, strangely enough, we are hardly conscious that what he is suffering is partly the agony of losing this world and of dying. As for the weird of Everyman, the dramatist has never shown it taking shape in the days of Everyman's carefree living. As for the agony of Everyman, it lies, in large part, in a growing spiritual recognition that the things of this world which he has possessed and depended upon are now failing him in his great need and are not worth possessing. It may hardly be said to lie in regret at their loss. Neither does it lie in what may with any great truth be called the pangs of physical dissolution. We do not see Everyman writhe in sickness. His limbs fail and his strength wanes, but he notices such things very little and only as a warning that his time of spiritual preparation is short.

Mundus et Infans, printed in 1522, but possibly written before the close of the fifteenth century, is the first of the extant English moralities which does strive to make something of physical suffering as retribution. However, it does not dramatize the visitation of death and it does not leave mankind in suffering unrelieved. Like all its predecessors it has a merciful denouement. Its scope is the whole pilgrimage of the life of man, but the traditional action of that sort has in this play undergone much simplification. The thirty-three characters of *The Castle of Perseverance* are here reduced to five.

Infans (his name changes as he passes the seven-year milestones of life upon the way to Manhood) enters the world and goes before the throne of Mundus, knowing that he has been gotten in sin and that even now at birth he must begin to seek death. But at this point he has no spiritual counselor; it costs him no struggle to bow before Mundus and promise to serve him. After all, he is naked and hungry, and who is there but the World to give him clothing and food? The dramatist lets us feel that this is not exactly a fall into sin, but rather a natural absorption of childhood and youth in the things of the world without which humanity would not be humanity. By good service rendered to Mundus the child eventually gains the name of mighty Manhood. He is dubbed knight; he has rich array; he has lordship over knights in towers and over ladies in bowers; he is the conqueror of many far countries. He boasts that he has power over the very stars in their courses, that emperors and kings yield to him, that there was never baron born who was his equal, and that he is certain of maintenance by the King of Pride, the King of Lechery, and their fellows representing the other five Deadly Sins.

In short, he is, in his proud eminence, an entirely fit subject to attract the lightning and to become the object lesson of a *De Casibus* tragedy. The dramatist partly develops such a tragedy. Conscience comes to Manhood as spiritual adviser. His teaching wins Manhood from the seven sinful masters one by one; first, of course, from Pride, against whom remembrance that even the prince may fall into misery is particularly efficacious:

> And thynke on Kynge Robert of Cysell,
> How he for pryde in grete pouerte fell
> For he wolde not Conscyence knowe.[41]

But must he give up all mirth, asks Manhood? By no means, answers Conscience. Mirth in measure is always good; it is Folly of whom Manhood must beware, for Folly is the essence of all the sins. Hence, Manhood turns for the moment to the pursuit of his salvation, though, significantly enough, he does not plan—and this is even according to the instruction of Conscience—to practice Contempt of the World. He will allow Mundus his place in the scheme of things, and it is to be noticed that he includes holy things:

> But yet wyll I hym not forsake,
> For mankynde he doth mery make.
> Thoughe the Worlde and Conscyence be at debate,
>   Yet the Worlde wyll I not despyse;
> For bothe in chyrche and in chepynge
> And in other places beynge,
> The Worlde fyndeth me all thynge
>   And dothe me grete seruyse.[42]

Now comes Manhood's fall from his high position and the loss of all his worldly blessings. He allies himself with Folly, as we have had only too good reason to fear that he would from the emphasis which Conscience has placed upon the danger in Folly. Folly has much skill in threading the delights of the world (his particular home is London) and he soon gets Manhood to employ him as servant. So Manhood leaves the stage, led by Folly toward immoderate pleasure, deafened to the counsel of Conscience. At last Manhood reënters, his name changed to Age, his body old and broken, and, as he thinks, his soul irretrievably destined for Hell. He has a racking cough and he groans in the pain of debility and disease. He has lost all his rents and his riches. At London he thought to live freely by borrowing and never paying, but justice overtook him, set him in the stocks, and clapped him into Newgate Prison. Nothing remains for him but the last act of desperation, suicide. He is saved by Perseverance, the brother of Conscience, who changes the name of Age to Repentance and gives the salutary counsel that God always has mercy upon even the worst of sinners when repentance is sincere.

Thus, as it makes its alliance with *De Casibus* tragedy, *Mundus et Infans* fixes on Folly, instead of Fortune, as the author of man's misfortune; and this exchange means that man himself is here an effective mover in a world where all is not irrational, where man's wisdom and unwisdom do produce results according to natural laws. Man rises to high place by service rendered to the world in the world's ways, but though that service leads him to sin, we are distinctly to understand that his active life is not inherently sin and that it is not inherently folly. When full-formed conscience comes to man in his maturity, he is capable of maintaining himself in a right measure of worldly achievement and honor by steering his course wisely. Embracement of folly brings in its train physical suffering and downfall. So much for the theater of the world, a truly tragic theater. Beyond that is a theater with which tragedy has properly nothing to do, and into this second theater the moral play is still impelled to take us, though it does not

THE DEATH OF LUCRECE

From Laurent de Premierfait's translation of Boccaccio's *De Casibus*,
MS Royal 14 E v, late fifteenth century.

actually force entrance. For it is still unwilling to stop with the loss involved in a human downfall and to leave its audience to find purgation of pity and fear in acceptance of that loss. It must still give assurance that the loss is as nothing when one knows that the soul is yet to be saved through mercy.

v

To draw useful distinctions between the run of fifteenth- and the run of sixteenth-century English moralities is not difficult, and, as it happens, 1500 is almost exactly a pivotal date. For one thing, the fifteenth-century moralities which are preserved to us are all mainly intent upon grasping human nature in some form of abstraction standing for mankind as a whole (we hardly need to make exception of *The Pride of Life*), but almost immediately after the new century has opened we find plays in which the grasp weakens and in which the protagonist tends to lose the abstract quality of *Humanum Genus*. For another thing, closely bound to the first, the so-called "full-scope" morality, attempting to embrace man's pilgrimage through life from infancy to old age, is typical of the fifteenth century to its very end, but from the beginning of the sixteenth century it loses appeal. As we enter the sixteenth century we commonly find that moralities are called "interludes." Difficult as the word "interlude" may be to define, its use after 1500 often indicates new form and spirit in the moral drama."

The keynote of the fifteenth-century moralities is other-worldliness. The extreme abstraction of their protagonists is as much a part of that otherworldliness as is the merciful nullification of tragic catastrophe through spiritual salva-

P

tion. A word must here be said about the medieval fondness
for abstraction and the closely related medieval fondness
for allegory, both of which the moralities helped in such
generous measure to satisfy and both of which are so foreign to the ruling taste of modern readers.

If we take them when they have the aura of seriousness
most about them, medieval abstraction and medieval allegory are both truly logical manifestations of Neo-Platonic,
Augustinian, Christianity. In large proportion they retain
their religious validity at the heyday of the moral drama,
just as Augustinian otherworldliness in general retains at
that time a large share of its validity. The abstract view of
life produces in the earlier Middle Ages the philosophy of
Realism, which finds basic truth not in things but in a universal quality binding things together, and which proceeds
by gradations of minor abstract groupings to the one great
abstract grouping of all things in God. The allegorical view
of life minimizes individual significance in the things of
this world and frequently possesses the same temper.

In the Middle Ages the allegorical view of life is partly
a heritage from Greco-Roman philosophy, just as the view
of the world as inherently irrational and meaningless is
partly such a heritage. It is instructive to consider the *Psy-
chomachia* of Prudentius (b. 348), a long poem upon the
struggle between virtues and vices and the battle between
Christianity and paganism, as an influential early Christian
allegory pointing the way to the medieval moral drama.
But even in the pagan world we may find Hellenistic philosophy turning more and more toward allegorizing. To
the pagan Sallustius," as the old religion makes its last fight

against the new, the whole material world is much as it will be to the mass of Christians for many centuries to come, "a great myth, a thing whose value lies not in itself but in the spiritual meaning which it hides and reveals."[45]

For the people who created them and for those who enjoyed their presentation on the stage, the early moralities were thus capable, at least, of being something more than mere tissues of "the cobwebs of theoretical divinity." The allegorical was the most commonly accepted medieval method of approaching profound reality, not for the intellectual man alone, but for the common man also; as, indeed, the intricate decoration of Gothic cathedrals for the purpose of giving popular instruction and enjoyment bears abundant testimony. As for the abstraction of human nature in the moralities and the minimizing of what is to us the realism of individual human character, this had adequate sanction from the Neo-Platonic Realistic spirit. The medieval philosophy of Realism was quite able to regard "the totality of similar individuals as constituting a real unity, the totality of men as a generic unity, *unus homo in specie*."[46] In the figure of Mankind walking the stage, there seems to have been, even for the most ignorant among the fifteenth-century audience, less of the shadow than there is for us and more of the satisfying substance of reality. If we take the matter otherwise, we are brought to the absurd conclusion that the moral drama was in general, and not merely on particular occasions, forced down the people's throats by an intellectual and ecclesiastical conspiracy.

It only remains to add that the concreteness attained so early in the mystery is hardly to be called a realism of the "modern" variety. The mystery was simply drama which began to discover interest in worldly life, but which never came to the point of making a thoughtful search for the meaning of worldly life *qua* worldly life. The morality was drama which came to this point quickly. It found, rather paradoxically, that to discover the meaning in worldly life was at first to employ quite fully the spiritualizing processes of medieval Realism, and to occupy itself chiefly with abstracting and allegorizing life.

Before English drama could go far upon the road toward tragedy it needed to learn that the poetic discovery of life's inner nature is not dependent upon abstracting and allegorizing. It needed to learn that the dramatic poet's most severe but most rewarding task is the revelation of human universality by the very act of creating authentic human individuality, that Hamlet truly can be Hamlet magnificently and pitiably alone, yet at the same time Hamlet-Everyman. Creation by English drama of truly responsible human individuality in a tragic setting was deferred until the sixteenth century. The share which the sixteenth-century morality had in this development must be our next consideration.

Chapter VI

TRAGEDY AND THE ENGLISH MORAL
PLAY: SIXTEENTH CENTURY

CHANGES of form and purpose in the English morality of the sixteenth century produce many plays
of which little or no account need be taken in this
chapter. Where plays show a tendency to become primarily
comic interludes and to minimize serious didacticism, there
is obviously a forking of the ways leading from the morality
toward comedy and tragedy. Where humanistic secular
didacticism copies the dramatic methods of religious didacticism and produces educational interludes like John Ras-
tell's *The Nature of the Four Elements* (*ca.* 1517), the
result is an amusing and instructive record of new interests
in an age of rapid intellectual growth, but such things as
the truancy of man from the classroom pursuit of learning
and the winning of him back again do not lead us toward
the profounder truths of mortal suffering and mortal destiny. Finally, where religious or political partisanship in
an age of violently changing loyalties turns to the writing
of moralities, the controversial result is sometimes, as one
might expect, far removed from the elemental drama of
human life. In short, our attention must now be confined
to a critically selected number of later English moralities,
and some even of the selected number, interesting for technical reasons, will be upon a rather low level so far as ethical
significance of the action is concerned.

As has been said in the preceding chapter, the morality

almost immediately at the opening of the sixteenth century
loses dramatic need for the fully abstract hero of the earthly
pilgrimage. This loss seems to show some of its worst effects
in *Hyckescorner* (*ca.* 1513), in which we find the old
Humanum Genus removed from the scene and a drama
constructed—or patched together—without any true protagonist to take his place. Opposed to the forces of good,
who are Pity, Contemplation, and Perseverance, are three
characters who may be called evil, but who are hardly
the equivalents of any of those beings presented in earlier
drama as working to entangle man's soul. The three are
Freewill, Imagination, and Hickscorner. They seem much
more like different types of corrupted mankind, or, the first
two at least, like corrupted aspects of the human soul, and
remind one of the fifteenth-century play *Mind, Will, and
Understanding,* in which Anima, the human soul, is at-
tended by the three "mights" of the play's title, who are
liable to corruption, and who, as the play progresses, are
indeed changed to evil in distinctive ways. In *Hyckescorner*
the three subjects of corruption are already reduced to evil
at the beginning. Freewill, as he himself says, has power to
choose good or ill, but his choice is all for ill, for fighting
and chiding and drinking. To match this perversion of
man's power of will, Imagination seems to be a perversion
of man's power of reason, for he boasts that he is skilled in
the planning of devious ways to get money and in the
twisting of right into wrong by intellectual legerdemain.
He is a clerk and can escape the halter by reading his neck-
verse. Hickscorner, however, is simply a bawdy sinner of
nondescript character. It is difficult to see that this interlude,

as has been suggested, gives basis for constructing a hypo-
thetical early form of the conflict of vices and virtues in the
morality, a form in which no figure of mankind was represented.[1] As a matter of fact, mankind is represented in
Hyckescorner, though piecemeal and not in abstract fullness, and the play gives many signs of being purely and
simply a product of disintegration. The author seems to
have thrown overboard the old unifying principles of the
morality and to have acquired none of the new principles
which were soon to show themselves plainly.

Lacking a protagonist as it does, *Hyckescorner* makes little real advance in the individualizing of human character
that could have significance in a tragic setting. Its three
scapegraces are perilously close to being merely three bad
boys who will not listen to the admonitions of virtue, who
play pranks on their sad-faced elders, and who get into
trouble. Two of them, Freewill and Imagination, are finally
converted, somewhat as the mights of the soul are converted
in *Mind, Will, and Understanding.* Hickscorner, who, by
being nondescript as an aspect of man's corrupted soul, almost becomes a human individual free from the burden of
abstract meaning, and who might have been made an arresting central character in the play, really plays a part no
more important than that played by either of his fellows,
and in the end he simply wanders off not to come back.
He thereby misses a conversion and an extension of mercy
which would seem to have been his due.

But the play does give some indication of a growing impulse in the moral drama to entertain thoughts of a justice
with tragic possibilities and to let such thoughts sap the

strength of the traditional glorification of mercy. The con-
versions which *Hyckescorner* metes out do not have the
old solemnity; and the words of Pity at the beginning of
the action describe a debased and sorry world for which the
preachment of God's mercy seems to have lost much of
its usefulness and even to have become a stumbling-block.
Men must beware:

> They trust so in Mercy, the lanterne of bryghtnesse,
> That no-thynge do they drede Goddes Ryghtwysnes.[2]

Of an utterly different order is John Skelton's *Magnyfycence* (*ca.* 1516). Here the English morality as it departs
from the older spirit of otherworldliness and of complete
abstraction first achieves a large measure of consistent new
purpose. And in this play, though a tragic catastrophe is
averted by merciful restoration of the central character after
his fall, the moral drama takes a long step toward tragedy.
As it does so it finds that a close alliance with *De Casibus*
story can be profitable.

The protagonist of *Magnyfycence,* instead of being representative of mankind in the large, is representative of one
class of mankind, the princely. There is much to arouse our
suspicion that the play was aimed in the general direction
of King Henry VIII as a veiled warning against Wolsey and
the perils to which his guidance might lead,[3] but if it was
so aimed, Skelton took care, for very good reasons, to make
the political application of his allegory none too exact. He
undertook to dramatize the fall of a more or less typical
prince and to moralize the fall with broad generalities.
Among the earlier of Skelton's writings are some verses

upon the death of Edward IV in which the once proud king is represented as telling his story, speaking from the grave and beginning with this plea:

> *Miseremini mei,* ye that be my frendis!
> This world hath formed me downe to fall.

The manner and the moral tone are those characteristic of the *De Casibus* story when it most earnestly contemns the world; as we shall see, these verses by Skelton were incorporated in the *Mirror for Magistrates* when the age of Elizabeth found fresh impulse for the writing of tragical poems. In *Magnyfycence* the fall of his typical prince brings from Skelton many echoes of the conventional ascetic philosophy which he had put into the mouth of Edward, but this philosophy often has a peculiar lack of consonance with the moving spirit that informs the play. At heart, Skelton's *Magnyfycence* is the most worldly of the English moral plays up to its time, and not merely by reason of its passages of low comedy or salty realism, but also by reason of the philosophical basis upon which the dramatist builds his story.

Skelton's mainstay is the *Nicomachean Ethics* of Aristotle. In giving meaning to the drama he leans toward Aristotle's coolly measured acceptance of the world as contributing to the "good life." The typical prince is named Magnificence and is the embodiment, so far as he fulfills his ideal self, of the two Aristotelian virtues of magnificence and liberality, somewhat modified for the combination.[4] This means that Skelton is decidedly not setting out to picture a world for ascetic Christians to scorn, one in which the climbing of princes to high place and their efforts to

maintain themselves in worldly prosperity are to be regarded as egregious folly because the gifts of Fortune are
despicable. On the contrary, he is thinking of a world in
which it is good for princes to gain high place and to gather
and dispense the worldly gifts of Fortune so long as these
things are done with true greatness of spirit and under the
noble rule of measure. The background of values is so different from that of the ascetic Christian-Stoic world that
happiness has now become something which is not wholly
limited to an inner spiritual integrity. Happiness is ultimately of the soul, but, in the words of Aristotle himself:
"Nevertheless happiness plainly requires external goods
too, as we said; for it is impossible, or at least not easy, to
act nobly without some furniture of fortune. There are
many things that can only be done through instruments,
so to speak, such as friends and wealth and political influence."[15] The Christian-Stoic had maintained that nobility
required no "furniture of fortune" whatever.

Thus Magnificence is represented by Skelton as a prince
happily endowed with wealth at the hands of Fortune and
possessing the capacity for directing a noble course between
extremes of action. As a generous man he may be expected
to avoid niggardly handling of his wealth, but he must also
avoid the vice of prodigality to which his nature is prone.
As a generous prince he may be expected to show the peculiar virtue of magnificence, a virtue which the common
man could not practice even if he would. Aristotle makes
this almost a matter of genius: "The magnificent man is
like a skilled artist; he can see what a case requires, and can
spend great sums tastefully."[16]

The action is complicated and the play is longer than the usual interlude of its time, but a brief outline may serve to show how Aristotle fares when his ethical theory has the sometimes dubious support of didactic conventions established by moral drama and *De Casibus* tragedy. The entrance of Magnificence is preceded by a debate between Felicity (i.e., Wealthful Felicity, happiness resulting from wealth) and Liberty (i.e., satisfaction of the desires or the will) over the possibility of their existing together. Measure undertakes to arbitrate between them and decides that both are necessary to happiness, especially to the happiness of a prince, but that they must submit to his (Measure's) rule. Liberty accepts the decision only with reluctance, after Felicity has made forecast of the evils which may descend upon them, and which, as we find, do descend in the course of the play. As Felicity says:

> For, without Measure, Pouerte and Nede
> Wyll crepe vpon vs, and vs to Myschefe lede;
> For Myschefe wyll mayster vs yf Measure vs forsake.[7]

The great source of virtue, then, is reason, which gives man power for the moderation and intelligent use of the lower faculties. Refusal on man's part to be virtuous, or reasonable, can lead to physical retribution according to laws of cause and effect. The possible tragedy which Felicity sketches is rational to the last degree.

Like the Mankind of the earlier moralities, Magnificence is at first strong in his desire to follow virtue. He accepts Measure as chief counselor and as controller of Felicity and Liberty, especially Liberty. He fully intends to lead the good princely life. To undermine his good intentions there is no army of evil captained by Satan, but there is a body of Vices headed by Fancy, a character who may be taken as the opposite of Measure and as the representative of wanton excess. Magnificence allows himself to be deceived by a forged letter and by the old trick of changed names for the Vices. Fancy creeps into his confidence as Largesse, and the Vices conspire to ruin him. It is not long before the king abandons Measure and hands Felicity over to the control of Fancy and Liberty. This is the turning-point of the action. The king is elated and feels that he has climbed to the top of worldly bliss. He is like the ambitious man in a *De Casibus* tragedy, or like the king in *The Pride of Life*. He boasts that he is beyond the reach of Fortune and that he is peerless among historic princes of the world, whom he calls to our minds at great length. He even lets himself take amusement with Folly.

Suddenly comes reversal. Fancy hurries upon the scene to say that the king's favorites have made away with Felicity and that they have brought Adversity to court. Adversity enters and announces in no uncertain words that he is the stroke of God, humbling the proud and punishing all who follow their fancies and fall into evil ways. His punishments are of many sorts, including plagues and diseases, bereavement, legal condemnation, murder, and sudden death. Sometimes he strikes where there is no cause, just to try men's patience, but nowadays he usually has good cause. He seizes Magnificence, beats him to the ground, and despoils him of his goods and raiment. Then he hands the king over to Poverty. Despair enters, and recommends suicide. Mischief comes close at heels to proffer knife and halter. But the king is mercifully saved from suicide through Good Hope, Redress, and Circumspection. He is given fresh garments, he is lectured on the folly of trusting dishonest counselors, and his feet are placed upon the path that will lead once more to material prosperity.

It is obvious that in *Magnyfycence* there appears a fully recognizable Nemesis to visit physical punishment upon erring humanity. Under Skelton's hand the avenging quality in the figure is far from being the vague thing that it is in the Mors or Death of earlier moral drama. Here we find confident expression of the conception that there is a mundane scheme of justice working through life according to individual deserts.

One might think that Skelton could have small place for the Christian figure of fickle Fortune in this rather well-ordered Aristotelian world. But not so. The spirit of *De Casibus* tragedy has a very real power over Skelton, and as he brings Adversity to bear upon the king he turns gladly to the achieving of typical *De Casibus* effects. As we have noticed, the king reaches a height of self-confidence which corresponds to the apex of the pyramid of worldly activity in several of Boccaccio's tragedies, and he then boasts conventionally that he is beyond the power of Fortune. When Adversity stands over the fallen Magnificence, his moralizing speech includes the line:

> Beholde howe Fortune on hym hath frounde.[8]

And when Poverty comes to the king, the royal unfortunate hears much talk about the wanton turning of Fortune's

wheel at the same time that he is rebuked for not taking in
good part a punishment from God which he has deserved.
The king even proceeds to the bewailing of his lot in the old
set terms, accusing Fortune of having no steadfastness in
her friendship. Finally, the play actually ends, despite its
generous measure of neo-Aristotelian paganism, with an
emphatic epilogue *de contemptu mundi*. The moral here
is hardly to be distinguished from that which Boccaccio or
Lydgate in their most ascetic manner might have drawn
from the fall of royal magnificence:

> Sodenly thus Fortune can both smyle and frowne,
> Sodenly set vp, and sodenly cast downe.
> . . . .
> To day a lorde, to morrowe ly in the duste:
> Thus in this worlde there is no erthly truste.[9]

Skelton is carried away by this conventional condemnation
which he has conjured up for things worldly; but, to do
him justice, he has made some slight explanatory preparation for its inclusion in a play which bases itself upon Aristotle's balanced worldly wisdom. As he makes Felicity say
in the beginning, man can have much control over material
prosperity by the use of reason, but man must always remember that wealth is not eternal and that he must not fix
his affection upon it too strongly:

> A man may haue Welth, but not as he wolde,
> Ay to contynewe and styll to endure.[10]

Nothing, of course, could be more judicious, but it is far
milder justification for scorn of the world than was wont

to be offered by those who felt that all desire for material wealth was folly.

In certain ways, then, we may find remarkable advances made by Skelton toward the kind of dramatization of misfortune brought upon a royal personage that will later appear in Elizabethan chronicle-tragedy. Magnificence is merely a type, however much Henry VIII may have served for the artist's model, but at least he is given some class distinction from mankind in general and he is exposed to a peculiarly royal kind of misfortune, which comes upon him chiefly through his own characteristic faults. Perhaps the worst that can be said of Skelton the dramatist is that the peculiarly royal course of action and the peculiarly royal misfortune which he has chosen for Magnificence fall far short of being heroic and deeply significant. A tragedy, or even a moral play, making its stage the royal exchequer viewed as an arena for the exercise of policy or principle, and striving to present with dramatic intensity the conduct of a king in spending his money, would seem to be foredoomed to a certain lack of vitality and of larger ethical meaning, despite the theoretical attraction which the subject had for Aristotle. In short, *Magnyfycence* shows some academic tendency toward that departure from the main issues of human life which throws many moralities of the sixteenth century outside the sphere of our consideration.

II

In moralities which come after *Magnyfycence* there is stronger and stronger testimony that tragic justice working through laws of cause and effect is beginning to be a reality to men's minds. The character Adversity conceived by Skelton is followed upon the English morality stage by a long line of similar characters, and details of physical retribution come to be presented with sharply increasing dramatic strength. However, two notable plays written before the accession of Elizabeth, *The Enterlude of Youth* and R. Wever's *Lusty Juventus,* show the sixteenth-century tendency to make the protagonist less broadly abstract and at the same time show not at all the sixteenth-century tendency to make him suffer physical retribution. In spite of the fact that *Lusty Juventus,* the later of the two, is staunchly Protestant in temper and goes out of its way to make argumentative points for the new faith, both plays have something of the fifteenth-century benignity. They tell a simple story of spiritual adventure, in which Youth falls into the pitfalls toward which he is peculiarly enticed by his nature, experiences contrition, and wins divine forgiveness. The Youth of *Lusty Juventus* is carefully instructed according to good Protestant doctrine that it is in no sense according to his deserts—which are vile—that he is shown mercy. Yet the divine hand dealing physical retribution for sin, which the Protestant spirit so often imagined with especial force, has not been laid upon him.

In contrast, the plays of that bitterly disputatious Protestant, John Bale, frequently show the hand of God's vengeance as ever ready to fall upon sin and strike it down. The world which Bale then sets upon the stage is indeed different from one which has been left by God to the governance of Fortune. It is a world in which the Hebrew God of vengeance is a fiercely direct mover of physical event. In *A*

THE DEATHS OF VIRGINIA AND APPIUS
From Laurent de Premierfait's translation of Boccaccio's *De Casibus*,
MS Additional 35321, late fifteenth century.

Comedye Concernynge Thre Lawes, of Nature, Moses, and Christ (written in 1538, according to the undated first edition), Bale brings evil, generously given a papistical color, to a well-deserved end. The three laws indicated by the title are degraded through Infidelitas as the chief embodiment of vice. Vindicta Dei falls upon Infidelitas and conquers him with flood, fire, and sword. Deus Pater, before he restores the three laws, makes plain the moral:

> As ye have seen here, now I have striken with fire
> The pestilent vice of Infidelity,
> So will I destroy, in the fierceness of mine ire,
> All sects of error, with their enormity."

In the *Chefe Promyses of God* (printed in 1577 with the note that it was "compyled" in 1538), which he entitles "a tragedye or enterlude" instead of a comedy, Bale runs the course of humanity's sinful suffering from Adam to the coming of Christ. He gives almost the entirety of seven acts to the various accumulations of divine wrath visited upon erring humanity, to the stayings of the divine wrath for the good few, and to the promises made by God to Noah, Abraham, Moses, and others in the vain hope that men would turn from evil—all leading up to God's final determination to break man's stubborn heart with a supreme act of mercy. Thus the promise is given to St. John the Baptist that Jesus shall die for mankind. And in *Kynge Johan* (not printed until 1838, but written in its first form in the late 1530's), a play which must come up for further discussion in connection with chronicle-tragedy, Bale is not content until he has condemned Sedition, the villain of the piece, to be hanged

Q

and to have his head impaled upon London Bridge. A character named Nobility then reminds us that God's retribution for sedition has left many tragedies on the pages of history and that he personally will accept the warning:

> I consydre now, that God hath for Sedicyon
> Sent pōnyshmētes great, examples we haue in Brute
> In Catilyne, in Cassius, and fayer Absolon
> Whóme of their purpose, God alwayes destytute,
> And terryble plages, on them ded execute
> For their rebellyon. And therfor I wyll be ware,
> Least hys great vengeaūce, trappe me in suche lyke snare.[12]

Nobility, with his list of great ones fallen for cause, thus makes a miniature "mirror for magistrates."

The antipapal Scot, Sir David Lyndsay, also has good use in his *Ane Satyre of the Thrie Estaits* (*ca.* 1540) for the chastening divine hand and likewise lets lessons be drawn from the falls of mighty ones who were given to evil. The play is exceedingly long and exceedingly complicated, but at the center of the action is a Rex Humanitas who reminds us somewhat of Skelton's Magnificence. Lyndsay's Rex is corrupted by evil companions and reduced to a life of sensuality. Good Counsel tells him forcefully that kings and princes are brought to mischance for good reason:

> Quha haldis me at delusioun,
> Sall be brocht to confusioun:
>   And this I understand,
> For I have maid my residence,
> With hie Princes of greit puissance,
> In Ingland, Italie and France
> And monie uther land.[13]

Then, at the end of the first part of the play, Rex Humanitas is saved from his evil companions and from his iniquity by Divine Correction, who gives him again the reminder that kings and other famous men have fallen for just cause. Let him remember, for example, how "King Sardanapall" fell for lust. The same Divine Correction attends to the hanging of the Vices at the end of the play.

A Nemesis of quite different sort is introduced into *Respublica* (1553), that curious and not wholly unsuccessful attempt to construct a moral play with the Commonwealth of England as the central character. The author, in the prologue, makes no secret of his intention to have the allegory apply to the political situation in which he finds his country, but his characters maintain the abstract names customary in the morality. Also they maintain a large degree of abstract significance. The widow Respublica, born to tribulation as she is, has in a sense the composite character of all cities and states which take life from the worldly activity of mankind. Like men, they are born to fall and to die, according to the nature of the mortal round. It is as natural that the author of *Respublica* should put himself into a certain degree of harmony with the spirit of *De Casibus* tragedy as it is that the author of *Magnyfycence* should do so. Cities and men are equally good subjects from which to draw the *Ubi Sunt* moral, whether the moralist is pagan or Christian. As Seneca concludes after asking the stock *Ubi Sunt* question for the great city-states of the past: "What I say about cities I say also about their inhabitants."[14] What the writers of moralities and of *De Casibus* tragedies had said about humanity belonging to states, the writer of *Res-*

publica seeks to say about the abstract state: it can be assailed
by the power of evil and by the power of mortality, and it
can fall. But the dramatist distinctly belongs to an age in
which the fall of a state, as well as the fall of a prince, is
beginning to be examined for rational cause and not left to
Fortune; to an age likewise which can imagine justice operating in the mortal theater of affairs and not only elsewhere.
It is thus that "the Goddess Nemesis" enters the play, sent
by God to redress wrong; and there is no harm, as the
author serves notice in the prologue, in thinking of her as
the new ruler of England, Queen Mary.

The author's patriotic optimism, in natural combination
with his willingness to accept the morality convention of
merciful denouement, keeps *Respublica* from becoming unrelieved tragedy. The widow Respublica is found upon her
first appearance to be in the throes of unhappiness. She
enters with the familiar complaint of those who have descended on Fortune's wheel:

> Lorde, what yearethlye thinge is permanent or stable,
> Or what is all this worlde but a lumpe Mutable?
> Who woulde have thought that I from so florent estate
> Coulde have been browght so base as I am made of Late?[15]

She recites an *Ubi Sunt:* Where are Troy, Babylon, Athens,
Corinth, the empire of the Medes and Persians? All mortal
things are subject to decay. But she does not draw the formerly inevitable lesson that the world is therefore to be surrendered as incalculable and that man's gaze is to be fixed
on Heaven. She concludes that the world is to some degree
calculable and that states may be observed to fall for good

reason, namely, lack of good government. Hence there is hope for her widowhood:

> But lyke as by default quicke ruine dothe befalle,
> So maie good governemente att ons recover all.[16]

Through the greater part of five acts Respublica is pitiably taken advantage of in her laudable desire to find good rulership. She falls before the blandishments of Avarice, the chief of the Vices, who calls himself Policy and leads her to think that he is the quality of which she is in need. But God—the God who often needs to punish but delights to forgive—hears her prayer for aid. The Four Daughters of God (Misericordia, Veritas, Justitia, and Pax) now play rôles in an earthly instead of a heavenly drama, a drama strangely altered from that in which mankind's salvation was the issue. Justice arrests the four Vices and refers their punishment to the Goddess Nemesis. Misericordia succeeds partially in her plea for mercy, but Avarice is condemned to be pressed "like a sponge." Thus Respublica is restored to the good estate which she had before possessed.

It is already apparent from the dramas which have been passed in review that acceptance of the world as revealing a measure of justice according to natural law and order, an acceptance through which Elizabethan tragedy was eventually to attain nobility of outlook, did not necessarily tend to ennoble the moral play. The same thing may be said of De Casibus tragedy. The discovery of a mundane scheme of tragic order led writers at first to the crudest ideas of poetic justice and often to the most crassly materialistic application of those ideas. Nothing could be more crassly materialistic, for example, than a morality concerned with merely pecuniary prosperity and misfortune, as imagined for the typical ordinary man absorbed in getting and spending. Such a morality is to be found in *Impacyente Poverte* (printed in 1560), which probably was written in Queen Mary's reign, about the same time as *Respublica*.

This play still clings to the merciful denouement, though it reduces its hero to much physical suffering. Impatient Poverty first appears upon the stage complaining in angry voice that a knave has wanted to arrest him for a debt of forty pence. A character named Peace gives him some highly profitable advice, urging him to abandon his sins of envy and wrath because they are great hindrances to worldly success. The matter is as plain as A B C: Poverty is so full of wrath and envy that he can "growe no grace," but if he will forsake sensuality and be governed by reason, as Peace will instruct him, he shall "come to rychesse, wythin shorte space." Poverty sees the light of truth—that one who is good will also be rich; and he perceives conversely:

> That pouerte and miserye that I my lyfe in lede
> It is but onely punishemente for my mysdede.[17]

So Poverty is converted. Peace puts a new garment on him and starts him out on the path to material felicity, even wagering upon the result by immediately changing his name to Prosperity. But Prosperity must remember to avoid evil, and he must remember to give plentifully to the poor, since this is simply practical wisdom:

> For euerye peny that so is spente
> God wyll sende the double.[18]

Of course Prosperity falls by the wayside, but only after he
has acquired wealth by the practical means which have
been shown him. He meets his old acquaintance Envy, who
enters into his confidence by calling himself Charity, and
finally he is led to accept Misrule, under the false name of
Mirth, for a servant. They all take the familiar morality
route to the tavern and its evil delights, the chief of which
in this play is gambling with dice. The conclusion is fore-
gone. Prosperity is stripped of his wealth, to the tune of
£2,000. Then he comes upon the stage under his old name
of Poverty, lamenting the loss of all his goods and warning
all young men to take warning by his misfortune. A sum-
moner hales Poverty into court for his great sins of envy
and slander; the sinner is publicly degraded and does penance "aboute the place" with a candle in his hand. His misery is so great that he desires the relief of death. At last he
again meets Peace, who does not at first recognize the miserable wretch. Peace points out that it is a plain case of just
suffering brought to pass by the sufferer's own fault:

> Thou art well punyshed for thy trespasse
> By thyne owne sensuall and vndyscrete operacyon
> Hath brought the to all thys trybulacyon.[19]

Poverty repents, reforms, gets a new garment again, is once
more called Prosperity, and once more starts upon the road
to material felicity.

Though it is hard to imagine an ethical outlook more of
the earth earthy, more uninclined to contemn the world
for a lack of trustworthiness, yet the otherworldly spirit of
the first moralities rises like an unlaid ghost at the end of

the play. It is with some sense of shock that we find the dramatist concluding with a moral in contempt of the world, written with gusto and with no apparent insincerity. Why, he asks, after his ardent attempt to answer just the question which he poses, should men trust in this world where the gayest of us all is but worms' meat! The sole excuse for his moral which the dramatist might successfully offer to a Christian of the former age would be his incidental exposure of certain corrupt and unjust practices in the ecclesiastical court before which Poverty is tried.

III

The logical next step for the English morality to take toward tragedy was the representation of unrelieved catastrophe for an erring representative of humanity. The step had been indicated as imminent by the meting out of punishment to the Vices, who, as they had assumed something of human at the expense of supernatural quality, had often attracted to themselves the retribution of villains; by the increasing attention which had been given to momentary retributive suffering for the central character; by the progressive loss of validity which had been suffered by the merciful denouement; and, in general, by the increasing faith which had been shown in a world order of justice.

Certainly by the first years of Elizabeth's reign the unrelieved catastrophe was a well-established form of conclusion for the English moral drama. It was accomplished for minor figures, though not for what should probably be considered the central figure, in the anonymous play *Nice Wanton* (printed in 1560, and possibly written before the death of Edward VI in 1553). Like Thomas Ingelend's *The Disobedient Child* (*ca.* 1560), *Nice Wanton* is a derivation from the humanistic school-drama of the Continent.[20] It was perhaps suggested by the *Rebelles,* a comedy published in 1535 by the Dutch Latin writer Georgius Macropedius, and it aims, again like *The Disobedient Child,* to make plain the need for parental control over children. The English author successfully introduces much of the English morality manner into a simple story of a mother and her badly disciplined children, who are fully individualized characters, not abstract morality ones. But by far the most important of the changes which he makes in his borrowed material, if he is indeed borrowing ideas from the *Rebelles,* is his substitution of a double catastrophe for that part of an essentially comic denouement in which wayward children are saved from disaster.[21] Of a family of three children he shows two, a boy named Ismael and a girl named Dalila, posting upon the road to ruin even so early as their school days. Barnabas, the third child, is as wonderfully good and obedient as the others are bad and disobedient. The mother is faced from the beginning with the duty of correcting the perilous tendencies of Ismael and Dalila, but she refuses out of softheartedness. They are corrupted by an evil companion, a Vice named Iniquity, and both die disgraceful deaths, the boy hanged for felony, burglary, and murder, and the girl diseased with the pox, which she has contracted in the public stews. Iniquity is punished along with Ismael. A curious abstraction named Worldly Shame exults when the mother is goaded by the sense of her dereliction to the point of attempting suicide. But the good son, Barnabas, saves her by taking the office assumed by the ministering Virtues in the older moralities. He preaches that what she has undergone is obviously punishment from God and that she must accept it in the belief that her sins may be forgiven. Also he consoles her with the news that Dalila has died repentant under his care and that her soul at least has been saved. If the mother is properly to be regarded as the central character of the play, the one who has most moral responsibility for the course which the action takes, then the author of *Nice Wanton* has followed previous morality tradition in refusing to consummate a major catastrophe which he has indicated. Otherwise, however, he has shown an unwonted severity in his presentation of retribution for sinning humanity. He has given to the story a cast of petty tragedy.

The early Elizabethan dramatist W. Wager, of whom nothing is known aside from his plays, shows severity that is much more thoroughgoing. In *The Longer Thou Livest, the More Foole Thou Art* (*ca.* 1559), which enforces a similar school-drama moral with respect to parental control of children, but which has more completely than *Nice Wanton* the style and form of the English morality, Wager abandons all effort to save the central character. His work is called in the title "A very mery and Pythie Commedie"; it is also called "A Myrrour very necessarie for youth, and specially for such as are like to come to dignitie and promotion," a characterization which hints strongly that the author or printer had in mind the *Mirror for Magistrates*. William Baldwin's *Mirror,* inaugurating an Elizabethan revival of *De Casibus* tragedy which will be discussed in following chapters, was published in 1559, and if we may judge by Wager's Protestant approval of a "new order" recently established in England, *The Longer Thou Livest* was written about this very time, soon after the accession of Elizabeth.[22] There can be no doubt that Wager turns his drama to one of the purposes of *De Casibus* didacticism and lets it serve as a warning for the vicious man elevated by Fortune to high place in the land. But his protagonist is a type, and he is careful to say that he means no particular person.

The Longer Thou Livest is the story of Moros, a fool. The very fact that Wager conceives and names him so cuts the play off from any development of tragic sympathy. From beginning to end it is an exercise in condemnation. After a prologue preaching the importance of education and the responsibility of parents for the correction of children, especially when the children "by birth are like to have gubernation in publikque weales," we find Moros falling into the ungentle hands of Discipline, Piety, and Exercitation. He enters as a carefree and happy youth, singing gay songs and thinking of play. The Virtues are sad to find that his parents have taught him no better way to spend his time. Indeed, he has been taught something much worse. He has been reared in "idolatry"—that is, in the religion of Rome. At first the Virtues maintain that even a fool may profit by their instruction, but later they have their doubts. They pour their doctrine into him, vainly try to get him to repeat it by rote (very low comedy), beat him generously, and never for a moment treat him with the sad sufferance shown by the Virtues in the fifteenth-century moralities. The fool is to be reformed by force, and the Virtues have a pitiably blind faith that humanity can be made good by external pressure. Moros never has change of heart. He accepts with alacrity the escape provided by the Vices under the leadership of Idleness, and the stage is cleared after sharp comment by Discipline.

While Moros is carousing with his evil companions, Fortune opens new action leading to a *De Casibus* catastrophe. She enters boasting of her power and declares that to prove her might she will elevate Moros, the mere popish fool, to high position, even to a wise man's seat. This she does. Piety comments that the times are evil, but that there is no reason to doubt that God is only biding his time. Virtuous men may have evil speed and fools may be put into places of ease, wealth, and honor, but God will shortly subvert the works of sin. It is to be noted that Fortune here is not the irrational ruler of earth permitted by a rational God to be whimsical in order that men's minds may more surely turn to Heaven. She is simply the spirit of the topsy-turvy evil times, over which right is soon to prevail.

Thus Moros becomes an elegant and influential gentleman, a very silly and shallow oppressor of good people who come under his control, going his foolish way with evil associates while Discipline comments ominously that such as he shall "be beate with an yron rodde." When Moros has grown old in his iniquity, the long-delayed retribution descends upon him. "Entre with a terrible visure Gods Iudgment."[23] Fools must learn by experience that a God of vengeance is over them. A curt and obviously perfunctory invitation to repentance is refused, and Moros is stricken with the sword of judgment. Confusion assumes custody of the fallen great one, now become "a pesant of al pesantes," and leads him forth to a generous portion of both the physical and the spiritual wages of sin:

> Cum forth of thy folly to receiue thy hyre,
> Confusion, pouertye, sickenes, and punishment,
> And after this life eternall fyre.[24]

So, says God's Judgment, does God throw down iniquitous rulers. So did he throw down tyrants in the past, who need not be named because they are in every man's mind. So has he thrown down fools full of spite in more recent times; "in this world [we] haue seene their reward." Here and elsewhere in the play there is obvious reference to the previous sufferings of Protestants under a hostile government. The point is carefully made that Moros is not a "natural," or innocent, but a malicious fool refusing to listen to reason, and that he is therefore morally responsible for his wicked deeds.[25] His fall has been justly earned.

One might say that Wager was led to abandon the merciful denouement simply because of an inordinate desire to excoriate his ecclesiastical opponents as they appear in the person of Moros, were it not for a second play from his pen which has been preserved to us. This is *Inough Is as Good as a Feast,* rediscovered in 1919 at the sale of the Mostyn library. It was printed without date about 1565 and was probably composed about 1560. Here Wager demonstrates that his severity is not necessarily bound up with a partisan bitterness of spirit. His temper is still definitely Protestant, but in the main he is not writing a controversial drama; rather, he is writing a drama of retribution which in essence could draw approval from many Christians of the day, ir-

respective of their ecclesiastical allegiance. Therefore, partly
by lack of original handicap in conception, it is a much better play than *The Longer Thou Livest*. The author shows a
dramatic inspiration in the vivifying of his action which he
has not shown before, and the catastrophe has a detailed
execution and a moving appeal which is remarkable in a
drama that holds to the morality tradition.

The theme of *Inough Is as Good as a Feast* is man's acquisition and use of earthly riches; yet its ethical outlook is
upon a far higher level than that of *Impacyente Poverte*. It
allies itself with *De Casibus* tragedy in a more legitimate
manner than does *The Longer Thou Livest,* and has much
to say about the tragic perils of worldly ambition. The hero
of the piece is Worldly Man, who faces us at first "stout and
frolicke," arguing with Heavenly Man and Contentation
that it is his duty to take good care of himself in this world
and good care of the treasure with which he is endowed.
Heavenly Man preaches that love of riches infects humanity with the incurable sickness of ambition, to the jeopardy
of the soul, and he outlines a *De Casibus Virorum Illustrium*
in the regular style:

> As for the treasure that you possesse heer,
> Through ficklenes of Fortune soon fadeth away:
> The greatest of renown and moste worthy Peer,
> Somtime in the end falleth to misery and decay.
>   Recorde of *Dionisius* a King of much fame,
> Of the valiant *Alexander*, and *Ceaser* the strong:
> Recorde of *Tarquinus* which *Superbus* had to name:
> And of *Heliogabalus* that ministred with wrong,
> To resite them all it would be very long.
> But these be sufficient plainly to prooue:
> How soon and vncertainly riches dooth remooue.[20]

But it is instructive to see how Wager turns the edge of this time-tested moralizing, lacking as he does a truly ascetic scorn for the world. In his heart of hearts he knows that the mortal scheme is not merely an evidence of Fortune's fickleness. Just as he does in *The Longer Thou Livest,* he allows that Providence may bide its time, to take vengeance upon wrongdoers and to set earthly matters right, but he will not allow that God leaves all earthly affairs to Fortune, especially when ambitious men spill innocent blood in religious persecution. He makes Contentation allude to such evildoers and express a pious faith:

> But God I trust shall disapoint their intent,
> And ouerthrowe the power of fading treasure:
> And cause vs al to wish for the heauenly pleasure.[27]

In short, Worldly Man is warned that ambition can bring its train of punishment on earth and that justice does not wait for the other life. For the time being, Worldly Man accepts the warning and concludes that he will be contented with only that amount of worldly goods which will satisfy honest needs: enough is indeed as good as a feast. He will study under his good advisers to be a heavenly man.

At first he is not unsuccessful in following the new course. He consorts contentedly with a companion named Enough, who is "poorly arayed." But he is soon assailed by Covetousness, the peculiarly insinuating leader of a band of Vices, and he is soon conquered. Particularly is he impressed by the specious argument that if he had more wealth he could better give alms according to his Christian duty. Thus Worldly Man puts his foot upon the ladder of wicked ambition. Among the Vices whom he takes for companions are names which show colors of the new age: Inconsideration, disguised under the name of Reason because "men now a dayes to reason doo trust," and Ghostly Ignorance, the popish ghostly father of Inconsideration, disguised under the name of Devotion. Heavenly Man closes this episode as a chorus, commenting that Worldly Man now begins to kindle the wrath of God.

We are spared the details of Worldly Man's rise to high position. We enter immediately into an episode in which bitter complaints by type-characters named Tenant, Servant, and Hireling reveal that Worldly Man is a landlord of hard and grasping ways, grinding the faces of the poor who come under his hand. Covetousness, disguised as Policy, is now Worldly Man's steward. Both steward and master scorn the complaints of the sufferers, and when Hireling declares that God hears the prayers of the oppressed and roots out the prosperity of the unrighteous, Worldly Man sneers. What cares he for the people's curses so long as his riches increase? He will enlarge his already fine barns and will get hold of a certain "little tenament" belonging to a poor neighbor. He has reached the apex of ambition by allowing himself to be ruled by Reason and Policy, and in conventional *De Casibus* fashion he finds himself unique:

> Oh policy, how glorious my buildings doo shine:
> No gentlemans in this contrey like vnto mine.[28]

It is a fit boast to draw the tragic destroyer. Off stage, Worldly Man suddenly hears the voice of a Prophet, a Jeremiah speaking for his special benefit: Beware! The earth

must know that man is but clay, that death comes to all, and
that just punishment comes to the idle servant of God.
Worldly Man feels a weakness creep through his sinews,
he waxes sick, he sits down to sleep. Behind him appears
God's Plague. This is very plainly not a Death who strikes
all men in the same spirit:

> I am the plague of God properly called,
> Which commeth on the wicked sudainly:
> I go through all townes and Cittyes strongly walled,
> Striking to death and that without all mercy.[29]

Worldly Man comes to his senses with the realization that
he is beyond the mercy of God and is doomed. There is a
futile bustle in his household, a coming and going of steward, chaplain, and physician, who are made much of by the
dramatist and effectively presented in both the sober and
the comic spirit. Worldly Man gets to the point of making
a will. "In the name of—of—of—"; he gets no farther. He
dies miserably and goes to Hell, not even being suffered to
put God's name in a will. It is a radically different ending
for the human sinner from that exhibited in *The Castle of
Perseverance* at a time when the morality was all for mercy.
There humanity also dies in full occupation with the sin of
covetousness, but he is not unable to make the saving call
for forgiveness. *Inough Is as Good as a Feast* ends with the
coming on of Satan to rejoice in the increase of his kingdom
and to carry off on his back the much-praised Covetousness;
with the inevitable moralizings by the Virtues; and with a
glimpse of the happiness of Heavenly Man in his goodness.

After Wager, the unsaved sinner appears with frequency
in moral plays, though the convention of mercy can still

R

exert some appeal for the moral dramatist and likewise, apparently, for his audience. But the morality in Elizabeth's reign is obviously drawing near the end of its service as a literary form. With few exceptions it shows distinct loss of ability to attain unification in a central character, and it shows a related tendency to rambling diffuseness. In still another of the many later moralities dealing with worldly wealth, *The Triall of Treasure* (*ca.* 1567), two characters named Lust and Just divide the representation of humanity much more than do Worldly Man and Heavenly Man in *Inough Is as Good as a Feast,* where Worldly Man is unquestionably the protagonist. On the one hand, Lust gives the dramatist an opportunity to bring upon the stage the type of character representing God's vengeance which by this time had become popular. Because of his life given thoughtlessly to baser inclination and because of his joy in the possession of Lady Treasure, Lust is reduced to dust by God's Visitation, who declares that to those of evil life he brings sickness, perturbation, pain, and destruction. On the other hand, Just gives the dramatist an opportunity to show the good life rewarded materially in this world. There is much low comedy, and the general effect of the play is far from true edification.

Division between the good and the bad in humanity also appears in Ulpian Fulwell's *Like Wil to Like* (printed in 1568 and probably written not long before). Here there is further division of the bad into so many different characters that the action has little unity except in the character of the Vice. This Vice, Nichol Newfangle, one of the gayest of his kind, is content with a series of minor seductions worked upon characters named Ralph Roister, Tom Tosspot, Pierce Pickpurse, Cuthbert Cutpurse, Philip Fleming, and Hance. Fulwell shows himself decidedly prone to chronicle small beer and develop low comedy. However, the play at least pretends to sternness in the finding of unrelieved retribution for evil. Its title in 1568 advertizes that it declares "what punishment followeth those that wil rather folowe licentious liuing, than to esteeme & followe good councel: and what great benefits and commodities they receiue that apply them vnto vertuous liuing and good exercises." The worst of the punishments which it represents or reports is hanging for thievery, and the least is sickness of the gout acquired through dishonest pleasures of the flesh. At the end, when Newfangle has ridden away on Lucifer's back, Virtuous Life points to the honor and dignity which he has obtained by honest living.

The lowest stage of rambling diffuseness into which the English morality was capable of falling is well represented by two plays printed at the beginning of the last quarter of the sixteenth century. They are George Wapull's *The Tyde Taryeth No Man* (printed in 1576) and Thomas Lupton's *All for Money* (printed in 1578). In spite of their literary failings, however, they are worth some attention as further demonstrations of the tendency in the later morality toward worldliness and unpitying harshness.

The title of Wapull's offering is the much-repeated watchword of Courage, the play's Vice. There is no such thing as the soul, preaches Courage, and man can expect nothing after death. Therefore let us go catching and snatching for worldly goods as the tide of life offers them, for in truth the tide tarrieth for no man. But if the reader is inclined to think that Wapull means to imply through Courage that all worldly activity is vicious and that only ascetic denial of the world is virtuous, he is to be disabused. Courage himself says that when he inspires men to mundane activity, he produces not only evil, in which he has his delight, but also good. There can be courage which is truly noble:

I meane corage to win worship and fame.[30]

Properly speaking, there is no central action in which Courage makes demonstration of his power to seduce humanity; there is only a heterogeneous collection of incidents. But the action with which the play opens and to which it returns at the end after its devious wanderings is somewhat reminiscent of Wager's *Inough Is as Good as a Feast*. By a curious character named No Good Neighborhood, a landlord named Greediness is prevailed upon (for a price) to dispossess a tenant from his rightful holding. Later we have a glimpse of the same Greediness as a usurer, given an opportunity by Courage to lend money to a needy gentleman at the most ruinous rate of interest and according to the sharpest and most dishonest practice. At the end of the play Courage reports Greediness as dead and gone to Hell in sin and despair, without any remembrance of God and without any opportunity to find mercy. Courage himself, after a struggle, is seized upon by Faithful Few, Authority, and Correction, and led away toward capital punishment. In only one episode of the play do we find the traditional merciful denouement. A character named Wastefulness is led into riotous living, loses his goods, despairs, is about to commit suicide, and is saved by the able ministrations of Faithful Few.

Even more lacking in dramatic cohesion is Lupton's *All for Money,* which, as its title serves notice, is yet another exploitation of the pecuniary theme attractive to an age that was meeting the ethical problems of material prosperity and rapidly turning away from ascetic denial of the world. Through a succession of ill-assorted incidents with ill-assorted characters it preaches that greed is corrupting all the activities of mankind in the new order of society. Yet the prologue staunchly maintains that money is not evil *per se* and that mankind need not forswear the very real blessings of its acquisition:

> Thus the creature of God is not euill of him selfe
> But through our misuse from good to euill conuerted:
> Euen so money ill vsed is a most wicked pelfe,
> And also as good where well it is bestowed.[31]

What man must therefore learn to avoid is the "tragedie" which comes through misuse of money and which he can forestall if he will amend his faults:

> And because that euery man of money is so greedie
> Our Authour a pleasant Tragedie with paynes hath now made,
> Whereby you may perceyue, All thing is for money.
> . . . .
> In hearing vs attentiuely we craue but your ayde,
> Beseeching God, the hearers that thereby shal be touched,
> May rather amend their faultes, then therewith be grieued.[32]

Lupton obviously uses the word "tragedie" with the vaguest of critical consideration. The title of his play characterizes the work as "a moral and pitiful comedie." Neither as tragedy nor as comedy has it any real effectiveness, but his dominant occupation is unquestionably with the sort of tragic retribution which his prologue indicates.

Furthermore, Lupton takes a leaf out of the literature of *De Casibus* tragedy and uses it most curiously for one of his many episodes. At the conclusion of the drama two Boccacesque ghosts rise from Hell to relate brief stories of their evil lives and their punishments. After Sin, the Vice, has commented finally upon the way in which the audience has seen Money, with the help of Pleasure and Sin, sending men to Damnation, "Judas commeth in like a damned soule, in blacke painted with flames of fire, and with a fearfull vizard, speaketh as foloweth." He tells the classic story of the thirty pieces of silver which brought his downfall. Next comes Dives, in like dress, to speak in much the same manner. He loved money so greatly that he never gave to Lazarus, and he is now punished forevermore. Damnation comes upon the stage to drive the poor souls away to Hell, "and they shall make a pitiefull noyse." Godly Admonition drives home the moral that mercy cannot successfully be called upon after death has come to the sinner.

IV

We have seen how the English morality, as it gave way to secularization, found its central character not in the broadest abstraction of humanity but in the class abstraction or in the typical representation, and how it could even give a rather high degree of individuality to some of its minor characters. We have also seen how, along with the morality's acceptance of a secular reality, there came a tendency to dwell upon mundane suffering and a consciousness of lawful order in that suffering which steadily developed as a tragic sense. In some of the later plays the moral drama retreated from the otherworldly reality of broad abstraction only to lose all need for any central representative of humanity whatever and lapsed into mere conglomeration, but the way had been in large measure prepared for the reception of a truly individualized protagonist upon whom a developing tragic sense might be brought to bear. Nothing was more natural than that the individualized protagonist should be discovered in history or legend. *De Casibus* tragedy, with which the moral drama had made a sympathetic alliance, had long ago pointed the way to an effective moralizing of the historic and legendary lives of great men. Furthermore, the vaguest knowledge of the ancient stage was sufficient to give the hint that dramatic figures were to be discovered in records of the past. Nor was the discovery very difficult to make even without guidance. How successfully the English moral drama entered this field of history and legend, we must now consider.

When the morality reached the point of taking concrete characters from history, it was fated quickly to give place to a secular order of drama that should not be moral drama at all in the medieval sense. Yet in England, as in France, the "historical" morality has left examples enough to establish its very real share in the development of tragedy. One may even say that it achieved tragedy, however crude, almost wholly without benefit of those classic dramatic principles which its age was beginning to revive. It is useless to ask whether this development could have been carried very far by native force alone. It is sufficient to say that in England it was preparation of no small importance for the historic pageantry of the tragic stage in the time of Shakespeare. For England no less than for France it is true that the historical moralities "attestent le goût que l'on avait déjà pour les pièces sérieuses, pathétiques, historiques et d'action limitée: elles ont préparé le succès de la tragédie."[33]

An arrestingly early historical morality in England is John Bale's *Kynge Johan,* apparently written in its first form before the autumn of 1536, recast and acted for Cranmer in January, 1539, and revised even so late as the first years of Queen Elizabeth's reign.[34] But the spirit of *Kynge Johan* is far from being an indication that even before the death of Henry VIII the English stage was beginning to be interested in the pageantry and the tragedy of national history for their own sakes. The play was written as a violently partisan argument in favor of Protestantism, and King John was chosen for its hero because representation of his struggle against the pope for independent power could provide all the dramatic opportunity which Bale desired for vilification of the Roman church. Naturally, Bale permits the king to assume the colors of stainless nobility. This royal champion of Christian truth, as Bale sees that truth, fights a losing action and is overwhelmed by evil forces from abroad and by evil forces at home. He dies with Christ-like pardon on his lips for the monk (Dissimulation) who poisons him. Bale does not try to arouse in his audience anything like the tragic pity which can recognize failings as well as nobilities in the object of its sympathy. Nor does Bale in any way

present King John in *De Casibus* fashion as the pitiful subject of Fortune's whimsicality. The plain truth is that Bale
has little to say in the language of tragedy and that his main
purpose does not that way lie. It must be added that the
play also shows incomplete purpose in the presentation of
individual human beings. The king alone maintains his
integrity as a historical person. Other historical characters
easily shift into abstractions, the pope himself becoming for
a time Usurped Power.

It was not until the first years of Elizabeth's reign that
the English stage produced those examples of the historical or legendary morality with distinctly tragic implication
which have been preserved to us. Among them we may
include John Phillip's *Pacient and Meeke Grissill* (1558–
1561), though it is entitled a "commodye" and though it
accepts the happy denouement of the traditional Griselda
story. It brings the long-suffering wife back into the full
favor of her husband, but in Grissill's woes it lays itself out
to discover tragic meaning. Here again the moral drama
manifests sympathy with certain traditions of *De Casibus*
narrative. Grissill is guiltless, and her fall from high place
raises the medieval problem of unmerited misfortune happening in an evil world. The play has a Vice, Politic Persuasion, who becomes a sort of morality Iago, poisoning the
mind of a more than ordinarily loving husband against a
virtuous and more than dutifully loving wife. After Gautier
has raised Grissill to eminence from poverty-stricken surroundings and has boasted to Politic Persuasion (whom he
has accepted as a member of his household) that he has
found a wife with extraordinary virtues, we see the Vice

setting to work to bring about her confusion. The Vice hates her because she is good. He finds in her only a beggarly upstart; her father is an old fool and she has no drop of noble blood in her veins. He slyly gets Gautier to test all this boasted virtue, and furthers his plotting by an appeal to the husband's selfish pride. Women always want to rule, says he, and they need to be taught their lesson. As Gautier robs Grissill of her children and cruelly lets her think that they have been murdered, the Vice praises him for now proving himself a man indeed. The final stroke of injustice is prepared, and Gautier banishes Grissill from his house. Politic Persuasion rejoices in this "sudden fall" from greatness, and Rumor appears upon the stage to emphasize a De Casibus moral: Fortune is fickle and the world full of mutability,

> As nowe by Lady Grissill doth playnly appeare,
> For shee is nowe throwne, from the top of prosperytie.[35]

But there is little further implication that misfortune comes by chance. Grissill herself is at pains to tell her father not to blame Fortune for their woes; she would have him realize that God has given them adversity simply to test them. The joyful issue out of all these misfortunes leaves the tragic moralizing of the play unimpaired.

The "tragical comedy" *Damon and Pithias* (*ca.* 1565), so characterized by its author, Richard Edwards, because, as he says, it mixes mirth with care, also deals with misfortunes which are overcome happily. It dramatizes the adventures of the famous exemplary friends upon the level of romance rather than upon the level of tragedy or moral

drama. Its use of classic story, however, in drama which follows the native tradition with effective introduction of English low-comedy characters, is a foreshadowing of much
that was to follow in Elizabethan tragedy.

It was in classic story that the English morality, so far as
we may judge from surviving examples, discovered matter
for its last and most promising tragic development. It is in
three "classical" plays of the 1560's that the morality stands
closest to those popular tragedies which are immediately
pre-Shakespearean. These three plays are *A new Tragicall
Comedie of Apius and Virginia,* by "R. B." (printed in
1575, entered in 1567–1568), *A Newe Enterlude of Vice
Conteyninge the Historye of Horestes,* by John Pickering
(printed in 1567), and *A lamentable Tragedie, mixed full
of plesant mirth, containing the life of Cambises king of
Percia,* by Thomas Preston (printed without date, but entered in 1569–1570).

Apius and Virginia is utterly uncouth and undistinguished in poetic execution, but its dramatic conception and
structure are worth considering. Not least of its claims to
attention is the fact that it is a rather ingenious adaptation
of Chaucer's *Phisiciens Tale.* The dramatist seems even to
have let Chaucer provide suggestions for the particular business of making the story into a morality and a tragic drama.
The background and the spirit of the production are naturally quite different from those of the sophisticated later
play upon the same subject in which Webster had a hand.[36]

In 1566, William Painter published a paraphrase of the
tale of Appius and Virginia as it is told by Livy,[37] but though
R. B.'s play may have been written soon afterward, it shows

no inspiration from Painter's *Palace*. Nor does it show inspiration from Livy directly. It has all the coloring of that medieval version of the story which came to Chaucer from Jean de Meung's *Roman de la Rose*,[38] a coloring which is distinct from that of medieval versions in Boccaccio, Gower, and Lydgate.[39] In this version Icilius, the betrothed lover of Virginia, does not appear, and Virginius, instead of stabbing his daughter to the heart, severs her head from her body and makes of it a gory present to the lustful judge. The beheading, which Jean de Meung may or may not have invented, is accepted gladly by the Elizabethan drama-tist and is made much of for its melodramatic quality. Per-haps the most convincing single bit of demonstration that the dramatist made use of Chaucer's *Phisiciens Tale* is given by correspondence in a minor matter of poetic adornment. Chaucer at the beginning of his narrative embarks upon an elaborate eulogy of Virginia's beauty and goodness, for which there is no counterpart in Jean de Meung's story. Vir-ginia, says he, was created by an extraordinary effort of Nature, who worked in blessed accord with the "Former principal":

> For nature hath with sovereyn diligence
> Y-formed hir in so greet excellence,
> As though she wolde seyn, "lo! I, Nature,
> Thus can I forme and peynte a creature,
> Whan that me list; who can me countrefete?
> Pigmalion noght, though he ay forge and bete.
> Or grave, or peynte; for I dar wel seyn,
> Apelles, Zanzis, sholde werche in veyn,
> Outher to grave or peynte or forge or bete,
> If they presumed me to countrefete."
>
> (C, 9-18)

In *Apius and Virginia* these lines have an obvious echo.
Judge Apius, at his first appearance, when he soliloquizes
upon the effect of Virginia's beauty upon his peace of mind,
declares:

> By beuty of *Virginia,* my wisdome all is trudged,
> Oh perelesse Dame, oh passing peece, oh face of such a fature.
> That neuer erst with bewty such, matched was by nature:
> Oh fond *Apelles* pratling foole, why boastest thou so much?
> The famost peece thou madst in Greece, whose liments were such
> Or why didst thou deceued man, for beuty of thy worke?
> In such a sort with fond desire, where no kinde lyfe dyd lurke,
> With raging fits thou foole ran mad, oh fond *Pigmalion,*
> Yet sure if that thou sawest my deare, the like y" couldst make
> none."[40]

Having caught the method, the dramatist makes further
learned embroidery of his own. Here and elsewhere he
gladly welcomes an opportunity to show what he can do
with classic allusions.

Despite such increase of learned embroidery, the action
of *Apius and Virginia* has no more classic authenticity than
the action of Chaucer's story. After a prologue in which
the persons who are gathered "this Tragidie to heare" are
exhorted to extract abundant moral profit from the play,
Virginius appears, praising Heaven for his domestic bliss.
He is on his way to a temple to thank the gods for the exceptional sobriety and goodness of his wife and daughter. He
encounters these paragons of virtue, also on their way "to
church." The mother knows that she is about to die, but she
rejoices that Virginia is a child who needs no correction
and can be trusted to walk in the right way of life. Mother,

father, and daughter exchange ardent vows of affection for one another and sing a song whose burden is appropriate:

> The trustiest treasure in earth as wee see,
> Is man, wife and children in one to agree.[41]

A Vice, Haphazard, is next introduced in a scene of byplay with three low-comedy characters (Mansipulus, Mansipula, and Subservus) which ends with a second song as empty of edification as the first is full of it. The main course of the action now begins with the entrance of the hopelessly enamoured Apius, who has apparently just seen Virginia. He soliloquizes upon his passion in the manner already indicated. So far the dramatist, with generous elaboration and with shameless injection of low comedy, is following the first few lines of Chaucer's story proper:

> This mayde up-on a day wente in the toun
> Toward a temple, with hir moder dere,
> As is of yonge maydens the manere.
> Now was ther thanne a justice in that toun,
> That governour was of that regioun.
> And so bifel, this juge his eyen caste
> Up-on this mayde, avysinge him ful faste,
> As she cam forby ther this juge stood.
> Anon his herte chaunged and his mood,
> So was he caught with beautee of this mayde;
> And to him-self ful prively he sayde,
> "This mayde shal be myn, for any man."
>
> (C, 118–129)

Neither Livy nor Jean de Meung tells of a visit made to the temple by Virginia and her mother. Livy says that after the lust of Appius had been aroused, Virginia was seized in accordance with his orders as she was going to a school in

the Forum accompanied by her nurse. Jean de Meung tells
of nothing even remotely similar.

If it is instructive to see a moral dramatist at work upon
these dozen lines of Chaucer, it is both curious and instructive to see him fall in with the three lines immediately following in the *Phisiciens Tale*. Chaucer says of Appius:

> Anon the feend in-to his herte ran,
> And taughte him sodeynly, that he by slighte
> The mayden to his purpos winne mighte.

Certainly the author of *Apius and Virginia* could easily
have provided work for his Vice as a corrupter of the
enamoured judge without any suggestion from Chaucer,
but the fact remains that he uses his Vice just as Chaucer
hints that he might. It is difficult to imagine that he did
not get aid and comfort in some degree from the way in
which Chaucer unwittingly seconds the suggestion of conventional morality practice. After the soliloquy of Apius,
the dramatist arranges a scene between Apius and Haphazard in which the Vice tells the lustful judge how easily
his desires may be satisfied if he will turn to trickery. Apius
has only to instruct someone to claim Virginia as a slave and
to say that she was abducted by Virginius. In the further
development of this scene the dramatist evolves a striking
variation in morality technique. He finds the means for a
crude representation of inner struggle in a character impelled toward tragedy, and he thereby enters a level of dramatic conception much more "modern" than that of the
early moral dramatists. As Apius greets the proposal of
Haphazard with enthusiastic approval he is suddenly aware

of conscience. The stage direction reads: "Here let him make as thogh he went out and let Consince and Iustice come out of him, and let Consience hold in his hande a Lamp burning and let Iustice haue a sworde and hold it before Apius brest." Thus Apius is made to face himself with the realization that his choice may bring a tragic retribution:

> But out I am wounded, how am I deuided?
> Two states of my life, from me are now glided,
> For Consience he pricketh me contempned,
> And Iustice saith, Iudgement wold haue me condemned:
> Consience saith crueltye sure will detest me:
> And Iustice saith, death in thende will molest me,
> And both in one sodden me thinkes they do crie,
> That fier eternall, my soule shall destroy.[42]

But Haphazard is able to nerve Apius for the doing of evil by arguing contemptuously that Conscience and Justice are but thoughts, without any true reality. The plot is laid that Claudius shall be the man to get Virginia away from her father by the trickery already contemplated. Apius now stands firm in what he plans, in spite of further warning from Conscience.

With the same degree of general indebtedness to Chaucer's story, the play goes to its conclusion. Claudius pleads to have Virginia as his rightful "thrall" (the word is used by both Chaucer and the dramatist); Judge Apius, giving Virginius almost no chance for defense, decides that the father may no longer have custody of his daughter; and Virginius goes to his home, where Virginia awaits him. The placing of the final scene between father and daughter within the house of Virginius is one of the ways in which Chaucer goes beyond Jean de Meung, who does not localize the scene at all. (Livy says that Virginia was with her father when Appius made his decision, and that her father led her aside into a street, where he stabbed her with a knife snatched from a butcher's booth.) Chaucer's affecting dialogue between Virginius and Virginia seems to have stimulated the dramatist to do his emotional best. He lets the daughter throw her arms around her father's neck just as Chaucer describes her as doing, but he undertakes a refinement of pitifulness in representing the actual beheading. In Chaucer, Virginia swoons and thus gives Virginius an opportunity to strike the blow under less harrowing circumstances; in the play, she quails at the last moment and is able to submit only after her eyes have been bandaged. When Virginius comes to Apius to present the bloody head, the dramatist also attempts an improvement. He has Apius condemn the father to be killed with the same knife that has beheaded Virginia, instead of condemning him to be hanged. The ensuing seizure of the unjust judge, his suicide in prison, and the punishment of Claudius with exile at the merciful request of Virginius are according to Chaucer's (and the usual) ending of the story, except for their adaptation to a morality setting.

This final bit of adaptation leaves us in no doubt that so far as the play is the tragedy of Apius, it is conceived as a tragedy of direct retribution for an evil course of action well considered and responsibly pursued. When Apius has condemned Virginius, his course is run. Justice and Reward enter upon the stage and confront him, speaking in unison:

We both are ready here at hande, to worke thy fatall fall.[43]

S

No move is made to offer him mercy in the spirit of the earlier moral drama. Reward merely announces that Apius' just desert is "deadly death." As for Haphazard, he too gains his reward, and is hanged. All this is a logical manifestation of that fondness for retribution whose development we have followed in sixteenth-century drama. But here, as in his use of Haphazard, the dramatist received aid and comfort from Chaucer, who adorns his *Phisiciens Tale* with a moral which begins:

> Heer men may seen how sinne hath his meryte!
> Beth war, for no man woot whom god wol smyte.
>   (C, 277–278)

It is a moral not unknown in *De Casibus* tragedy, as we have observed, but not the dominant moral; and in Chaucer's *Monkes Tale* a dramatist interested in mundane retribution would have found less support.

So far as *Apius and Virginia* is the tragedy of Virginia, it is certainly no tragedy of retribution, but it is just as certainly no tragedy of whimsical Fortune. Like the guiltless heroine of Phillip's *Pacient and Meeke Grissill,* the guiltless Virginia is brought to grief by dramatically motivated forces which we are invited to analyze. And the lesson of her undeserved misfortune is in no sense the advisability of scorning a mutable world and fixing the eye upon a stable Heaven. On the contrary, the lesson is that the reputation of such outraged virtue has enduring quality. At the end of the play the figure of worldly Fame promises that Virginia shall have everlasting honor and renown.

Pickering's *Horestes,* appropriating as it does one of the most fruitful themes of Greek tragedy, is a sufficiently notable production among the English moralities of the 1560's. But it gives no indication of having taken either dramatic form or tragic significance under direct inspiration of classic drama. It is rightly to be considered as a product of the native spirit, sophisticated by no more than a minimum of learning. Though Pickering shows some general knowledge of classic legend, his main dependence for the action of the play is upon Caxton's *Recuyell of the Historyes of Troye,* translated from the French of Raoul Lefevre and first printed *ca.* 1475." The crudity of his versification is even more marked than that of R. B. in *Apius and Virginia,* but his utilization of a medievalized classic story for a morality-tragedy is in some ways more ingenious, and his ethical scope is in some ways broader. *Horestes* can claim distinction because of its earliness in the long line of Elizabethan tragedies of revenge.

Following Caxton, Pickering makes the revenge of Horestes a matter of medieval warfare, with knights leading an army against a walled city; "go & make your liuely battel & let it be longe eare you can win ye Cittie," is one of the stage directions. The Vice, however, who lets us know at the end of the play that he is properly to be called Revenge, furnishes a kind of motivation for which there is no counterpart in Caxton. We see him at the opening of the play rejoicing that there is prospect of warfare to be waged by Horestes and in the meanwhile engaging upon a minor, low-comedy, business of fomenting strife. He gets two clowns, Hodge and Rusticus, into a fight by saying that the dog of one has killed the hog of the other. He soon has his chance at larger game. He finds Horestes musing upon his father's murder and immediately begins to urge him toward revenge. At the corresponding point of the story in the *Recuyell,* Caxton says simply: "Whan Horrestes the sone of kynge Agamenon that was had foure & twenty yere of age the kynge ydumeus that had nourysshid hym made hym knyghte and maad a grete feste of the new chyualerye of horrestes. And than horrestes prayd hym that he wold helpe hym wyth his peple to take vengeance of the deth of his fader and to recouere his lande. The kynge ydumeus delyuerd to hym a thousand knyghtes wyse and hardy."[45] Later, we hear: "Horrestes had an answer of the goddes that he hym self shold take vengeance of his moder by hys handes notwythstandyng she was closid in the cyte."[46] Pickering's introduction of the Vice into this setting is a first step toward reviving for the Orestes saga some of those ethical implications which had once converted it into great tragedy. In the play, Horestes is made to doubt that he should kill his mother and to call upon the gods for guidance. Thus the Vice gets his opportunity. He declares that he comes as a messenger of the gods to announce that Horestes must achieve revenge, that he was himself present at the divine council where the issue was decided, and that among the gods he is known as Courage. The Vice even suggests in a rather notable pair of lines that he is to become a sort of "other self" for Horestes:

> And I as gyde with you shall go, to gyde you on the way,
> By me thy mind ther wrathful dome, shal be performd in dede.[47]

All hesitation on the part of Horestes is quickly overcome, not only by the Vice's ancient trick of changing his name to that of a Virtue, but also by the counsel of King Idumeus.

Idumeus makes his entrance to a strain of tragic moralizing in the *De Casibus* manner. He observes how the fall of Agamemnon, that once proud prince, shows the insecurity of those who bear the scepter. When he hears that Horestes is planning revenge for Agamemnon's murder, he is first concerned, as much as was Horestes, to establish the righteousness of the act, and then, as in Caxton, he gives Horestes a thousand knights for the campaign.

It is manifest that Pickering sets out with some care to make the revenge of Horestes an evil course of action and Horestes an unwitting sinner, blinded as so many protagonists in the moralities are blinded with the conviction that evil is not evil but good. The dramatist is appealing to the Christian teaching that vengeance belongs to God and not to man, no matter how justly it is called for. In effect he is laying the foundations for a tragedy that could show vengeance recoiling upon the righteous avenger, exacting some measure of retribution for sin even though the sin was committed with full belief in a divine sanction. The approach has a certain crude resemblance to that of Aeschylus in his Orestean trilogy, apparently a quite fortuitous result of applying the Christian code of ethics to the story.

But though Pickering reveals promising possibilities at the opening of his action, he does not in the least proceed to their realization. He is content in the remainder of the play to write a bald tragedy of Clytemnestra and Egistus. At all times he is ready to stop for a comic interlude, and some of his comedy has slapstick effectiveness. Horestes and his knights ravage Clytemnestra's kingdom and capture both the queen and Egistus. Egistus is hanged on the stage by being turned off a ladder in good Elizabethan style, and Clytemnestra, after pleading with her son for mercy, is taken off the stage for execution. Pickering makes much of the tragic retribution which has come to these two sinful lovers. At last they have "wrought their own decay." As for Horestes, he is tried by Menelaus for the crime against nature which he has committed in slaying his mother and for the cruelties of his warfare, but he easily gains acquittal. He is allowed to keep the kingdom which he has won and is given Hermíone, the daughter of Menelaus, to wife. Pickering ignores the sinfulness of private vengeance which he has been at such pains to indicate and resolves the problem for Horestes by nothing more than the excuse which Horestes gives to Menelaus in the *Recuyell:* "Horestes excusid hym therof sayng that that he had doon the goddes had comanded hym."[48] Caxton permits this excuse to have real validity by never implying that the command was actually other than divine. Pickering may have intended from the first to extend mercy to Horestes, somewhat in the old morality manner. If so, he could have made a consistent drama by having his protagonist show the usual contrition and gain the usual divine forgiveness. One must suspect that when Pickering approached the end of his labor he had wearied of effort at originality and simply allowed Caxton to carry him through. He saw fit, in conclusion, to let Truth moralize the play as a tragedy showing sure retribution for the following of unrighteous and personal desires—with what application to Horestes one is left to wonder. The application to Clytemnestra and Egistus is, of course, plain enough.

THE REVENGE OF ORESTES
From Boccaccio's *De Mulieribus Claris,* 1473.

The third of the "classical" morality-tragedies, Preston's
Cambises, suffers like Pickering's *Horestes* from the author's disinclination to depart very far from the book in
which he finds his story. What book this is can be demonstrated beyond question. In 1539, Richard Taverner published *The Garden of Wysdom,* a compilation of anecdotes
concerning various great men of classical antiquity. It
proved popular and went through new editions into the
1550's. Taverner had an M.A. in Greek from Cambridge,
and his literary work in general was humanistic translation and adaptation. He had a bent for moralizing the material which he compiled. The larger part of the contents of
The Garden of Wysdom is translation from the *Apophthegmata* of Erasmus, but about a third of Book II, which was
published separately from Book I in the same year, is other-

wise obtained. In this *Secōd booke of the Garden of wyse-dome, wherin are conteyned wytty, pleasaunt, and nette sayenges of renowmed personages,* one section which cannot be traced to Erasmus is "Of Cambyses."[49] The account of the Persian king here given is closely followed by Preston in the serious scenes of his play.

If one considers what Taverner does with Cambyses, one can well understand how Preston, seeking matter for a moral play, could have been caught by it. In a short section dealing with "The Egyptians," Taverner praises the extreme care taken by certain Egyptian kings to obtain incorruptible judges and then furnishes an end link with his next section by alluding to "a certayn iuge of whome I shall nowe make relation." Thus he begins his section "Of Cambyses" with the story of the unjust judge Sisamnes. He sagely remarks: "Cambyses Kynge of Persia was otherwyse a verye wycked and cruell tyraunte. Yet there is no prynce of so disperat an hope of so naughtye a lyfe, but that at the lest waye other whyles doth some honest acte."[50] In all the histories, he says, Cambyses is commended for one good deed: when the king learned that Sisamnes, a deputy of his in Asia, had allowed bribery to corrupt justice, he put him to death and commanded that he should be flayed. The skin of Sisamnes was placed over the judgment seat, and the son of Sisamnes, who succeeded to his father's office, was thereby constantly admonished to be upright in his dealings. "Thys exemple," says Taverner, "teacheth them yᵗ beare offyce & rule to remēber, yᵗ god suffereth not iniustice nor iniury vnreuenged." But, he proceeds, since he has begun to talk of Cambyses, who otherwise lived a very tyrannous and wicked life, he may as well report certain of his notorious crimes and his end, so that rulers may take further example. For though Cambyses at the beginning "subdued & conquered Egypte, yet anone he forgatte all goodnes and degendred quyte & cleane frō the renowmed & excellent vertues of hys father." The crimes of Cambyses which Taverner sketches are three. First, when Prexaspes, one of his chosen counselors, urged the king to abandon his besetting vice of drunkenness, Cambyses appealed to other lords of the realm, and when they flattered him instead of seconding Prexaspes, he visited terrible punishment upon his counselor. He commanded that the young son of Prexaspes be brought before him. The king, after he had "throughly washed hys braynes wyth wyne," shot the boy through the heart with an arrow, and had the transfixed heart cut out to prove that he was no drunkard. Second, Cambyses murdered his own brother Smerdis lest he might at any time be king. Third, he sinned against nature by marrying his "owne suster germayne," and then he put her to death. At a feast with this queen he arranged a combat between a young lion and a dog for pleasure and sport. Another dog of the same litter as the first broke his bonds to help his brother vanquish the lion. When the queen shed tears and reminded the king that he had treated his own brother otherwise, he slew her. "Wherfore," concludes Taverner, "not long after, wyth a greuouse vengeaunce, God plaged him. For as he was comming out of Egypte in to Persia, when he shulde mownt on horsbacke, his swerd felle out of the skaberd and sore wounded hym in suche wyse that he dyed of it. This exēple testifyeth, that god woll not longe suffre tyrantes to reygne."

All this is to be found in Herodotus, though it is not there related in the same order and though some of the minor details are different. In Herodotus the story of Sisamnes is told in a separate book following that in which the three crimes appear, and the three crimes are not described in Taverner's sequence.[51] Wherever Taverner got the matter for his section on Cambyses, it was doubtless not directly from Herodotus, and the same thing may be said of his moral attitude.[52] His "plague of God" moralizing is somewhat reminiscent of the pointed way in which Herodotus says that the sword of Cambyses gave the king a fatal wound in the thigh, in that part where he had once stabbed the Egyptian god Apis, but Taverner's moral manner is essentially one which the skeptical Herodotus does not in the least attempt.

Here, then, Preston could find a moral play and a tragedy of sorts very neatly made to order, with even the moralizing fully supplied according to the fashion of the day for discovering examples of God's vengeance. That he made thorough use of the opportunity is proved by the fact that he offers the good deed and the three crimes nearly as they are in Taverner, and exactly in Taverner's order, for the serious action of *Cambises,* emphasizing the one good deed done by the king just as Taverner emphasizes it and upon occasion employing distinctive words and phrases to be found in Taverner. Preston more than once makes the garrulous Vice direct attention to the one good deed of the king, as in the following lines:

> As he for the good deed, on the Judge was commended,
> For all his deeds els he is reprehended.[53]

The places in which Preston's words and phrases are the same as Taverner's are few but noticeable. In dramatizing the story of Prexaspes (Praxaspes in the play), Preston seems definitely to have kept his finger on the text of *The Garden of Wysdom* and let it provide some of his wording. Taverner has Prexaspes say to the king "that the Persians praysed hym very much, but thys one thyng dyspleased them, that he was so subiecte to the vyce of dronkēnes." Preston gives this speech to Praxaspes as:

> The Persians much doo praise your grace, but one thing discommend:
> In that to wine subiect you be, wherin you doo offend.

Taverner's king asks his lords "whether in any thyng he were worthy to be reprehēded." Preston's king asks:

> Am I worthy of any crime once to be reprehended?

Finally, Taverner's king says to the father that the murdered child's heart is well hit, "wherfore he mought esteme full well herby, yᵗ he was no drōkard." Preston's king comes about as close to saying these very words as he could come in a line of morality verse:

> Esteem thou maist right well therby, no drunkard is yᵉ King.[54]

The play might have been far better if Preston had not found it so easy to let Taverner's arrangement of anecdotes take on dramatic meaning and be sufficient in themselves for the main business of the action. Preston might otherwise have been stimulated to the discovery of further material in history or legend and to purposeful organization. Yet, disconnected anecdotal structure was relatively no great

blemish upon a play in the 1560's, and if the level of achievement demanded by his age be considered, Preston must
be praised. He recognized tragic possibilities in an outrageously cruel protagonist stalking through a succession
of bloody crimes to a bloody doom, and hit for the first time
an Elizabethan dramatic taste to which Marlowe and the
immature Shakespeare were to cater. Also, he utilized Taverner with a kind of shrewd economy.

Preston's modicum of dramatic shrewdness makes itself
plain at once in the dramatization of his first incident, that
of Sisamnes. Taverner begins with the punishment by Cambyses of the unjust judge simply because his comment on
Egyptian kings and Egyptian judges has led him to do
so. He does not place this one good deed among the first
exercises of power by the Persian king; he tells of it as an interlude in the king's later viciousness. As he observes, Cambyses began his reign by approaching the greatness of his
father Cyrus in another matter, that of conquering Egypt.
Preston magnifies the incident of Sisamnes and combines
it with the conquest of Egypt to make them both together
represent the level of statesmanship and goodness at which
the king began his reign and from which he declined and
fell. He lets the king appoint Sisamnes as his deputy at
home when he departs for Egypt. Also, Preston uses Sisamnes quite effectively in introducing the inevitable Vice, in
this play named Ambidexter because he "plays with both
hands," doing both good and evil though always intending
mischief. Ambidexter helps to corrupt Sisamnes, and later,
of course, speeds the king upon his mad career of crime.
In intervals between the more serious scenes, Ambidexter

turns to orthodox low comedy with such company as the ruffians Huf, Ruf, and Snuf, and the country bumpkins Hob and Lob. In his character as a politic player with both hands, getting much evil done but some good, Ambidexter is a legitimate extension of Taverner's ruling idea that good may somehow come to be done in the midst of vice.

The final moralizing of the action Preston leaves practically as it is in Taverner, except to make sure that it shall not suffer for any lack of emphasis. His king dies with these last words:

> A iust reward for my misdeeds, my death doth plaine declare.

Ambidexter, deserting a scene in which he can do nothing more, reminds us that events have worked neatly toward their logical conclusion and that he has rejoiced to point out their working all along:

> I did prognosticate of his end by the Masse.

And one of the lords of the court immediately makes the moral triply sure:

> A iust reward for his misdeeds, the God aboue hath wrought:
> For certainly the life he led was to be counted nought.[55]

In *Cambises,* the English morality comes to the climax of its concern with mundane retribution and truly becomes simple tragedy, without any of the older morality spirit which stood in the way of tragic finality. Preston's play has no touch at all of mercy. It centers in a single concrete sinner and leaves him with the utmost lack of hesitancy to the wages of sin which his acts might be expected to gather in this world.

By its unification in the melodramatic fall of a single tragic figure, *Cambises* has a certain effective superiority over either *Apius and Virginia* or *Horestes,* even though its structure is loosely episodic. All three plays are plainly from the same popular mold. Each lacks division into acts and scenes. Each has its lone Vice who gives some impulse to the major action and who draws with him into the play a troop of comic figures from vulgar life. Each has generally a marked distinction in versification between the "heroic" scenes and the scenes of low comedy, giving to the former a measure which may be scanned as seven-foot iambic and to the latter a measure which may only be scanned as tumbling verse. Each is in the fullest sense native to the English stage; the author of each is so far from being directly stirred by classic learning that he is content to depend almost wholly upon a single secondary source in English for his classic subject-matter.

Scorn for the failure of these three plays to show, either by form or by choice of subject-matter, a broader classic background than they do can easily obscure their very real achievement. They demonstrate that English popular drama at the beginning of Elizabeth's reign was ready to profit by the example of classic tragedy because English popular drama had been able to develop a crudely tragic force of its own. But before their promise was to be converted into established reality; the popular taste for tragedy was to be further confirmed in nondramatic literature.

Chapter VII

THE "MIRROR FOR MAGISTRATES"

Now, as the English moral play, by shifting concern from God's saving mercy to God's avenging justice, entered more and more into the domain of tragedy, England revived the Boccacesque tragical story. With that revival, which centered in the *Mirror for Magistrates* (first published in 1559) and which found strength that perhaps surprised the begetters of the *Mirror,* the problem of tragic retribution proved to have a fresh urgency. Denial that the world of the flesh had its perceptible laws of tragic cause and effect was still in conflict with affirmation, but affirmation was gaining greatly in confidence. The expression which Elizabethan nondramatic tragical story gave to this affirmation before the last decade of the sixteenth century and the inspired discovery which was made by the *Mirror* that British history and legend were an almost inexhaustible well of tragical matter, waiting to be drawn upon, constituted vitally important preparation for the establishment of tragedy upon the Elizabethan public stage. First the original *Mirror* and later its extensions and imitations taught the Elizabethan public that tragical moralizing had newly moving appeal when brought close home by being appended to the storied misfortunes of a Richard II or an Owen Glendower; the public soon demanded a recanvassing of universal history as well as the canvassing of British history that had been hitherto neglected in tragical narrative. Well into the seventeenth century, *De Casibus* tragedy maintained a degree of popularity, even when it was over-shadowed by stage tragedy.

Pointing the way to the *Mirror's* use of British history, John Skelton, perhaps as early as the closing years of the fifteenth century, found *De Casibus* tragedy in a subject that was of particular and immediate interest to English-men.[1] His verses *Of the Death of the Noble Prince, Kynge Edwarde the Forth* were possibly among the first that he wrote. But the poem is not one of retribution: it is given to the teaching that death comes to all of us, even the greatest. Its somber force, which makes it worth comparing with the well-known *Ubi Sunt* ballade of François Villon, is en-hanced by an effective refrain:

> Et, ecce, nunc in pulvere dormio.

I sleep now in dust, says Edward, but as a mortal creature I could have expected to do so. How may one trust in mor-tality, since on this earth all things die and have recourse to the earth of nature? Fortune raised me to a place among the great, but she exiled me from life when I was loathest to go; and where now are my victories, my riches, my castles? Where are Alexander, Samson, Solomon, Absalom? Why should the spirit of mortal be proud? *In manus tuas, Do-mine!* Of sin or frailty and its consequences upon earth, Edward says nothing. His lesson is entirely one of humility and his penance is only for the pride of life:

> I haue played my pageyond, now am I past;
> Ye wot well all I was of no great yeld.[2]

Also pointing the way toward the *Mirror,* and doing so more definitely because of the monitory tone which he

adopted, Sir David Lyndsay drew from the Scottish history
of his time *The Tragedy of the late most reuerende father
Dauid, by the mercie of God Cardinall and archbishoppe
of sainct Andrewes,* published at London without date but
probably very soon after the death with which it deals.
David Cardinal Beaton was assassinated on May 29, 1546.
Lyndsay tells of sitting in his oratory and taking up the book
of John Bochas, where he finds much matter to make him
muse upon the falls of the mighty. Cardinal Beaton in red
raiment and fine velvet suddenly appears before him, grievously wounded and begging to have his pitiful story recorded as he knows Bochas would record it were Bochas
still alive. In the main the tragedy which is told is one of
deserts, with the direct judgment of God upon sin for its
theme. As the ghost admits, the cardinal had little intellectual or spiritual qualification for his post and was the author
of much wrong, the result of which was a just punishment
that by example should lead princes and prelates to reform.
The poem is decidedly antipapist, but not so viciously so as
the epistle to the reader added by Robert Burrant, which
makes the comment that England is the better off for the
death of one more evil servant to the Whore of Babylon.³

Such single poems as Skelton's and Lyndsay's are, of
course, only casual attempts to make local history into *De
Casibus* tragedy. A more sustained attempt was made by
George Cavendish. Some part of his tragical poetry seems
to have been written after the year in which the *Mirror* was
published, but much of it at the time when the original
Mirror was being composed. His *Metrical Visions* contain
laments by the ghosts of great men and women recently

T

dead in England, covering the period from the death of Wolsey in 1530 to that of Queen Mary in 1558. They remained in manuscript until 1825.' In the *Visions* there is much talk of irrational Fortune, but there is also an undertone of recognized guilt. Wolsey, for example, laments that his deceit was met with deceit and that his end had aspects of retribution, though his tragedy is occasion for lengthy comment in dispraise of the world and its uncertain ways. Anne Boleyn humbly hopes that death has expiated her sin. Thomas Lord Cromwell finds both guilt in himself and treachery in Fortune, as though Fortune's fickleness were somehow accountable for his own deeds of willful commission. To Henry VIII is given a confession of lustfulness and lechery amazingly frank when one considers the fact that Henry's immediate descendants had supreme power over Cavendish while he was writing. It is not surprising that the book was not published in its author's day. From Henry, as from Wolsey, Cavendish draws with large satisfaction the lesson that ruling greatness, even in the midst of the luxuries of life which it may command, must go the way of all flesh.

The same George Cavendish is the author of a prose life of Wolsey which must be called primarily a very effective biography, but which is also an ambitious tragical composition spread upon a canvas wider than that of the usual tragical poem and done with a notable skill in the analysis of character.' It, too, was written about the same time as the original *Mirror,* and likewise, so far as is definitely known, suffered the necessity of delayed publication in print, although through circulation in manuscript it yielded matter for Shakespeare's *Henry VIII.* In its first extant edition, that of 1641, garbled for political purposes, the work is entitled *The Negotiations of Thomas Woolsey, The Great Cardinall of England.*

Cavendish had been a gentleman usher in the household of Wolsey, and he possessed the wit to make excellent use of what he had seen at first hand of his master's magnificent rise and cataclysmic fall, a subject for *De Casibus* tragedy— and for dramatic tragedy—*par excellence.* With admiration and sympathy, yet with artistic detachment that makes the narrative all the more powerful, he tells first of Wolsey's rapid climb "uppe fortunes whele." Wolsey, the son of a poor man, enters upon the field of strife where the world's prizes are distributed. He has no greater endowment than a quick brain. His capacity for learning helps him to Oxford. Then his shrewdness furthers his fortunes as he adapts himself with clear foresight to the slightest needs of those whom he serves, until the king realizes that there is royal need for such a man. As the king's chaplain, then as Archbishop of York, then as Cardinal, Wolsey is always sedulous to further the king's desires, sensual or ambitious. Now who so great as Wolsey the Chancellor of the Exchequer? He has met the world, and it is his. He luxuriates in silver crosses that are carried before him; in masques and all manner of pageantry; in servants by hundreds; in cloth of gold; in stuffs of velvet, satin, damask, taffeta, grosgrain, sarcenet; and in other material things not in Cavendish's remembrance.

But Fortune views Wolsey's magnificent estate and turns to the consideration of means whereby his high port may

be abated. To speak more concretely, as Caven
able to do, Wolsey's course of action has not only
succession of his triumphs, but has also stored a
animosity in Mistress Anne Boleyn, in certain
kingdom, in the king himself. The time com
reservoir is full to overflowing, and in an insta
swept away from all that has been his. He is br
ness and dies. It is not the fall of outright evil
dish sees here when he is not talking about
ways of Fortune, but the fall of a noble man
escape a certain misapplication of effort in wh
that make us men have a hand. He tells ho
was found next Wolsey's body after his de
Cavendish, this man in his time of authority
the haughtiest man in all his proceedings th
he had more respect to the worldly honor of 1
he had to his spiritual profession. We are lef
ing that this prince of the Church who cou
shirt and at the same time be the haughti
both deserved his heroic place in the worl
his tragic fall, the fact that his tragedy is
the frame of Fortune's wheel being only
importance. In short, we are left with the
that comes of following a tragedy subtl
have pity and fear not so much because of
ness against a cruel world as because of
against it, which was so much greater tha
heroic man, yet could not be perfect. Tha
spearean tragedy.

What may be called dramatic instinct i

matter for Shakespeare's *Henry VIII.*[c] In its first extant edition, that of 1641, garbled for political purposes, the work is entitled *The Negotiations of Thomas Woolsey, The Great Cardinall of England.*

Cavendish had been a gentleman usher in the household of Wolsey, and he possessed the wit to make excellent use of what he had seen at first hand of his master's magnificent rise and cataclysmic fall, a subject for *De Casibus* tragedy— and for dramatic tragedy—*par excellence.* With admiration and sympathy, yet with artistic detachment that makes the narrative all the more powerful, he tells first of Wolsey's rapid climb "uppe fortunes whele." Wolsey, the son of a poor man, enters upon the field of strife where the world's prizes are distributed. He has no greater endowment than a quick brain. His capacity for learning helps him to Oxford. Then his shrewdness furthers his fortunes as he adapts himself with clear foresight to the slightest needs of those whom he serves, until the king realizes that there is royal need for such a man. As the king's chaplain, then as Archbishop of York, then as Cardinal, Wolsey is always sedulous to further the king's desires, sensual or ambitious. Now who so great as Wolsey the Chancellor of the Exchequer? He has met the world, and it is his. He luxuriates in silver crosses that are carried before him; in masques and all manner of pageantry; in servants by hundreds; in cloth of gold; in stuffs of velvet, satin, damask, taffeta, grosgrain, sarcenet; and in other material things not in Cavendish's remembrance.

But Fortune views Wolsey's magnificent estate and turns to the consideration of means whereby his high port may be abated. To speak more concretely, as Cavendish is well able to do, Wolsey's course of action has not only created the succession of his triumphs, but has also stored a reservoir of animosity in Mistress Anne Boleyn, in certain lords of the kingdom, in the king himself. The time comes when the reservoir is full to overflowing, and in an instant Wolsey is swept away from all that has been his. He is broken by sickness and dies. It is not the fall of outright evil that Cavendish sees here when he is not talking about the insecure ways of Fortune, but the fall of a noble man who cannot escape a certain misapplication of effort in which the faults that make us men have a hand. He tells how a hair shirt was found next Wolsey's body after his death. Yet, says Cavendish, this man in his time of authority and glory was the haughtiest man in all his proceedings that then lived; he had more respect to the worldly honor of his person than he had to his spiritual profession. We are left with the feeling that this prince of the Church who could wear a hair shirt and at the same time be the haughtiest man living both deserved his heroic place in the world and deserved his tragic fall, the fact that his tragedy is stretched upon the frame of Fortune's wheel being only of conventional importance. In short, we are left with the sort of emotion that comes of following a tragedy subtly dramatic. We have pity and fear not so much because of Wolsey's weakness against a cruel world as because of Wolsey's strength against it, which was so much greater than that of the unheroic man, yet could not be perfect. That way lies Shakespearean tragedy.

What may be called dramatic instinct is abundantly evi-

dent here in the finesse of Cavendish's method of presentation, a finesse that is the more effective because it seems
effortless. The greatness and the frailty of the cardinal he
simply presents in the action; he does not require labels to
make us feel what he wishes to convey. He uses dialogue
liberally and sets the scenes for it deftly. By recounting
omens and premonitions, such as the falling of Wolsey's silver cross upon the head of Bonner and Wolsey's remark of
"Malum omen," he contrives to give something of that inti-
mation so often given by Greek and Shakespearean tragedy
that the stage of the action is not merely the world's stage,
and that invisible powers have concern with the drama.

II

The *Mirror for Magistrates,* which came to have a repro-
ductive power entirely lacking in these early efforts at
British tragedy, was conceived merely as an appendage to
Lydgate. Lydgate's *Fall of Princes* had maintained secure
popularity through the fifteenth century and into the sixteenth. Besides being copied in numerous manuscripts, some
of them sumptuously executed, it was twice printed before
the middle of the sixteenth century, first in 1494 and then
in 1527, both times by Pynson. Apparently at some time not
long after 1550 a printer was inspired with the idea of again
putting forth the *Fall of Princes* and of procuring from
some available writer or writers of the day "a memorial of
suche Princes, as since the tyme of King Richard the seconde, haue been vnfortunate in the Realme of England," the
"memorial" to be used as an extension of Lydgate's classic
that would give it new and particular appeal to English

readers. It has been argued that this printer was Edward Whitchurch, but Whitchurch's successor, John Wayland, gives us by implication to understand that the idea of extending Lydgate was his own.[7] The plan was never to be carried out according to its original conception. The *Fall of Princes* was put forth by Tottel in 1554 and by Wayland at nearly the same time (1555?). The "memorial" of English princes appeared in Wayland's edition only as a part title at the end of some of the copies, except for its share in a variant general title which has been discovered in one copy.[8] As it was being printed the matter to have been included under the part title had been suppressed, obviously because the authors, in their zeal for commenting upon history, often got upon dangerous political and religious ground.[9] But in 1559, the prohibition having been removed so far as the work in general was concerned, a large part was safely printed and given to a reading public by Thomas Marsh as *A Myrroure for Magistrates,* independent of the *Fall of Princes*. Lydgate's book was never again reprinted until the twentieth century. It was eclipsed by the *Mirror* and by the host of tragical poems that were the *Mirror's* progeny.

Chief among those engaged to write the tragedies of English princes was William Baldwin. We have his own word for it that he did not regard the task lightly, and that he only consented to provide what the printer desired when he was assured of aid from other writers who were brought to have an interest in the project.[10] Baldwin was of serious moral bent. In the later, extended, *Mirror* he is alluded to as "a Minister and a Preacher"; we find that he took orders, probably between 1559 and 1561, became Vicar of Tortington in Sussex, probably in 1559 or 1560, and Rector of St. Michael le Quern in Cheapside in 1561." He had been associated with Whitchurch in the publication of books connected with religious reform in England, and Whitchurch had published in 1547 Baldwin's highly edifying compilation, *A treatise of Morall Phylosophie, contaynyng the sayinges of the wyse,* which continued to be reprinted through the first quarter of the seventeenth century and went into twelve editions. Thus through Baldwin, as the editor and chief author, if not also through Whitchurch, as the printer to whom Baldwin ascribes the original plan, the *Mirror* came honestly by a severe morality that often went beyond the morality of the *Fall of Princes* in insistence upon tragic retribution.

That such dwelling upon tragic justice met a growing taste of the age is indicated by the way in which Lydgate himself had come to be magnified by his printers as a preacher of retribution. The titles of the four editions of his *Fall of Princes* tell the story. At first the work was offered merely as a praiseworthy collection of tragedies. In neither the titles nor the colophons of his editions of 1494 and 1527 does Pynson indicate that it draws a lesson from vice punished duly. He simply advertizes it as "descriuinge" or "fructuously tretinge vpon," in compendious fashion, "the falle of princis princessis & other nobles." But Tottel, in 1554, sees fit to make plain that in Lydgate the reader may find vice as well as Fortune producing tragedy. He advertizes: *A Treatise excellent and compēdious, shewing and declaring, in maner of Tragedye, the falles of sondry most notable Princes and Princesses with other Nobles, through ye muta-*

bilitie and change of vnstedfast Fortune together with their most detestable & wicked vices. And Wayland, in the edition that was to have included the *Mirror* as an extension into English history, offers: *The tragedies, gathered by Ihon Bochas, of all such Princes as fell from theyr estates throughe the mutability of Fortune since the creacion of Adam, vntil his time: wherin may be seen what vices bring menne to destruccion, wyth notable warninges howe the like may be auoyded.* The implication here would seem to be that mutability of Fortune is actually only another name for reward according to deserts, and that men may avoid mutability by virtuous living.

Baldwin will have no mistake about the "chiefest end" of the *Mirror.* In his epistle "To the Nobilitye and all other in office" he ventures an opinion that Justice is the grand virtue. God has established it with his highest name, and God honors kings, together with their delegated authorities, by calling them under his own name, gods. If you who are magistrates are unfaithful to your trusts, your shameful presumption will be grievously punished. How God has plagued evil rulers in other nations you may see in "Boccas" as translated by Lydgate. How he has dealt with some of our own countrymen, your ancestors, "for sundrye vices not yet left," you will see in this book:

> For here as in a loking glas, you shall see (if any vice be in you) howe the like hath bene punished in other heretofore, whereby admonished, I trust it will be a good occasion to move you to the soner amendment. This is the chiefest ende, whye it is set furth, which God graunt it may attayne. . . . And although you shall find in it, that sum haue for their vertue been enuied and murdered, yet cease not you to be vertuous, but do your offices to the vttermost: punish

sinne boldly, both in your selues and other, so shall God (whose lieutenauntes you are) eyther so mayntayne you, that no malice shall preuayle, or if it do, it shal be for your good, and to your eternall glory both here and in heaven, which I beseche God you may covet and attayne. Amen.[12]

It is thus that a conception of rational morality and of tragic justice on earth begins to conquer Contempt of the World and brings as its corollary a conception, not of mutable glory on earth and changeless glory in Heaven, but of eternal glory both here and in Heaven. The book is a "mirror" because princes and others in authority may find in it not so much a reflection of life's lawlessness here below, which will repel their eyes and turn them upward, as a reflection of life's law both here and above, which they may well take to heart. The title given to the edition of 1559 certainly does not forget the mutability of the world, but it puts the retribution of the world first: *A Myrroure for Magistrates. Wherein may be seen by example of other, with howe greuous plages vices are punished: and howe frayle and vnstable worldly prosperitie is founde, even of those, whom Fortune seemeth most highly to fauour. Fælix quem faciunt aliena pericula cautum.* The Latin motto adequately enforces the lesson of retribution.

The form under which the lessons of the *Mirror* are conveyed is substantially that of Boccaccio and Lydgate except in one important respect. Boccaccio conjures up a pageant of ghosts who beg that their misfortunes shall be made known, but who normally allow their stories to be told for them. Lydgate does the same. But the authors of the *Mirror*, representing the unfortunates as eloquent in the moral analysis of their ills, make the ghosts tell their own stories in the form of complaints. There is thus in the *Mirror* a certain dramatic effectiveness which Boccaccio and Lydgate do not reach.

Baldwin tells in his epistle "To the Reader" how, when associates have been found to share his labor, the group gathers for consultation. He himself comes bearing Lydgate's translation of Boccaccio. It is decided that they must find someone to whom the unfortunates can make their moan, and Baldwin is quickly elected the receiver of complaints to "vsurpe Bochas rowme." The company opens "suche bookes of Chronicles as we had there present." Then George Ferrers begins the discussion. He marvels that Boccaccio and Lydgate forgot so many miserable princes of Britain and thinks that it would even be a good work "to searche & dyscourse oure whole storye from the fyrst beginning of the inhabitynge of the yle." But that cannot be done at the moment. The present labor must begin with the time of Richard II, where Lydgate stopped. So, says Ferrers, planning the first of the *Mirror's* stories as a tragedy of retribution: "I wyll take upon mee the miserable person of syr Robert Tresilian chiefe Iustice of Englande, and of other which suffred with him: therby to warne all of his authorytie and profession, to take heed of wrong Iudgementes, mysconstruyng of lawes, or wrestyng the same to serue the princes turnes, whiche ryghtfullye brought theym to a myserable ende."[13]

The heading of the story is well in accord with Ferrers' intent: *The Fall of Robert Tresilian chiefe Iustice of Englande, and other his felowes, for misconstruyng the lawes, and expounding them to serue the Princes affections.* But in this opening tragedy, as in so many of the eighteen other poetical complaints which, interspersed with prose links, complete the first edition of the *Mirror,* a philosophy in contempt of the world of action comes up from the past to offset a philosophy that would sift virtuous from evil worldly action and condemn only the evil action. Tresilian, clearly enough, is made to realize that he fell not because any great man may fall, but because he was a guilty great man. Yet he is also made to declare that riches and promotion "be vaine thynges and vnsure"; wherefore:

> Esteme not worldly hyre, thynke there is a treasure
> More worth than golde or stone a thousande tymes in valure
> Reposed for all suche as righteousnes ensue,
> Whereof you cannot fayle, the promys made is true.[14]

Of the nineteen stories in the *Mirror* of 1559 (the tragedies of Duke Humphrey and his wife listed in the table of contents are not included here and appear for the first time in 1578) a good majority may be said to be primarily tragedies of retribution for sin or fault. A few stories discover and moralize upon sin or fault in such mild fashion as to leave their tragedies mainly to another way of presentation. Only three, the last three stories of the collection, are, properly speaking, not tragedies of retribution at all. It does not appear that the different tragic philosophies expressed by the *Mirror* of 1559 are ascribable to different theories consistently maintained among its contributors; nor does it appear that its tragic philosophies are not at times warped by political considerations. But it seems certain that Baldwin did more of the writing for this edition than any other author and that, though the extent of his work cannot be determined definitely, he was prone to moralize tragedy as just desert. The story of Clarence, however, which is one of those most certainly his, is the tragedy of a man wholly innocent.[15]

The vices by which men fall in these stories of the original *Mirror* are plainly and not subtly analyzed. Mowbray, who was banished by Richard II "and dyed miserably in exyle," was guilty of treachery, pride, and envy. Tragic justice was sure:

> See Baldwin see, the salarye of synne,
> Marke with what meede vile vyces are rewarded.
> Through pryde and envy I lose both kyth and kynne.[16]

Richard himself, whose fall is recorded in the next tragedy, was a king who ruled all by lust and made little of justice, right, or law. Princes, take warning from what happened to him; curb your vices and do not trust flatterers. James I of Scotland deserved the wrath of God for forswearing himself. The Duke of Suffolk, who caused the death of the good Duke Humphrey, was worthy of destruction, and his ghost considers that vice and good fortune are not natural companions:

> Good hap with vices can not long agree,
>   Which bring best fortunes to the basest fall,
>   And happiest hap to enuy to bee thrall.[17]

What we may call tragic faults, with some attempt at distinction from tragic vices, are confessed freely by complaining ghosts, sometimes along with their sins. The younger Mortimer was killed because he rashly despised the naked Irish as fighters, and the Earl of Warwick had too much boldness to avoid mishap. But the fault most often dwelt upon is that of ambition or aspiration. On one side this failing may go so far as to entail sins with which aspiration seeks to further itself, and on the other it seems to be little more than that embracement of the world's activity or that climbing upon Fortune's wheel of which Boccaccio and other medieval writers had been wont to show the folly. The younger Mortimer in the second tragedy of the collection sees Fortune and sin, ambition and vice, as allied, or even merged, causes of calamity for the other Mortimer:

> In whom dame Fortune fully shewed her kynde,
> For whom shee heaves shee hurleth downe as fast:
> If men to cum would learne by other past,
> This cosen of myne myght cause them set asyde,
> High clymyng, brybyng, murdring, lust, and pryde.[18]

It may be difficult to say just where and how the passion for climbing upon the ladder of the world's material rewards ceases to be merely common folly, according to ascetic interpretation, and becomes an unbalanced particular appetite,— a fault in character akin to vice, according to a more worldly rationalistic interpretation,—but we find the *Mirror* frequently and quite naturally making the change.

Thus Fortune is more and more plainly made to surrender the mystery of her ways and to work according to laws which men may analyze and understand. Thomas of Woodstock, Duke of Gloucester and uncle of King Richard II, was unlawfully murdered. Fortune raised him and Fortune lowered him at her will; she put him upon a scaffold, which she made ever higher and more flimsy until he was like "one on a stage attendyng a playe," unconscious of his frail support until the timber collapsed. Yet, unlawfully murdered though he was, we may understand his tragedy as a result of his excessively aspiring character, which actually led to his "mating" of the king when he called a parliament without royal authority. Here is not Fortune at work, but a willful fault in Gloucester, for it does not fit a subject to have his own way. Owen Glendower, too, was one of Fortune's "owne whelpes." Yet we must remember his tragic faults. He was open to the seduction of false prophecies, and at the end of his complaint he denies that external fate was the cause of his tragedy:

> Byd Princes flye Colprophetes lying byll:
> And not presume to clime aboue their states,
> For they bee faultes that foyle men, not their fates.[19]

These faults that foil men, not their fates, are a concern of other stories in Baldwin's original collection that talk of Fortune with no less restraint because they do recognize characteristic faults.[20]

Mowbray, who attributes his tragedy primarily to the sins of treachery, pride, and envy, makes a notable delimitation of Fortune that may be found, assumed or expressed, elsewhere in the *Mirror* of 1559:

> I blame not Fortune though she dyd her parte,
> And true it is she can doo lytell harme,
> She gydeth goods, she hampreth not the harte.[21]

The idea that Fortune has control over the material rewards of the world but cannot direct the soul's will toward good or evil, is, as we have found, right medieval doctrine even when Fortune is held up as most powerful. But where true ascetic despite for the world might maintain that the soul's will to evil is punished with dramatic effectiveness only in an afterworld, Mowbray obviously holds that it works toward tragedy in this world. Chance or fate operating upon man's surroundings may set the stage for tragedy, but it is the inner man upon his own responsibility who carries the action through to a tragic harm that is not merely loss of goods. A shadow of Shakespearean tragic philosophy has already fallen upon Mowbray.

That shadow has also fallen upon Jack Cade, whose tragedy tells how he, "traiterously rebelling agaynst his Kyng, was for his treasons and cruell doinges wurthely punyshed." The ghost of Cade plunges into deep philosophical water with the very first stanza of his complaint, and it must be granted that he swims well:

> Shal I cal it Fortune or my froward folly
> That lifted me, and layed me downe belowe?
> Or was it courage that me made so Ioly,
> Which of the starres and bodyes grement growe?
> What euer it were this one poynt sure I know,
> Which shal be mete for euery man to marke:
> Our lust and wils our evils chefely warke.

> It may be wel that planetes doe enclyne,
> And our complexions moue our myndes to yll,
> But such is Reason, that they brynge to fine
> No worke, vnayded of our lust and wyl:
> For heauen and earth are subiect both to skyl:
> The skyl of God ruleth al, it is so strong,
> Man may by skyl gyde thinges that to him long.

> Though lust be sturdy and wyl inclined to nought,
> This forst by mixture, that by heavens course,
> Yet through the skyl God hath in Reason wrought
> And geuen man, no lust nor wyl to course
> But may be stayed or swaged of the sourse,
> So that it shal in nothing force the mynde
> To worke our wo, or leaue the proper kynde.[22]

Hence Cade concludes that when we yield to lust and will and attribute that yielding to Fortune, we need to know ourselves better. We should call the blame our own. But even after he has made it plain that not Heaven alone but also the world has a rational order which man may know and by which he may guide himself, and that man is the final author of his own woe whatever inclinations external forces may give him,—even then Cade remembers, and turns his argument toward, a philosophy that would have the world given up entirely. As Boccaccio does in the *De Casibus* when he tells the story of Fortune and Poverty, Cade concludes that the man who follows his guiding reason to such a degree that he "medleth not with any worldes affaires" is the man who is surely safe. The unusual excursion into philosophy taken by the author of Cade's tragedy gets due recognition in the comment of the end link. "By saint Mary," says one of Baldwin's company to the author, "if Iacke were as well learned, as you haue made his oracion, what so euer he was by byrth, I warraunt hym a gentylman by his learnyng."[23]

The last three tragedies of the collection require some consideration by themselves. As has been said, they deal with men who through no specified fault were borne down by calamity. The last tragedy of all is Skelton's *Edward*

IV, acknowledged as his and introduced as worth being accorded a place in the *Mirror.* That, of course, has originally the ascetic Christian moral in all fullness. "What creature is borne to be eternall?" Not even the king in all his pride of place. But the general spirit of monitory morality in which the *Mirror* has been undertaken is strong enough to give Skelton's poem a heading that Skelton himself does not justify: *Howe king Edward through his surfeting and vntemperate life, sodainly died in the midst of his prosperity.* Skelton gives no cause at all for Edward's end except frail mortality.

The other two of these three concluding tragedies are stories of outraged innocence. That of Edward IV's younger brother, the Duke of Clarence, shows Fortune's rigor exercised in pitiful manner upon a man who was murdered:

> Thus drounde I was, yet for no due desert,
> Except the zeale of Iustice be a crime.[24]

The tragedy of Henry VI, which tells how that "vertuous prince was, after many other miseries, cruelly murdered in the Tower of London," likewise offers an innocent sufferer, but not for blind pity and decidedly not to teach any lesson that Fortune works blindly. The ghost of the king is made capable of a disquisition upon the causes of tragedy that for interest can only be compared with the philosophizing of Jack Cade. Henry, like Cade, reasons upon that trinity of fate which Boccaccio and so many other men in the Middle Ages had recognized. Men say that our fate issues from the stars, from Fortune, from God. If, says Henry, we use Fortune as a general term for our fate and make "sterres

U

therof the markes," then we can say that God is behind all
and that our fate is God's will. In any other sense "skath
causers skyes be none."

> Thus of our heavy happes, chiefe causes be but twayne,
> Whereon the rest depende, and vnder put remayne.
> The chiefe the will diuine, called destiny and fate,
> The other sinne, through humours holpe, which god doth
>   highly hate.[25]

So, says Henry, misfortune may be the appointment of God
for the good man's exercise, but it may also be the well-
deserved punishment of vice, and that, of course, is in large
part brought about by the man himself "through humours
holpe." Cade's occupation with the "complexions" and
Henry's with the "humours" are early manifestations of an
Elizabethan compulsion to search for the springs of human
action rationally, a compulsion which grew rapidly and
lent of its force to the development of dramatic tragedy.[26]
The author of Henry's complaint, like the author of Jack
Cade's, gets tribute from his company for philosophizing,
as indeed he well might. He too helps to visualize a world
in which tragedy may come to pass through the conjunction
of fate and deliberate human action.

It is obvious, then, that though the *Mirror* of 1559 inherits
the figure of Fortune from medieval tragical story and frequently talks conventionally of her incomprehensible ways,
it never travels far from a guiding belief in the comprehen-
sibility of tragedy. Again and again its authors return to an
attack upon the tragic mystery, with a persistence that Boccaccio and Lydgate do not have and with far stronger conviction that there is a "salary of sin" paid here upon earth

or that there is a chartable course whereby man's faults bring him down to ruin. The external impulse toward tragedy has its recognition from them. Call it Fortune, the stars, or, more properly, God. But the internal impulse, chiefly the lust and the will (in the sense of carnal appetite) which man may choose to follow or not to follow, has grown for them to be the more effective cause of tragedy. The idea that tragedy is the natural portion of any man in high place, simply because he has climbed upon Fortune's wheel and must meet the downward turn eventually, is still present. The correlative idea that true safety lies in lowly positions and in scorn of ambitious action is also present. But these ideas are now overshadowed by others which will even allow that an ambitious prince, by studying the lessons of tragical stories, may avoid tragedy.

III

The extension of the original *Mirror* began four years later, in 1563. Baldwin, apparently with George Ferrers as his chief lieutenant in the collection and arrangement of material, then added eight new tragedies to the nineteen which already had been published.

Most of the new tragedies discover sins or faults in their subjects, but it happens that the two which are most famous are based upon the philosophy that tragedy merely issues from the world's mutability and is an evil which men may no more avoid than they may avoid death. The first of these is the complaint of Henry, Duke of Buckingham, offered, along with the well-known "Induction," by Thomas Sackville, the ablest of all the writers connected with the *Mirror*.

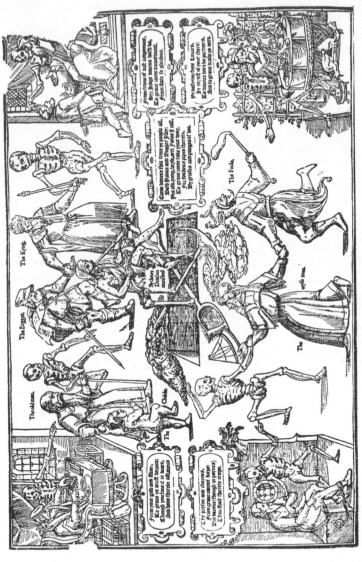

AN ELIZABETHAN DANCE OF DEATH

Sackville does not make Buckingham accuse himself. False Fortune overthrew him when he least suspected danger, and men may gain from the story of his fall the old lesson that all flesh must be humble:

> Euen kinges and kesars byden Fortunes throwes,
> And simple sorte must bear it as it is.[27]

The second is the complaint of Jane Shore, by Thomas Churchyard, which was later to become so popular and to have so much honor in the way of imitation that Churchyard was to find it advisable to claim and establish its authorship. The discovery which Churchyard made was that the prince's mistress could be as moving a subject for tragedy as the prince, and could have a special appeal in her femininity. Boccaccio and Lydgate had given some recognition to famous women as tragic figures, but hitherto the authors of the *Mirror* had been severely content to recognize only men. Whether through sentimentality or through proneness to see the world as merely mutable, Churchyard makes almost nothing of the sin which might be credited to his heroine. Jane Shore, we are given to understand, was married too young and to a commonplace man. It is true that she left her husband for the king, but at the height of her career she did much good by befriending unfortunates and presenting them to her royal lover. She was overthrown by Fortune, and the moral is that persons in low place must not climb, that those need not fear who look not up aloft, and that those who leave the quiet life in the dale below must expect the wind upon the highest hills. A similar sentimentality mixed with true human sympathy is written large

in many of Churchyard's other works. Also, a full capacity
to see mortality in orthodox *De Contemptu Mundi* fashion
is made plain in his early effort called *A Myrrour for Man
Where in he shall see the myserable state of thys worlde,*
published before 1553. Its beginning lives up to the title:

> O man remember, from hence thou shalte passe
> Lyke as thy fygure, ones sene in a glasse
> Doeth vanysshe awaye.

The next extension of the *Mirror,*[28] that by John Higgins
alone, which was first published in 1574 and called *The
First parte of the Mirour for Magistrates, containing the
falles of the first infortunate Princes of this lande: From
the comming of Brute to the incarnation of our sauiour
and redemer Iesu Christe,* is perhaps the most significant
attempt to carry on Baldwin's work. It is even more consistently given to the display of tragic justice than the series of
tragedies gathered by Baldwin.

At some risk of making the unsubtle and rather casual
Higgins into a philosopher, it may be asserted that his address "to the Nobility and all other in office" is a more forceful turning away from Contempt of the World than any
previous theorizing upon tragedy to be found in connection with *De Casibus* storytelling. That Higgins, by his lack
of subtlety, overdoes his reaction against the conception of
irrationality in tragedy and brings tragedy too narrowly
down to earth, will, I think, be apparent. His zeal for rationality is a sign of the increasing temerity which men of
his age were bringing to the solution of the tragic problem.
Baldwin in the introductory address to those in authority

admits that men who are virtuous may yet be brought into misery; but not Higgins.

Baldwin, as we have seen, erects justice as the chief of the virtues and hopes to show that, frequently, persons high in authority are punished by God for injustice and for vices in general. Higgins spreads the four cardinal virtues, the so-called Senecan virtues, before his noble readers and commends all four with the help of classical authority. But the virtue of temperance he glorifies particularly. He is a disciple of the pagan teachers of the golden mean. The world and its ambitions, its stimulations to the seeking of honor, glory, and renown, its covetings and its desires—all these, he would have it, do not lead to tragedy of themselves. Distinctly he implies that to be safe one does not have to resolve that he will never climb upon Fortune's wheel. It is all a matter of the reasonable control which one has over one's climbing. "For to couet without consideration: to passe the measure of his degree: and to lette will run at randon, is the only destruction of all estates. Else howe were it possible, so many learned, politike, wise, renoumed, valiaunt, and victorious personages, might euer haue come to such vtter decaye."[20] How, indeed, Higgins may ask, if he is going to discard the simple answer already made by so many Christians that such is the nature of the world. He offers for our consideration such test cases as Alexander the Great, Caesar, Pompey, Cyrus, and Hannibal. All these "felte the rewarde of their immoderate and insatiable lustes," not merely of any lust for power at all. Alexander desired too many triumphs; Caesar and Pompey might have been satisfied with a due measure of victories and not have fallen to civil dissension. And so on to the conclusion that these princes "had neuer come to suche ende, but for wante of temperance."

Practice the other three virtues of justice, prudence, and fortitude by all means, Higgins charges those in high place, but join with them this noble virtue of temperance and know that then, if grace be added, it is impossible "euer to fall into the unfortunate snares of calamitie or misfortune." Ambition is to be defined not as a desire for honor, rule, dominion, and superiority, but as an "immoderate" desire for these things. "I haue here (right honorable) in this booke (which I am so bold to dedicate to your honors)," says Higgins in a last attempt to vindicate the world of action which princes must perforce enter, "only reproued foly in those which are heedelesse . . . and excesse, in such as suppresse not vnruly affections."[30]

In the sixteen stories which are introduced by this rational analysis of the nature of tragedy, all taken from the legendary history of early Britain beginning with Albanact, son of Brutus, Higgins is by no means averse to using the conventional figure of Fortune. Albanact opens his complaint as "first of all the Princes in this lande" whom "flattering Fortune slyely could beguyle." However, Higgins is at heart committed to the idea of poetic justice. When he comes to the conclusions of his tragedies, he is almost always unwilling to let calamity pass without comment upon its legitimacy. The God of justice is in his Heaven, as Higgins often makes the complaining ghosts remind us. The woes of Humber prove this to be true:

> For God is iust, iniustice will not thriue:
> He plagues the prowde, preserues the good aliue.[31]

Those of Manlius prove that

> If ether vice or vertue we abande:
> We ether are rewarded, as we serue:
> Or else are plaged; as our deedes deserue.[32]

The Seven Deadly Sins can, of course, be brought into this picture of immediate justice in the mortal world. The tragedies of Elstride and Sabrine are causes for comment that pride and lust quickly get their due rewards and that children born in unlawful wedlock seldom thrive. But Higgins is most fond of demonstrating that miseries of men and women spring from lack of due regard for measure,—from the faults of rashness, overweening ambition, and intemperance,—as we should expect from his introductory address to the nobility. Humber, King of the Huns, was not only sinful; he was also rash in not biding upon his own soil and in trying to conquer Britain. Morgan, Forrex, and Porrex were inordinately ambitious. And King Bladud went to the amazing extreme of building wings with which to fly. Against a stiff wind he was even able by practice to rise a little from the ground. But because of his rash folly and his lack of decorum especially ill-becoming in a prince, he fell upon a temple of Apollo and broke his neck. The moral is plain for all to see. We should not climb too high for fear of tumbling down.

The tragedy of fault in which we may see folly working out its own destruction can even become for Higgins the tragedy of excessive and unbalanced virtue with a faint hint of Shakespearean irony in the misdirection of human nobility. The story of King Morindus, as Higgins tells it, is trivial, but it is nevertheless the tragedy of a prince who fell through inordinate courage. The moral carries us back to Higgins' theories concerning the four cardinal virtues:

> Here maist thou see of fortitude the hap,
> Where Prudence, Iustice, Temperaunce hath no place:
> How sodainly we taken are in trap,
> When we despise good vertues to embrace.
> Intemperaunce doth all our deedes deface,
>   And lettes vs heedlesse headlong run so faste,
>   Wee seeke our owne destruction at the last.[33]

While *The First Parte of the Mirour* was being printed in 1574, Higgins added the tragedy of Irenglas, making seventeen tragedies in all.[34] Here he takes occasion to make an unfortunate prince deny the reality of Fortune in a discussion which is no mere moral tag and which is as earnest as similar discussions by Jack Cade and Henry VI in Baldwin's *Mirror*. Irenglas came to his death not in heroic battle, but in a quarrel with a friend which arose from their folly. Some who have fallen talk of themselves as fools of Fortune, says he, but the truth is that

> No fortune is so bad, our selues ne frame:
> There is no chaunce at all hath vs preseru'de:
> There is no fate, whom we haue nede to blame:
> There is no destinie, but is deseru'de:
> No lucke that leaues vs safe, or vnpreseru'de:
>   Let vs not then complayne of Fortunes skill:
>   For all our good, descendes from goddes good will,
>   And of our lewdnes, springeth all our ill.[35]

One feels that this is a fit summary of Higgins' secure faith in a too complete tragic justice.

By this year 1574, which saw Higgins' venture into tragedy based upon the earliest legendary history of Britain, the

Mirror was safely established in popularity, and its destiny, not only as a work which would grow by accretion but also as a work which would have the honor of much imitation, began to be apparent. In 1574 began the long line of those imitations which were never printed in any extended edition of the *Mirror* proper, but which often made able contributions to the *Mirror's* tradition. Usually these were single tragedies, not collections. It will be well to leave them for later consideration and to survey briefly the continued growth of the *Mirror* itself. One may survey thus briefly because, though the *Mirror* acquired new editions and issues until so late as 1620, and though many more tragedies were added to it, the later work tends to show a falling off in vitality. The temptation to monotonous and insincere repetition was in the nature of the *Mirror's* conception.

The next ambitious extension of the *Mirror* was from the pen of Thomas Blenerhasset and was published in 1578 as *The Seconde part of the Mirrour for Magistrates, conteining the falles of the infortunate Princes of this Lande. From the Conquest of Cæsar, vnto the commyng of Duke William the Conquerour.* Higgins planned to continue in his labor, and did continue, but Blenerhasset forestalled him in publication of further legends. Printed as Blenerhasset's work was, in the shop of Richard Webster, and not in that of Thomas Marsh, who had printed all the parts of the *Mirror* written hitherto, it was in truth an imitation poaching upon Marsh's preserves. It was not gathered up with the rest of the *Mirror* until the edition of 1610. Blenerhasset offers twelve tragedies, beginning with the story of Guidericus, who was killed by a thunderbolt as a manifestation of Heaven's vengeance, and ending with the story of King Harold, whose fall showed that even Harold's admirable manhood and good policy could not keep the English crown from William, the rightful heir. Blenerhasset's performance is sadly undistinguished. One feels that Baldwin and his fellows, and Higgins too, are often moved to enthusiasm as they discover meaning in tragedy, but one feels that Blenerhasset engages upon workaday versification. Whether by nature or by cue from Higgins, he makes a large majority of his tragedies show that vice is punished on earth, but he does not see so often as Higgins the fault of intemperance.

In 1587, Henry Marsh, the assign of Thomas Marsh, gathered together his property in the *Mirror* and printed it with a title similar to that of 1559. Many new stories by John Higgins were added to the number already published, and one, the tragedy of Wolsey, by Thomas Churchyard. The moral interests here shown by Higgins are much the same as those shown in his first attempt at supplementing Baldwin's *Mirror*.

The last extension of the *Mirror* came with the publication of the inclusive gathering printed by Felix Kyngston in 1610. To this edition Michael Drayton contributed the tragedy of Lord Cromwell, and Richard Niccols contributed ten tragedies "of such princes especially famous who were exempted in the former Historie," to which he gave an induction and which he called *A Winter Nights Vision*. Niccols also contributed *Englands Eliza,* a long poem having nothing to do with tragedy.

In his induction, Niccols represents himself as walking forth on a winter's day and viewing the dead life of trees and herbage. These teach him that all things on earth are subject to change: the oak teaches that strength passes and the lily that beauty fades. He goes to his bed at night and reads the *Mirror for Magistrates*. There also he finds the truth which the day before has shown him—that beauty, strength, wealth, vain pomp, and all mortal things are subject to Death's dart. The virtuous and the vicious prince are in this alike. So far, we may say, he is a good follower of the oldest *De Casibus* conventions. But, proceeds Niccols, the names of princes are not condemned to death if some writer may be found to keep their memories green. He proposes in his verses to eternize certain princes exempted by the older contributors to the *Mirror*. At midnight, Fame appears to him with her golden trumpet. Then Memory appears, who says that he must be her penman this night and that she will summon the exempted heroes to tell their stories.

Such sadness at the mortality of beauty and greatness and such clinging to fame as at least one of the earthly things which may escape death, is far removed from the spirit of Boccaccio in his *De Casibus,* even though Boccaccio does permit himself to defend Alcibiades for desiring honor and glory. Boccaccio apologizes when he magnifies fame, but Niccols and many others of his age do not. The mutability of Niccols is the mutability of Spenser in his *Complaints* and of Shakespeare in his *Sonnets,* though he falls far short of their ability to make us feel irretrievable loss in the decay of beauty and greatness. It is, in short, a mutability of the later, thoroughly established, Renaissance. Niccols' glori-

fication of fame, especially his assertion that it can have
deathless embodiment in poetry, follows that polite convention which Spenser took from the Pléiade and helped to
popularize in *The Ruines of Time:*

> But fame with golden wings aloft doth flie,
> Aboue the reach of ruinous decay.
> . . . .
>
> Then who so will with vertuous deeds assay
> To mount to heauen, on *Pegasus* must ride,
> And with sweete Poets verse be glorifide.

The ways in which Niccols finds his princes worthy of
deathless remembrance are widely tolerant. The tragedy of
King Arthur, with which he opens his collection, is made
to teach us to dare the earning of fame through the cultivation of eminent virtues. No matter how insecure the proud-
est states of man may be, names as glorified as Arthur's are
always secure. But princes have acquired the right to commemoration in tragedy through other means than the practice of Arthurian virtues. Many have done so by being the
undeserving subjects of excessive cruelty, which fate and
their fellows have exercised upon them. Edmund Ironside
and Alfred, his brother, were betrayed and killed in horrible ways, Alfred with torture, which Niccols is glad to
describe at length. King Edward II, not especially blame-
worthy, was also tormented to death. King Edward V and
his brother, the two young princes, were cruelly smothered
by Forrest and Dighton. In his taste for horrors such as
these and in his proneness to see a cruel fate overwhelm
mankind, Niccols is a sort of Webster among writers of seventeenth-century nondramatic tragedy. He can even pity

King John, who, though he killed Prince Arthur, has had
far too much scandal talked about him and must be allowed
to attribute his fall to his "false subjects vndeserued hate."
Yet Niccols is able to see King Richard III as one who suffered just punishment:

> Th' ambitious Prince, whose hand vniustly gripes
> Anothers right to make himselfe a King,
> Suffers the smart of many Furies stripes:
> Th' internall worme his conscience still doth sting,
> His soule t' a fearful iudgement death doth bring.[36]

It is only infrequently that he views tragedy thus.

Under the hand of Niccols, *De Casibus* tragedy forgets
the retributive justice of Baldwin and of Higgins, except
for occasional echoes, and tends to turn back toward irrational mutability, but it shows almost nothing of ascetic
Christian Contempt of the World. It participates in the
worldliness of its age, though not in the worldliness of the
moralist who would reduce tragedy completely to rational
comprehension. Niccols, if we are to take this work of his
seriously, is one who would tell us not that man should
refrain from attaching himself to the insecure things of
earth, but that since man actually is attached to them, their
mutability and decay are matters to arouse melancholy.

Chapter VIII

THE PROGENY OF THE "MIRROR"

THE PROGENY of the *Mirror for Magistrates*—that is, those independent poems which follow the general medieval tradition of tragical storytelling, but which have some particular, often acknowledged, inspiration from Baldwin and his fellows[1]—also bear witness that the tragedy of mundane retribution, not the tragedy of mundane irrationality, had the stronger power of perpetuation and growth in Elizabethan England. Discussions or exemplifications of tragic justice in numerous writings other than close imitations of the *Mirror* help still further to demonstrate how vital for the age was the question of such retribution. It was a time when the marvelous operation of God's wrath and the inescapable operation of God's laws against wrongdoing, as evidenced in worldly event, were often brought to men's attention in the ballads sung on the streets and in the books sold on the stalls, to say nothing of the sermons preached in the churches.

In 1574, the year in which John Higgins published his extension of the *Mirror* called the *First Parte,* Richard Robinson put forth the first separate collection of tragical falls imitating the manner of the *Mirror.* It is notable as a gathering of tragical stories dealing entirely with famous unfortunates justly punished. The title avows the moral purpose of the book in the plainest terms: *The rewarde of Wickednesse Discoursing the sundrye monstrous abuses of wicked and vngodlye worldelinges: in such sort set downe*

*and written as the same haue beene dyuersely practised in
the persones of Popes, Harlots, Proude Princes, Tyrauntes,
Romish Byshoppes, and others. With a liuely description
of their seuerall falles and finall destruction. Verye profitable for all sorte of estates to reade and looke vpon.* Robinson, as he says himself, was servant in household to the Earl
of Shrewsbury, and helped to keep watch over Mary, Queen
of Scots, when as a prisoner she was entrusted to his lord's
hands. He offers these tragedies as a fruit of his vigils. That
the fall of the unfortunate queen turned his thoughts toward such subjects, he does not say.

Robinson's literary light is of the palest, a fact for which
he apologizes in conventional but perhaps quite honest
fashion. He feigns that on a night in dreary December Morpheus leads him to Pluto's kingdom, and his induction
thereby invites comparison with the inductions of Sackville
and Higgins in the *Mirror.* The tragedies which follow,
as Morpheus and Robinson make a Dantesque pilgrimage
through Hell, are told by a medley of guilty souls, including, among others, Helen, Medea, Tantalus, Tarquin, Pope
Alexander VI, and Pope Joan. Robinson's taste for the tortures which may properly be assigned to the vicious after
death makes him somewhat neglectful of the operations of
justice in mortal life, but that he believes in such justice is
obvious enough. Tantalus, for example, whose complaint is
startling for its well-documented sermon upon sin, confession, and repentance taken out of the Christian Fathers, was
plagued by the gods for a cause which "the Poets haue mis-
tolde." Tragedy came to him, not for slaying his son Pelops
and serving him as meat to the gods, but for oppressing the

X

poor people of his country through extortion and covetousness. Thus Tantalus is converted into a practicer of one of
the Seven Deadly Sins and into a mirror for magistrates.
His ghost begs that those in authority may be made to take
good heed by his example not to oppress the poor and not
to earn their subjects' hate. Otherwise, death will come and
reward them full well. Robinson is especially conscientious
in description of tragic rewards gained by the sins of popery,
but even here, where his heart seems to be most engaged, he
has small capacity for anything but ineptitude. He simply
serves in his humble way as a sign of the fervor which the
conception of tragic justice was beginning to arouse.

There is but one other imitation of the *Mirror* in the form
of an independent collection of tragical poems with a framework specially devised.[2] It is Anthony Munday's *The Mirrour of Mutabilitie, or Principall part of the Mirrour for
Magistrates. Describing the fall of diuers famous Princes,
and other memorable Personages. Selected out of the sacred
Scriptures,* which was published five years after *The Rewarde of Wickednesse,* in 1579. Munday's collection is as
completely given over to the punishment of evil as Robinson's, and its bearing upon tragedy is greater because the
punishment presented is thoroughly of this world. In literary craftsmanship Munday has the advantage of Robinson, but his work will not bear comparison with the best
in the *Mirror.* His trading upon the title of the *Mirror* and
his following of the *Mirror* are quite different from Blenerhasset's. Blenerhasset, it is to be remembered, published his
Seconde Part of the Mirrour the year before Munday published this *Principall Part.* Blenerhasset's work, though it

was not issued by the rightful printer of the *Mirror*, was a true extension of the book and was eventually canonized. Munday's was an imitation not at all adapted for attachment to the *Mirror*. Munday was an obsequious timeserver, as is proved by his betrayal to death of the Catholics who had befriended him and provided his education.[3] It happens that a good deal of his smallness and deviousness of character appears in the rather irrelevant story of his journey to Rome told in "The Epistle Dedicatory" of *The Mirrour of Mutabilitie*.

The fact that Munday shows himself a timeserver and a hypocrite adds to the significance of his *Mirrour* as an indication of popular taste. He is out to give his readers the most schematic proof that calamity is always true reward for wrongdoing, and the supposition is that he thinks they will like it. First he follows the obvious device of telling one tragedy for each of the Seven Deadly Sins, prefacing each tale with an adornment of monitory verses whose initial letters spell the sin which leads to tragedy. In King Nebuchadnezzar the sin is pride; in King Herod, envy; in King Pharaoh, wrath; in King David, lechery; in Dives, gluttony; in Judas, avarice; in Jonah, sloth. The sins have much of the conventional medieval flavor, but as a proud child of the new learning Munday makes an appeal to Marcus Tullius Cicero, "flourishing floure of all Eloquence," as the great authority upon their effects. It was from Cicero, who exhorts so well "to auoyd the vices which are incident to the weakned minde," that he got his inspiration. He says nothing about the writers of the Church. Thus the avoidance of the Seven Deadly Sins, primarily not because they ruin man's soul but because they ruin his career on earth, becomes a worldly-wise rule of life. As Munday says in the introduction to the second part of his book, he compacts with the sins "their due obtayned hire."

In the second part of his book, Munday gives eleven miscellaneous examples of tragedy incurred through sin, or fault, or both. The causes of tragedy range from murder and cruelty to incontinency and rashness. The result is a curious mixture of injunctions not to sin and injunctions to be cautious.

But *The Mirrour of Mutabilitie* is most remarkable because here for the first time an author of a collection of *De Casibus* tragedies so pointedly neglects the figure of Fortune that he almost leaves Fortune out of account. As we have found, the authors of the *Mirror for Magistrates* are glad to minimize or deny Fortune's power, but they are no less willing to keep her name alive, if only for the purpose of poetic adornment. In *The Mirrour of Mutabilitie* one will read far before he finds any mention of Fortune at all.[4] Justice (or God) usually takes her place, as in the concluding stanza of the complaint of Adonijah, son of David, who brought tragedy upon himself by ravishing his sister:

> Now Lordings see my proud presumpteous hart,
> What liew I gaynd in recompence for all:
> See Justice scornd at my vnlawfull part,
> And from the top did headlong make me fall.
> I which was Sonne vnto a famous King:
> By pamperd pride my ruin great did bring.[5]

Here is the headlong fall from the height, but not from the height of Fortune's wheel. Here is fatal scorn of Justice, not of Fortune. The famous prince falls through pride, not because pride makes man most subject to Fortune, but because pride tempts man into unlawful action, which is justly punished. It is the complete metamorphosis of that tragic philosophy which contemns the world as amoral into that which embraces it as moral.

One may well ask, then, what meaning the "mutability" of his title can have for Munday. Certainly it has not the older meaning of irrational change. It, too, has gone through a metamorphosis. For an example of Munday's "mutability" let us take the complaint of King Ptolemy Philometor. Ptolemy murdered his son-in-law and gained a kingdom to add to his own. Thus he won delight "as braue as beaten Golde," to which he had long looked forward. But behold how "this pomp to short a time did last"—not, we notice, because pomp is by nature hollow, but because here it was won through evil. Ptolemy died in grievous case within three days after his triumph, and the moral is not that all Ptolemies have insecure thrones, but that this Ptolemy chose a tragic course of action and reaped the whirlwind from that which he had sowed:

> See heere the wight whose folly made him fall:
> In seeking that which did return his thrall.[6]

In short, mutability has turned into a dramatic progress from cause to effect.

II

The span of five years (1574–1579) which produced the collections of Robinson and Munday also produced the first poems written as single complaints which can with certainty be called imitations of the tragedies in Baldwin's *Mirror for Magistrates*. In the previous years following the publication of the *Mirror* a Robert Sempill, about whom little is known, had been writing ballads upon recent events in Scottish history and getting them printed in the north. Some of these, printed in the late 1560's and early 1570's, are tragical, but they were probably not inspired by Baldwin's collection. Three of the ballads ascribed to Sempill conjure up the ghosts of their tragic subjects. In *Ane Tragedie, in forme of ane Diallog betwix Honour, Gude Fame, and the Authour heirof in ane trance* (1570), James, Earl of Murray, Regent of Scotland, appears to the author sorely wounded, but does not tell his own story. In *The Testament and Tragedie of vmquhile King Henrie Stewart of gude memorie* (1567), and in *The Bischoppis lyfe and testament* (1571), the dead return to review their falls much as the ghost tells his story in Lyndsay's tragedy of Cardinal Beaton.[7] Sempill can discern something of justice in the tragedies which he celebrates, but his mind dwells for the most part on the mutability of a disorderly world, which is

> Lyke to ane Schip that saillis on the seis
> Tost with winds & wallis Innauigabill.[8]

Though Sempill does not seem to have acquaintance with Baldwin's *Mirror,* he shows acquaintance with the "morall buke, the Fall of Princes," written by "the worthie Bocas."[9]

Thomas Churchyard, however, the contributor of the tragedy of Shore's wife to the *Mirror* of 1563, both knew Baldwin well and was glad to acknowledge inspiration from the *Mirror* when he published, in 1575, a tragical poem independently. In *The Firste Parte of Churchyardes Chippes,* which is a medley of "fayned fancie," "dollfull discourse," and what not, he includes *Syr Symon Burleis Tragedie, who liued in the xi. yeer of King Richard the second.* Just as Churchyard inaugurates a style of feminine tragedy in his story of Shore's wife, so he inaugurates here a popular style of opening for those single poems which frankly imitate the tragedies of the *Mirror.* "O Baldwin! why have I been neglected; why should not my tragedy also be told?" asks the ghost, in effect. Burley appeals to Baldwin in vain; he reproachfully leaves that famous worthy sitting in a bower of laurel leaves and procures Churchyard as recorder of his sorrowful life. What Churchyard records is in all ways a tragedy contemning the world and in no way a tragedy of justice. Burley was true both to God and to the crown, and his fall shows that no surety grows out of anything that is here on earth possessed. Churchyard, as we have already seen, inclines to be a moralist of the older order when he is not merely a sentimentalist.

Not so Ulpian Fulwell, who also imitated the *Mirror's* tragic manner in 1575. Into *The Flower of Fame. Containing the bright Renowne, & moste fortunate raigne of King Henry the viii,* which is a heterogeneous collection of historical matters, Fulwell introduces two brief complaints, the first "of King James of Scotlande, who was slayne at Scottish Fielde, Anno 1513," and the second "of King James; Sonne vnto King James before mentioned." The first complaint particularly is a tragedy of just deserts, of "guerdon due." King James broke his sacred vow. Fulwell introduces this tragedy by announcing that it follows the style of the *Mirror,* and he makes the king allude to the *Mirror's* growing popularity:

> Why have not I a place among them left,
> Whose fall each tong with dayly talke revyves?[10]

Even more plainly not of the older order is George Whetstone as he appears in *The Rocke of Regard,* published in the following year. This, too, is a collection of miscellaneous pieces including matter which owes something to the *Mirror.* The spirit of the book in general, while not averse to "honest pleasure" and "wanton devises," is that of the sure and, shall we say, youthful believer in tragic justice. It advertizes, among other things, "the wretched end of wanton and dissolute liuing" and "the miseries that followe dicing ... with diuers other morall, natural & tragical discourses."[11] The first of those poems here included which show the wretched end of sin is *The disordered life of Bianca Maria, Countesse of Celaunt, in forme of her complainte, supposed at the houre of her beheading for procuring the murder of Ardissino Valperga, Earle of Massino.* It tells a story which appears in Bandello. Although this is the complaint of a living unfortunate, it seems quite definitely to have taken character from the ghostly complaints of the *Mirror.*

Bianca records first her rise to "weare dame Fortunes crowne" and then her "filthie fall." She begins with words which apparently ask comparison for her story with the famous stories of the *Mirror* and their kind:

> Among their falles, by wanton fate untwist,
> Let my lewde hap remembred be I pray.[12]

But Whetstone's writing of Dame Fortune and wanton
fate is merely conventional adornment. In his address "to all
the young Gentlemen of England" he expresses the pious
hope that "who so noteth . . . the issue of the Countesse
of Zelants hate, may happely feare to execute a strumpets
bloudie revenge," and the story is in fact constructed to bear
the countess' moral at its conclusion: the moral that

> due desert, by lawe and justice lead,
> Did dome my misse with losse of my poore head.[13]

It is Whetstone's distinction to have discovered and used for
De Casibus tragedy an exotic story of lust, ambition, and revenge with all the motions of intrigue in the best Italian
style, a story of such sort as was to be enormously popular
upon the later Elizabethan stage. The circumstantial detail
which he introduces into the speeches incident to the action
has much of the later dramatic color.

Cressids Complaint, which immediately follows that of
the murderous countess in *The Rocke of Regard,* and which
is less plainly marked by the *Mirror's* style, has equal recognition of tragic retribution. As she is about to die, the leprous
Cressid, reduced to poverty and misery, offers a warning to
others tempted as she was:

> But (ah!) in vaine, I frame excuse by fate,
> When due desart doth worke my overthrowe;
> Ne was I first by fortune stauld in state,
> My roome by byrth did high renoune bestow,
> Though wicked life hath wrapt me now in woe:
> A warning faire, a myrour full of mone,
> For gadding gyrles a bone to gnaw upon.[14]

For such a picture of Cressida sunk into the mire of prosti-
tution and smitten with leprosy after her faithless desertion
of Troilus, Robert Henryson is, of course, mainly responsible. His well-known continuation of Chaucer's *Troilus* in
the *Testament of Creseyde* was printed in Thynne's 1532
edition of Chaucer and was often taken to be Chaucer's
own work. But a host of Elizabethan writers contributed
to the debasement and punishment of that Cressida whom
Chaucer had left little reproached and wholly unpunished.
The story of Troilus and Cressida as it was extended, retold,
or alluded to between Chaucer and Shakespeare is a record
of that increasing satisfaction in the discovery of mundane
justice which turned *De Casibus* tragedy more and more
away from Contempt of the World. Henryson had been
severe with Cressida and had represented her as stricken
down in the midst of her folly by inexorable retribution,
but he had still been capable of sympathy for her, light-o'-
love though she was. Later and cruder moralists blackened
her character quite without sympathy in their willingness
to make her story prove that vice brings plagues and that
virtue brings happy ends. Thus the name of Cressida became a byword.[15] Whetstone in *Cressids Complaint* is simply going with the tide.

In 1579, Churchyard returned again to *De Casibus* tragedy in his *A General Rehearsall of Warres*, also known by
its running title of *Churchyardes Choise*. To a military pot-
pourri of "sieges, battailes, skirmiches, and encounters," he
adds, as he advertizes in his title, "some Tragedies and Epi-
taphes"; frankly speaking, they are "as many as was necessarie for the firste booke." In one of these added poems,

called *A Pitefull complaint, in maner of a Tragedie, of Seignior Anthonio dell Dondaldoes wife, somtyme in the duke of Florences Courte,* he turns like Whetstone to the Italian scene and makes a lustful and unfaithful woman bemoan her fate. In another, called *A heauie matter of a Englishe gentleman and a gentlewoman, in maner of a Tragedie,* he makes a gentleman whose life has led him to prison curse the Fortune that has turned his game to grief. Both poems have the indefiniteness and the slack sentimentality of the author at his worst. Each is a complaint by a subject to whom death has not yet given relief from misery. A ghostly complaint of better order is *A Pirates Tragedie, beyng a gentleman of a verie good house.* Here even the pitying Churchyard, who is usually ready to ascribe misfortune to the wanton way of the world, records a tale of tragic justice as a stern warning to evildoers. He would "shewe the miserable life of a Rouer, whose wretched desire of other mens goodes brings open shame and a violente death." The shade of the gentleman who came of such a good house, yet fell to piracy, appears to Churchyard in the best *Mirror* tradition and tells the story of his buccaneering in order to keep the necks of other men from the hemp.[16]

Such tragic matter as this and such treatment as Churchyard gives it can only pass as unheroic when not "domestic." Churchyard's poetic concern with the private woes of people little known, or unknown, to fame and his attempt to tell their stories in the manner which he had learned as a contributor to Baldwin's *Mirror* represent a breaking down in *De Casibus* tragedy of its decorum as falls of princes. Even in the story of Shore's wife Churchyard develops the domestic touch. If he does not usually train with the new order of writers who would see the operation of dramatic justice in tragedy, he at least belongs to a new order who would expand tragic subject-matter to include the misfortunes of common humanity. He certainly does not scorn, as Giles Fletcher (the elder) does later,

> To write of women, and of womens falles,
> Who are too light, for to be fortunes balles.[17]

Immediately after the half-decade, ending in 1579, which produced so many variations in the manner of *De Casibus* tragedy, close imitation of the *Mirror* seems to have ceased for several years. The *Mirror* itself, which had had no less than eight extensions or refurbishings, counting Blenerhasset's, from 1571 to 1578, was allowed to stand from 1578 to 1587 without a new edition. But the question of the justice which may be manifested in those calamities of earth that had often been ascribed to unjust Fortune was by no means put aside.

In 1580, Anthony Munday again capitalized the idea of mundane punishment for sin and did what he could, in an obviously hasty compilation, to make such retribution vivid, this time not in tragical stories of outstanding figures from the past, but in news stories of ordinary human beings and of marvelous happenings from the present. The result was a journeyman's labor in prose called *A View of sundry Examples. Reporting many straunge murthers, sundry persons periured, Signes and tokens of Gods anger towards vs.* This makes free with a kind of thing that was stock in trade for the ballad-maker of the day. It deals with earthquakes, blaz-

THE MURDER OF ARDEN OF FEVERSHAM

From the *Complaint and Lamentation of Mistresse Arden*, a ballad.

ing stars, and other portents; with monstrous children who have two heads or speak prophetically at the moment of birth; and with celebrated murderers. Here are reminders that many men and many cities have fallen for sin aforetime and that God is serving notice of fresh wrath. Fortune is disregarded. Sodom and Gomorrah, Jerusalem, Nineveh, and other once fair but now ruined cities, concludes Munday, should remain in our memories to make us turn from evil. The many examples of murder and the just reward for murder which the book contains seldom take more than the barest narrative form, but they are murder tragedies in the germ, and dramatists were later to use exactly such material in plays like *Arden of Feversham, A Warning for Faire Women,* and *A Yorkshire Tragedy.* Also, this citing of sundry examples to prove God's watchful justice on earth was to be done later in Thomas Beard's *The Theatre of Gods Judgements* (1597), and in John Reynolds' *The Triumphs of Gods Revenge, Against the crying, and execrable Sinne of Murther* (1621), prose collections much more solid and less journalistic than Munday's and much more given to moral philosophy. In such writing as this the stern Jehovah has eclipsed the God of mercy magnified in the early moral plays. Thomas Beard protests: "The greatest part of men go clean contrary [to God's commandments], they dream vpon mercie, mercy, & neuer thinke vpō iustice & iudgement."[18]

Though Munday himself did not trade upon the *Mirror* in such exemplification of God's wrath taken from the run of the day's news, the possibility of so doing was inviting. In 1584 the bookseller Thomas Hacket, for example, put forth an anonymous pamphlet in prose called *A most rare and wonderful Tragedy of all other in our age most admirable, of the life and death of a miserable usurer of Fraunce, which hanged himselfe in Hell streete, betweene the Cittie of Niuers in Fraunce and S. Peter le Moustier, on theyr Christmas-eue last past. A woorthy warning for all couetous Vsurers and miserable Misers, how to eschewe the vile vice of Auarice.* That such a tragedy, too, is a "mirror" the author announces in a preface: "Here haste thou (Gentle Reader) a Tragedie for the rarenesse there of no lesse pleasaunte then for the terror Tragicall, which may be rightly named, *A Mirror for Misers,* or A glasse for greedy Gatherers, in which if thou reade with iudgment, thou shall perceiue, howe horrible a vice Auarice is.... I haue deliuered thee the reporte thereof as it was in French."[19] But the "report" has nothing of the form of the *Mirror for Magistrates.* In spite of the high moral tone of its title it descends to gross pleasantry and is in all ways merely an ephemeral catchpenny production.

A far more respectable "mirror" exploiting the popular taste for tragic justice at this time when the closer imitation of Baldwin's tragedies had temporarily ceased is Robert Greene's *The Myrrour of Modestie, Wherein appeareth as in a perfect Glasse howe the Lorde deliuereth the innocent from all imminent perils, and plagueth the bloudthirstie hypocrites with deserued punishments,* which was also published in 1584. The story is that of Susanna penned out in prose "more largelie then it is written among the Apocripha."

III

It was in the late 1580's and the early 1590's that tragedy began to take full shape as popular drama upon the English public stage, and it is likely that the resounding success with the playgoers which Marlowe and Kyd taught dramatic tragedy to achieve helped to stimulate a new and more sophisticated fashion for imitation of the *Mirror*. During the last decade of the sixteenth century the literary ability which was drawn into the writing of single tragical poems was sometimes of high order, but, as will duly appear, literary sophistication did not always bring increase in tragic perception.

This revived imitation of the *Mirror's* form of tragedy began with two writers of widely different abilities.[20] In 1592, Samuel Daniel first published *The Complaint of Rosamond,* appended to his *Delia,* and in the same year William Wyrley published in his *The True Use of Armorie* two tragical complaints by the ghosts of a Sir John Chandos and a Sir John de Gralhy. Of Wyrley's tragical poems little need be said except that they are dull, arising as they do from the

author's interest in the election of his two knights to the
Order of the Garter at its founding by Edward III, rather
than from interest in tragedy as tragedy. They acknowledge
their imitation of the *Mirror,* whose authors have won
"eternal praise," and talk of the fickleness of Fortune in
banal fashion. But of Daniel's *Rosamond* something more
must be said. It demonstrates that its author had power to
perceive dramatically the progress which imperfect humanity can make toward catastrophe. Also, it shows a certain
delicacy and ease of touch that is unusual in the tradition
of *De Casibus* tragedy. Daniel was soon to turn to the writing of dramatic tragedy, taking his stand upon the side of
those who despised the rough vitality of the public stage
and sought more artificial excellence in pseudoclassical exercises. As it happened, his French-Senecan play *Cleopatra*
was joined in publication with *Delia and Rosamond Aug-
mented* in 1594.

Daniel ushers before the reader the poor afflicted ghost
of Rosamond, the mistress of Henry II. There is at first a
touch of elegant sentimental trifling. Rosamond comes to
declare that her soul cannot obtain transport to its sweet
Elysian rest except by the waftage of pitying sighs from lovers on earth. Shore's wife, she complains, has aroused such
pity that the woman even passes for a saint—pity which
could more justly be given to herself. Perhaps Daniel's Delia
will deign to read this story of poor Rosamond and offer up
her sighs along with those of other readers. But with this
gallant linking of Rosamond and his Delia out of the way,
Daniel lifts the story to a plane which is not sentimental,
even though it is highly sympathetic. Arresting for one who

would look from tragical narrative to tragical drama is
the balance of opposing forces within the character of Rosamond by which Daniel contrives a truly dramatic suspense.
The hesitation and the sore inner conflict incident to Rosamond's yielding to Henry are made the most of: she stood
"ballanc'd equally precize" till her frailty weighed her down
to sin. That which followed—the torture of conscience
joined with the torture of detestation for the royal lover, the
discovery by the queen, and the poisoning of Rosamond—
is represented as a chain of events in which shame followed
sin, and ruin was duly found.

Was Rosamond, then, responsible for her tragedy? The
balance of power which Daniel constructs for fate and character is even more arresting than the balance of opposing
forces which he erects within the self of Rosamond. Upon
the richly wrought casket which Henry gave to Rosamond
the day before she yielded to his wooing she saw prefigura-
tion of her destiny in a representation of the afflictions of Io,
beloved of Jove. One would think that such presage of her
harms and her fall might have helped her to avoid tragedy.

> But Fate is not preuented, though foreknowne.
> For that must hap, decreed by heauenly powers,
> Who worke our fall, yet make the fault still ours.
>
> Witnesse the world, wherein is nothing rifer
> Then miseries vnken'd before they come:
> Who can the Characters of chaunce decipher,
> Written in cloudes of our concealed dome?
> Which though perhaps haue beene reueal'd to some,
>   Yet that so doubtfull (as successe did proue them)
>   That men must know they haue the Heau'ns aboue
>   them.[21]

Y

So Rosamond was responsible for her tragedy, though fate, dimly revealed, also played its part in the action. Fate worked her fall, yet made the fault still hers. Thus *De Casibus* tragedy is schooled to talk a subtle language of destiny which approaches quite nearly to that employed by some of the greatest dramatic tragedians. There is here none of the cruder dichotomy of external compulsion and internal will. External fate and internal urge seem to flow into each other, and almost to operate as one force, in a tragic scheme where our falls are, it is true, worked from without, but only by subscription of our responsible selves.

The Complaint of Rosamond laid hold upon the imagination of its day and was several times republished. What Churchyard had begun in his tragedy of Shore's wife it consolidated and bettered, and it raised emulation. In 1593, the year following its first printing, Anthony Chute made Churchyard's heroine narrate her misfortunes once more in *Beawtie dishonoured written vnder the Title of Shores Wife*. Also in 1593, Thomas Lodge annexed *The Tragicall Complaynt of Elstred* to his *Phillis,* as Daniel had annexed *Rosamond* to *Delia;* and Churchyard, thinking it was high time to revive his credit as the founder of this fashion, refurbished his *Shores Wife* and included it in *Churchyards Challenge,* along with certain other tragical poems,[22] "because Rosimond is so excellently sette forth" and because doubters of his authorship had worried him. In 1594, Shakespeare himself, in *Lucrece,* told a tragedy in poetic narrative which owes something to *Rosamond,*[23] though it is not, like these others, autobiographic and closely imitative of the *Mirror's* style. Also in 1594, Michael Drayton published his *Matilda. The faire and chaste Daughter of the Lord Robert Fitzwater,* offering Matilda as the virtuous resister of King John, worthy for her tragic end to be remembered with Lucrece and far more worthy of remembrance than Rosamond, Shore's wife, and Elstred, who had allowed themselves to be overcome by lustful importunity.

Where a temptation to sentimentality is yielded to in such stories as these—where the occupation of the authors with a feminine world of hopes and fears in which the central figure does not act so much as she is acted upon leads simply to tender emotionalism—the tragedy is drawn away from the most vital consideration of the ways of fate. It then has very little of the serious purpose with which *De Casibus* storytelling began. An easy flow of tears and an elegant flow of verses are all that is desired. Daniel, as we have seen, escapes from sentimentality to something worthy of high commendation. Lodge, in *Elstred,* lends himself so little to sentimental palliation of his heroine's faults that he allows her to make an eloquent charge against Fortune as "nurse of fools," "impugner of preuentions," and "supposed soueraigne through our vaine construction":

> It was not thou (tho worldly wits accuse thee)
> That sette *Mount Gibel* of my plagues a burning:
> It was not thou, my conscience doth excuse thee,
> It was my sinne that wrought myne ouer-turning,
>> It was but iustice, from the heauens inflicted
>> On lustfull life, defamed and conuicted.[24]

But Drayton shapes his story of Matilda as out-and-out sentimental melodrama, with the wicked king persecuting the heroine's father to make him break down her virtuous resistance. This is neither a medieval tragedy contemning the world in which virtue can be so put upon, nor a medieval saint's legend of chastity, but simply a tearful tale. Shakespeare in *Lucrece,* with a similar theme of chastity outraged and little more than the same "literary" impulse to tell the story, makes inimitable poetic adornment justify his work. It is a justification through virtuosity.

Let us look forward to three tragical poems of the early seventeenth century, all of which are tragedies of women told more or less in the fashion which was set by Churchyard and which was given wider popularity by gallant poets of the 1590's.[25] They are: David Murray's *The Tragicall Death of Sophonisba* (1611); Thomas Sampson's *Fortunes Fashion, Pourtrayed in the troubles of the Ladie Elizabeth Gray, wife to Edward the fourth* (1613); and Patrick Hannay's *Sheretine and Mariana* (1622).

Murray printed his *Sophonisba* in company with his sonnet series *Caelia,* as Daniel and Lodge had published tragical poems accompanied by sonnets. The story is told in the third person and not as a complaint. It strives to extract the last drop of emotion from the famous decision of Hasdrubal's daughter both to escape from Roman captivity and to keep faith with her lover Massinissa by drinking poison. Upon the morning of the day fated to be her last she by chance arrays herself in black. The author makes his sensuous best of her beauties as he describes her dressing. When she receives the potion from Massinissa, she enters upon a long and pitiful debate on the demands of Life and Honor. Such youthful beauty as is hers, which we have seen in luxurious detail, is the beauty of Life, and Life demands love.

Honor demands death and the chastity of the grave in which there is no loving. Thus, so fortunately dressed in black, she chooses Honor, dies, and, in violation of all decorum, becomes "a votresse vnto loues-foe, chastity." One is inevitably reminded of Marston's play *The Wonder of Women Or the Tragedie of Sophonisba* (1606), which, though it discovers sterner tragedy in the story, also discovers sadness in such enforcement of chastity by death and luxuriates in it shamelessly.

Sampson's story of Lady Elizabeth Gray is told in the words of her ghost, "newly risen out of her graue." Both in form and in spirit it is closer to the manner of Baldwin, but it, too, makes the most of injured innocence and offers an abundance of pathetic detail.

In *Sheretine and Mariana,* Hannay, who is another poet apparently the more ready to inject sentiment into tragical poetry by reason of being a sonneteer,[26] tells of young love thwarted, and the tale is all tenderness and "bitter brinie teares." In far-away Hungary, Mariana pledges herself to Sheretine. Sheretine goes to the wars and Mariana is compelled by her parents to marry another. Sheretine returns, is convinced that Mariana is utterly faithless, seeks a solitary place, languishes, and dies of "heart-killing Care." First Mariana and then her husband commit suicide. Mariana finds that her ghost cannot be freed, until, like the ghost of Rosamond, it tells its pitiful history.

In these poems, particularly Murray's and Hannay's, the heroic spirit with which *De Casibus* tragedy began reaches its thinnest dilution. The authors show no desire to flee from the world and little desire to scan the mysteries of either God or the world. They welcome the opportunity to explore broken hearts.

To return to the sixteenth century, we find that Giles Fletcher (the elder) in 1593 so far recognized this new fashion in *De Casibus* tragedy and so far deplored its tendency toward softness and triviality that he took occasion to scorn it in *The Rising to the Crowne of Richard the Third*. This tragical poem he annexed to his love sonnets gathered under the name of *Licia,* though obviously with no intention of implying that it might appeal to the tender emotions. He makes Richard say, as a prelude to his story, that his tragedy is stately matter such as cannot be compared with the trifling misfortunes of Shore's wife and Rosamond, or even with the pitiful fall of Elstred, who at least was a queen. He, Richard, has lost his match at tennis played with Fortune. But he played as a man should, not as one of these women would, and the upshot of the action is not to be greeted with sentimental tears:

> Nor weepe I nowe, as children that have lost,
> But smyle to see the Poets of this age:
> Like silly boates in shallow rivers tost,
> Loosing their paynes, and lacking still their wage.
> To write of women, and of womens falles,
> Who are too light, for to be fortunes balles.[27]

It is unfortunate that after giving due credit to such an introduction one can only add that Fletcher's tragedy of Richard has very little of the force and weight that he invites us to find. It is brief, and it talks rather weakly of the power lying in the hand of Fortune.

Of other tragical poems written late in the sixteenth century and early in the seventeenth something must still be said. Among the less significant are Richard Williams' *The Camplaynte of Anthonye Babington,* a glorified ballad, surviving in manuscript, upon the death of a Catholic conspirator against Queen Elizabeth, which by its allusion to Rosamond seems to have been written not long after 1592;[28] John Weever's *The Mirror of Martyrs, or The life and death of that thrice valiant Capitaine, and most godly Martyre Sir Iohn Old-castle knight Lord Cobham* (1601), a ghostly complaint presented as coming from Elysium, which has an echo (st. 4) of Shakespeare's *Julius Caesar; The Legend of Mary, Queen of Scotland,* a ghostly complaint, surviving in manuscript, which has been attributed to Thomas Wenman and which by allusion to Sackville as still alive shows that it was written not later than 1608;[29] Gervase Markham's *The Famous Whore, or Noble Curtizan: Conteining the lamentable complaint of Paulina, the famous Roman Curtizan, sometimes M[es.] vnto the great Cardinall Hypolito, of Est* (1609), which is not primarily sentimental, despite the fact that Paulina has a place in the tradition started by Jane Shore; and Richard Niccols' *Sir Thomas Overburies Vision* (1616), in which the ghost of Sir Thomas and the ghosts of the murderers who poisoned him in the Tower tell their stories.

As for Michael Drayton's *Peirs Gaueston, Earle of Cornwall his life, death, and fortune,* published with an undated title page, but probably put forth very soon after it was entered on December 3, 1593, and his *Tragicall Legend of Robert, Duke of Normandy,* published in 1596 along with the "legends" of Matilda and Gaveston, they are more than ordinarily competent pieces of poetry. The celebrator of Matilda's harrowing misfortunes is even here not free from the temptation to excessive pity; he has a delicacy and a sophistication which frequently lead him far away from the severity of the older *De Casibus* tragedy and of much contemporary tragedy on the stage. Yet in these works he cannot be called shallow. In his highly pitiful *Legend of Robert,* the sympathy is undeniably well placed and its expression honestly moving. Drayton represents himself as walking forth one morning to relieve his melancholy and as seeing the ghost of the cruelly wronged Duke of Normandy, who was blinded and tortured after his brother had robbed him of the English throne while he was crusading in Palestine. The poet hears the larger part of the tragic story told in an ensuing dispute between Fortune, who is conventionally carefree, and Fame, who is tender and loving to such outraged virtue. Again we see a later tragical poet showing no impulse either to contemn the world or to explore his subject's actions but making much of the recompense which worldly fame may offer for unjust calamity.

The tragedy of Gaveston is somewhat sterner. It has rather curious relationship with the tragedies of inordinate ambition to which the contemporary stage was given. Gaveston admits that he had:

> Selfe-loue, Prides thirst, vnsatisfied desire,
> A flood that neuer yet had any bounds.[30]

So, "with this deuill [of ambition] being once possest," he came naturally to desire selfish application of power. But Drayton has hard work making the sycophantic favorite of

Edward II into a Richard III and finally lets him lapse into
a pitiable state that is more natural. After Gaveston's death
the many-headed mob which had hated him alive shed
many tears for him, and the king mourned grievously.

In his epic poem *The Barrons Wars* (1603), which is his
Mortimeriados (1596) rewritten, Drayton has little to say
of Gaveston, but much of Edward II and Mortimer. They
appear as quite firmly shaped tragic figures. With a combination of frailty and intemperate will the king drives toward his ruin. Mortimer rises with towering ambition only
to fall through overreaching himself.

This poem of Drayton's, *The Barrons Wars*, and Daniel's
*The Ciuile Wars between the two houses of Lancaster and
Yorke* (1595), are exploitations in epic literature of that
tragical interest in British history which the *Mirror* had
fostered. They arise from a growing desire for more detailed
presentation of British heroic themes, and are one of the
signs that the *Mirror's* form of moralized narrative had by
this time served its best uses. But before that form was completely superseded, a few poets tried to meet the changing
taste of the age by giving to the tragical complaint the ambitious scope and the colorful detail of the epic or the drama.

Among the apotheosized tragical complaints which re-
sulted from this widening of scope is Thomas Storer's *The
Life and Death of Thomas Wolsey Cardinall* (1599). Feeling the need of an articulate form for a work so long as
this, Storer divides his tragedy into three parts: "Wolseius
aspirans," "Wolseius triumphans," and "Wolseius moriens."
Thereby he marks sharply the outlines of that pyramid of
tragic ambition, or of tragic embracement of the world,

which even so early as Boccaccio is indicated as the most naturally effective structural form for *De Casibus* tragedy. There is first the incline upward, then the apex of triumph, then the slope downward to calamity. The traversing of the pyramid corresponds to progress around the circle of Fortune's wheel. The effect which such pyramidal structure of tragical story had upon the form of Elizabethan dramatic tragedy, differentiating it sharply from that of Greek tragedy, should be kept in mind. More will be said of this later.

Storer gives some indication that his hero had the tragic fault of unchecked pride and unmeasured ambition, but his tragic philosophy frequently proceeds upon the medieval assumption that the only sure way to avoid calamity is to smother ambition wholly and live the life of retirement. After invoking Melpomene, the tragic muse, Storer lets Wolsey tell in his own words of his lowly origin, his first sure conviction that he had great powers with which to rise in worldly undertaking, and his rapid demonstration of those powers. Wolsey was "drawne in chariot of Desire" while ambition led the way. Yet philosophy from the first reminded him that the unambitious life is holier and wiser:

> Experience holdes the *Tragique Poet* wise:
>   That rather chose mong Corsicke rockes to dwell,
>   Then in the pompe of *Caesars* court excell.[31]

It was thus that "reason sought to stale ambitions hould," but all his care was to flourish, all his desire to gain. Storer gives him no consciousness of fault at the time of his fall. Fortune's wheel revolved, and

> Neuer did Fortune greater instance giue,
> In what fraile state prowd Magistrates do liue.[32]

Thus, despite its elaborate dress, this story of the rise and fall of Wolsey is a simple tragedy told very much in the orthodox ascetic manner.

The same cannot be said of *The Historie of Edward the Second* by Sir Francis Hubert. The work was published in 1629 under this title, but appeared in the preceding year, in briefer form, under the title of *The Deplorable Life and Death of Edward the Second.* According to the author's testimony in 1629, it had been completed some twenty years before.[33] Hubert's poem, too, has an epic introduction and runs to great length; it occupies 664 stanzas and 166 pages in the edition of 1629. But Hubert, unlike Storer, is bent primarily not upon showing that the state of magistrates is frail, but upon showing that the state of unworthy magistrates is frail. He is uncompromising in his judgment that Edward fell according to natural laws which may be discovered. He annexes to the story of Edward a short poem called "The Authors Noli peccare," beginning:

> Forbeare to Sinne: God hath thee still in sight.

And in the introduction he delivers himself of a philosophy of tragedy which is an unconditional denial not only of the power of Fortune but even of the mystery of fate. He speaks of Edward conventionally as "in highest fortunes, cast by Fortune downe." Then he corrects himself hastily:

> Did I say Fortune? Nay by Folly rather,
> By vnrespect vnto the rules of State.
> For let a Prince assure himselfe to gather
> As he hath planted: eyther Loue, or Hate.
> Contempt, or Dutie: not the workes of Fate,
>   Much lesse of Fortune, but of due respects
>   To Causes, which must needs produce effects.

> As if a Prince doe draw his plat-forme right,
> And then with courage builds vpon the same,
> His ends proues happie: But by ouersight
> Hee that is weake, wholly subuerts the frame
> Of his owne building, and doth Idly blame
>   Fortune, the seruant to deseruing merit,
>   But the commander of the abject spirit.

Yet it is only fair to add that though Hubert abolishes the mystery of fate, he at least acknowledges, and quite handsomely, the mystery that lies in that universal human weakness which is so different from divine perfection:

> Where as our humaine actions all are mixt,
> Men liue in motion, so do theyr designes;
> Nothing is simply good, or firmely fix'd.
> All haue defects: Nature it selfe declines,
> Darknes oft clouds the clearest Sun that shines.
>   Our purest streames are not without their mud
>   And we mistake, what oft we take for good.[34]

A third of these later epic-tragedies, Christopher Brooke's *The Ghost of Richard the Third* (1614), soars above the others both in the manner of its setting forth and in the philosophical choric comment which it attaches to the narrative. It is introduced to the public by a string of commendatory verses from a most distinguished body of poets, including William Browne, George Wither, and the dramatists Ben Jonson, George Chapman, and Robert Daborne. It is not too great praise to say that Brooke's abilities sometimes justify their commendation by these friends, conventionally high-flown though that commendation is.

Brooke's *Richard* goes far beyond the ordinary stories of the *Mirror* in attempt at subtle and sustained analysis of tragic event. It is divided, like Storer's *Wolsey,* into three parts—the rise, the triumph, and the fall—though the titles of the divisions are somewhat obscure: we are asked to consider Richard's "Character," his "Legend," and his "Tragedie." The "Character" has especial significance, for it shows Brooke's instinct to lay a foundation for all that happened to Richard by making the youth father to the man and by making the constitution of both youth and man bring tragedy as an inevitable sequence. The egregious villainy of Richard thus becomes more than simple evil for which there is simple punishment; it becomes a thing with increasing life, able to grow monstrously until it turns and feeds upon itself to its own destruction. The conception has true greatness, and Brooke often brings true poetic imagination to its carrying out, though his taste sometimes is for the tawdry, as in such lines of Richard's as these:

> My tongue in firie dragons spleene I steepe,
> That acts, with accents, cruelty may sound;
> At once the furies snakes hist in my breath,
> When I kist Horror; and engender'd Death.[25]

Richard is made to discuss his study to be great, his careful policy, his Machiavellian support of religion only to enslave the people, and his sailing of a swift course upon a swelling tide where he was "driu'n with ambitions gale." So he comes to discuss his triumph and fall, matters growing from his responsible acts but also matters ruled by a larger fate:

> Thus haue I character'd my spirit and state
> In generall termes, next shall yee heare apply'd
> The sequell of mine actions, to that fate,
> Which heau'n ordain'd, as justice to my pride.[26]

By skillful policy he gained the heights, and all within the realm bowed the knee to him, but by skillful policy he could not make himself secure. The downward turn of royal fortune began with the rise of conscience, of doubt, of cramping fear natural to one who had dyed his hands in blood. These things weakened Richard's powers

> and did engender
> Confusion, horror, and blood-thirsting care
> Which passion (mixed with distraction) render.[37]

He bade himself

> Cut knotty doubts, and bars of all restraint,[38]

and added to the well-considered crimes which he had already committed one of different order, a superfluous and infinitely revolting outrage conceived in panic. He murdered the harmless princes in the Tower. Then, while Richard sank farther into paralyzing fear, "the Lancastrian line, that scarce was seene ... begins to raze the line of Yorke." Disaster followed disaster, and finally Richard, with every faculty corrupted by fear, melancholy, and distraction, was smothered in ruin and death. As he says, his descent gathered impetus by its own movement, and his progress toward calamity demonstrated a linking of cause with effect and of human choice with external fate

> Where guilt giues terror, terror mischeefe lends,
> And mixe their malice with my fatall starres.[39]

There is nothing like this carefully wrought tissue of tragic analysis elsewhere among the tragical poems through which we have pursued our course, and Brooke's *Richard,* one of the very last of these works in date, is a fitting climax to their line. It is probable that without Shakespeare's *Richard III*[10] and other dramas of the time to teach him, Brooke could not have done what he did. According to its title page, his work is one "containing more of [Richard III] than hath been heretofore shewed: either in Chronicles, Playes, or Poems."

One more comment may be made upon these three epic-tragedies, Storer's *Wolsey,* Hubert's *Edward,* and Brooke's *Richard*. It happens that they represent conveniently three main tragic philosophies with which we have to deal in these chapters. Storer leans toward one absolutism, that otherworldliness which makes tragedy an inexplicable accompaniment of any ambitious worldly activity. Hubert leans toward the opposite absolutism, that worldliness which makes tragedy fully explicable as reward of sin or error. Brooke finds inspiration in a marriage of explicability and inexplicability which nondramatic tragedy had done something to further and which tragedy on the Elizabethan stage, as we shall see, had just brought most truly into being.

IV

The demonstration of mundane justice, which we have found tragedy in the *Mirror* and in its imitations increasingly drawn to undertake, was frequently attempted apart from tragedy in the moral philosophy of Elizabethan England. As the sixteenth century gave way to the seventeenth, disquisitions upon the world as moral disorder still had their hearing,[11] but they were receding before confident pronouncements upon the world as moral order. The Middle Ages, in spite of their fondness for what might be expressed through the figure of Fortune, had known good and sufficient arguments against the existence of Fortune: in the Fathers of the Church there was weighty authority on the side of denial. This earlier denial of Fortune was above all else aimed to establish God's omniscience and omnipotence. But for good medieval Christians it was in the main sufficient to have simple faith, or to prove metaphysically, that ultimately all was order, and it was unnecessary to demonstrate scientifically that some of this order was manifest on earth. Scientific demonstration of order on earth is exactly what we find later moral philosophy often attempting. God, of course, was still presented as the mover of justice, but often as a mover who had chosen mortal lieutenants and instituted physical laws for the punishment of evil in advance of the punishment to come after death. As *The French Academie,* a popular translation of a moral and philosophical work by Pierre de la Primaudaye, expresses this concept in 1594: "And as himselfe [God] commeth in judgment to take vengeance, so hee woulde have them that supplie his place among men, unto whome hee hath committed the sworde for the defence of·the good and punishment of evill doers, to followe his example. But whether they doe so or no, there is no sinne that can avoide punishment, and that findeth not a Judge even in him that committed it, to take vengeance thereof by meanes of the affections, which God placed in man to·that ende."[42]

Thus God had commissioned magistrates,—for whom Baldwin's collection of tragedies was a "mirror,"—and if the magistrates should prove unfaithful servants, God had also provided that evil men should punish themselves through their "affections" or "passions," that is, through their own inner disorders. The passions—for example, anger or revenge—could be studied, and their effects could be foretold, partly through physiological and psychological discoveries of an alliance between the passions and the humors of the body. Hence the conception of tragic justice was supported by a medical and psychological science which had ancient foundation in the Middle Ages, not to mention the classical world, but which was being extended and applied with a materialistic zeal that the Middle Ages had not possessed. The stimulus which this cast of thought could give to the creation of dramatic character in tragedy is obvious. The perils which it could have for tragedy when it was accepted in too confident simplicity are also obvious, and have already been noticed.

With a philosophy that did not scorn the world, men found a way to defy Fortune that was far different from the way of the Stoic or Christian-Stoic. They entered Fortune's realm and strove to take it away from her. Following Machiavelli, they might be cavalier and somewhat lightly cynical, arguing that "it is better to be adventurous than cautious, because Fortune is a woman, and if you wish to keep her under, it is necessary to ill-use her."[43] Following Bacon, they might have faith that the human capacity for reducing the mystery of Nature could also reduce the mystery of Fortune, and by the same method, namely, by patient observation of the infinite number of tiny details which make the whole: "The way of fortune is like the milken way in the sky; which is a meeting or knot of a number of small stars; not seen asunder, but giving light together. So

Z

are there a number of little and scarce discerned virtues, or rather faculties and customs, that make men fortunate." By implication these words from Bacon's essay "Of Fortune" mean that a refined knowledge of human character and the results of its actions is our key to tragedy.

Another Elizabethan essayist, exactly contemporary with Bacon, offers notable denial that mischance is a mystery into which we cannot see. Sir William Cornwallis in an essay "Of Feare," published in his *Second Part of Essayes* (1601)," is disdainful of signs and portents supposedly boding calamity. "I remember," says he, "a speach of *Cassius* to a South-sayer that wished him not to fight with the *Parthians* vntill the Moone had passed *Scorpio,* hee answered, hee feared not *Scorpio* but the *Archers;* These things are least of all to bee feared, they begge feare that picke them out of these occasions." And as for the fear of Fortune: "There are no mischances, there is no fortune, there is no miserie in our humaine liues, except we looke into the feeblenesse of our merits, & our Creators bountie, in other things we are deceiued by imagination, the circūstances of things are more then themselues."

How surely Cornwallis is thinking of each man as the responsible author of his own tragic misfortune, will appear in a passage from his *Discourses vpon Seneca the Tragedian* published in the same year as his *Second Part of Essayes.* If his logic and his syntax break down under the weight of philosophy which they carry, at least his drift away from Seneca's fatalism is clear enough:

That our actions are called, and rightly called humane, here is the reason; fortune gouernes them: which word, though the fancy of

Poets hath giuen a bodie to, and made her blinde, and a goddesse;
yet is she neither a goddesse, nor a separated essence: for there are
millions of fortunes, yea as many as there are men, euery man his
owne fortune; but the word expresseth chance, and by chance wee
are gouerned, for so must they needes bee that allowe not their de-
signes premeditatiō without order: it is a shift to set vp fortune, and
the imputation of fortunes preposterous and disorderly working,
it is our owne fault; since nothing commeth from vs marshalled
with iudgement but as our sences catch vp euery obiect destinated
to their functions, without all choyse or regard; so suffer wee our
selues to ingrosse the commandements of lust and appetite, to embrace euery thing that they see, and to deuoure poyson, so it promiseth but sweetnes.

I can not say wee goe without meanings, but without the true
meaning I may: for superfluously taking the suruey of things not
penetrating the depth, we neuer taste of any thing but the scumme
and top of things. Hence come the exclamations of the world, the
shipwrackes of all estates, and to comprehend in a word that might
fill pages, all that we call calamity, & think worthy of the bewayling.[45]

In such a philosophy as this, which anatomizes the medieval Fortune into millions of fortunes and would show that
each man constructs a fortune which is his and no one else's
due, there is a basis upon which Shakespearean tragedy of
character may be built, though Shakespearean genius may
not be disposed to imply that by premeditation man can
free himself wholly from calamity.

Chapter IX

THE ESTABLISHMENT OF TRAGEDY
UPON THE ELIZABETHAN STAGE

ESTABLISHMENT of tragedy upon the Elizabethan stage
was accomplished after two major manifestations
of formative energy. The first of these, in the opening decade of Elizabeth's reign, produced English translations for almost all of Seneca's plays in rapid succession; it
produced *The Tragedie of Gorboduc* (1561–1562), *Jocasta*
(1566), and *The Tragedie of Gismond of Salerne* (1566–
1567),[1] plays which are truly landmarks in their varied
utilization of classic dramatic tradition upon the English
stage, even though theirs was not the public stage; it also
produced *Apius and Virginia* and *Horestes,* and perhaps
Cambises, which have already been discussed as morality-
tragedies. The second major manifestation of energy, in ten
years or more following the appearance of *The Spanish Tragedie* (1585–1589) and *Tamburlaine the Great* (*ca.* 1587),
developed a sudden variety and an amazing breadth of
achievement. In play after play it gave to tragedy secure
foundation upon the public stage, frequently using Seneca
to advantage but not allowing him to devitalize the native
spirit, and it set the lines of most fruitful development for
the tragic drama of Shakespeare. At the outset of each
period, access of interest in stage tragedy was accompanied
by access of interest in *De Casibus* tragedy heralded by an
edition of the *Mirror for Magistrates* which had special importance—in 1559 the first edition by which publication

was accomplished, and in 1587 an ambitious collected edition of original and later legends.

From Elizabethan works of criticism it is plain that *De Casibus* tragedy was often in the minds of those sixteenth-century English writers who were rediscovering the meaning of ancient tragedy. The falls of princes which had been presented in the long succession of tragical stories beginning with Boccaccio were not forgotten when an Elizabethan critic attempted to characterize the matter and purpose of ancient tragedy. Thomas Lodge in his *Defence of Poetry* (1579) finds that the writers of Greek tragedy "did set forth the sower fortune of many exiles, the miserable fal of haples princes, the reuinous decay of many countryes." Sir Philip Sidney in his *Apologie for Poetrie* (1595) says that tragedy "with sturring the affects of admiration and commiseration, teacheth the vncertainety of this world, and vpon how weake foundations guilden roofes are builded," and the words receive a moral application more Christian than pagan which reminds us that Sidney, later in the same essay, admires the *Mirror for Magistrates* as "meetely furnished of beautiful parts." And the author of *The Arte of English Poesie* (1589)—whether George Puttenham, or his brother Richard, or some other—goes even farther than Lodge and Sidney in using the language of *De Casibus* tragedy to describe the ancient tragic drama. He writes: "But after that some men among the moe became mighty and famous in the world, soueraignetie and dominion hauing learned them all maner of lusts and licen- tiousnes of life, by which occasions also their high estates and felicities fell many times into most lowe and lamentable fortunes: whereas before in their great prosperities they were both feared and reuerenced in the highest degree, after their deathes, when the posteritie stood no more in dread of them, their infamous life and tyrannies were laid open to all the world, their wickednes reproched, their follies and extreme insolencies derided, and their miserable ends painted out in playes and pageants, to shew the mutabilitie of fortune, and the iust punishment of God in reuenge of a vicious and euill life."[4]

Moreover, Jasper Heywood, the first English translator of plays attributed to Seneca, gives definite indication that learned admiration for Senecan tragedy was entirely compatible with admiration for *De Casibus* tragedy. He introduces his *The Seconde Tragedie of Seneca entituled Thyestes faithfully Englished* (1560) with a long apology for his youth and humble attainments in which he pretends that after he has fallen asleep over a book on a dreary winter's day, the shade of Seneca appears and discusses with him the translation of the famous ten plays. Heywood is worshipful toward the master. He says that he has already translated the *Troas,* and if Seneca wants more of his services, he will gladly go on, but better men for the work could be found among England's literary wits. What about North, Sackville, and Norton? Also, there is Baldwin:

> There heare thou shalt a great reporte,
> of Baldwyns worthie name.
> Whose Myrrour dothe of Magistrates,
> proclayme eternall fame.[5]

If he had been writing three years later, Heywood might have added that Sackville was a sharer with Baldwin in the

Mirror's fame and had joined with Norton to produce in *Gorboduc* an English drama bidding for Seneca's highest commendation, which was based, like the *Mirror,* upon the national chronicles.

This coloring of classic tragedy with *De Casibus* tragedy and this uniting of admiration for the one with admiration for the other was natural. For the cultivated Elizabethan the classic art of tragedy was usually well represented, even represented preëminently well, by the plays attributed to Seneca. In these plays he could find something of the same spiritual satisfaction that he had found in the *Fall of Princes* or the *Mirror for Magistrates* because he was uncovering there an important source of Christian tragical moralizing. They could lead him not only into a world of dramatic form which he had grown ready to appreciate, but also into a world of tragic philosophy which was at many points so similar to his own that he was able to feel much at home there. When he did not know, as Roger Ascham knew,[6] that Aeschylus, Sophocles, and Euripides were greater than Seneca, he frequently seems to have been blind rather than merely unable to read Greek or to get Greek plays in any sort of translation. It seems to have been highly difficult for him to carry sympathetic understanding farther into the realm of classic tragedy than the province nearest to his own familiar realm of *De Casibus* tragedy. His taste was supported by the enthusiastic Senecan revival which had already taken place on the Continent.

As the Senecan was made to join with and yield support to the native presentation of tragedy, the two themes of ambition and revenge came to possess outstanding popularity and importance. Often ambition and revenge were merged into a single theme of revengeful ambition. In these themes there was solid basis for union between the Senecan tragic conventions and the native, and they were bound to be attractive for their dramatic effectiveness, but the reader of plays immediately antecedent to Shakespeare will do well to remember that ambition and revenge did not interest the Elizabethan public merely as conventional themes for drama. Elizabethan moral philosophy in general had much to say of ambition, the typical manifestation of Renaissance wordly aspiration, and much to say of revenge.

"What are the elements and grounds of all euill?" asks Thomas Crewe in the catechism which he entitles *The Nosegay of Morall Philosophie* (1580). "Enuie, pride, auarice, and ambition," is his answer.[7] Thus ambition bids fair to become one of the deadly sins, or at least a major cause of deadly sin. Says Geoffrey Fenton in his *Golden Epistles, Contayning varietie of discourse both Morall, Philosophicall, and Diuine* (1575): "As ambicion is the beastly nourse of couetousnesse, and both they creepe in in these dayes vnder a forme and maner of seueritie: So it can not bee but that man which desireth power, is an ill mayteyner of Iustice, and he that thirsteth for glory, runnes with great swiftnes into actions of iniuries and oppression."[8]

Can ambition, either as sin or as predisposition to sin, bring mundane retribution in its train? The first edition (in English) of Pierre de la Primaudaye's extremely popular *French Academie, wherin is discoursed the institution of maners, and whatsoeuer els concerneth the good and happie life of all estates and callings* (1586) makes emphatic

answer: "And no doubt but for the most part, iust punishment for example to mē, foloweth such an ambitious passion, whereof there are infinite examples both in the Greeke
and Latin histories." This is echoed in almost the same
words by Henry Roberts in his *A Defiance to Fortune, Pro-
claimed by Andrugio, noble Duke of Saxony, declaring his
miseries* (1590): "But no doubt for the most part, iust punishment follow the ambitious, for example to others, whereof there are vnfaigned histories, which mention the same."
Roberts comes to the pious conclusion that we should "detest ambition whiche is an infinite euill, and companion of
pride, so much hated of God and men."[10]

Naturally, ambition shows itself with particular force
and has particularly tragic consequences among the great
princes and rulers of the world. The chapter "Of Ambition"
in *The French Academie* makes reference in its opening
words to the passionate desire to rule that caused "the strāge
tragedie of the Romane Emperors" and includes the statement that "the desire of hauing more (saith *Plutark*) is a
vice common to Princes and great Lords, which, by reason
of ambition and desire to rule, bringeth foorth in them
oftentimes an vnsociable, cruell, and beastly nature."[11]

As for revenge, it belongs to God, as Elizabethan moral
philosophy staunchly maintains. Consequently, private vengeance is nothing other than sinful, and the God who re-
pays sin with mundane punishment may even curse the man
who becomes a divine instrument in taking vengeance upon
another sinner.[12] Also, revenge, like certain other tragic sins,
has a peculiar affinity with ambition. The picture in its completeness is sketched with skillful economy by Joseph Hall

in "The Characterism of the Ambitious," a division of his *Characters of Vertues and Vices* (1608):

> Ambition is a proud couetousnes, a dry thirst of honor, the long-ing disease of reason, and aspiring and gallant madnesse. The am-bitious climes vp high and perillous staires, and neuer cares how to come downe; the desire of rising hath swallowed vp his feare of a fall.... But now when hee finds himselfe desperately crossed, and at once spoiled both of aduancement and hope, both of fruition and possibilitie, all his desire is turned into rage, his thirst is now onely of reuenge.... Hee is in the common body as a Mole in the earth, euer vnquietly casting; and in one word is nothing but a confused heape of enuie, pride, couetousnesse.[13]

For John Reynolds, in *The Triumphs of Gods Revenge* (1621), there is a tragic trinity of ambition, revenge, and murder well established in human experience. Their retri-bution is certain, for "if our contemplation dive into elder times, and our curiositie turne ouer the variety of ancient and moderne Histories (as well Diuine as Humane) wee shall finde that Ambition, Reuenge, and Murther, haue euer prooued fatall crimes to their vndertakers."[14]

These ideas of ambition, or revengeful ambition, and its consequences have patent relationship with the Christian ascetic ideas of worldly aspiration and its train of insecuri-ties. But they are far from being encouragements to ascetic denial of the world. They imply that the fall of the ambi-tious man should be regarded as a just outcome of a com-plexly sinful course of action rather than as a result of Fortune's disfavor. They add to the growing conception that the world shares somewhat with Heaven in the scheme of divine justice and is to that extent good.

The purely ascetic scorn of the world as a realm of absolute injustice is to be found surviving, however, in a moral poem by Anthony Copley called *A Fig for Fortune* (1596), which reveals in another fashion the interest that tragic ambition and revenge might have for a theater audience of the time. The poem provides occasion for moralizing in a tale of an "Elizian out-cast of Fortune" (subject of Eliza's), who is discovered ranging on his jade Melancholy through the desert of Affliction. The wanderer meets Cato's ghost, who advises suicide. He next meets the spirit of Revenge, who counsels courageous resistance to evil fate. He suspects that both are spirits not of good but of evil. Changing his steed for one called Good Desire, he sets forth upon a new course and reaches Mount-Sion, the Temple of Peace, where a hermit catechizes him and urges Christian contempt for worldly vanities. Then, celestially armed by an angel, he participates as a champion in the overthrowing of Doblessa (Fortune) when she advances with her company to make a raid upon the temple.

The counsel here given by the spirit of Revenge is a most eloquent piece of seduction to the vital, instead of the moral, enjoyment of tragedy. It gives testimony that the tragedy of ambition and revenge would not have been so attractive as it was to the Elizabethan audience if only moral enjoyment had been found in it. Ambition and revenge could be counted upon to contribute heroic activity to life and to the stage. Under their influence men lived dangerously, bravely, dramatically. In Copley's poem, Revenge does nothing so base as merely to encourage in the outcast of Fortune a hope that ambitious effort will restore him to prosperity. The evil counselor pictures the glory of manly struggle for the world's prizes and dwells finally upon the glory of tragic misfortune itself when the man of ambitious spirit is overthrown and yet will not consent to be conquered, perhaps even in death:

> To be faire Fortunes euer Carpet-darling
> Is femall glorie: But Reueng'd disgrace
> That's truly Masculine, and rich triumphing:
> Al peace-content is too too cheap and base:
>   What manhood is it still to feed on Chickins
>   Like infant nurse-boys in nice Fortunes kitchins?
>
> Giue me the man that with vndaunted sperit
> Dares giue occasion of a Tragedie:
> And be content for his more after-merit
> To be downe beaten from felicity:
>   To th' end that with a fierce amount he may
>   Re-blesse himself in spight of Fortunes nay.
>
> T'is braue to plunge adowne into the deep
> And so vp-bound againe aboue the waue,
> To be continually a mountain-sheep
> Is Cockrell-like, it is a dung-hill braue:
>   The crauin Cocke is hartlesse from his hill,
>   Shame to be so that hast a manly will.
>   . . . .
> The gallant man vnhorst amidst his foes
> Fightes to the death his latest wrath away
> And when he can no more: with mops and mowes
> He flouts both them, and Death, and Destinie:
>   So if not Victor, yet vnvanquished
>   He dies to euerlasting liuelihed.[15]

This doctrine, despite its moving spirit of Elizabethan adventurousness, is made to yield before the time-tried teaching of the hermit that man must resolutely despise the world and fix his eyes upon Heaven. For injustice is natural to the world, and only in the next world will the just tribunal be found. Ambitious effort here below is folly:

> Then vp to heauen amount thy true ambition
> And as for earth out-care it in contrition.[16]

Elizabethan moral philosophy turns again and again to consideration of what are known as the "passions," the "affections," or the "perturbations" of the human soul, among which ambition and revenge may be counted. They are the "motions of the mind," not necessarily evil in themselves, which may produce disorder in man's spiritual constitution, and they are often conceived to have connection with the humors of the body, so that their consideration may be medical as well as moral.[17] Certain basic passions may be thought of in pairs, as: love and hatred, desire and aversion, joy and sadness, hope and despair, courage and fear. The lore of the passions has a long history going back into medieval and classic thought, and from both medieval and classic philosophy the question of how the passions should be mastered is inherited by Elizabethan writers. The tendency of asceticism they find to be toward the suppression of passions—some passions, at least—for the avoidance of evil; the tendency of nonascetic rationalism toward the control of passions by measure. As espousal of the world and its ways comes into stronger and stronger acceptance, Elizabethan moral philosophy shows more and more favor for the classic doctrine of the golden mean. Ambition, for example, is often allowed to have aspects of good. *The French Academie,* even after it has drawn attention to the just punishments of the ambitious passions recorded in history, is careful to add that we are permitted to struggle for excellence when we do not go beyond our strength and when we have regard for the general welfare of our fellow men.[18]

But neither Stoic defiance of the world nor Aristotelian measured acceptance of the world is quite equivalent to a main tradition of Christian doctrine, and there is some attempt at recognition of this fact. Joseph Hall in one of his *Epistles* (1608), "Of the Contempt of the World," distinguishes between "a Stoicall dulnesse, and a Christian contempt."[19] And Thomas Rogers, introducing *The Anatomie of the Minde* (1576) with a chapter "Of the Perturbations in generall," rejects as untrustworthy guides both of two great "sectes of Philosophers, namelye, the *Stoikes,* and *Peripatetions,*" though these "haue bene the Fathers and protectours of Philosophie."[20] One gathers that Rogers sees nothing to praise in any ascetic doctrine, since he condemns the Stoics for attempting to geld man of that which is grafted and planted in him by nature when they will not permit him to be moved any whit, for anything. In taking vices out of man, the Stoics take virtue also, for "except there bee passions and perturbations in man, ther is no place for vertue."[21] But the Peripatetics, to whom one might expect Rogers to turn with approval for their ideal of rational balance, are interpreted by him as likewise falling into serious error. His conception of·sin as something absolutely forbidden by God is the basis of his disapproval:

Now the *Peripatetions* saye that a man shoulde be affectioned, but yet *modicè* meanly, and in his passions keepe a measure: As though that then he should fall into none offence. But, as he offendeth as well which goeth softlye, as he which runneth, if they both wander and be out of the waye: euen so is he as well to be reprehended, which is subiect to perturbations, though it be but in measure, as he which immoderately doth serue them, if both be vnlawfull. For as directly to walke is good, and to goe astraye daungerous: so to be moued with affections to a good purpose is commendable, but to an yll ende and purpose altogether damnable. For a more illustration, the burning desyre of the fleshe, though it be without measure, as lōg as it is in lawfull Mariage, is without blame: but if it once desire another mans wyfe, though it be not in such burning, and vehement wyse is a most horrible crime.[22]

And it is the same, Rogers argues, with anger and covetousness, for other illustrations. Nevertheless, as he proceeds to discuss such perturbations later in his book, he comes very close to saying, as many of his contemporaries incline to say, that lack of measure is a primary cause of evil.

In short, Elizabethan moral philosophy shows great variety between its ascetic and its rationalistic or worldly judgment of evil. To many writers it is hardly clear whether ambition and certain other passions that may bring mankind to tragedy are to be completely shunned or are merely to be ruled according to the doctrine of the golden mean. There is always the impulse, however, to espouse the world for a greater and greater degree of meaning as a theater of retribution, whether the retribution is for sin or for lack of measure. Though the shifting lines of newly revived classic philosophies, of Christian asceticism, and of Renaissance rationalism weave much confusion, they also make for a new subtlety and breadth of moral order. In tragedy written for the stage, as it goes through the phases of its establishment, both the confusion and the promise of new order are reflected far more strongly than in *De Casibus* tragedy of the same period.

II

Gorboduc was acted at the Christmas revels of the Inner Temple in 1561–1562, and before the queen at Whitehall soon afterward. The historical importance of the play for its division into five acts, for its use of the Senecan chorus, the Senecan messenger, and other Senecan technique, for its use of dumb-shows which are perhaps influenced by Italian drama but are obviously related to the native spectacles in city pageants and court masques, and for its discovery of blank verse as a fitting measure for dignified English drama, has been given all due recognition. It is the first tragedy in English aiming at anything like classic "regularity." But it is very far from being an orthodox academic exercise after the Senecan model, and this is not merely because it scorns the unities of time and place with hardly less abandon than the later popular drama.

The authors, Thomas Norton and Thomas Sackville, quite obviously entered upon their work intending to point a moral that is essentially not Senecan. There is every indication that they honestly desired to give an object lesson to Queen Elizabeth showing the evils which might ensue in the realm of England if succession to her throne should be left unsettled. From the chronicles they chose the story of the legendary British king Gorboduc and of his sons Ferrex and Porrex, between whom he divides his kingdom before his death. The fifth act of their play is a doleful presentation of general mischiefs and miseries, of civil wars, murders, and all manner of wrongs, to which England is left helplessly exposed after Porrex has slain his brother, the queen has slain her surviving son, and the people have slain both Gorboduc and the queen in the turmoil of jealous ambition and revenge excited by Gorbuduc's willful departure from the usual course in disposing of his rule. In the development of the action the authors are glad to accept every opportunity for rhetorical moralizing in the Senecan form of long and tiresome speeches. For a moment they are so "classical" as to let Gorboduc attribute the misfortunes of his house to the vengeance of the gods, pursuing the Trojan race even into Britain.[23] But the tragedy is made to depend in sober truth upon no vindictive divinity. Nor is it furthered by any vengeful Senecan ghost. It hangs upon the well-considered and wholly responsible act of Gorboduc. This unwise act brings evil consequences just as sin might bring them. The lesson is that the misfortunes of a king and his realm could have been avoided by right action.

In the execution of its seriously controversial purpose *Gorboduc* at times reminds us strongly of the moral plays. For one thing, since it is as much the tragedy of a commonwealth as of a king, it enforces a moral concerning the decay of kingdoms which has some relationship to the moral of a play like *Respublica* (1553). The fifth act, before which all the principal characters have met their deaths, is a gross violation of dramatic unity except as it indicates that the authors conceive the kingdom itself to have a sort of dramatic entity. For another thing, the formal balancing of the good and evil counselors given to Gorboduc and to each of his sons is Senecan with a difference; it reproduces much of the effect obtained in the moralities when the forces of good and the forces of evil struggle for the human soul.[24]

A A

Gorboduc also betrays a native background in verses which echo the *Mirror for Magistrates*. We are reminded that Sackville had an interest in the *Mirror,* though contributions from him were not published until 1563. The chorus at the end of the first act serves notice that Gorboduc

> A myrrour shall become to Princes all,
> To learne to shunne the cause of suche a fall.[25]

Over some of the moralizing elsewhere in the play the 1559 edition of the *Mirror* appears to have cast a general influence, especially the moralizing in the fifth act. The long closing speech by Eubulus, secretary to Gorboduc, is a summary comment upon the tragedy, beginning with a ponderous annunciatory

> Loe here the end of *Brutus* royall line,
> And loe the entry to the wofull wracke.[26]

It has the style of such lines in the *Mirror* as those with which Henry VI concludes his legend:

> Lo, here the heauy haps which happened mee by heape,
> See here the pleasant fruites that many princes reape.[27]

Thus, though *Gorboduc* is a Senecan play and though learned theory takes sponsorship for the formality of its scenes, it has a healthy measure of attachment to the popular tragic tradition of its day and age. It may hardly be said that Sackville and Norton have allowed Seneca to choose their subject for them or do their basic thinking for them. The rivalry of Ferrex and Porrex which they present has some resemblance to the rivalry of Polynices and Eteocles in Seneca's *Phoenissae,* but the success of the *Mirror for*

Magistrates and a definite political purpose are more likely
to have influenced them primarily in the choice of their material. Because of their political purpose they follow the lead
of that native tragic moralizing which emphasizes retribution; royal responsibility must be impressively indicated to
Elizabeth. The bond of necessity which holds a Senecan
protagonist to some horrific course of unwilled action is
therefore never a reality in *Gorboduc*. Neither is Fortune,
Senecan or Christian. Gorboduc and his sons are firmly
implanted in the world of the later English morality and
of the nonascetic *De Casibus* legend, where responsible
human acts effectively produce suffering according to a
material law and order reflecting the spiritual. The play has
so little Senecan pessimism for the world and so little Christian scorn of the world that its patriotic last lines are no
violation of its general spirit:

> Of iustice, yet must God in fine restore
> This noble crowne vnto the lawfull heire:
> For right will alwayes liue, and rise at length,
> · But wrong can neuer take deepe roote to last.[78]

Looking forward to the favorite themes of Elizabethan
tragedy upon the popular stage, *Gorboduc* has much to say
of "climbing pride," of "lust to reign," of "ambitious minds
with gaping hope," of private vengeance, and of God's vengeance therefor. Neither ambition nor revenge, however, is
at the center of the tragedy. Gorboduc himself is no more
guided by them than Shakespeare's Lear. By his lack of
wisdom and his refusal to follow good counsel he simply
releases such forces in others for the destruction of his kingdom. Even Ferrex and Porrex, avid as they are for worldly

power, hardly make us think of Richard III. But in Fergus, Duke of Albany, who appears only in the last act, there is very plainly a Richard III in little. For him the thought of the prostrate kingdom is a spur to unprincipled action, as he lets us know in a Richardian soliloquy where he resolves "to venture life to winne a crowne." He is the forerunner of a dramatic type of ambition which in the hands of popular Elizabethan dramatists is given far larger proportions than any type of ambitious tyranny in Seneca's plays and is granted the center of the stage.

In *Jocasta,* by George Gascoigne and Francis Kinwelmershe, *Gismond of Salerne,* by Robert Wilmot and several others, and *The Misfortunes of Arthur,* by Thomas Hughes, the lead of *Gorboduc* is followed and various new adaptations of Seneca to English use are made under the auspices of the Inns of Court. *Gismond,* which may have been presented as early as 1566, the same year as *Jocasta,* was rewritten as *Tancred and Gismund* by Wilmot and published in 1591. *The Misfortunes of Arthur* was published in 1587 under the title, *Certaine deuises and showes presented to her Maiestie.*[29]

Jocasta was published as the translation of a tragedy by Euripides, but it is well removed from the Greek in both letter and spirit, and it inaugurates no emulation of Greek drama upon the Elizabethan stage. Truth requires the statement that "in England the national drama develops without any more direct intrusion of Greek influence than could be exerted by Gascoigne's English version of Dolce's partly Senecanized translation of a Latin rendering of the *Phoenissae* of the most Senecan of the Greeks, Euripides."[30] The recension of the *Phoenissae* in Dolce's *Giocasta* (1549) is a forced adaptation of Euripides to the Gothic taste in tragedy by use of Seneca. The English translation from the Italian goes even farther in compelling Euripides to take on Gothic color. Both adaptations reveal the inability of their age to enter very far into the subtler spirit of Greek tragedy. Especially in the moralizing added by the translators is this inability plain.

The matter of the *Phoenissae* of Euripides is, of course, substantially that of the Senecan play which may have encouraged the authors of *Gorboduc* in the choice of their subject. The success of *Gorboduc,* with its theme of brothers warring for a kingdom, perhaps led Gascoigne and Kinwelmershe to the choice of *Giocasta* for translation and production. But without the example of *Gorboduc,* and even without the aid of Dolce's *Giocasta,* they might well have found a peculiar attraction in the original *Phoenissae,* granted that they could have compassed a translation. As a classic drama it is unusual in that it is filled with action. Moreover, it has in Oedipus a commanding tragic figure for the support of Senecan and *De Casibus* moralizing upon the insecurity of worldly eminence, and in his sons, Eteocles and Polynices, excellent object lessons in tragic ambition. Many possibilities, as it happened, had already been realized and exploited by Dolce. His translation, without very large departure from the dialogue of Euripides, both Senecanizes the drama and makes of it a fall of princes. On his own responsibility Dolce gives Jocasta in the opening lines of his first act a lamentation upon her debasement "da l' alto e Real stato."[31] In his Senecan choruses at the ends of his acts

he offers much moralizing upon ambition, upon the folly
of worldly activity, and upon Fortune's wheel, which has
no counterpart in Euripides. His final chorus seizes upon
Oedipus as a type of fallen prince and might in all ways
have done service in Boccaccio's *De Casibus*. In the English
translation it begins:

> Example here, loe take by *Oedipus,*
> You Kings and Princes in prosperitie,
> And euery one that is desirous
> To sway the seate of worldlie dignitie,
> How fickle tis to trust in Fortunes whele.[32]

Its point of departure in the text of Euripides is the moving
speech of Oedipus upon the cruel irony of his exile from
Thebes after the benefits which he has conferred upon the
city and the honor which he has gained there. Euripides
himself concludes the *Phoenissae* with a very brief chorus
which makes no comment upon the action and is merely a
graceful hope that he may always be worthy of victory in
tragic poesy.

Gascoigne and Kinwelmershe follow Dolce rather faithfully, though they betray some misunderstanding of their
text and make some additions.[33] They find it natural to in-
tensify Dolce's moralizing for English readers by alluding
to the *Mirror for Magistrates* or by phrasing after its style.
"The argument of the Tragedie," as they give it, would let
us know that

> Creon is King, the type of Tyranny,
> And Oedipus, myrrour of misery.[34]

A marginal note opposite the speech of Oedipus upon his
exile presents him to our attention as "A mirrour for Magis-

trates." And an epilogue supplied by Christopher Yelverton is a warning to the "high-aspiring minde" and to "ambitious wightes" which neatly blends the Senecan commonplaces with those of the *Mirror.* The dumb-shows added as introductions to the acts, where original contrivance is most in evidence in the English production, adequately do their share to color the play according to a native taste in tragedy not to be satisfied by Seneca alone. The first dumb-show strangely foreshadows *Tamburlaine* when it represents "vnto vs Ambition, by the hystorie of *Sesostres* king of *Egypt,* who beeing in his time and reigne a mightie Conqueror, yet not content to haue subdued many princes, and taken from them their kingdomes and dominions, did in like maner cause those Kinges whome he had ouercome, to draw in his Chariote like Beastes and Oxen, thereby to content his vnbrideled ambitious desire." The second dumb-show spectacularly plays up the revengeful enmity between the ambitious sons of Oedipus as a lasting force which even divides the flame when their corpses are burned together. The fifth dumb-show brings upon the stage the medieval figure of Fortune, who interchanges the positions and the apparel of two slaves and two kings brought forth upon leading-strings.

The spirit of Senecan fatalism asks for acceptance in these Inns of Court dramas, along with Senecan structure, and is obviously a subtle influence operating against the making of their tragedy into mundane retribution for freely willed sin according to nonascetic Christian conception. Where such fatalism joins peacefully with the native spirit of tragedy it naturally falls into something like ascetic medieval moralizing, contemning the material world as a realm in which even princes have no hand in shaping their fortunes and in which heavenly justice has no part. The authors of *Jocasta* are more or less bound by the fact that they are translators, but even when they assume freedom they succumb to this combined philosophy. The authors of *Gorboduc* in the main escape from it, more because they have a political purpose than because they wish to show the "plagues of vice." Gorboduc is not at all a vicious figure, whatever one may say of the sons and their mother. The authors of the last two plays in the group certainly do not completely escape, but at times they do their best to escape.

Thus we find that both *Gismond of Salerne* and *The Misfortunes of Arthur* can frequently speak the language of those stories in the *Mirror* which dwell upon mundane punishment for the responsible sinner. They do so in spite of the fact that they employ the Senecan tricks of dramatic composition more fully than do the other two plays. *Gismond* dramatizes Boccaccio's story of Ghismonda and Guiscardo (*Decameron*, first novel of the fourth day) and apparently has direct indebtedness to the Italian.[35] The spirit of Boccaccio's *novella*, however, is much changed. The amour entered into by the young widow who has been restrained from marriage by a selfish father is now matter for something other than a sad story which ought to arouse sympathy in all true lovers. Its results—the murder of the lover by the father, the sending of his heart to Gismond in a cup of gold, and Gismond's drinking of poison from the cup—are held up as a warning against lust. The second chorus of the play condemns Gismond for her failure to

show the chaste steadfastness of such famous women as
Lucrece and Penelope. The fourth chorus urges all lovers
to walk in the path of chastity and sinlessness that was followed by Petrarch and his lady, and to realize that glory
instead of tragedy will then be their portion. Such senti-
ments fly in the face of the supernatural beings who, partly
under the inspiration of Dolce's *Didone* (1547) and partly
according to general Senecan convention, are offered as
machinery for the tragedy, and who would imply that the
struggling human creatures of the action are merely puppets under the control of whimsical forces. Cupid appears
at the opening of the play as a slighted and petulant divinity of the type familiar in Seneca and not unknown in
Euripides. His designs for the ruin of Gismond are furthered later by Megaera, a Fury of Hell, who explains her
presence by telling how the gods have lightly played poli-
tics with humanity as a pawn. She has been sent by Pluto,
who owes a debt to Cupid because Cupid has helped him
to win Proserpine. Pluto has also been moved by the demand for revenge made by the spirit of Gismond's husband, and, all in all, has decided to make Cupid "lord of
his will." The play is thus a patchwork of Christian morality at odds with Senecan fatalism. In one sentence Megaera
juxtaposes the two conceptions of tragedy:

> Furies must aide, when men will ceasse to know
> Their Goddes: and Hell shall send reuēging paine
> To those, whome Shame frō sinne can not restraine.[36]

Here man's punishment for not knowing his gods, in view
of the political background which Megaera has just pic-

tured, has no more to do with right and wrong than it usually has in Seneca himself. The revenging pain for the sin of unchastity is quite another matter.

In *Gismond of Salerne* the ghost of the husband takes no place upon the stage for the execution of his revenge. He is only the subject of remark in a line or two of verse. But in *The Misfortunes of Arthur* a Senecan ghost comes upon the Elizabethan stage in full regalia, ushering into the play a host of Senecan passages which at times make it little more than a mosaic of extracts.[37] In this, the second of the Inns of Court tragedies to be based upon the legendary history of Britain, Gorlois, Duke of Cornwall, rises from the infernal deeps to glut himself with vengeance. Because King Uther Pendragon despoiled him of his wife, fathering the twins Arthur and Anne, and then slew him in battle, he must see that evil overwhelms the royal line. He claims the characters in the play as "engines" of his hate. If they are engines of such hatred, they are also useful engines of Christian morality. Mordred, son of Arthur by an incestuous union with Anne, is an ambitious villain, admitting that right is not on his side, but willing to dare everything against Arthur to win the queen and the kingdom. On the part of both Arthur and Mordred there is much talk of chance. Yet after the fatal clash of armies, the dying Arthur addresses the dead Mordred in these terms:

> Well: since both Heauens and Hell conspir'd in one,
> To make our endes a mirror to the worlde,
> Both of incestuous life, and wicked birth:
> Would Gods the *Fates* that linckt our faultes alike,
> Had also fram'de our minds of frendlier mouldes.[38]

Thus Senecan fatalism changes into a philosophy rather suggestive of Christian predestination, which would emphasize human responsibility for sin even under Providence. At the end of the play the ghost of Gorlois professes himself well pleased with the way in which his "revenge" has meted out punishment for vice. The drama so easily becomes a tragedy of retribution to Arthur for his sin of incest and to Mordred for his criminal ambition that its matter can with truth be advertized as one which

In tragike note the plagues of vice recounts.[35]

In this one of the four plays, at least, the Christian, or Hebraic, God of justice tends strongly to overshadow the Senecan machinery of supernaturalism.

The Inns of Court dramatists, as we have seen, were in various ways closely in accord with popular taste. It may not be said that their learned predilections led them to take refuge in an ivory tower. They practiced much that was too artificial and too flatly pretentious for vital stage drama, but at the same time they did their work in English, the "vulgar" tongue, and when they prepared Seneca for English—though not vulgar—reception, they manag... quently enough to let him talk and think in the native style. They decidedly earned a right to be considered as helping to fill the main stream of Elizabethan tragedy.

III

Dramatic development of the theme of ambition to such a degree that it could be truly dominant, a development written large in the popular destiny of Gothic tragedy, took place in even more academic surroundings than the Inns of Court. In that period between the earlier and the later bursts of dramatic activity in Elizabeth's reign when tragedy was still awaiting secure establishment upon the public stage, Thomas Legge, master of Caius College, Cambridge, and twice vice-chancellor, produced his trilogy *Richardus Tertius*. It was acted at Cambridge in March, 1580 (1579 according to the old reckoning). The subject, drawn from fairly recent national history, was a sufficiently remarkable one for university Latin drama. Subject and able exploitation together gained for Legge's play a large contemporary fame. With its discovery of the unifying dramatic force and the profound dramatic appeal which lay in the destructive ambition of Richard III, it was prophetic of high success for English chronicle tragedy.

Renaissance Latin tragedy before Legge had already provided some such historic central figure as Richard III, a figure of criminal ambition heightened beyond the Senecan conception of tyranny represented by Lycus in *Hercules Furens* or by Atreus in *Thyestes*. By the middle of the fifteenth century three Latin plays in imitation of Seneca had been written in Italy. The earliest of these, the *Ecerinis* (1314) of Albertino Mussato, had found its subject not in classic story but in almost contemporary history. Its action is the career of Ezzelino III, tyrant of Padua, his rise to hold the scepter after he has discovered that Satan is his father and may be invoked for aid, his fiendish cruelties, his death. In English university drama, however, there had been nothing truly comparable with Legge's venture.[40]

In *Richardus Tertius* the fatalistic spirit of Senecan tragedy once more finds out the ascetic spirit of *De Casibus* tragedy and unites with it by a natural affinity. The union results in a hybrid dramatic conception in which it is sometimes difficult to say whether the Senecan has been subdued to the native spirit or the native to the Senecan. Legge's Richard lacks entirely the willful force of Shakespeare's Richard. He is one who is driven rather than one who drives; he is so far from showing proud self-confidence that he is shaken by fear at all stages of his ambitious course. Yet he is not a cog in a mass of Senecan machinery. Behind the tragedy there are no gods or goddesses actuated by personal spite, and there is no ghost to start the action, himself perhaps drawn unwillingly from the depths of Pluto's kingdom to preside over the mechanical dance of other puppets. Toward the end of the play Furor appears briefly to urge Richard toward his destruction, but here there is only mild and unsustained use of a Senecan Fury. Legge offers plentiful imitation of Seneca in phrasing and in certain other matters, but not in the structure of his work as it implies tragic interpretation of Richard's character.

This structure is simple. *Richardus Tertius* may be called a trilogy because it is divided into three actios, each of five acts, for presentation on three several evenings, though each actio, strictly speaking, is scarcely to be thought of as a play by itself. The first is Richard's rising toward the crown, including the removal of Hastings and ending with the debasement of Shore's wife from the high position that she occupied under the former king; the second is his attainment of the crown, ending with the spectacle of his coronation; the third is his decline and fall, beginning with the outrageous murder of the princes in the Tower and ending with his death in the battle with Richmond. Here are no classic unities. The pageant of history is spread before us in epic as well as dramatic fashion, with a host of characters and much change of scene. At the center of it all is Richard, first attaching himself to Fortune's wheel and rising with its revolution, then seating himself at the top of the wheel's reach, then falling from the height as the wheel continues its motion. Some who are in his train fall as he rises, and some fall as he falls. There is a constant chorus of outcries against false Fortune, from a Hastings, from a Buckingham, or from Richard himself. Such outcries may have the phrasing of Senecan moralizings upon the fickleness of Fortuna, but they issue from human beings placed in an almost purely medieval setting. Legge's tragedy of Richard might well be one out of Boccaccio's *De Casibus,* much expanded in dramatization. It retains faithfully the Boccacesque pyramid of ambition and marks off plainly its three formal divisions: ascent, apex, descent. Thus Legge's three actios are like the "Wolseius aspirans," the "Wolseius triumphans," and the "Wolseius moriens" of Thomas Storer's *The Life and Death of Thomas Wolsey Cardinall* (1599) and the three similar divisions of Christopher Brooke's *The Ghost of Richard the Third* (1614). Both of these tragical poems have already received attention.

In marking for Richard a reversal of Fortune's favor after the medieval style, Legge was supported by certain passages of moral comment in those chronicles upon which he depended for his material." Much of the chronicle tradition, however, as well as the later dramatic tradition,

made the story of Richard a tragedy of conscience, giving
him a capacity to realize his responsibility and to suffer
inwardly for crimes which he had willfully committed.
Readily as Legge used the structure of the Boccacesque
tragedy of Fortune, he may possibly have let learned sympathy with Seneca really determine him when he chose to
make Richard so definitely a driven creature instead of a
driving force.[42] Certainly Legge's protagonist has no more
conscience and no more responsibility for his acts than an
Atreus or a Jocasta under Senecan manipulation. *Richardus
Tertius* forecasts the colorful pageantry and the effective
sweep of the best tragic drama on the Elizabethan popular
stage, yet does not forecast the dynamic conceptions of human character achieved on the stage of Shakespeare.

Chapter X

THE ESTABLISHMENT OF TRAGEDY
UPON THE ELIZABETHAN STAGE
(*Continued*)

SOON AFTER 1585, the floodgates of Elizabethan tragic drama were opened, and from that time forward a rapidly filling stream flowed across the popular stage. By the end of the sixteenth century, probably, Shakespeare had written *Julius Caesar* (*ca.* 1599), a play in which he clearly stands poised between immaturity and maturity in tragic perception. Thereby he had helped to mark a limit to the period of primary development for the popular tragic drama. The crowded years at the close of the century are now to be scanned. Amidst their oscillating and often repetitive achievements, we shall serve the purpose in hand if we fix attention upon main divisions of tragic manner and examine representative plays.

In the very forefront of this popular movement in tragedy, and obviously possessing key importance, we find Christopher Marlowe's *Tamburlaine* and Thomas Kyd's *The Spanish Tragedie,* the one a drama of ambition and the other a drama of revenge. Both took the fancy of the theatergoing and the reading public in the highest degree and left indelible impression upon many succeeding plays. Which of the two came first it is perhaps impossible to determine. Some conservative opinion, including that of Sir Edmund Chambers, would give the honor to *Tamburlaine* (*ca.* 1587). Whether such opinion is right or wrong, there is a certain fitness in approaching the tragic drama of the late 1580's and the 1590's through *Tamburlaine* and those plays with which it has a pronounced measure of kinship. This is because Marlowe's famous conqueror play is representative of something which needed little help from Renaissance Seneca to achieve dramatic power in new form. It has native feeling much more simply and obviously than *The Spanish Tragedie,* and it urges upon our understanding with all the authority of true poetic genius the fact that serious popular drama as it outgrew the manner of the morality possessed great promise.

As a play contributing to English tragic tradition, however, *Tamburlaine* is curiously distorted. It has a very real relationship with the native tragedy of the past and with the popular tragedy of the future; on the title page of the first (1590) edition, it is designated as "two Tragicall Discourses." But, whether or not through mere carelessness, the entry in the Stationers' Register (August 14, 1590) makes it "twooe commicall discourses," and the "discourses" might, indeed, be called somewhat comic in a medieval sense, since there is no true catastrophe for Tamburlaine. The Scythian shepherd walks upon the necks of captive kings to unbelievable success after unbelievable success. He dies in the fullness of years, but he never falls, and no one need feel that his end is other than "prosperous." Nevertheless, the fact remains that never before was there a medieval comedy like this, a medieval tragedy reversed, a rebellious violation of all that *De Casibus* tragedy had set out to convey.

What of the power of Fortune and the insecurity of those ambitious men who enter her realm? Ascetic medieval tragedy had had much to say on this matter. *Tamburlaine* surrounds what had thus been said and turns it upside down. The young poet Marlowe erects a hero who has all the possible effrontery of self-confident youth, and he makes him brave Fortune, throw humility to the dogs, seduce us from Contempt of the World with eloquent poetry—and prosper. Tamburlaine himself never lets us rest from hearing that he holds "the Fates bound fast in yron chaines," that it is his own hand that turns Fortune's wheel about,

> And sooner shall the Sun fall from his Spheare,
> Than *Tamburlaine* be slaine or ouercome.[1]

This demands lightning from Heaven; but lightning never strikes. Others agree that Tamburlaine is supreme and that his merits combine with fate to make him so:

> Nature doth striue with Fortune and his stars
> To make him famous in accomplisht woorth:
> And well his merits show him to be made
> His Fortunes maister.[2]

Their words prove true. He is Fortune's master to the last. He attaches himself to her wheel and then commands its movement to his liking, rising to the sweet fruition of kingship and refusing to let that fruition turn bitter because death claims his beloved queen. Zenocrate's death merely produces "impassionate furie" and a further display of grandeur, an outfacing of death itself with the preservation of her embalmed body "not lapt in lead but in a sheet of gold" as a royal memento. In all this we are infinitely far removed from the spirit of Boccaccio's *De Casibus* and of the Dance of Death. We are asked to have sympathy with an espousal of worldly life that is almost childish, or savage, in its heedless thoroughness, and we see that Marlowe is utterly beyond making excuses for liking the "divine" aspiration of a hero.[3] *The French Academie* (1586), one of the many works in which Marlowe could have found some account of Tamburlaine's career,[4] makes peace with the *De Casibus* tradition by saying in its chapter "Of Fortune" that the Scythian shepherd was exceptional for the way in which he remained supremely happy after his conquering rise. It implies that contemplation of his career cannot be very edifying. Marlowe, of course, makes no such comment. We may be sure that in giving himself to the poetic magnification of such an exception he is, indeed, the exact opposite of apologetic.

Marlowe obviously takes delight in showing tragic possibilities for Tamburlaine only to reject them. When Bajazeth, the captive emperor of the Turks, has brained himself against the cage which Tamburlaine has provided for him and when the Turkish empress has followed her lord to a like release from ignominy, Zenocrate knows not only pity but also tragic fear. Let Tamburlaine, she says, fighting "for Scepters and for slippery crownes" and sleeping each night with conquest on his brows, behold this great Turk and his empress, how they are fallen. May Heaven pardon Tamburlaine's contempt of earthly fortune and his ruthless cruelty. Otherwise, he may fall as his captive princes have fallen, and so may she herself. This note of tragic expectation is sounded near the end of the first part of the play. In the second part Marlowe goes farther in suggesting the tragic reversal which he refuses to carry out. Bajazeth has a son, Callapine, also taken prisoner by Tamburlaine. In the first act of the second part he escapes and bends his energies to the gathering of an army and the execution of revenge for his father's death. He becomes a recurrent threat to Tamburlaine. By the third act, when he has been crowned Emperor of Turkey, and kings have sworn allegiance to him, he is confidently hoping, and we are fearing (since Marlowe's hero has our sympathy), that through him Fortune "will now retaine her olde inconstancie" and show it upon Tamburlaine. But Marlowe builds up the force of Callapine only to make it come to nought in pure fiasco. Twice the Turk flees from Tamburlaine in defeat. The last time furnishes matter for mere farce. Tamburlaine, old and diseased but still holding at bay his "slaue, the vglie monster death," rides in his chariot drawn by captive kings. He is told that Callapine, with an army again, is in the offing. From the business of dying and properly disposing of his dominions the conqueror for a moment turns his attention: "Alarme, Tamb. goes in, and comes out againe with al the rest." We learn that at the mere sight of him the opposing forces have melted and run away. It is a fitting final show of Tamburlaine's high astounding quality, always magnificent and at the same time always more or less ludicrous.

It is common knowledge that Marlowe had a reputation for "atheism." Just what degree of seriousness may have lain behind the iconoclastic remarks upon religion which he apparently made so freely to his acquaintances does not appear in the doubtlessly garbled and highly colored complaint laid against him by Richard Baines. That Marlowe had found honest doubts in his soul sufficient to keep him from taking the holy orders for which his residence at Cambridge had prepared him, and which his scholarship required him to take, it is reasonable to assume. But at least it is plain that after he reached London he took a certain youthful delight in shocking simple piety by unrestrained conversational comment upon religion in general and Christianity in particular. And in *Tamburlaine* he shows something of the same youthful delight in letting himself go. He glorifies outrageously all those things that ascetic *De Casibus* tragedy had held up to the view of good Christians as lacking in true glory and worthy only of contempt. Here he took a long step beyond that acceptance of the world, common enough in his time, which interested itself in tragedy working through mundane law. He gave himself completely to a drama of untrammeled worldly success. Needless to say, Marlowe outgrew this young man's worship of pomp, or he could not afterward have written the tragedies that he did write. Occupation with the business of holding Fate fast bound in iron chains was far behind him before he died.

Unbalanced though Marlowe's genius is when it shows itself in *Tamburlaine,* it is unquestionably genius of high promise, and the ludicrous dramatic effects into which it falls have a saving quality. We may smile at them, but we are not inclined to smile in scorn. For by this play Marlowe means something that is essentially not cheap or tawdry. The aspiration of his conqueror hero is somehow sidetracked in satisfaction with crowns and scepters and other baubles. Yet it starts with the contemplation of faculties in man which can hopefully strive to comprehend the world and all the restless spheres in their "wondrous Architecture."

It must have truly moving force for any age which views the material world as at least one theater for man's courageous effort.

The conqueror plays written most directly in imitation of Marlowe have little of Marlowe's saving grace. Robert Greene's *The Comicall Historie of Alphonsus King of Aragon* (*ca.* 1587), which has almost nothing to do with history, makes Venus preside as prologue over the king-trampling exploits of a hero who has a softer side in love than Marlowe's hero. Like *Tamburlaine* it recognizes the moralizings of *De Casibus* tragedy only to nullify them, except for minor characters. Alphonsus takes service with the King of Naples, who is eventually to be swept from his path, and his ascent begins:

> Thus from the pit of pilgrimes pouertie
> *Alphonsus* ginnes by step and step to climbe
> Vnto the toppe of friendly Fortunes wheel.[6]

Though petty kings know Fortune's frown, Alphonsus always gains her smiles. He talks, like Tamburlaine, of mastering Fortune, of clapping her up within a cage of gold, but his Tamburlainean thunder is unconvincing. In all ways he shows himself the creation of a young poet more lightly ballasted than Marlowe, though skillful. Alphonsus wins his climactic crown and his princess from Amurack, the Great Turk. The Oriental scene, as Marlowe had revealed, possessed a colorful fitness for the conqueror play. The anonymous productions *The First Part of the Tragicall Raigne of Selimus* (1591–1594) and *The Warres of Cyrus King of Persia* (of about the same date as *Selimus*) also follow Mar-

lowe's lead into Eastern fields of ambition. Each takes its
hero through astounding deeds or outlandish tyrannies to
a position secure from catastrophe. *Selimus* especially is an
orgy of cruelty. The spirit in which its hero's conquering
is done is that which passed for Machiavellian among the
Elizabethans. Selimus believes that religious teachings and
the laws of morality were invented only as "bug-beares to
keepe the world in fcare" in order that it might be held
under the tyrant's yoke. He himself is beyond being duped
by such things, and he sees no reason why the truly great
man should not be guided by worldly Nature instead of by
some imagined God who would restrain the ambitious:

> Why should we seeke to make that soule a slaue,
> To which dame Nature so large freedome gaue?[7]

Apparently he is justified in his philosophy. He finally
exults as a succcssful traveler through weary places who
finds dangers overpast. There is promise by the dramatist
that applause would bring a second part to the drama, with
"greater murthers." Probably retribution for Selimus, or a
change of Fortune, was far from the dramatist's mind.

Interest in the ambitious conqueror for success alone was
never so great among the Elizabethan audience, however,
as to check the development of tragedy. The age of Marlowe was far from having forgotten that Fortune or other
forces could lower man's pride as well as raise it. If anything, the dramatic spectacle of Tamburlainean ambition
seems to have stimulated new desire in the public theaters
for the dramatic spectacle of tragic ambition and to have
encouraged rapid development of that spectacle through

wide variations of form, from the simplest tragedy of Fortune's wheel to tragedy of psychological complexity in the
linkage of character and event.

II

By 1599, Thomas Dekker could produce *The Pleasant Comedie of Old Fortunatus,* a play dealing with rise and fall
under the rule of Fortune which has very little of the medieval seriousness of purpose and much graceful lightness of
spirit. But in this formative period of the 1580's and 1590's
plays are not wanting which lay emphasis in most primitive fashion upon the wholly inscrutable ways of Fortune
and which have the most primitive kind of *De Casibus* plot
structure. Even when they show some Senecan or other
sophistication, they tend to represent the earliest conceptions of Gothic tragedy. Mingled with or quickly followed
by plays of far more advanced conception, they are vivid
reminders of the distance which Gothic tragedy traveled
in the course of its evolution. One of the first of these is
Thomas Lodge's *The Wounds of Ciuill War. Liuely set
forth in the true Tragedies of Marius and Scilla (ca.* 1588),
in which very little happens that is not referable merely to
the perilous chances of high place. Fortune, "the wayward
Ladie of this wicked world," as the younger Marius calls her
with Christian rather than Roman feeling, is constantly in
the thoughts and upon the lips of the characters. The story
has little unification; it turns into a record of the violent
ups and downs of two ambitious climbers and their satel-
lites. Marius rises to command against Mithridates in Asia.
Fortune's wheel turns, and Marius finds himself in exile,

while Scilla (Sulla) exults that the "blindfold mistris" has put him in the place of Marius. While Scilla wars against Mithridates, the wheel turns once more and Marius is back in Rome as consul. Just as he captures honor and success, and is about to slaughter his political enemies, he dies, for no apparent cause. Scilla returns in triumph and seizes the reins of power, boasting that the planets at his birth "could entertain no retrograde aspects." But when he hears that Marius the younger has stabbed himself, he is suddenly smitten with a perception that worldly power is vanity. He will retire to low position and learn how to die, since die all men must. He gives up his axes and rods, takes affecting leave of his wife and daughter, and dies, like Marius, for no apparent cause. Despite its basic moral that the wicked world is given over to whimsical Fortune, the play is not above presenting worldly ambition with some of the Marlovian coloring. The conqueror Scilla returning from the war against Mithridates "in his chare triumphant of gold drawen by foure Moores" is highly reminiscent of Tamburlaine.

It is worth while to compare *The Wounds of Civill War* with another Roman tragedy picturing the round of Fortune's wheel, though this was presented upon the academic instead of the public stage. The anonymous *Tragedie of Caesar and Pompey Or Caesars Revenge* was "priuately acted by the Studentes of Trinity Colledge in Oxford"; it was entered in 1606, but it may well have been written in the earlier 1590's. Its speeches show academic origin in a fulsomeness of rhetoric and of classical allusion; yet there is little more of the true classic spirit shown by the univer-

sity drama than by Lodge's. For example, Caesar, smitten
with love for Cleopatra, boasts of his greatness in the accents
of *Tamburlaine*. The tragic structure is simply the rise of
Caesar beginning with Pharsalus, his fall, and his revenge,
over which he presides as a ghost. It is notable, especially so
in an academic play, that the ghost leads us to think as
much of the *Mirror for Magistrates* as of Seneca, and is,
indeed, an excellent example of one more way in which
medieval and Senecan tragedy could join forces.

While Caesar climbs to the top of Fortune's wheel he has
in a conquered rival an object lesson to show him the dangers which follow such rising, as Scilla has in Lodge's play;
and at Pompey's death his "compassion draws forth Princely
teares." He says that he knows he will himself fall from
prosperity, because those on the heights always do fall.
When Caesar has been assassinated and his followers are at
outs among themselves, his ghost appears upon the stage
to bewail his fortune and to berate his friends for fighting
each other while they should be uniting to get revenge for
his death. The ghost also appears to Brutus on the eve of
battle, as Plutarch gives him a right to do, and in the end
exults over the downfall of the conspirators. What this
ghost has of *De Casibus* character is shown in such a speech
as the following, which could easily serve as the beginning
of a ghostly complaint to Baldwin in the *Mirror,* granted
that Baldwin might imagine himself at Rome:

> Out of the horror of those shady vaultes,
> Where Centaurs, Harpies, paynes and furies fell:
> And Gods and Ghosts and vgly Gorgons dwell,
> My restles soule comes heere to tell his wronges.

Hayle to thy walles, thou pride of all the world,
Thou art the place where whilome in my life
My seat of mounting honour was erected,
And my proud throane that seem'd to check the heauens.
But now my pompe and I are laid more lowe,
With these asosiates of my ouerthrow,
Here ancient *Assur* and proud *Belus* lyes,
Ninus the first that sought a Monarches name.

And so on to the fallen rulers of Rome, including Marius
and Sulla:

Ambitious *Sylla* and fierce *Marius*,
And both the *Pompeyes* by me don to death,
I am the last not least of the same crue,
Look on my deeds and say what *Caesar* was.[8]

At the height of his career he was struck down with three-
and-twenty wounds. Then what, he asks, avails his former
grandeur? In spite of the preachment urging us to scorn
the world as ruled by irrational change, there is some attempt in the play to show that Caesar's fall was retribution
for the bloodshed of his ambitious career.

III

The tragedy of ambition with primitive principles of structure was well represented on the Elizabethan stage by plays
drawing upon British history, or upon what was accepted
as history in the chronicles. Such chronicle drama as
The Famous Victories of Henry the Fifth (1588 or earlier)
might be merely spectacular patriotism mixed with unsubtle comedy, serving a commemorative purpose on the secular stage somewhat comparable with that served by the

mystery on the religious stage. But a dramatist scanning the chronicles with a new play in mind found no lack of stimulation to the construction of simple tragedy. The pages which he turned were often filled with failures of national and personal ambitions, many of which had received moral tags from the chronicle historians. Moreover, there was always the unforgettable *Mirror,* with its tragic exploitation of the British scene, to furnish powerful example.

Tragedy of exceedingly primitive, not to say incomplete, conception appears in *The Life and Death of Iacke Straw, A notable Rebell in England,* which is possibly of about the same date as *The Famous Victories.* The anonymous author gives the play no real unity in the person of his hero; especially in conclusion he is of two minds whether he is writing of a notable rebel or of a notable rebellion in the reign of Richard II. Jack Straw's career is ended in the third act; a fourth (and last) act merely chronicles the punishment of the remaining rebels and praises the fairness and goodness of the king's actions. There is an abundance of clownish comedy in connection with the rustic rebellion, and there is an obvious implication that dignity and right are on the side of the king's law and order. Yet some sympathetic attention is given to the development of tragic character in the leading rebel, for Jack Straw is presented as a man much wronged when he rises against the state. With a horde of armed followers at his back he changes from a righter of grievances into a blustering bully crying that he is as good as a lord and will be one. He is then talked of contemptuously as a man of low degree who has become unruly through ambition. Eventually there is some attempt to make him an example of fallen pride. Typical *De Casibus* moralizing, however, is conspicuously absent.

In *Jacke Straw* some would find the hand of George Peele.° If Peele's hand is really there, it performs a far more naïve kind of tragic experimentation with historical material than that performed in his *The Battell of Alcazar, fought in Barbarie, between Sebastian king of Portugall, and Abdelmelec king of Marocco* (*ca.* 1589), even though *The Battell of Alcazar* also fails to achieve an effective tragic unity. *Jacke Straw* has so much of the unsophisticated native style that it fully deserves the name of "enterlude" given to it by the Stationers' Register. For its scenes of low comedy it even uses tumbling verse in the manner of the moral plays. *The Battell of Alcazar,* on the contrary, has more than a little sophistication. It has dumb-shows, and it introduces Act II with three ghosts crying "Vindicta!" and seeking revenge. Also it is by way of making an ambitious adventurer, Captain Thomas Stukeley, who was reputed in some quarters to be the illegitimate son of Henry VIII, into an English Tamburlaine. But though Tom Stukeley is made to talk in the best Scythian tradition of his brave mind which must never cease to aspire, of his determination to choose a kingdom among all the continents that bound the world, and of his preference for being king of a molehill rather than the richest subject of a monarchy, his historic ineffectuality is something of a clog upon the dramatist's expansiveness. Moreover, though Stukeley takes the front of the stage when he dies, and reviews at length the adventures of his colorful career, he is not the true center of the action. The play is exactly what it is called in a second title:

"The Tragicall battell of Alcazzar in Barbarie, With the death of three Kings, and Captaine Stukley an Englishman." In other words, it is a wholesale offering of heroic business in romantic foreign fields where ambition, stirred by

> Honor the spurre that pricks the princely minde,
> To followe rule and climbe the stately chaire,[10]

leads to the fall of three princes and the end of a grandiloquent upstart. The struggle for the crown of Barbary is between Muly Mahamet, "the negro Moor," who is "black in his look and bloody in his deeds," and his uncle, the "good" Abdelmelec. The king of Portugal aids the usurper Muly Mahamet and draws Stukeley into the venture when the Englishman puts into Portuguese waters with a fleet which is primarily intended for the capture of Ireland in the interests of Catholicism. The deaths of these principal contenders for empire make a multiple catastrophe which is little more than a martial spectacle of blood.

How such multiple tragedy as this, which still has much of the nonselective character of the chronicles, may become a sort of dramatic section of the *Mirror for Magistrates* and offer its several fallen great ones in a moralized *De Casibus* procession is shown by *The Lamentable Tragedie of Locrine* (*ca.* 1591), which is one of the earliest of the so-called apocryphal Shakespearean dramas.[11] This play boasts much superficial sophistication and has with reason been counted as strongly marked by Seneca. It has two ghosts seeking revenge for blood, it has a presiding spirit of revenge in the Goddess Ate, it has much Senecan declamation, and it has the dumb-shows of English Seneca as evolved by the Inns of Court in the 1560's. But it also has unashamed native affiliations in some rather effective scenes of low comedy, and its general structure can by no means be explained merely as Senecan. Obviously the author knew the *Mirror,* in particular the part first published by John Higgins in 1574, and obviously the *Mirror* served him in more ways than by simply directing him to tragic material of tested popular appeal. In a very real sense it helped to shape his tragedy.

Higgins' first five legends, of Albanact, Humber, Locrinus, Elstride, and Sabrine, cover the action of the drama. Behind these is matter in the chronicles, upon which the dramatist depended in large measure directly.[12] The most concrete indication that he also depended upon the matter in Higgins' legends is to be found in what he writes of Turnus, the follower of Brutus.[13] Here, it seems, we may accept a plain debt to the *Mirror* for a small bit of fact as well as for the spelling of a name. But the more important common ground held by *Locrine* and the *Mirror* is in tragic design and in tragic philosophy. Instead of reaching unity in the character of Locrine, the play tends to be a dramatized series of Higgins' legends, a string of medieval tragic falls. And the morals which it yields for the constant succession of deaths are substantially those supplied in the *Mirror.*

The tragic comment which Higgins allows to his plaintive ghosts is often enough utterly commonplace. Certainly the author of *Locrine* did not need to learn from him that the world is unstable, that the poor are farthest from annoy, and that great men, like tall trees, are most shaken by blasts and most smitten by lightning. Such ideas were anybody's property. It is not the general likeness of the moral observations, then, so much as the correspondence in application that is noteworthy. After he has given Brutus' dying harangue, Higgins philosophizes at length upon the inescapable character of death. In the play at the same point the old warrior Corineius offers similar comment on mortality:

> For fatall *Mors* expecteth all the world,
> And euerie man must tread the way of death.[14]

In the *Mirror,* Albanact falls before Humber just when he considers himself "an heauenly happy wight," and although Higgins has elsewhere made it plain that Albanact's fault is rashness, the subject of mishap assails Fortune with rhetorical reproach. In the play, Albanact outdoes the *Mirror* but preserves its spirit in railing against the injurious Fortune who fails "thus in the prime of my felicitie." When in turn Humber is overtaken by tragedy, the play and the *Mirror* unite closely in moral spirit. The dramatist has used the opportunity to introduce a Senecan ghost of Albanact in pursuit of Humber. Not content with the revenge theme, he gives the ghost righteous observations upon the character of Humber's sins. The result is a ghost who shouts "Vindicta!" in the most approved Senecan style and at the same time makes a general moral justice contribute to the satisfaction of his personal desires:

> Loe here the gift of fell ambition,
> Of vsurpation and of trecherie.
> Loe here the harmes that wait vpon all those
> That do intrude themselues in others lands,
> Which are not vnder their dominion.[15]

This "intruding" upon others' lands is definitely a moral offense which Higgins allows Humber to confess:

> Thou mayst thyselfe perceiue, somwhat by mee,
> Let neither trust, nor treason, trayne forth yee,
>   But bee content with thine estate, so shall
> No wrath of God procure thy haplesse fall.
>
> If thou bee foraine, bide with in thy soyle
> That God hath giuen to thee and thine to holde.[16]

Finally, both Higgins and the dramatist direct attention to the fruits of Locrine's lawless love, though Higgins, who is more consistently attracted by the idea of poetic justice than the dramatist, is in this matter more explicit. These correspondences between *Locrine* and the *Mirror* are, of course, not the sort to prove that the dramatist had John Higgins' work constantly before him as he wrote. It is not difficult to see how a popular work like the *Mirror* could have been to an Elizabethan playwright a pervasive influence rather than a source of material.

By far the most forceful of such early attempts to deal with tragical history in the mass is comprised in the three parts of *Henry VI* (1590–1592), the last two of which are closely related to *The First Part of the Contention betwixt the two famous Houses of Yorke and Lancaster* and *The true Tragedie of Richard Duke of Yorke, and the death of good King Henrie the Sixt.*[17] Whatever share Shakespeare may have had in this sweeping together of man's inhumanities to man practiced in the Wars of the Roses is usually regarded as his earliest dramatic work. And if Shakespeare's hand was actually dominant in the shaping of the produc-

CC

tion, he already showed signs of dramatic power. For in a pageant of chronicled tragedies, one pursuing the other with simple iteration, there can be an epic weight, quite different from the weight of the more narrowly unified tragedy, but genuinely effective. In *Henry VI* the finer possibilities of multiple tragedy are often realized.

Throughout the trilogy we follow the ill-fated kingship of Henry, but the most constant theme is England torn by civil war. Coming and going upon the scene are men and women who hope to profit by the bitter animosities of the struggle, who have their little day of rising ambition and success, and who quickly fall. The civil war is a forced draft fanning all those fires of worldly aspiration which the ascetic tragedy of the Middle Ages sought to quench. It favors all the criminal propensities in ambitious humanity. England as pictured under its influence is very much like the world pictured by medieval Contempt, a trackless forest filled with wild beasts and robbers, where the struggle for place is merely madness with horrible accompaniments. Sometimes the good man falls (Humphrey, Duke of Gloucester); sometimes the evil (Suffolk, destroyer of Gloucester). Henry himself is in it all, yet not of it all. He is a spiritual opposite to those around him who have lusts for power and domination; he loves peace and he has manly pity for suffering. He is hardly drawn as a weak man, and he is certainly not drawn as basely or miserably weak. He is simply a king who cannot use the strong hand of domination because brutality repels him. The ironical result is that cruel things happen in his realm which might never have happened if he had been willing to use cruelty on his own account in taking the reins of government—Duke Humphrey's murder, for example.

Henry thus is able to fill the place of an ascetic medieval chorus, scorning the ambitious life which produces such a succession of tragic falls. But this is not a drama showing the otherworldliness of medieval asceticism or offering its religious morality. Though Henry has some saintly quality, he is only a secular saint, one who would retire from an evil world, yet one who has no sure other world of goodness for his retreat. His scorn of the world leads therefore to despairing philosophic inactivity. No scene in which we find him is more pointed with such despair than that in which he has been chidden from the battle by his queen and by Clifford because they feel that he is useless in such enterprise, as, indeed, he is. While he sits upon a molehill contemning the state of kings and reviewing the happiness of which the lowly state is capable, fringes of the battle come into his view. "Alarum. Enter a Son that hath killed his Father, with the dead body." Also, "enter a Father that hath killed his Son, with the body in his arms." Before his eyes these nameless common soldiers both discover what they have done, and the king learns that when ambitious overlords fly at each other's throats, even the lowly state may be no happy retreat:

> O piteous spectacle! O bloody times!
> Whiles lions war and battle for their dens,
> Poor harmless lambs abide their enmity.
>   (Part Three, II, v, 73–75)

Primitive tragedy of a quite different sort appears in *The True Chronicle Historie of the whole life and death of*

Thomas Lord Cromwell (entered and printed in 1602; probably written some few years earlier). Here, though dramatically significant character drawing is of the slightest, the dramatist is pressed by the biographical nature of his task toward the creation of a unifying central figure. It is one of the apocryphal Shakespearean dramas which are least like anything that we should expect from even the immature Shakespeare. The attempt which it makes at giving some degree of tragic structure to the biography of Cromwell relates it closely to those ascetic *De Casibus* narratives in which men rise and fall upon Fortune's wheel only because the world is full of lawless instability. Yet the ascetic theme utterly lacks the spiritual force which it may have in a medieval tragedy. We gain the impression that the author either knows no better theme to follow in presenting the career of Cromwell or that he is content with a conventional view suitable to the purpose of making Cromwell a good man sinned against. For Cromwell here is something of the Protestant martyr that he is in Foxe's *Actes and Monuments*. As a boy in his father's smithy he shows himself moved by ambition, declaring that if Wolsey, the wonder of the age, can rise to the heights after being born a butcher's son, so can he soar from baseness. But the dramatist gives him no power of will to bring about his rise and no qualities of selfish scheming. Cromwell travels on the Continent, he does many good deeds, and eventually, when the play is half done, he is raised suddenly to great power in England. Observers of his career, remembering the recent fall of Wolsey, expect for him the same reversal of Fortune. They are not disappointed. Envy overthrows him, and he pro-

vides his own chorus of contempt for a world of struggling
ambition in his farewell to his son:

> Marke, boye, the last words that I speake to thee.
> Flatter not Fortune, neither fawne vpon her;
> Gape not for state, yet loose no sparke of honor;
> Ambition, like the plague see thou eschew it;
> I die for treason, boy, and neuer knew it.[18]

In two other plays of about the same date, loosely composed chronicle biography tends to have a tragic outline
based upon the irrational revolution of Fortune's wheel,
emphasizing first a spectacular rise to greatness from com-
parative obscurity and then a sudden fall. One of these, *Sir
Thomas More* (*ca.* 1596), preserved in manuscript and of
more than ordinary interest because a part of the script is
possibly Shakespeare's, is a much finer piece of work than
Thomas Lord Cromwell. Its chief figure frequently stands
before us as a man of innate power, able to sway other men,
to inspire their affectionate confidence, and to rise to the
level of true greatness. Also, his solemn decision to look
at suddenly gained "honor, office, wealth, and calling" as
having serpent natures dangerous to his soul and as being
wholly transitory makes him more profoundly a scorner
of the world than Cromwell and gives his tragedy honest,
rather than conventional, medieval meaning. He has much
of the combination of merry staunchness and religious humility shown by the historic More in both his writings and
his actions. But the play makes small dramatic capital of
the problem of conscience which More cannot solve except
with the loss of his head. This is partly, no doubt, because
there is dangerous religious controversy involved, but also

because the matter is regarded simply as a *De Casibus* reversal of Fortune. More dies with some of the most effective Gothic mingling of the comic and tragic spirits of which sixteenth-century English tragedy is capable. For the other of these two plays, *The Famous Historye of the life and death of Captaine Thomas Stukeley* (probably 1596), the most that one can say is that it is a rather incoherent gathering of Stukeley's erratic adventures in England, Ireland, Spain, Rome, and Africa. Since it sets out to be Stukeley's biography, it gives him wider scope than Peele's *The Battell of Alcazar*. As a chorus tells us, he rises upon the steps of high promotion while his stars are favorable, and he falls for no other reason than that clearest summer days have darkest nights and that everything must finish.

In none of the popular tragedies more or less given to the theme of ambition which have so far been discussed do we find much attempt to show ambition as introspective by reason of ethical self-consideration and finally open to the refined torture of conscience. Even when there is some disposition to moralize the fall of ambition as a well-deserved retribution, there is nothing but the most rudimentary dramatic process of linking character and event. The simplest medieval conception of rise under the favor of Fortune and fall under her disfavor is usual. Those tragedies of the period with pyramidal rise-and-fall structure which look farther into ambitious human character must come in for later discussion. In the meanwhile we may consider a wholly different fashion of dramatic construction which came very early to have importance for the development of technical skill in popular tragedy.

IV

The Spanish Tragedie (1585–1589) shows itself the head of a dramatic line as clearly as its contemporary *Tamburlaine* (*ca.* 1587). The two lines are so distinct in origin, although they quickly mingle upon the Elizabethan and Jacobean stages, that Kyd's greatest popular success is hardly to be thought of as competing with Marlowe's upon the same tragic ground. *Tamburlaine,* it is true, fails of being tragically catastrophic, but it occupies the usual ground of *De Casibus* story, as has already been said. It takes little color from Seneca and is built upon the medieval shape of Fortune's wheel. Its theme is power gained in the lists of heroic ambition, its lines of plot are broad and in no sense intricately joined, and its concern with the passion of love is the casual concern of a world predominantly masculine, where women are taken for granted as the spoils of the conqueror and have little weight in motivation of action. *The Spanish Tragedie,* on the contrary, cultivates a ground of "Italianate" court intrigue which had been touched by *De Casibus* story only in some such exceptional later production as George Whetstone's *The disordered life of Bianca Maria, Countesse of Celaunt, in forme of her complainte, supposed at the houre of her beheading for procuring the murder of Ardissino Valperga, Earle of Massino,* in *The Rocke of Regard* (1576). It takes much color from Seneca, though its theme of love, revenge, and blood is less lustful than the right Senecan combination. Its plot is an intricate one showing devious scheming for the attainment of various desires, in which check is met with countercheck. Kyd thus reveals the way to popularity for a new kind of tragedy presenting involved romantic intrigue instead of simple rise and fall.

Where *Tamburlaine* and other plays following more or less closely the usual *De Casibus* tradition tend to give the effect of biography, *The Spanish Tragedie* and its kind tend to give the effect of the crowded romantic novel. It is entirely possible that Kyd drew his story of fearful and wonderful happenings incidental to a war between Spain and Portugal from some romance now lost that had already distorted and embroidered history.[19] Though he shows real skill with dramatic situation, he shows neither the skill nor the instinct for confining and deeply channeling the stream of a tragic action; and the unity that he gives the play is only the clever unity of ingenious fiction which connects several lines of startling incident with a certain plausibility. Kyd's achievement, however, is not to be despised. His cleverness, meretricious though it often is, is a step taken upon the Elizabethan stage toward what in Shakespeare's hands is subtlety of dramatic joinery. *The Spanish Tragedie* is loosely constructed, but its joinery is not clumsy, as that in other plays of its time often is.

To talk of a serious tragic meaning for *The Spanish Tragedie* is mostly a labor of supererogation. Kyd's outstanding gift is an instinctive discrimination for utilizing incident melodramatically and for making his story into "good theater." Senecan though he is, he succeeds for the most part in escaping from the ponderous and pretentious seriousness in which Seneca's plays are apt to be stifled. Andrea, whose ghost presides over the play, has no reason for revenge that will bear scanning. He has suffered no horrible wrong. He

THE MURDER OF HORATIO IN "THE SPANISH TRAGEDIE"
From the edition of 1633.

has gone forth to battle and fallen in fair conflict. Nor is anything about his apparition calculated to make our flesh creep. He reports that he has gallantly gained favor from Proserpine, the Lady of Hell, after a viewing of Hell's horrors that was satisfying to curiosity rather than painful. And his conduct throughout the play toward his companion, Revenge, is that of a not too pressing gentleman. He is somewhat impatient, but he sits through an action which approaches what he is really desirous of seeing by a devious course of court intrigue and contention for love. Half the play is a leisurely, though not languid, introduction to the tragedy of Hieronimo's revenge for a murdered son, which a dramatist with profounder tragic instincts than Kyd's might have begun sooner. At the end, Andrea's joy over

[393]

the punishments to be meted out in Hell to many of the long list of dead is a harmlessly melodramatic "hate" offered to the audience for those characters to whom the playwright has denied romantic sympathy.

In short, it seems to be Kyd's faculty in *The Spanish Tragedie* to interest us but not to disturb us by the presentation of direful circumstances. He seems to suffer no real disturbance himself. In the midst of blood and thunder he is singularly free from morbidity and gives us the feeling that he is merely immersing himself in life's violence with youthful and rather innocent zest. Youthful and zestful as *Tamburlaine* is, it is the work of a mind much less innocent, far more capable of questioning life for meaning. Thus the revival of Seneca for the popular stage in this fortunate venture by Kyd is not in the least a revival of pessimistic Stoicism. Something of that kind is to come later, in the seventeenth century. Kyd's Seneca is thoroughly denatured— more so than the early academic Seneca of love intrigue embodied in *Gismond of Salerne*—with a naïve and essentially unphilosophic *joie de vivre*.

It is worth noting that when Kyd thus won popular success with an involved method of tragic construction, the spell of unsophisticated *De Casibus* tragedy showed its continuing strength in a peculiar manner. A ballad is extant which is based upon *The Spanish Tragedie* and which, to judge by the number of editions known, was in popular demand even in the early seventeenth century. It throws Kyd's drama into the simplest terms of *De Casibus* story. Here Hieronimo is a complaining ghost. He tells briefly of his rise to honor under Fortune's smiles (a matter in which

Kyd is dramatically uninterested) and then tells at some length of his fall under Fortune's frown (the matter which Kyd develops in the play but not with any eye for the moral of Hieronimo's fallen "greatness"). The language is in a well-worn *De Casibus* style:

> Hapless *Hieronimo* was my name,
> On whom fond fortune smiled long
> And now her flattering smiles I blame.[20]

Whether Kyd was capable of very much more profundity in the *Ur-Hamlet* than in *The Spanish Tragedie,* granted that the *Ur-Hamlet* was his, we may not know. Certainly there is no more profundity in *Solimon and Perseda* (ca. 1589–1592), based, like the play within the play of *The Spanish Tragedie,* upon Henry Wotton's *Courtlie Controuersie of Cupids Cautels* (1578), and attributable to Kyd upon fairly good grounds of style. Here there is even more interest in lovers crushed by cruel fate, there is the same lightly skillful touch in joining varied incidents of romantic fiction, and there is something of the same not overserious use of a chorus. Love, Fortune, and Death see the play and debate the question: Which has the most important power in the tragedy? There is less intrigue and more humor. The *Ubi Sunt* rumination of Basilisco, the braggart knight, which ticks off a list of great dead from Hercules to Pompey and concludes that since man's life is brittle as a glass, one does well to "play least in sight," is successful foolery with the medieval convention. It is not unworthy of comparison with Falstaff's famous meditation upon honor.

The dramatist who adapted Seneca to the popular stage with such success in *The Spanish Tragedie* also lent a hand in that introduction of French Seneca to English readers which was encouraged by the renowned Lady Pembroke. Kyd's *Cornelia* (printed in 1594) is a translation of Robert Garnier's *Cornélie* inspired by the countess' *Antonius* (printed in 1592), which is a translation of the same French author's *Marc Antoine*. Samuel Daniel and other followers of the countess produced original dramas in the academic form of French Seneca. Except for Kyd, this literary guild despised the popular stage. Its work was an unfruitful attempt to "elevate" English tragedy by a reactionary Senecan movement at a time when English tragedy was strongly bent upon working out its Shakespearean destiny. The characteristic note of the self-conscious reformer is sounded in Daniel's dedication of his *Cleopatra* (printed in 1594) to the Countess of Pembroke herself and to the memory of her brother, Sir Philip Sidney. He feels that he is a soldier fighting for a righteous cause

> Now when so many Pennes (like Speares) are charg'd
> To chase away this tyrant of the North;
> *Grosse Barbarisme,* whose powre grown far inlarg'd
> Was lately by thy valiant brothers worth
> First found, encountred, and prouoked forth.[21]

Fortunately the Gothic spirit, the "tyrant of the North," was powerful enough in England to escape mastery by Senecanism in any such way as this.

The exotic field of love, intrigue, and revenge entered by *The Spanish Tragedie* is assayed for the popular stage in widely varying fashions, but usually in darker mood, by *Titus Andronicus* (printed in 1594), with its story of a father's revenge and its nearer though still not very sophisti-

THE REVENGE OF TITUS ANDRONICUS

From *The Lamentable and Tragical History of Titus Andronicus*, a ballad.

cated approach to the fulsome repulsiveness of Senecan lust
and bloodshed; by Marlowe's *The Jew of Malta* (*ca.* 1589),
with its less central interest in love or lust; by *Alphonsus
Emperour of Germany* (printed in 1654 as by Chapman,
but conceivably written in the sixteenth century originally),
with its cultivation of revenge for a father murdered; by
Lusts Dominion; or, the Lascivious Queen (printed in 1657
as by Marlowe and perhaps first written earlier than 1600),
with its scheming Moor somewhat similar to Aaron in *Titus
Andronicus;* and by John Marston's two parts of *Antonio
and Mellida* (1599), with their intricate trumpery which
includes a father's ghost bent upon revenge and which
foreshadows certain developments of sophistication in the
tragedy of love in the earlier seventeenth century. The star-
crossed lovers in *Romeo and Juliet* (1594–1595), slaves of
Fortune in the play very much as they are in Arthur

Brooke's poem *The Tragicall Historye of Romeus and Juliet* (1562), have some kinship with the romantically ill-fated pair in *Solimon and Perseda*. And, among Shakespeare's later and greater tragedies, *Hamlet* and *Othello* are partly metamorphoses of the Kydian, or post-Kydian, drama of intrigue, though *Hamlet* has a distinctly developed rise-and-fall action and a unity as a drama of revenge to which *The Spanish Tragedie* cannot pretend. It is Marlowe's genius that makes the popular conception of Machiavelli, as a devil of worldly irreligiousness, preside over villainous intrigue in such drama and replace the Senecan ghost. The use of the spirit of Machiavel to speak the prologue to *The Jew of Malta* and foster the action is a successful stroke in the translation of the Senecan language of revenge into a Renaissance language of revengeful ambition. The sort of conscienceless villainy charged to Machiavellian philosophy by many moralists of the age becomes a stock-in-trade of Elizabethan tragedy.

With such drama of exotic intrigue and bloodshed, capitalizing the passions of love and revenge, the "domestic" drama of murder seems to have points of close contact. *The Lamentable and True Tragedie of M. Arden of Feuersham in Kent* (printed in 1592), the best of its kind and apparently the first, has persistently invited comparison with Kyd's known work and has persistently invited ascription to Kyd. At least, Kyd shows a willingness to employ his pen in the journalistic reporting of a crime like that committed against Arden. His pamphlet called *The trueth of the most wicked and secret murthering of Iohn Brewen, Goldsmith of London, committed by his owne wife, through the prouocation of one Iohn Parker whom she loued* was published in 1592, the same year as *Arden of Feversham,* and was listed by the same bookseller. Another play of this kind, *A Warning for Faire Women* (printed in 1599), which deals with the murder of a husband in much the same fashion as *Arden of Feversham* and achieves much the same realistic effectiveness, has a well-known induction evidencing the popularity of the Kydian drama of intrigue. History, Comedy, and Tragedy introduce the action by a contest for dominance on the stage. Tragedy is victorious, though Comedy satirizes shrewdly the occupation of Tragedy with tyrants who obtain crowns by violent cruelties, with plotters who stab one another, with howling choruses, and with filthy whining ghosts who scream, "Revenge! Revenge!" It is Tragedy's honest regret, expressed in confidence to the audience, that her offering of the day does not have heroic and colorful trappings in the style satirized and is especially lacking in both the substance and the trappings of personal revenge. Her implication is that this homely drama of homicide, proffered *faute de mieux,* has at least a place as a poor relation in the family of *The Spanish Tragedie.* Interest in the dramatic possibilities of murder with middle-class setting must have been stimulated by ballads and by moral compilations showing God's judgment upon sin in horrible examples. But it is likely that Kyd and his romantic followers strengthened an impulse toward dramatizing famous murders of everyday life and helped particularly to inspire the domestic tragedy of guilty love and bloodshed.

Both *Arden of Feversham* and *A Warning for Faire*

Women have a simpler structure than *The Spanish Trag-edie*, though the simplicity is not that of the *De Casibus* pyramid. The conspiracies of crime are merely less complicated and the checks to intrigue which increase the dramatic tension less intricate. The two plays are closely similar in their implication of supernatural forces. In each, the dramatist has conceived the action as a series of attempts made upon the life of an ill-fated husband which are frustrated by apparently miraculous combinations of circumstances until finally this supernatural resistance is broken down and the victim meets his death. Then follows retribution in the hanging or burning of the criminals, which is distinctly edifying. Arden is cursed toward the end of the play by a sufferer from his sharp dealings in land, and his death follows soon after. Also, his body is found upon the ground which he has unjustly taken, and grass refuses to grow upon the spot for two years. But the playwright uses such things casually and rather bunglingly. In the story of Arden's murder recorded for the year 1551 by Holinshed the cursing and its apparent result are mentioned. Of previous supernatural protection accorded to Arden nothing is said. The dramatist seems to have had some independent taste for the development of a supernatural tragic background on the domestic plane of old wives' tales. The same can be said for the author of *A Warning for Faire Women,* who deals with a murder chronicled in bare detail by both Holinshed and Stowe for the year 1573.[22]

V

There remain for consideration a number of plays produced in these years just before the turn of the century which we may segregate, perhaps not too arbitrarily, as showing some manifest attempt to deal with the inner tragedy of character. They promise in a particular way the deepening of characterization and the close union of character and event that we associate with Shakespearean tragedy of the seventeenth century. In varying degrees they make for dramatic penetration into the recesses of human nature and for a definite carrying of the tragic scene into the soul of man, to the accompaniment of introspective analysis by the protagonist. Sometimes these plays show the strong and firmly willful soul racked by conscience. Sometimes they show the weak and infirmly willful soul worn down by ineffectual assaults upon the pale of its desire. Even when they lack complexity they deserve the name of spiritual tragedies in a peculiar sense.

Here the versatile genius of Marlowe again leads the way, and not in one order of drama alone, but in two. His *The Tragicall History of D. Faustus* (*ca.* 1588) and his *The troublesome raigne and lamentable death of Edward the second, King of England: with the tragicall fall of proud Mortimer* (*ca.*1592) are spiritual tragedies of willful strength and willful weakness, respectively.

In *Faustus*, Marlowe takes the worldly ambition, forgetful or defiant of Heaven, which *De Casibus* tragedy had presented in terms of desire for material things and makes it an infinite craving of the human spirit for things impon-

DD

derable. The sweet fruition of an earthly crown so much coveted by Tamburlaine is only a minor desire for Faustus. It is true that there is a certain irony in the tragedy (even if the effect results, in part, from corruption of the play) connected with Faustus' inability to gain anything but the most unheroic material triumphs by his dearly bought magic power. He can think of becoming "great Emperor of the world," but he has no real taste for the consistent effort that would be necessary for this consummation. Fitfully he expends upon vulgarly base and childishly undirected satisfactions those powers that could have conquered physical kingdoms. Yet the truly consuming desire in Faustus is for knowledge that shall transcend the limitations of the imperfect world. Impatient with the slow and at best unsure processes of philosophy, physic, and theology, he determines to cut their bonds of restraint by means of magic and to ride in triumph through the kingdom of the mind as Tamburlaine would ride in triumph through Persepolis. He sells his soul to Mephistophilis that he may do so, and because, unlike Tamburlaine, he is made to realize that his course is evil and that his fruits of conquest are hollow, he is tortured by conscience and sinks under the weight of despair. His worldly presumption has led him to seek the easy pleasures of knowledge, which are of the mind, instead of the difficult satisfactions of wisdom, which are of the spirit. Very early after he has signed away his soul he finds that Mephistophilis can give him only shreds of encyclopedic fact concerning the motions of the planets, and will not even talk of the deep mystery of their being. Also, magic can bring the great art and the great thought of the

past to the perception of Faustus as cleverly staged pageantry, but can do nothing more. The "deede of gift of body
and soule" has hardly been delivered to Mephistophilis before Faustus addresses himself in darkest dejection:

> Faustus, thou art damn'd, then swordes and kniues,
> Poyson, gunnes, halters, and invenomd steele
> Are layde before me to dispatch my selfe,
> And long ere this I should haue slaine my selfe,
> Had not sweete pleasure conquerd deepe dispaire.
> Haue not I made blinde *Homer* sing to me
> Of *Alexanders* loue and *Enons* death,
> And hath not he that built the walles of *Thebes,*
> With rauishing sound of his melodious harp
> Made musicke with my *Mephastophilis?*[23]

To the very end of the term nominated in his bond, however, such pleasures as these which he mentions help to
keep Faustus from the repentance that would cleanse his
soul or from destruction of his life. The last of them, just
before the devils hale him away to Hell, is provided by the
famous apparition of Trojan Helen.

Faustus seems to be written with the desire to widen and
extend, instead of rebel against, the authority of medieval
doctrine concerning the means of damnation. The language of the moral play is readily available for Marlowe's
purpose, and he accepts it. Faustus falls into sin, a good
angel and an evil struggle for his soul, he is urged to repent
before it is too late, and he is urged toward suicide when he
most despairs of salvation. Ostensibly he is damned for the
sin of black magic, forbidden of God. All this an audience
could understand in the light of conventional moral drama.

But behind it Marlowe attempts to go far deeper than the conventional moral dramatists into spiritual tragedy. Though the play as we know it is doubtless debased, it lets us see that Faustus is really damned because, although he has the nobility to aspire toward true wisdom, he nevertheless allows himself to snatch at the counterfeit. Spiritual disintegration follows at once, and the evil spell is never broken until

> Cut is the branch that might haue growne ful straight,
> And burned is Apolloes Laurel bough,
> That sometime grew within this learned man.[24]

Probably more than a year or so before Marlowe's *The troublesome raigne and lamentable death of Edward the second, King of England* (*ca.* 1592) comes the anonymous play, in two parts, *The Troublesome Raigne of John King of England* (printed in 1591). It foreshadows *Edward II* in more ways than by its title, and it asks comparison with another of Marlowe's plays in the preface addressed "To the Gentlemen Readers." King John is urged upon the public who have entertained Tamburlaine so gladly; he is put forward as a warlike Christian gentleman, instead of an infidel Scythian. The author of *The Troublesome Raïgne of John* can hardly have intended very close competition with *Tamburlaine*. The historic John was a poor subject for a dramatist with any such purpose. The first part of the play does show John as a rather grandiloquent leader of English forces warring against France, an ambitious strengthener of his claim to a throne, and, in his own judgment at least, a match for "the Arche prowd titled Priest of Italy." But already much that is utterly foreign to the spirit of *Tamburlaine* has appeared in the drama; toward the end of the first part a vacillating ruler has replaced the royal warrior. John has reached the height of his career and proudly taken stock of his achievement:

> Now warlike followers, resteth ought vndone
> That may impeach vs of fond ouersight?[25]

He has been "reproclaimed and inuested King." Immediately thereafter we find him shaken profoundly by the prediction of his fall made by the Prophet of Pomfret. He now shows the cruelty of vicious weakness rather than that of vicious strength, not only against the prophet, but also against young Arthur, claimant to his throne:

> The brat shall dye, that terrifies me thus.[26]

We leave John, in this first part of the play, rejoicing inanely that his evil designs upon Arthur have been blocked by an underling who refused to execute his charge. The king has had a taste of the barons' wrath after a report of Arthur's death, and he is happy that a chance to placate them has been forced upon him.

The second part of the play begins with the actual death of the imprisoned Arthur, which happens ironically without any planning by the king, as Arthur is trying to escape, but which impels the barons just as effectively toward revolt. John goes utterly to pieces. As the rebels ally themselves with France to overcome him, he bends the knee to Rome, but this cannot save his life. He is poisoned by a monk in payment for his spoliation of the monasteries and dies in physical and spiritual agony. Long before his misfortunes have come to a head he has frequently known the burden of conscience. He has cursed the crown and then cursed his will that made the crown his care. He has confessed his sins to himself and declared them both the cause of England's misery and the reason why he cannot prevail against the pope. He has cried for death and thought that "death scornes so vilde a pray." At the end he reviews "a cattalogue of sinne, wrote by a fiend in Marble characters," and searches his soul with eloquent questioning:

> How haue I liu'd, but by anothers losse?
> What haue I loud, but wracke of others weale?
> Where haue I vowd, and not infring'd mine oath?[27]

The play has many faults. Probing of King John's character is by no means always skillful or revealing, and dramatic craftsmanship is often slipshod. But when one considers its early date, its achievement seems remarkable. King John is followed through a long rise to consolidation of temporal power and through a long descent to ruin, the first part of the play being the rise and the second the fall. The outline is similar to that of *De Casibus* tragedy built upon Fortune's wheel. Yet the author makes nothing whatever of the medieval Fortune, even rhetorically. Those in the play who suffer reverses suffer them without cursing any such easily blameable figure of fate. Even Constance, the mother of Arthur, whose tongue is "tunde to storie forth mishap" and who does not neglect to mention the sorrows of Dido and the wrack of Troy, curses only her enemies, not Fortune. King John himself liberally finds the causes of his ills in his own soul. All this at a time just before 1591, when the truly medieval Fortune was still much in the minds of dramatists, is sufficiently noteworthy. Even more noteworthy is the attempt to show the disintegration in King John's character and the connection of that disintegration with his tragic end. John rises to what height he attains by a burst of effort to command. We feel this to be not magnificent but on the whole kingly. In the course of his rise the young Arthur, who stands between him and the security of the throne, has fallen into his hands as a prisoner of war. With the vicious move to put Arthur out of the way comes the turning-point in his career. Following logically come the barons' revolt, the destruction of John's peace of mind, and the unnerving of his better powers. The development of the catastrophe through the second part of the play is in large part psychological, and in spite of its crudenesses it seizes upon our imagination. King John is rightfully entitled to consideration as one of the precursors of Macbeth on the Elizabethan stage. He gives something of the same paradoxical impression that Macbeth gives of being morally responsible for his own destruction even though he is so heavily fated to destroy himself that the lines of his destiny can be read by prophecy.

Marlowe's much-praised *Edward II* is another study of tragic weakness in a king who cannot dominate his barons, but it is a true innovation in its choice of a protagonist so consistently and pathologically weak as Edward. Needless to say, it is better poetry than *The Troublesome Raigne of John,* though the creator of *Tamburlaine* in subduing his style to the demands of psychological subtlety has not freed himself from faults of immaturity. It is perhaps useless to ask whether the Marlowe we know, who has so many blind spots, and particularly a blind spot for feminine character, could ever have come to anything like mature Shakespearean perception of the human soul. But we must acknowledge that in *Edward II* he achieves a concentration upon a central tragic figure and a sustained psychological penetration of that figure such as no dramatist before him had achieved and such as Shakespeare the beginning dramatist could later study with profit. In this approach to the finer ends of tragedy, however, Marlowe is handicapped gravely by his choice of a protagonist thoroughly deficient in dynamic quality, whom he cannot make us admire until the end of the play, and then merely as a man capable of some final dignity in hopeless suffering. He has even chosen to make Edward weaker than he was in history, partly by minimizing a measure of martial valor which Holinshed allows to him. The poet's early interest in ambitious climbing strength and the Machiavellian acquisition of power here remains only for the creation of Mortimer, a foil to Edward and frequently an unconvincing stage villain, who falls from the top of his flight with a conventional *De Casibus* curse for "base Fortune" and her wheel.

The tragedy of Edward is made more poignant by the fact that for him there is markedly no such satisfaction as there is for Mortimer in cursing Fortune. One might expect him in the misery of weakness, if not in the effrontery of robustness, to unpack his heart against Fortune, and in the lightness of his understanding to rail the more readily against the world as governed by irrational forces. But light-brained though he is, he seems unable to rid himself of a vague feeling that there must be reason in the scheme of things. Again and again he tortures himself with thought upon the enormity and seeming outrageousness of the suffering which he, a king, must undergo. It is pitifully scattered thought and it penetrates hardly at all into the mystery. Nevertheless, it is fumblingly persistent.

But even though Edward's tragedy is one of almost un-relieved weakness, it has a rising and falling action curiously similar to that of a *De Casibus* tragedy of ambition. Though Edward is never the conquering king that John is in the first part of *The Troublesome Raigne,* though he is infirm of purpose from the very beginning, yet he has a consum-ing desire which impels him to gain a certain degree of royal success. The center of his world is his favorite, Gaves-ton; and for Gaveston, base and unworthy, yet capable of calling forth something more than merely debauched af-fection, the king is almost willing to give up all else. He cannot bring himself, however, to give up kingship. To the very end of his career he holds with fretful certainty to the idea that he is a king and that somehow nothing can change that fact, not even deposition. He is forced by his barons to banish Gaveston; he gets Gaveston back; he takes the field against the barons, is defeated, and cannot save the captured favorite from death. So much may be regarded as a long and vacillating preparation for what now takes quick shape as a rise to triumph. But the triumph is brief and hollow. It is also bitterly ironic, for only now that Gaveston is dead and cannot be won, is Edward nerved with power enough to defeat the rebels. He kneels, vows vengeance, and actually carries it out—all, that is, except the most important part. He imprisons Mortimer, instead of beheading him at once with the other captured rebels. It is the sort of tragic failure to push purpose completely home at the high moment of opportunity which Gothic tragedy readily makes much of, from Boccaccio's story of Hannibal in the *De Casibus* to Shakespeare's *Hamlet*. Just as Hamlet's refusal to kill the praying king sets a falling action in motion, so does Edward's refusal to execute Mortimer. For Mortimer escapes to France, joins forces there with Edward's queen, who has long ago encouraged him to aspire toward her favors, and brings the king to his fall, to his lingering torture, and to his death. As he falls Edward finds in himself now a "dauntlesse minde" curbed by ambitious Mortimer, and now a mind "murthered" by Mortimer, but never suspects the frailty of mind which inevitably works his ruin after destiny has given him the scepter. As he is basely murdered in a dungeon foul with muck, he cries in his unchanged simplicity:

> Know that I am a king, oh at that name
> I feele a hell of greefe: where is my crowne?[28]

A fourth in this line of early psychological tragedies which are either from the pen of Marlowe or closely connected with Marlowe's work is *The True Tragedie of Richard the Third* (printed in 1594). It is a play not without crudity, but in many ways it is arresting for the historian of English drama. Marlowe himself never combines the cruel aspiring force of a Tamburlaine or a Machiavellian villain with the capacity of a Dr. Faustus for conscience-stricken introspection. The author of *The True Tragedie* makes the combination. Also, from the accepted work of Marlowe the modified Senecan ghost, so logically useful to the English popular tragedy of ambition and revenge, is wholly absent. In *The True Tragedie* the Senecan ghost finds his place within a Marlovian setting.

The True Tragedie is definitely a drama of retribution for egregious sin, but by attempting to present the inner rather more than the external quality of retribution the author contrives to arouse a certain amount of that pity which always comes with the understanding of human nature, however monstrous its deeds. His display of psychological knowledge is simple, but it has its finer moments. The ghost of the murdered Duke of Clarence heads the piece with a brief Senecan cry for the blood of vengeance, after which Poetry and Truth lead us to view the death-bed of King Edward and the undertaking of Richard to gain the crown. Then follows the swift rise of the aspirant to a point midway in the play which is the top of Fortune's wheel. Richard, however, is not one to leave all or lay all to Fortune. He talks of Fortune's being so ready to follow his lead that he no sooner devises "but she sets abroach," and he is strongly conscious that this devising of his own is evil and that for it he must count the cost. He concludes that to be king for a day, even to hear the title of "Your Majesty" given him but once, is worth all that the cost may be. Thus having taken thought for the consequences and thus having steeled himself to put the thought away from him, he follows the course which he has set. He has the princes murdered in the Tower and embraces whatever crime is necessary for the attainment of his goal. But no sooner does he reach the goal

than with fresh urgency the cost bedevils him. This time he
is shaken to the depths of his soul by a vision of horror:

> Meethinkes the Crowne which I before did weare,
> Inchast with Pearle and costly Diamonds,
> It turned now into a fatall wreathe
> Of fiery flames, and euer burning starres,
> And raging fiends hath past ther vgly shapes,
> In Stygian lakes, adrest to tend on me,
> If it be thus, what wilt thou do in this extremitie?
> Nay what canst thou do to purge thee of thy guilt?
> Euen repent, craue mercie for thy damned fact,
> Appeale for mercy to thy righteous God.[29]

Like Faustus, he does not repent. Richmond takes the field
against him. The screws of conscience are tightened as his
fortunes fail; he falls into delirium and imagines the ghosts
of his victims gaping for revenge. In short, he knows more
and more surely

> The hell of life that hangs vpon the Crowne,[30]

but Hell, here and hereafter, he regards to the very end of
his career as not too high a price to pay for the kingship.
Just before he is slain by Richmond he takes refuge in the
"golden thoughts" that bid him keep his crown and die a
king: "These are my last, what more I haue to say, ile make
report among the damned soules."

The author of *The True Tragedie* knew the *Mirror for
Magistrates* and depended upon it in writing the scenes
dealing with Shore's wife.[31] These comprise a *De Casibus*
interlude with much of the sentimentality and the outcry
against cruel Fortune to be found in Churchyard's famous
legend of Jane Shore as printed in the *Mirror*. But for Rich-

ard himself the dramatist used various material, with a passable instinct for anything which would help him to write the tragedy of a consciously evil nature. The torturing conscience of Richard he was able to find in the chronicles, ready for dramatic development.[32]

<h1 style="text-align:center">VI</h1>

It is in some part upon what had been achieved by the category of dramas just discussed that Shakespeare builds in *Richard III* (*ca.* 1593), *Richard II* (1595–1596), and *King John* (*ca.* 1596). Yet it is an odd fact that in two of these works the dramatist who was so soon to be the author of *Hamlet* and *Macbeth* frequently neglects the opportunity to lead his protagonists into painful soul-searching. If we compare *Richard III* with *The True Tragedie,* we find that Shakespeare has tried to make much less of Richard's conscience and humanity than the other dramatist. He has given his hero an almost incorrigible gaiety in the doing of evil which makes the man unforgettably theatric. The two plays join at many points in having Richard lend a forceful hand to the shaping of his destiny and in taking him beyond the medieval and Senecan realm of Fortune in which Legge's *Richardus Tertius* had placed him. But that Shakespeare makes use of *The True Tragedie* is by no means certain.[33] When Shakespeare comes to write *King John,* he obviously has an increased ability to make us feel subtlety in human-impulses. He is strangely disinclined, however, to probe the tragic character of John. There can be no question that he keeps *The Troublesome Raigne of John* before him as he writes, that, indeed, his work is a recasting of the old play. As we have seen, the earlier dramatist finds much psychological interest in the breakdown of the king. Yet Shakespeare very obviously finds little. He condenses the two parts of the old play into one action, and does not reach his dramatization of Arthur's death and the real beginning of John's fall, which opens the second part of the old play, until the end of the fourth act. All that he gives us of John's quaking terror before the assaults of conscience is to be found in the second scene of the fourth act, where the king mistakenly believes Arthur dead. After Arthur's death *King John* hastens to a conclusion in which the king plays a rôle markedly cut down and in which conscience-stricken introspection by the king does not take place at all. Where the second part of the old play gives the king speech after speech of self-examination, the later acts of *King John* give him nothing of the kind. Particularly do we notice the change when Shakespeare's John dies in purely physical agony instead of an agony of both illness and self-realization.

This neglect of opportunity, it is true, has a different quality in *Richard III* from that which it has in *King John*. Shakespeare accepts Richard completely as a subject for tragedy, and writes his tragedy zestfully. He does not accept King John completely as a subject for tragedy. He consistently magnifies the part of the Bastard Faulconbridge found in *The Troublesome Raigne of John*, raising up a character of courage and integrity, lighted by humor, to demand our sympathetic interest at the expense of the weak and vicious king. It may even be argued that the bastard is the true hero of *King John*, and that the play is planned as a patriotic chronicle drama more than as a tragedy.

In *Richard II,* however, Shakespeare really takes up the challenge offered by Marlowe in *Edward II.* It is a tragedy in which a weak but headstrong king, with what Holinshed calls "the frailtie of wanton youth," helps to work his own destruction by a succession of highly characteristic blunders. And it is one in which the protagonist, like Edward II, probes his inner being after misfortune has fallen upon him, but never attains self-realization. He is only capable of anatomizing his suffering and cannot get beyond it to anatomize its causes. Again like Edward, he has a certain pitiful nobility in his bewilderment. He is a king fallen from the heights to depths of indignity, and the spectacle of such violent change in fortune fascinates him. He shows poetic power in presenting it to himself and to others.

When we see it through the eyes of Shakespeare, the spectacle is one in which Richard's character much outweighs Fortune as the cause of his tragedy, but when we see it through the eyes of Richard, the spectacle is almost purely that of the Boccacesque tragedy of Fortune, except for lack of the medieval religious connotation. The structure of the play is well calculated to aid its protagonist in calling to our minds the round of Fortune's wheel. In none of the other tragedies of Shakespeare do we find such use of the form, the manner, and the conventional phrases of medieval tragical story in all its simplicity. Yet Shakespeare manages with much success to add the complexity of a psychological study to this simplicity.

In the third act we find that Richard has run a course of rising action and has begun his descent. Pressing behind him upon the turning wheel, rising as he falls, comes Boling-

broke. Later, when Richard surrenders the throne, Shakespeare finds for his hero another medieval poetic figure
than that of Fortune's wheel with which to express the dramatic relationship of the rivals. This is the well-known figure of Fortune's buckets.[34] The abdicating king, in the pain
of giving up his rule before he has "shook off the regal
thoughts" wherewith he reigned, addresses Bolingbroke:

> Give me the crown. Here, cousin, seize the crown;
> Here, cousin,
> On this side my hand and on that side thine.
> Now is this golden crown like a deep well
> That owes two buckets filling one another;
> The emptier ever dancing in the air,
> The other down, unseen and full of water:
> That bucket down and full of tears am I,
> Drinking my griefs, whilst you mount up on high.
>
> (IV, i, 181–189)

When the turn comes, Richard immediately adds himself to the company of those fallen princes who have been
the subjects of *De Casibus* story, and, further, sees his place
as king in the Dance of Death:

> For God's sake, let us sit upon the ground
> And tell sad stories of the death of kings:
> How some have been deposed, some slain in war,
> Some haunted by the ghosts they have depos'd,
> Some poison'd by their wives, some sleeping kill'd;
> All murder'd: for within the hollow crown
> That rounds the mortal temples of a king
> Keeps Death his court, and there the antick sits,
> Scoffing his state and grinning at his pomp;
> Allowing him a breath, a little scene,
> To monarchize, be fear'd, and kill with looks,
> Infusing him with self and vain conceit

As if this flesh which walls about our life
Were brass impregnable; and humour'd thus
Comes at the last, and with a little pin
Bores through his castle wall, and farewell king!
Cover your heads, and mock not flesh and blood
With solemn reverence.   (III, ii, 155–172)

He returns to this thought when he says farewell to his
queen in the fifth act. His story is to be among the lamentable tales told round the fire on winter's tedious nights and
will "send the hearers weeping to their beds." Richard comes
to a full rejection of the pride of life; he comes to feel that
any solemn reverence for flesh and blood is but hollow
show. Contempt of the World here, however, has almost
nothing of the meaning that it had in the Middle Ages. It
is the hopeless bitterness of a broken man, turning hardly
any thought toward a stability in Heaven after an irrational
instability has been found on earth. It is true that he talks
with his last breath of his mounting soul and the gross flesh
which dies, but this seems the merest lip-service.

It can hardly be doubted that Shakespeare gives *Richard
II* its strong cast of *De Casibus* story and its exactly balanced
form, with the fall of one prince counterweighted by the
rise of another, upon an impulse furnished by Holinshed.
In more than one place Holinshed, as he writes his sober
account of Richard's fortunes, moralizes after the fashion
of the *Mirror for Magistrates*. A passage which particularly
invites consideration is the following:

This suerlie is a verie notable example, and not vnworthie of all
princes to be well weied, and diligentlie marked, that this Henrie
duke of Lancaster should be thus called to a kingdome, and haue
the helpe and assistance (almost) of all the whole realme, which

EE

perchance neuer thereof thought or yet dreamed; and that king
Richard should thus be left desolate, void, and in despaire of all hope
and comfort, in whom if there were anie offense, it ought rather to
be imputed to the frailtie of wanton youth, than to the malice of his
hart: but such is the deceiuable iudgement of man, which not regard-
ing things present with due consideration, thinketh euer that things
to come shall haue good successe, with a pleasant & delitefull end.
But in this deiecting of the one, & aduancing of the other, the proui-
dence of God is to be respected, & his secret will to be woondered at.[35]

Building his play in accordance with Holinshed as the
"deiecting of the one, & aduancing of the other" contestant
for a crown, Shakespeare allows us to wonder less than
Holinshed at "secret" ways of fate. Knowing not only Richard but also Bolingbroke as Shakespeare makes us know
them, we penetrate in large degree the subtle workings of
their destinies.

Turning from Shakespeare's *Richard II* and *King John*
to his *Julius Caesar* (*ca.* 1599), we may see, as I have already
said, the first sign of accomplished maturity in English
tragedy and of its entrance into an enlarged domain which
is, as a whole, beyond the scope of these chapters. This play
heralds for English tragedy the attainment of a capacity
truly comparable with that of Greek tragedy, a capacity not
to be shown, of course, by the run of dramatists in the early
seventeenth century, but by Shakespeare supremely and by
some others in lesser degree. Shakespeare's Brutus asks admission to the ranks of those creatures of poesy who work
out some tragic destiny in the grand manner of profound
irony, not as pawns of Fortune or the gods, nor as magnificently defiant sinners, nor as headstrong weaklings, but as
men of heroic strength or goodness whose most admirable

qualities lead them into suffering. They are often forced to take the wages of what has the appearance of evil action and yet is not to be called evil action in all simplicity because it is dictated by their nobility. This is so with Brutus. Before his appearance we find no protagonist upon the English tragic stage in whom greatness of soul is thus linked with misfortune. He does not have the power of introspection given to the protagonists of Shakespeare's major tragedies, and his drama has less depth than theirs, but he belongs with them and not with the melodramatic villain Richard III or the blindly rash weakling Richard II. *Julius Caesar* has the rise-and-fall structure reminiscent of Fortune's revolving wheel; the fortunes of Brutus and his associates are at their height in the third act. Also, it is definitely in the line of popular dramas built upon ambition and revenge. The Senecan ghost of Caesar in search of revenge is developed with the authorization of Plutarch, and the theme of ambition, coloring the famous orations of Brutus and Antony, is developed without such authorization. But the play utilizes medieval and Senecan conventions only to transcend them in the manner of seventeenth-century Shakespearean tragedy.

Thus, by the end of the sixteenth century, English drama had developed an ability to focus upon human character as a progressive shaper of unhappy destiny, whatever the participation of fate or chance in the making of destiny, and to reveal with subtlety the inner man as a theater of suffering. It had not forgotten the medieval and Senecan Fortune nor the all too simple laws of tragic cause and effect which had been promulgated by the later *De Casibus* story and the later moral play. Sometimes it could still occupy itself with these in the old ways. Nevertheless, by probing the human mind and soul it had found a way leading out of the shallows and toward the depths of tragedy.

Chapter XI

CONCLUSION

WE HAVE FOLLOWED through its major nondramatic and dramatic forms of expression the growing tragic genius which Shakespeare was to dominate and transform. It should now be possible to view that genius in the large and to fix upon certain of its salient characteristics. To glance forward as well as backward and to take the principal tragedies of Shakespeare somewhat within the field of general consideration will be necessary, though the tragic art of Shakespeare in all its individuality, in all its complexity of shading and gradation of meaning, must remain outside the field of special consideration.

One very simple fact should be at once recognized. The Christian European spirit which one may call Gothic is strongly bent upon concluding tragedy with death and giving it a final seal of authenticity in death. In its religious Contempt of the World it dwells upon the ills of mankind as having their origin in the Garden of Eden with the sin of Adam. Chief among these ills, that toward which the others all tend, is the death of the body. Hence, death becomes for the Gothic mind a primary symbol of the imperfection in mortal life. It is thought of as a necessary culmination of tragic adventure. In a sense all Gothic tragedy, in the hands of Boccaccio and in the hands of his successors, is a Dance of Death. Thus it is that popular Elizabethan tragedy gives death an honorable place upon the stage, a dire claim to respect, and a power of finality in the dra-

matic scheme of things. Concerning Shakespearean tragedy Professor A. C. Bradley has said with his usual lucid
directness: "On the one hand (whatever may be true of
tragedy elsewhere), no play at the end of which the hero
remains alive is, in the full Shakespearean sense, a tragedy;
and we no longer class *Troilus and Cressida* or *Cymbeline*
as such, as did the editors of the Folio. On the other hand,
the story depicts also the troubled part of the hero's life
which precedes and leads up to his death; and an instanta-
neous death occurring by 'accident' in the midst of prosperity would not suffice for it. It is, in fact, essentially a tale
of suffering and calamity conducting to death." Between
De Casibus tragedy of the Middle Ages and Shakespearean
tragedy there is, as we have seen, a long development in
artistic and philosophic perception. But through it all,
death, whether dramatically prepared for or not, is peculiarly the final concern of Gothic tragedy.

Greek tragedy knows something of the physical picture
of death and certainly does not attempt to deny the physical
indignities of death, but, for whatever reason, it does not
with open freedom cultivate those indignities on the stage,
and it does not use them as an essential element in the por-
trayal of human limitations. Gothic tragedy, on the contrary, does so cultivate and use them, and eventually it gains
artistic triumph with them. It cultivates all sorts of physical horrors,—not alone those connected with death,—yet it
reaches a spiritual height comparable with that reached by
Greek tragedy. Its level of highest attainment is far above
the morbid level upon which Seneca's tragedy of horrors
moves and wholly has its being.

Even the aim with which Gothic tragedy begins is essentially nonmorbid. Medieval *De Casibus* tragedy, it is true, searches out and presents the same kind of physical horror that Seneca presents. Boccaccio, for example, welcomes a chance to tell in gruesome detail how Pompey was beheaded on the shore of Egypt, how his head was impaled upon a spear and exposed before the idle mob of Alexandria, how his body was at first tossed upon the sands unburied. A fifteenth-century illuminator of Boccaccio in the French version of Laurent de Premierfait takes the incident of the beheading as the one in Pompey's story most worthy of his attention (see illustration facing p. 96). He elects to show the headless body lying across the side of a boat, draining blood into the sea from its severed veins, and he takes care to show the bleeding stump of the neck in revealing full view. He paints Pompey's head held upon a spear by one of the assassins and does not forget the minor streams of blood which should flow from that. The same artist is stimulated to even greater care with gruesome detail by Boccaccio's story of Marcus Atilius Regulus, who was tortured upon a bed of spikes by the Carthaginians (see illustration facing p. 32). Other illustrators of such stories are unerringly attracted to the bloodiest and most horrible aspects of tragedy. Depicters of the Dance of Death pay the same sort of attention to the details of a putrefying cadaver. In short, medieval ingenuity seeks devotedly to let mankind see itself in disgustingly perishable flesh. To say that the literary man, the pictorial artist, or the public at which both aim their work never for a moment take morbid interest in all this gruesomeness would be to say that they are not human. But always there is a recognized larger justification for this employment with horror. The abasement of man active physically has deeper meaning because it helps the elevation of man active spiritually. However, in medieval tragedy man's spiritual power of achievement is thought of in terms that are, in large part, not of this world. Only with apologies and with lingering misgivings can Boccaccio suggest, in his admiration for Alcibiades, that worldly ambition may take impulse from, and be guided by, the "divinely aspiring mind."

Elizabethan tragedy early comes to realize the melodramatic appeal lying in the horrific drama of Seneca and sometimes strives to possess that appeal itself. But as an antidote to Senecan morbidity it inherits from the Middle Ages a sense of the contrast between physical ignobilities and spiritual nobilities which may be shown in man. And at its best Elizabethan tragedy, unlike medieval tragedy, can bear witness effectively to man's spiritual greatness, presenting it in terms of this world and bringing it most sharply to our understanding. When Elizabethan tragedy reveals that the same mankind which has capacity for spiritual nobility must live and die in a physical world productive of grossness and horror, it is able to raise in us a tragic qualm such as Seneca, with his shower of horrors upon men and women intrinsically ignoble, can never make us feel.

The major tragedies of Shakespeare often raise this qualm, two in particular with irresistible power. In *Hamlet* the work is done with least majesty, though with profound implication nevertheless. Hamlet himself throughout the play obviously experiences the qualm and falls into philosophical consideration of it upon the slightest impulse. He is hypersensitive to the grossnesses of flesh revealed by death and appreciates to the full the irony of their conjunction with the finenesses of spirit in man. "My gorge rises," he cries as he holds Yorick's skull, recoils from the odor of its decay, and thinks of the "infinite jest," the "most excellent fancy," which the mind once seated in that skull had contrived. Even the great Alexander, he realizes, looked like this in the earth—and smelt so. Rosencrantz and Guildenstern have dull perception of man's condition, but Hamlet has eyes painfully open to it: "What a piece of work is a man! How noble in reason! how infinite in faculty! in form and moving, how express and admirable! in action how like an angel! in apprehension how like a god! the beauty of the world! the paragon of animals! And yet, to me, what is this quintessence of dust?" These musings are legitimate secular descendants of the religious musings which produced the Dance of Death, the *memento mori,* and *De Casibus* tragedy. They have a peculiar power to move us because Shakespeare makes us feel with immediate certainty that Hamlet, the speaker, is himself noble in reason and infinite in faculty, even rounded with Yorick's faculty of infinite jest and most excellent fancy, and yet is quintessence of dust. Hamlet's mortal limitations are so far refined that they arouse endless debate among critics, but they conduct no less to death and to that "progress through the guts of a beggar" which he can so vividly imagine as the fate of royalty.

Hamlet's sensitiveness to other manifestations of fleshly grossness is just as keen. One need only mention his reactions to the drunken revelry of the Danish court and to his mother's comfortable callousness in the matter of hasty remarriage. He is almost monkish in his disgust, though he does not advance the religious sanction. Like the sincere monk, or like any sincerely ascetic contemner of the world in the Middle Ages, he saves himself from the accusation of mere morbidity because the contrast with the noble capacities of man is always in his mind. And his tragedy is saved from merely morbid appeal because this contrast is one of its foundations.

Shakespeare's greatest triumph in this kind, as in tragedy by and large, is *King Lear*. Here we have a world of terror accompanied by physical horror which at times is excruciating. It is a world which has almost reached the pass at which, as Albany says in his moment of realization,

> Humanity must perforce prey on itself,
> Like monsters of the deep.   (IV, ii, 49–50)

Shakespeare even resorts to a scene of blood and mutilation as unrestrained as the worst in Seneca or the worst in that Senecan melodrama of butchery *Titus Andronicus*. We are forced to be witnesses as Gloucester's eyes are gouged from their sockets and trampled under foot by a fiend in man's form, while a supporting fiend in woman's form stabs an interfering servant in the back. In Lear, the royal counterpart of the foolishly trusting Gloucester, we see a king reduced step by step to physical degradation. Whatever he contributes to his own fall is intensified and made the more effective by the rank cruelty visited upon him. Externally, he reaches the level of mad beggary exposed to the mad elements; as he takes physic for his pomp and tears off his

clothes, he cries, "Is man no more than this?" In Lear, and
to a lesser degree in Gloucester, we finally have proof that
man *is* more than a subject of such physical indignity. The
proof comes more dramatically than it does in Hamlet †
because there is here a gradual increase of inner nobility
through suffering, while in Hamlet there is rather a gradual revelation of that which is already possessed.

II

It is axiomatic that for great drama great audiences are as
necessary as great poets. Truly it is not easy to imagine how
the bawds, the thieves, the fishwives, and the apprentices,
whose tastes had more than a little influence in the public
theaters, could have helped to demand, and therefore helped
to create, the best Elizabethan tragedies. But in spite of what
Shakespeare and other dramatists of his time say against
the hydra-headed multitude and its cheaper concerns, the
good plays seem often enough to have been popular. The
groundling somehow made contribution to the beauty of
Elizabethan tragedy, as the common man made contribution to the beauty of Greek tragedy.[2]

We may well ask what could have been contributed by
the theatergoing multitude to the healthy spirit that per-
vaded Elizabethan tragedy until after the turn of the century and allowed the stage to approach the grossness of
death and physical suffering without essential morbidity.
The renowned horrors of *The Spanish Tragedie* and *Titus
Andronicus* are presented in a way that may be called
merely innocent. They are put before us carelessly, as
though they had little power to make the dramatists or their

audience brood upon them and quail before them. The horrors of Shakespeare's major tragedies are presented in a way that is not innocent, yet is not the way of fearful fascination. The Elizabethan tragic world outfaced death and horror, if not with medieval faith in another life, then with defiant carelessness or with gallant faith in this life despite its uglinesses. What part, then, could the groundling have had in such a world?

We may get some inkling of that part from the circumstantial detail in which several observers, both British and foreign, have recorded their opinion that the common Elizabethan Englishman showed an unusual fearlessness when he faced violent death in actual life. This common Englishman's manner of accepting death seems to have given him, even when he was a criminal, a truly remarkable reputation for gallant courage or largeness of spirit.

Early in the reign of Elizabeth, Sir Thomas Smith, a man of solid substance and wide experience in public service, gives his countrymen credit for a "neglect" of death that men of other countries may well envy. In his *De Republica Anglorum* (finished in 1565, printed in 1583), he says:

The nature of English men is to neglect death.... In no place shal you see malefactors go more constantly, more assuredly, and with lesse lamentation to their death than in England.... The malefactour, seeing there is no remedie, and that they be his countrie men, and such as he hath himselfe agreed unto it, do finde them worthie death, yeeldes for the most part unto it, and doeth not repine, but doth accomodate him selfe to aske mercie of God. The nature of our nation is free, stout, haulte, prodigall of life and bloud.[3]

The admirable phrase "prodigal of life and blood" might well be inscribed upon Elizabethan tragedy.

In the early seventeenth century John Barclay, a cosmopolitan Scot born in France, seconds Sir Thomas Smith but sees English neglect of death under another and, for him at least, not so praiseworthy aspect. Barclay's *Icon Animorum* (1614) is a Latin work yielding animated sketches of national character for the Europe of his day. His story of a nameless English soldier is worth full quotation (in translation by his contemporary Thomas May):

They [the English] contemne all dangers, and death it selfe with more courage, then iudgement: and hence it comes, that they are the best souldiers, when they are gouerned by wise Captaines; but when they goe on of their owne accord, possessed with the blindnesse of that desperate valour, they haue reason, after sad defeats, to accuse themselues more then their ill fortune. In the late warres of the Low-countries some Souldiers of the *Spanish* party were taken by the *Hollanders* and were to bee hanged, in requitall of the enemies cruelty, who had vsed their prisoners in the like manner. But the *Hollanders* did not entend to execute them all. Of foure and twenty (for so many were taken prisoners) eight onely were appointed to be hanged, and the rest to escape with life. There were lots therefore throwne into a helmet, and the prisoners were commanded to draw their fortunes, whosoeuer should draw a blanke, was to escape death; but whosoeuer should draw a blacke lot, was to be hanged presently. They were all possessed with a great apprehension of their present danger: especially one Spaniard with pittiful wishes, and teares, in some of the standers by did moue pity, in others laughter: There was besides in that danger, a certain Englishman, a common souldier, who with carelesse countenance, expressing no feare of death at all, came boldly to the helmet, & drew his lot; chance fauoured him, it was a safe lot. Being free himselfe from danger he came to the Spaniard, who was yet timorous, and trembled to put his hand into the fatall helmet; and receiuing from him ten crownes, he entreated the Iudges (oh horrid audacity!) that dismissing the Spaniard, they would suffer him againe to try his fortune. The Iudges consented to the mad mans request, who valued his life at so low a rate: and he againe drew a safe lot: a wretch vnworthy not onely of that double, but euen of a single preseruation, who so basely had vnder-valued his life.⁴

Barclay finds laudable characteristics in plenty among all the European races except the Spanish. When dealing with the Spanish he seems indisposed toward disinterested observation because of a hearty dislike. Certainly he is not trying to magnify the English at the expense of other races. He finds faults among the English, even in that prodigality of life and blood which Sir Thomas Smith praises; but he is careful to add that the English are not cruel.

Among foreign observers of sixteenth-century English character the well-known Renaissance figure Girolamo Cardano, or Hieronymus Cardanus (d. 1576), who traveled in England and Scotland, records an opinion on English fortitude in the face of death which agrees closely with that of Sir Thomas Smith. Both the English and the Scottish criminal particularly impressed him with the manner of their going to execution. The strength of the impression is obvious in his *Dialogus de Morte,* in which the speakers are Cardano himself and Joannes Petrus Albutius:

Alb. It is worth consideration that the English care little or nothing for death. And rightly so, since it is the last of all evils and must at some time or other be suffered. Moreover, it is a lesser evil to suffer once what must be suffered than to fear it many a time and often. . . . Is it not true, as is said of them, that they approach not only death but even execution with readiness and an easy spirit?

Cardan. Most certainly. They bid farewell to their dear ones, to their sons and their brothers, and kiss them affectionately. They make their last recommendations to them. They say that they are entering upon immortal life, where they will await those who belong to them, and they urge those in turn to cherish their memory. Without any pallor of countenance and without any tremors of the voice, they bear with constancy the extremities of death. . . . They are strong in war but they want caution. . . . They are faithful, liberal, and ambitious. But as for fortitude, the things done by the Highland Scots are the most wonderful. They, when they are led to execution, take a piper with them: and he, who is himself often one of the condemned, plays them up dancing to their death.

Alb. He proceeds less unsuitably perhaps than those who among us bewail death.[5]

Brief acknowledgment that the Elizabethan soldier was notably fearless of death is made by another foreigner, Emanuel Van Meteren. In his *Nederlandtsche Historie* (1599) he has occasion to say of the English, among whom he had lived as Dutch consul, that they "are bold, courageous, ardent, and cruel in war, fiery in attack, and having little fear of death." Van Meteren is not without a lively sense of English failings in other respects. He adds that the people "are not vindictive, but very inconstant, rash, vainglorious, light and deceiving, and very suspicious, especially of foreigners, whom they despise."[6]

In what these British and foreign observers say of the English neglect of death there is a glimpse not merely of a careless audacity, but also of a tragic dignity, in the full acceptance of death issuing from the courageous acceptance of life. Other records of the times confirm their judgment. One may well believe that the common Elizabethan criminal was often impressive under the gallows. In numerous accounts of Elizabethan hangings there are examples of the kind of thing which Sir Thomas Smith and Cardano admire. No matter how mean the malefactor, he had a leading and responsible part to play at the tragedy of his own execution, for his friends and enemies gathered to see him die. From the cart tail or from the ladder against the gallows he made a speech, preferably an edifying speech. If he could, he kept his knees firm and showed no "pallor of countenance" or "tremors of the voice." Usually, he seems to have achieved a simpler counterpart of the tragic dignity so often achieved by the offender of higher birth, brought to the block instead of drawn to the gallows.

III

In Gothic tragedy upon the Elizabethan public stage the liberal admission of comedy, often low comedy, is almost as characteristic as the liberal admission of gross horror and of death in its most physical aspects. The one admission may seem as unnecessary and repellent as the other to a critic inclined to be "Greek" or neoclassical in temper. Yet for the Elizabethan dramatist at his best both may serve certain profound purposes which have their inception in the very beginnings of Gothic tragedy. The one no less than the other may give a shock to the easy pretentiousness of man, raise his serious aspiration into high light through contrast, and bring to him the truly tragic qualm. It must be said at once, however, that medieval *De Casibus* tragedy, which has so much to do with the horror of physical suffering and death, has very little to do with comedy except in Chaucer's *Troilus and Criseyde,* and this work is an exceptional *De Casibus* tragedy in many ways. Something of grim humor may be found in various representations of the Dance of Death, and comic interludes have their place in medieval sermons. But the mingling of comic and tragic spirits which we know on the Elizabethan stage has behind it most definitely a dramatic tradition.

The juxtaposition of vulgar comedy and serious religious commemoration in the earlier medieval drama seems to have been made in the most natural manner. The loosely binding general theme of the plays is God and Man; and with Man go his limitations, even those which are grotesquely humorous. To say that the dramatists as a general rule composed comic scenes merely as sops to the multitude and introduced them into the mysteries with a feeling that thereby some measure of sacred spirit was sacrificed to an uncultivated audience, is to forget the gargoyles and other grotesqueries which had their place of significance in the decoration of the cathedrals. To say that some among the multitude may have been more interested in grotesqueries than in sacred history is, of course, another matter. In the moral plays comedy often appears with no more apparent lowering of the generally serious spirit and with even more dramatic justification for its inclusion. The quickly popular theme of the corruption of Mankind by the minor and less heroic forces of evil—by the Vices, who are seldom more than vulgar camp-followers in the army of Satan—provides low comedy that has truly tragic overtones. The Vices are largely human in character and they tend more and more to represent a kind of gross humanity rather than a spiritual force warring against good. In them man can often see his own flesh uninformed by soul, amoral rather than immoral, amiably mischievous rather than fearsomely vicious, without reason yet somehow comically shrewd, the

FF

clownish part of him that gets in his way and takes him down when he tries to be his nobler self.

Though comedy comes to take a major part of the stage in some of the later moralities and to have little articulation with what serious business still remains in these dramas, and though, when the convention of introducing comedy into serious matter is accepted for early Elizabethan tragedy, articulation is often crude, some instinct for making the "fool of flesh" give poignancy to the spectacle of mortal struggle always survives. It has recognizable manifestations in such early tragedies as *Locrine* and *Arden of Feversham*. And in *Sir Thomas More* it shows something of a new strength and subtlety, for here comedy, even a sort of low comedy, is often supplied by the protagonist himself—with historical justification.

Let us consider the effect in *Sir Thomas More*. More is in the Tower waiting for his execution on the morrow. "Maister Lieutenant," says he, "I haue had a sore fitt of the stone to night; but the king hath sent me such a rare receipte, I thank him, as I shall not need to feare it much." Later at the scaffold he remarks that he has come about a "headless errand," for he has not much to say now that he has arrived. He walks about the "most sweet gallery" and finds the air of it better than that of his garden in Chelsea. The audience waits, and he turns to it: "By your pacience, good people, that haue prest thus into my bedchamber, if youle not trouble me, Ile take a sound sleepe heere." He makes the customary final speech of the condemned man, that natural comment upon the preceding tragic action so common in the drama of the stage and in the drama of actual life which ended beneath the gallows or at the block: "I confesse, his maiestie hath bin euer good to me; and my offence to his highnesse makes me of a state pleader a stage player (though I am olde, and haue a bad voyce), to act this last sceane of my tragedie. Ile send him (for my trespasse) a reuerend head, somewhat balde; for it is not requisite any head should stand couerd to so high maiestie." The Earl of Surrey reminds More that he had better hold some conference with his soul, since his time is short. But it is More the mortal fool rather than More the soul that confronts the block. "I see it, my good lord," he replies to Surrey. "I dispatchte that business the last night. I come hether only to be let blood; my doctor heere telles me it is good for the headache." He forgives the executioner and takes his jesting self to death:

> Heere Moore forsakes all mirthe; good reason why;
> The foole of fleshe must with her fraile life dye.
> No eye salute my trunck with a sad teare:
> Our birthe to heauen should be thus, voide of feare.[7]

This, and much else in the scenes from which quotation has been made, is excellent fooling with the tragic business of death. Yet it is never fooling which makes the play as a whole deny the seriousness of that business. It contrives positively to have an opposite effect. Also, it emphasizes by contrast More's spiritual aspiration. The means for the true marriage of the low with the sublime, where the low can still be effectively itself without apology, is an artistic mystery possessed by the Gothic spirit.

The shock which mature Shakespearean tragedy delivers to man's pride through low comedy, like that which it delivers through physical repulsiveness, is strongest in *Hamlet* and *King Lear*. When the mature tragic Shakespeare feels no inclination to put the fool of flesh consistently near the center of the action, as he does in these two plays, he may still bring him upon the stage for an apt interlude, brief but strongly emphasized because it is introduced at a moment of the highest intensity. One need only mention the Hell-porter of *Macbeth* and the clown who, stumbling across the stage of *Antony and Cleopatra,* ministers to the Queen of Egypt a worm whose biting is "immortal," since "those that do die of it do seldom or never recover."

Hamlet, somewhat like Sir Thomas More, often combines in himself the fool of flesh and the noble spirit, though the contrasts are presented with much more fineness of shading. The gravediggers are brought before us for a low-comedy interlude the effect of which Hamlet alone could never compass, but even here he shares with them and is to a degree able to make one with them. At times of intense excitement, in situations like the laying of his father's ghost ("Well said, old mole! canst work i' the earth so fast?") or the watching with Ophelia of the king's action at the play ("Do you think I meant country matters?"), Hamlet shows entirely sufficient capacity for vulgar, sometimes bawdy, clowning. He is then his own irreverent Vice out of the old plays. His further capacity in comedy, extending to the graces of wit and of tender raillery, places such clowning in even higher relief than his magnanimity alone could place it.

In *King Lear,* articulation of low comedy with tragedy is no less close, and low comedy is used tragically with more

constantly artful force. Though Lear divides the part that
Hamlet plays and lets the Fool play jester, it is only to call
in a double. Inseparable from Lear throughout that part of
the play in which the old man descends into the most bitter
depths of tragic realization, the Fool is like another self of
the protagonist, listened to perforce even as another self
would be listened to. He searches as by inalienable right the
holes in Lear's fabric of mortal pride. The grossness of the
Fool is strangely touched with that unreasoning perception
of truth which folk-belief credits to the insane man and the
idiot, and it must always be felt as grossness with a pitiable
difference. It is a paradoxically delicate metamorphosis of
the Vice's shrewd irreverence and of the Vice's lack of rational soul or moral responsibility.

IV

The course by which Gothic tragedy gradually frees itself
from belief in a world of inherent disorder ruled by irrational Fortune and develops belief in a world which can
reflect the divine order of justice, or can show inherent law
and order, has been marked in the preceding chapters. The
belief in tragic justice produces many naïve implications
that humanity meets tragedy simply because it refuses to
follow a program of virtue that is an open book to any seriously questing person. But unsubtle ideas of tragic justice,
as we have seen, prepare the way for subtle ideas of the
manner in which tragedy comes to pass. They encourage
observation of cause and effect in human life, of the link-
ages between character and event—of many things, in short,
which must necessarily be recognized if tragedy is to have

truly dramatic structure. They help to make possible the Shakespearean tragic stage, though their distance from the mature Shakespearean conception of tragic inevitability, or from the Greek conception at its best, can hardly be over-emphasized.

We are justified in saying that the greatest Greek tragedy and the greatest Gothic tragedy never make tragic justice an entirely open book, and that they are in a certain sense unmoral, because they are concerned with much deeper ethical difficulties than those of squaring life with some simple and well-accepted moral code. When Shakespeare thus allies himself in profundity with the classic dramatists of Greece, however, he does so without any apparent bene-fit from Greek models and with essential distinction from them in manner. He is true to the Gothic spirit, even when he most transforms its less subtle ways of presenting the cir-cumstances leading to human catastrophe.

Frequently we feel that Greek tragedy—and we are apt to feel it most in those plays which have been counted most memorable—is built not upon the violation of some law which the universe has plainly established for man's guid-ance, but upon violation of some law not plainly established, or even upon man's inability to reconcile apparent contra-dictions in ethical laws. This is peculiarly a feeling of that tragic qualm which rises when accepted foundations of human action are unsettled by exploration.[8] The qualm is strong when we see Antigone confronted by two antagonis-tic duties, both powerfully sanctioned; but it is strongest perhaps when we find that divine forces having sway over mankind are in dire conflict concerning the path which an

Orestes should follow. Both divinity and humanity, though they may have good and just intentions, are then only struggling in darkness for guiding light, and tragedy seems inevitable for man, whichever course he pursues. His very gods have disagreed, each giving injunctions most plausibly justified, and the one god will punish him for following the other. Even the gods themselves may suffer tragedy for their lack of ability to reconcile the conflicting demands of goodness. It is good for Prometheus to benefit mankind in the way he does, but he must nevertheless undergo torture after his beneficial act because it is also good to obey the Zeus against whom that act is rebellion. When these things are presented to us without pessimism and with an implied hope of ultimate reconciliation, as notably in Aeschylus, we feel that the struggle is of the highest ethical importance, even though a clear and final tragic justice cannot be shown. We feel that we are witnesses at the first stages of painful birth for some more catholic ethical principle than has before been operative in our universe and found expression in human ideas of morality. Emphatically we are not uplifted here by any exposure of perfection in universal laws or their enforcement, but by an exposure of imperfection (so far as mortal eyes are concerned) working dynamically toward perfection with the accompaniment of agony.

In Shakespeare there is a comparable revelation of what one may call grandeur in the imperfection of good. As in Aeschylus or Sophocles, a distinction between good and evil is taken for granted, and at times we may even see acts which are very simply evil according to traditional moral judgment gaining apparent retribution for their authors.

But of the series of major tragedies beginning with *Hamlet,* only one—namely, *Macbeth*—may in any way be thought of as given over to the taking of downright evil toward exemplary punishment. Even so, *Macbeth* is far from being a *Richard III* and has a certain kinship of unmoral subtlety with other tragedies of the later group. At other times in Shakespeare we may see acts that rise from faults, or taints, or flaws, in character—qualities which would never be called good though they might not be called evil—leading their possessors inevitably to suffering. The later Shakespearean tragedies make much of these flaws, and hence tempt us strongly to explain the catastrophes by actions of the characters that are "wrong." Even while catastrophes have these aspects of retribution, however, they are apt to have another aspect as results of imperfection in human character. Here the imperfection is placed before us not as a taint in or falling away from goodness or nobility so much as a lack of balance, even a civil war of goods, in man's noblest nature. Under this aspect a catastrophe may seem to be partly produced by good itself—ironically, if one has what usually passes as the moral view of things. It is thus that Shakespearean tragedy joins Greek tragedy in the dramatic exploration of imperfection in good. It can raise in us a similar qualm, or moral vertigo, though it inclines to search and question not the good that lies in laws and principles under which man lives, but the good that lies in man's inner qualities.

One need not labor the well-known examples of this. In *Hamlet* we discover a protagonist who is at war with himself in all that we should call his noblest being. We are forced to make the conclusion that he might have escaped catastrophe if he had had narrower nobility, or if he had not been embarrassed, so to speak, with multiple nobility. Hamlet the man of fine intellectual perception is inimical to Hamlet the man of courageous instinctive action at points most crucial for his general success, though not, to make the irony more delicate, upon occasions like his boarding of the pirate ship. A man such as Fortinbras, admirable merely as a courageous doer, finally gets the kingdom and might well have had thorough success in Hamlet's place as an avenger of a murdered father. It deserves all possible emphasis that Shakespeare does not make Hamlet struggle with the inconsistency between a barbaric tribal code and the Christian code of morals in the matter of revenge, as a Christian Aeschylus might have made him struggle. There is never a sign that Hamlet or anyone else in the play recognizes this inconsistency, however much we may recognize it and be tempted to read the tragedy accordingly, or however much an Elizabethan auditor may have recognized it in the light of the current condemnation of revenge. Shakespeare is dramatically about other business.

Macbeth is quite unlike Hamlet in that he progressively degrades his nobility by embracing what he recognizes to be evil:

> For Banquo's issue have I fil'd my mind;
> . . . . and mine eternal jewel
> Given to the common enemy of man,
> To make them kings, the seed of Banquo kings!
>
> (III, i, 65–70)

Nevertheless, his ruin has more than a little of the causation just noticed for Hamlet's downfall. Ill-assorted qualities separately admirable seem to unfit Macbeth for rough and ready rule as a warrior king. He has real kinship with Hamlet as a man called to forthright action and bringing with him a delicacy of imaginative perception with regard to consequences which cramps direct action upon the more momentous occasions and even makes him appear superficially a coward. His imaginative perception is visionary and prophetic instead of intellectual, and it works against him with all possible force when stimulated by rising conscience through an evil course of action.

Shakespeare searches and questions the goodness of man's noblest nature by different but no less effective means in *Othello* and *King Lear*. The search does not expose inimical divisions in good, but it does expose the ways by which a disproportionate quality of good may help to make catastrophe inevitable. Faults Othello certainly has, but it is often difficult not to feel that his tragedy springs most deeply from his very magnanimity, with which he is so embarrassingly endowed that he trusts Iago. To say merely that Othello by this trust earns his suffering through a flaw in wisdom is not to take necessary account of that "intolerable" character which so many have attributed to the play. In Lear and in Gloucester there are also faults, but again the suffering which follows faulty action is intolerable according to any normal human sense of proportion. Throughout *King Lear* one can never forget that one is seeing the fate of parental love preyed upon and tortured the more readily by evil because it is expansively trustful.

By a course of its own, then, Shakespearean tragic drama attains delicate balance between an overwhelming assault

upon man's proud but imperfect moral security and a stimulating challenge to his faith in moral existence. The result,
especially in the assault upon human pride, is one which
fulfills rather than departs from the earlier impulses of
Gothic tragedy. Even the impulse to expose inherent imperfection in the mortal world which dominated Gothic
tragedy in its beginnings has some share of fulfillment.

For the tragic world must here be looked at under two
distinct guises. So far as the *individual* is concerned, the
world of later Shakespearean tragedy is assuredly not to be
embraced hopefully or to be regarded as achieving, or even
struggling toward, a gratifying show of decorum and of
poetic justice through natural law. The basest indignity
and injustice for the individual seem to be shockingly natural accompaniments of life in the flesh. The grossnesses of
flesh and of fleshly death, as we have found, are never far
from the poet's mind. Moreover, the nobility of man's spirit,
which contrasts so strongly with ignobleness in his flesh,
.and to which we look for a saving quality, is only human
nobility after all, divided against itself or unbalanced, and
able to command no just consideration from the forces of
mundane life. It seems even to turn these forces against the
protagonist ironically. All this is obviously reminiscent of
Contempt of the World. The disgusting odor of mortality
is strong. Pride is dashed for the good as well as for the evil.
Fortune, with her wheel, and the stars, with their emana-
tions, no longer are appealed to simply and seriously, but
they are still talked about poetically, and man's mortal being appears to be by no means truly free from some such
power, often whimsical. With reference to the individual

alone, the world is even more fiendishly unworthy of trust than it is in ascetic *De Casibus* tragedy, for it deceives us with infinite subtlety, toys with us, gives high intimations of law and order only to withdraw them, instead of wearing a thoroughly disordered look upon its face. It tempts us to find a neatly working key to Shakespearean tragedy in the moral responsibility which is there allotted to man without question: in the willful evil committed by Macbeth which so definitely works against him, in a sort of deadly sin of sloth for Hamlet, in courses of folly responsibly chosen by Othello and Lear. Or it tempts us to find such a key in some scientific principle. And it deserts us after we have done so.

But so far as *mortal life* without reference to the individual is concerned, the world of later Shakespearean tragedy has a quality which ascetic Contempt must of necessity not admit. It is here that Shakespeare embraces life for a show of beauty in dependability and is so little inclined to deny general goodness to the mortal scheme of things that he makes life magnificently heroic in its intolerance of evil. As Professor Bradley says, it is a very important fact that in the Shakespearean tragedy "villainy never remains victorious and prosperous at the last."[9] As he says further, in a discussion now classic, the life presented in Shakespeare's major tragedies is one which contends against evil as it would against a poison, struggles against it in agony, and eventually casts it forth, though it must rend itself in so doing and must tear out much good along with the evil. The good individual in the body politic must often suffer as much as, or more than, the evil individual through this agonized convulsion; or the good in an individual must be destroyed, and even help to destroy itself, because of the evil in him which is also to be destroyed. The process is quite other than one of weighing good and evil, determining relative merits, and administering rewards and punishments in due proportion. It is, indeed, a frightfully wasteful process, involving both order and disorder. After it has run its course, "what remains is a family, a city, a country, exhausted, pale, and feeble, but alive through the principle of good which animates it; and, within it, individuals who, if they have not the brilliance or greatness of the tragic character, still have won our respect and confidence."[10] The working force has had to lose "a part of its own substance,—a part more dangerous and unquiet, but far more valuable and nearer to its heart than that which remains,—a Fortinbras, a Malcolm, an Octavius. There is no tragedy in its expulsion of evil: the tragedy is that this involves the waste of good."[11] And life produces refined tragedy because "—at any rate for the eye of sight—the evil against which it asserts itself, and the persons whom this evil inhabits, are not really something outside the order, so that they can attack it or fail to conform to it; they are within it and a part of it. It itself produces them,—produces Iago as well as Desdemona, Iago's cruelty as well as Iago's courage. It is not poisoned, it poisons itself."[12]

Thus Shakespeare allays the tragic qualm which, by unsettling the very foundations of our moral conceptions, he raises in us. He purges our emotions of pity and fear by making us acquiesce without bitterness in catastrophe which at first sight may seem the result of goodness turning false to itself and aiding evil in the production of suffering with cruelly refined irony. It is not an easy reconciliation that he offers, any more than the reconciliation provided by Aeschylus, and perhaps somewhat less. It cannot even spare the life of a Hamlet as Greek reconciliation can spare the life of an Orestes. Death is a sure part of the tragedy because the tragedy is Gothic. All that Shakespeare alone will permit us to say is that the yoke of life is hard but supremely worth the bearing in the interest of general good. Ultimate reasons for its being hard are not brought to our perception.

v

Finally, Gothic tragedy is in nothing more patently different from Greek tragedy than in the structural forms evolved for its own peculiar purposes and given most subtle fitness for those purposes by Shakespeare. The two tragic arts may far more readily be united upon some general technical principle of function, even the purgation of pity and fear, than upon some general technical principle of unity.

In its nondramatic beginnings the tragedy of Christian Europe finds that what it has to say often falls by nature into a biographic form. In stories of ambitious human careers notable for the violent contrast of their rise and fall it finds that the full blow to a mortal pride involving attachment to the world and its transitory prizes is best delivered by recording both rise and fall with circumstantiality and making them equally vivid to the reader. Never far from the mind of author or reader is the figure of Fortune and her wheel. Frequently Boccaccio and his followers in *De Casibus* story quite obviously think of the scope of tragedy as the whole round of Fortune's wheel—the subject's attachment to the ascending side and his climbing thereby, his perilous enthronement after the ascent (emphasized as the turning-point of the tragedy), his decline upon and final precipitation from the descending side. The full untrammeled sweep of this biographic form is often seen in Elizabethan tragic drama, sometimes with the simplest ascetic ⅄ implication to be found in *De Casibus* narrative. Shakespeare eventually takes the tragedy of ascent and descent into the realm of supreme art.

In two of the four tragedies which have been commonly accepted as embodying his genius at its highest, Shakespeare builds a pyramid of rise and fall and balances its sides with delicacy and exactitude. They are, of course, *Hamlet* and *Macbeth*. If *Antony and Cleopatra* is to be made a fifth in the roll of honor, it must be grouped with *Hamlet* and *Macbeth* as another example of the same structural principle. Each of the three plays has a protagonist who is driven by an ambition or by a powerful impulsion toward some highly difficult accomplishment in a theater of worldly action. He aspires toward his desire and climbs step after step of ascent through almost exactly half the play. Just when he has attained the topmost level of his reach, something happens which lets us know in a flash of certainty that his course is to turn downward. He himself is filled with foreboding, though he continues to struggle toward his aim. More and more as he sinks away from his highest level of attainment his acts become those of desperation. The end is ruin and death accomplished through the gathered momentum of his fall. In the outline of the pyramid one may see the round of Fortune's wheel with a difference.

For in these plays Shakespeare is certainly not occupied with any such wholly mysterious tragic reversal as might be attributed to the averting of Fortune's face. Nor does he ever bring his subjects to any such point of elevation that they boast with highest satisfaction of their rise and meet with misfortune in the midst of a lulling prosperity. He partly gives the reversal a grimly logical causation—as we look back we can see that it was being prepared for in the ascending action—and never for a moment does he allow to the tragically aspiring spirit a sense of complete achievement.

This large lack of success for the protagonist combined with a very real measure of triumph Shakespeare dramatizes as resulting from a passionate urge which is decidedly not simple or homogeneous. The impulse cannot be followed single-mindedly by its possessor. It is at least a double urge, and the protagonist is fatally incapable of satisfying more than a part of it. Frequently the parts of the urge are at war among themselves, reminding us of another war which Shakespeare reveals within tragic character, the war between the goods.

Macbeth cannot remain satisfied with the kingship which he gains for himself. To sell his soul to the eternal enemy of mankind for that alone is to do worse than nothing, and he cannot rest with the thought that Banquo's issue, instead of his own, shall occupy the throne. He rises to the crown through two acts of the play, reaches for the rest of his ambition with a desperate hand, and then loses even that part which he has. When Fleance escapes from the murderers in the third act, we recognize that there is a turning downward of Macbeth's course.

Antony in a different way has two consuming desires, or, perhaps it would be better to say, two irrepressible grand passions. One is for military glory and the other is for Cleopatra. Whatever one may say of the good and evil involved (Shakespeare is distinctly not passing moral judgment upon Antony's love for Cleopatra as Dryden does), the two passions are tragically incompatible for the character that is Antony. He comes to the point where he might be content with military domination of something less than the whole world if he might also have Cleopatra. But fate will not allow him to confine his military ambition. He is linked to Octavius Caesar for a death struggle, his spirit

> Noble, courageous, high, unmatchable,
> Where Caesar's is not, (II, iii, 20–21)

yet forebodingly turned to water when he is near Caesar. Octavius knows Antony's greatness, acknowledges it generously; and as Caesar he simply cannot live in the same world with him without trying conclusions. Antony succeeds in combining possession of Cleopatra with military glory in the East; he makes her queen not only of Egypt but also of lower Syria, Cyprus, and Lydia, and to their sons he gives other far-flung kingdoms. Hardly has the news of this reached Rome, in the middle of the play, when the battle for world power at Actium is forced upon him. He allows Cleopatra and her ships to enter his battle line, and therein lies the inception of his ruin. Success in the combination of his two passions does not stretch so far.

For Hamlet we cannot mark thus definitely a double desire, but we know with great certainty that his aim is not single and that somehow his impelling forces are tragically

GG

incompatible. Through half the play his rise toward fulfillment of desire is a rise to success in demonstration that Claudius is the murderer of his father, as his prophetic soul and his father's ghost have led him to believe. This is his only measure of actual triumph through carefully planned effort, and he extracts from it the intellectual satisfaction which we should expect. Then when he finds Claudius at prayer and has the chance to kill him, just after reaching certainty about the king's guilt, he neglects to do so. This weakening of his purpose constitutes a large part of the Hamlet mystery. He conducts himself as one might who had converted hypothesis into proof as a detective exercise of the wits and could not develop enough interest in practical application to act effectively. But Shakespeare will not permit us to stop with such an explanation of Hamlet's delay. Hamlet himself gives a reason for his rejection of opportunity, and here a double desire somewhat similar to Macbeth's and Antony's puts in an appearance. Hamlet declares that he wants to take vengeance not only on the king's body, but also on his soul. He will combine both sorts of vengeance by killing the murderer at some grosser occupation than prayer, thus making sure of the soul's damnation. On the face of it, then, Hamlet is to bring ruin upon himself and upon others by reaching for the double, instead of the single, objective. Yet, Hamlet being what he is, we are bound to suspect that he may merely be inventing an excuse for delay, or giving a superficial reason to take the place of a deeper one. Moreover, this matter of sending the king's soul to damnation is insufficiently developed by Shakespeare for dramatic importance.

Gothic tragedy, as we have seen, does not limit itself to tracing the round of Fortune's wheel, the rise of aspiration nicely balanced by the descent. Fond as it is of emphasizing life's insecurity in that way, it knows and uses other methods of presentation. The protracted view of a downward course after a brief glimpse of prosperity is one of its offerings. The view of a downward course may include the spectacle of man letting himself be destroyed by the scheming of the world's evil forces, a kind of spectacle favored by the moralities as they incline toward tragedy. And partly with the aid of Seneca, the intrigues of love and revenge are made to yield various plots of ingenious complexity.

Shakespeare's *Othello* and *King Lear* are in no sense tragedies of rise and fall through aspiring action so far as their heroes are concerned. In each our attention is mainly fixed upon a long course of descent into suffering and death, and in each the protagonist is worked upon by fiendish evil. Iago draws his net about Othello like some Super-Vice out of the moral plays, and Othello slowly falls. There is nothing to relieve this descending action, once Othello has departed from the happiness which he finds in the first few scenes of the drama. *King Lear,* on the contrary, has such relief. Lear's brief moment of folly at the very beginning of the play exposes him to a whirlwind of evil powers which tear at him, strip him, and destroy him physically through the ensuing scenes. But spiritually Lear rises through the course of his anguish to a wisdom which he has never before approached, including a sympathetic appreciation of suffering among the world's unfortunates and a full realization of Cordelia's love. If one thinks again in terms of the moral play, it is as though Lear loses the world only to save his soul by confession and penitence. At the end he wants the pomp of kingship no more. Forgiveness from Cordelia helps to free him from the "wheel of fire" upon which he has been bound and to stop the tears that "do scald like molten lead." "Come, let's away to prison," he says to Cordelia,

> And take upon's the mystery of things,
> As if we were God's spies: and we'll wear out,
> In a wall'd prison, packs and sets of great ones
> That ebb and flow by the moon.   (V, iii, 16–19)

This ebb and flow of great ones by the moon which Lear calls to mind is a picture never forgotten by Gothic tragedy from its beginnings to Shakespeare. Like the more popular picture of the round of Fortune's wheel, it becomes a symbol so full of meaning that it even helps to give form to Gothic tragedy. Greek tragedy is willing to confine its scope to the action that immediately brings catastrophe and to let the audience feel all other motion indirectly. Gothic tragedy is normally not thus willing to limit its scope. It is keenly conscious of, and inclined to be directly concerned with, motion extended sweepingly through time and space in the theater of that active life which it first scorns and then tries more and more to understand.

General Bibliographical Note

Bibliographical information concerning the principal sources referred to may be found in the following works:

Attilio Hortis, *Studj sulle opere latine del Boccaccio con particolare riguardo alla storia della erudizione nel medio evo e alle letterature straniere. Aggiuntavi la bibliografia delle edizioni,* Trieste, 1879.

Eleanor P. Hammond, *Chaucer: a Bibliographical Manual,* New York, 1908.

Lydgate's Fall of Princes, ed. Henry Bergen (Carnegie Institution), 4 vols., Washington, 1923–1927; the same work (Early English Text Society), 4 vols., London, 1924–1927. (Vol. IV offers a bibliographical introduction.)

Mirror for Magistrates, ed. Joseph Haslewood, 2 vols., London, 1815. (Bibliographical introduction.)

W. F. Trench, *A Mirror for Magistrates: Its Origin and Influence,* Edinburgh, 1898.

D. A. Stauffer, *English Biography before 1700,* Cambridge, Mass., 1930. (Bibliography in conclusion.)

Willard Farnham, "The Progeny of *A Mirror for Magistrates*," *Modern Philology,* XXIX(1932):395–410.

E. K. Chambers, *The Mediaeval Stage,* 2 vols., Oxford, 1903. (Bibliographical appendix.)

E. N. S. Thompson, "The English Moral Plays," *Transactions of the Connecticut Academy of Arts and Sciences,* XIV(1910):291–413. (List of plays and their modern editions in conclusion.)

W. W. Greg, *A List of English Plays Written before 1643 and Printed before 1700* (Bibliographical Society), London, 1900.

F. E. Schelling, *Elizabethan Drama 1558–1642,* 2 vols., Boston and New York, 1908. (List of plays in conclusion.)

E. K. Chambers, *The Elizabethan Stage,* 4 vols., Oxford, 1923. (Bibliographical chapters in conclusion.)

The Cambridge History of English Literature, ed. A. W. Ward and A. R. Waller, Cambridge and New York, Vol. III (for the *Mirror for Magistrates*), 1909, and Vol. V (for drama), 1910.

A. W. Pollard and G. R. Redgrave, *A Short-Title Catalogue of Books Printed in England, Scotland, and Ireland and of English Books Printed Abroad 1475–1640* (Bibliographical Society), London, 1926.

In quoting from Chaucer I have used the Oxford text prepared by W. W. Skeat, and in quoting from Shakespeare the Oxford text prepared by W. J. Craig.

Throughout the notes which follow, full bibliographical details are given when a work is first cited for a chapter. The abbreviation *op. cit.* thus has reference to a previous note under the same chapter heading.

Notes to Chapter I

GRECO-ROMAN SURRENDER OF THE WORLD

[1] See Alexander Benazet, *Le Théâtre au Japon: Esquisse d'une histoire littéraire*, Paris, 1901; Marie C. Stopes and Joji Sakurai, *Plays of Old Japan, the "Nō", together with Translations of the Dramas*, New York, 1908; Ernest Fenollosa and Ezra Pound, *"Noh"; or Accomplishment*, New York, 1917. For a comparison with Greek tragedy see the last-named work, p. 102.

[2] Discussion of the folk origins of Greek tragedy and of tragedy in general has become highly involved. Convenient short introductions to the questions at issue, with bibliographical notes, may be found in D. C. Stuart, "The Origin of Greek Tragedy in the Light of Dramatic Technique," *Trans. and Proc. Amer. Philol. Assoc.*, XLVII(1916):173 ff., and in D. R. Stuart, *Epochs of Greek and Roman Biography*, Berkeley, Calif., 1928, p. 17.

[3] D. R. Stuart, *op. cit.*, pp. 16–17.

[4] Plutarch, *Solon*, 29.

[5] Chapter heading in *Five Stages of Greek Religion* (ed. 2), New York, 1925.

[6] See A. E. Haigh, *The Tragic Drama of the Greeks*, Oxford, 1896, p. 458; also Alfred Körte, *Hellenistic Poetry*, tr. Jacob Hammer and Moses Hadas, New York, 1929, pp. 276 ff.

[7] Edwyn Bevan, *Later Greek Religion*, London, 1927, p. xxvii.

[8] *Discourses*, III, v, 7–9. Translation by P. E. Matheson, Oxford, 1916. See also *Discourses*, IV, i, 99–103, where Epictetus allows that man has freedom only in the sphere of moral purpose and never in the sphere of worldly possessions.

[9] *Discourses*, I, xii.

[10] Translation by G. H. Rendall, *Marcus Aurelius to Himself* (ed. 2), London, 1898, ix, 39.

[11] Extract from *Stoicorum Veterum Fragmenta*, ed. Johannes von Arnim, Leipsic, 1903–1924, II, frag. 625, given in translation by Bevan, *op. cit.*, pp. 30–31.

[12] *Minor Dialogues together with the Dialogue on Clemency*, tr. Aubrey Stewart, London, 1912, p. 17. See also *Moral Essays*, ed. and tr. J. W. Basore (Loeb Classical Library), London and New York, I(1928):39.

[13] *Seneca's Tragedies, with an English Translation* by F. J. Miller (Loeb Classical Library), London and New York, 1916–1917, II:11.

[14] *Hellenistic Philosophies*, Princeton, N. J., 1923, p. 268.

[15] For those who would follow these ideas with a glance toward the Middle Ages, H. O. Taylor in *The Classical Heritage of the Middle Ages*, New York, 1903, and in *Ancient Ideals*, New York, 1913, is useful. See especially the latter work, I:372 ff.

[16] For a subtle discussion of this development see Edward Caird, *The Evolution of Theology in the Greek Philosophers*, Glasgow, 1904, II:171 ff.

[17] Walter Scott, *Hermetica: the Ancient Greek and Latin Writings which Contain Religious or Philosophic Teachings Ascribed to Hermes Trismegistus*, Oxford, 1924–1926, I:153.

[18] Caird, *op. cit.*, II:215.

[19] See, for example, *Enneads*, V, 3, 14, and VI, 9, 4.

[20] This fact is well emphasized by Gilbert Murray, *Five Stages of Greek Religion* (ed. 2), 1925, pp. 179 ff.

[21] Wilhelm Bousset, *Hauptprobleme der Gnosis*, Göttingen, 1907, pp. 351 ff.

[22] *Concerning Isis and Osiris*, extract given in translation by Bevan, *op. cit.*, p. 136.

[23] This document, I think, has all the importance which Professor Gilbert Murray gives to it when he translates it as an appendix to his *Five Stages of Greek Religion*, New York, 1925. It is edited and also translated by A. D. Nock, Cambridge, 1926.

[24] Tr. A. D. Nock, *op. cit.*, p. 21.

[25] Murray, *op. cit.*, p. 254.

[26] A work dealing in detail with the medieval figure of Fortune and its relation to the classical figure is H. R. Patch, *The Goddess Fortuna in Mediaeval Literature*, Cambridge, Mass., 1927. For a well-illustrated discussion of medieval art in this connection see Raimond Van Marle, *Iconographie de l'art profane au moyen-âge et à la renaissance . . . allégories et symboles*, The Hague, 1932, pp. 178 ff.

[27] The following works are particularly useful for bibliographical information concerning those matters of later classic philosophy which have been touched upon in this chapter: Eduard Zeller, *Die Philosophie der Griechen in ihrer geschichtlichen Entwicklung*, Teil III, *Die nacharistotelische Philosophie* (ed. 5), Leipsic, 1923 (a standard work with the fullest of documentation); R. D. Hicks, *Stoic and Epicurean*, New York, 1910 (select bibliography in conclusion); Edwyn Bevan, *Stoics and Sceptics*, Oxford, 1913 (prefatory notes); Cyril Bailey, *Phases in the Religion of Ancient Rome*, Berkeley, Calif., 1932 (appended notes); Eduard Zeller, *Grundriss der Geschichte der griechischen Philosophie* (ed. 13, revised by Wilhelm Nestle), Leipsic, 1928 (bibliography in conclusion to each section)—tr. L. R. Palmer as *Outlines of the History of Greek Philosophy*, New York, 1931 (bibliography in conclusion); Karl Vossler, *Mediaeval Culture: an Introduction to Dante and His Times*, tr. W. C. Lawton (2 vols.), New York, 1929 (lengthy and excellently classified bibliographical notes added in conclusion by J. E. Spingarn, covering all the main divisions of classic thought in connection with those of medieval thought).

Notes to Chapter II

GOTHIC ESPOUSAL AND CONTEMPT OF THE WORLD

[1] J. Huizinga, *The Waning of the Middle Ages: a Study of the Forms of Life, Thought and Art in France and the Netherlands in the XIVth and XVth Centuries*, tr. F. Hopman, London, 1924, p. 252.

[2] Charles H. Haskins, *The Renaissance of the Twelfth Century*, Cambridge, Mass., 1927, p. 6.

[3] Irving Babbitt, *Rousseau and Romanticism*, Boston and New York, 1919, p. 116.

[4] See Edward Caird, *The Evolution of Theology in the Greek Philosophers*, Glasgow, 1904, chapter on "The Influence of Greek Philosophy upon Christian Theology," II:347 ff.

[5] Extract from the Chronicle of Ralph, Abbot of Coggeshall, given by G. G. Coulton, *Life in the Middle Ages* (ed. 2), Cambridge, 1928, I:29 ff. For a brief account of the struggle which the Church made against a too rigid asceticism see J. O. Hannay, *The Spirit and Origin of Christian Monasticism*, London, 1903.

[6] E.g., see Huizinga, *op. cit.*, pp. 149 ff.

[7] The contrast is well made by G. G. Coulton, *Art and the Reformation*, Oxford, 1928, pp. 372 ff.

[8] Haskins, *op. cit.*, p. 17.

[9] *Ibid.*, pp. 19 ff.

[10] Huizinga, *op. cit.*, p. 124.

[11] B. P. Kurtz, "Gifer the Worm: an Essay Toward the History of an Idea," *Univ. Calif. Publ. Eng.*, II:240, 246 ff., 256.

[12] Émile Mâle, *L'Art religieux de la fin du moyen âge en France* (ed. 3), Paris, 1925, pp. 347 ff.

[13] T. R. Lounsbury, *Studies in Chaucer*, New York, 1892, II:232.

[14] Huizinga, *op. cit.*, p. 133.

[15] Mâle, *op. cit.*, pp. 352 ff.

[16] *Ibid.*, pp. 353 ff., 361. See also Eleanor P. Hammond, *English Verse between Chaucer and Surrey*, Durham, N. C., 1927, p. 126.

[17] Mâle, *op. cit.*, p. 356.

[18] F. P. Weber, *Aspects of Death and Correlated Aspects of Life in Art, Epigram, and Poetry*, New York, 1920, pp. 131 ff.; Mâle, *op. cit.*, pp. 347 ff.

[19] See S. R. Packard, *Europe and the Church under Innocent III*, New York, 1927, p. 13.

[20] See J. S. P. Tatlock, "Chaucer's Retractation," *Publ. Mod. Lang. Assoc.*, XXVIII (1914):521 ff.

[21] A-text, ll. 414–415. See Eleanor P. Hammond, *Chaucer: a Bibliographical Manual*, New York, 1908, pp. 381–382.

[22] For summaries of arguments see Hammond, *Chaucer*, pp. 291–292; R. D. French, *A Chaucer Handbook*, New York, 1927, pp. 247 ff.; and F. N. Robinson, ed., *The Complete Works of Geoffrey Chaucer*, New York, 1933, pp. 852–853.

[23] Lounsbury, *Studies*, III:332–334.

[24] But see Albert Hyma, *The Youth of Erasmus*, Ann Arbor, Mich., 1930, pp. 167 ff.

[25] Paynel's "Dedication."

[26] *The Life of Solitude by Francis Petrarch, Translated with Introduction and Notes* by Jacob Zeitlin, Urbana, Ill., 1924, p. 263.

[27] *Petrarch's Secret; or, the Soul's Conflict with Passion: Three Dialogues between Himself and S. Augustine*, tr. W. H. Draper, London, 1911, p. 14.

[28] *Ibid.*, p. 176.

[29] *Ibid.*

[30] *Phisicke against Fortune . . . Written in Latine by Frauncis Petrarch . . . and now first Englished*, tr. Thomas Twyne, 1579, fol. 251 *verso*.

[31] See *L. Annaei Senecae: Opera Quae Supersunt*, ed. F. Haase, Leipsic, 1872, III: 446 ff.

[32] Thomas Twyne, *trans. cit.*, fol. 42 *recto*.

[33] *Ibid.*, fol. 30 *verso*.

[34] *Ibid.*, fol. 90 *recto*.

[35] *Ibid.*, fol. 302 *recto* and *verso*.

[36] Title page.

[37] See *The Paradise of Dainty Devices (1576–1606)*, ed. H. E. Rollins, Cambridge, Mass., 1927, p. lxvi.

[38] *Ibid.*, p. xxxii.

[39] Ananda Coomaraswamy, *Buddha and the Gospel of Buddhism*, London, 1916, p. 144.

[40] See H. C. Warren, *Buddhism in Translations, Passages Selected from the Buddhist Sacred Books and Translated from the Original Pali into English*, Cambridge, Mass., 1922, pp. 298 ff., 359.

[41] See Mrs. Rhys Davids, *Psalms of the Early Buddhists. II. Psalms of the Brethren*, London, 1913, pp. 190, 23.

[42] See Henry Preble and S. M. Jackson, *The Source of "Jerusalem the Golden." Together with other Pieces attributed to Bernard of Cluny. In English Translation*, Chicago, 1910.

[43] *Discourses*, IX, 6; translation as given by Edwyn Bevan, *Later Greek Religion*, London and Toronto, New York, p. 145.

[44] See *Catholic Encyclopedia*, article on the Cross. The triumph of the crucified Christ is emphasized, though his sufferings are of course mentioned, in a notable twelfth-century comparison of the Church ritual with tragedy which has been brought to my attention by Professor J. S. P. Tatlock. The comparison, which is brief, begins as follows: "Sciendum quod hi qui tragoedias in theatris recitabant, actus pugnantium gestibus populo repraesentabant. Sic tragicus noster pugnam Christi populo Christiano in theatro Ecclesiae gestibus suis repraesentat, eique victoriam redemptionis suae inculcat." (Honorius Augustodunensis, *Gemma Animae*, Migne, *Patrologia Latina*, CLXXII:570.)

[45] See Émile Mâle, *L'Art religieux de la fin du moyen âge en France* (ed. 3), Paris, 1925, pp. 86 ff., 92 ff.

[46] *Ibid.*, pp. 92, 99 ff.

[47] *Ibid.*, pp. 108 ff., 117 ff.

[48] *Ibid.*, pp. 122 ff.

[49] *Ibid.*, p. 86.

[50] *Ibid.*, p. 87.

Notes to Chapter III

FALLS OF PRINCES: BOCCACCIO

1 See Henri Hauvette, *Boccace: Étude biographique et littéraire*, Paris, 1914, pp. 367 ff.; Edward Hutton, *Giovanni Boccaccio: a Biographical Study*, London, 1910, pp. 197 ff.; Silvio Segalla, *I sentimenti religiosi nel Boccaccio*, Riva, 1909, p. 62.

2 Hauvette, *op. cit.*, pp. 210, 324 ff.

3 For discussion of these dates see Hauvette, *Boccace*, pp. 210, 394, 396; also the same author's *Recherches sur le «De Casibus Virorum Illustrium» de Boccace* (Entre camarades. Publié par la Société des Anciens Élèves de la Faculté ès Lettres de l'Université de Paris), Paris, 1901, pp. 279 ff.; also Attilio Hortis, *Studj sulle opere latine del Boccaccio*, Trieste, 1879, p. 89, n. 2.

4 See my examination of Boccaccio's reputation in England, "England's Discovery of the *Decameron*," *Publ. Mod. Lang. Assoc.*, XXXIX(1924):129 ff. and 138.

5 Henry Bergen, ed., *Lydgate's Fall of Princes* (Early English Text Society), London, 1924, I:xii.

6 The original Latin may be found in Francesco Corazzini, *Le lettere edite e inedite di messer Giovanni Boccaccio*, Florence, 1877, pp. 298 ff.

7 See again "England's Discovery of the *Decameron*" (as cited in n. 4 above), pp. 126 ff.

8 See Hortis, *op. cit.*, p. 120.

9 Eleanor P. Hammond, *Chaucer: a Bibliographical Manual*, New York, 1908, p. 81. See also R. W. Babcock, "The Mediaeval Setting of Chaucer's *Monk's Tale*," *Publ. Mod. Lang. Assoc.*, XLVI(1931):207 ff. *Hygini Fabulae* have been edited by M. Schmidt, Jena, 1872.

10 Hauvette, *Boccace*, p. 401.

11 Hortis, *op. cit.*, p. 476.

12 Chap. LI. Translation from *The Ante-Nicene Fathers*, ed. Alexander Roberts and James Donaldson, Buffalo, N. Y., 1886, VII:321.

13 Bk. VI, Chap. XV. Translation from Aubrey Stewart, *Minor Dialogues together with the Dialogue on Clemency*, London, 1912, p. 181.

14 *Ibid.*, p. 175.

15 Bk. III, opening of pr. 5. The translation is that of Richard Lord Viscount Preston, London, 1695, p. 111. The passage is given the same importance as that which I have given it by B. L. Jefferson, *Chaucer and the Consolation of Philosophy of Boethius*, Princeton, N. J., 1917, pp. 85–86.

16 Ll. 5839 ff. See the collection of other examples in H. R. Patch, *The Goddess Fortuna in Mediaeval Literature*, Cambridge, Mass., 1927, p. 70, n. 3.

17 See E. K. Rand, *Founders of the Middle Ages*, Cambridge, Mass., 1928, p. 170. The verses in Boethius are Bk. II, met. 7. W. L. Renwick connects St. Bernard's verses with Spenser's *The Ruines of Time* and calls them "the fountain head of this mediaeval commonplace." See his edition of the *Complaints*, London, 1928, p. 191. For further notes on the theme see Patch, *op. cit.*, p. 72.

[18] Edition of H. E. Rollins, Cambridge, Mass., 1927, p. 6. See note on the poem and its Latin text, p. 181.

[19] Quotations from the *De Casibus* for this chapter are all from the second edition of Boccaccio's first version, printed at Paris for Jean Gourmont and Jean Petit early in the sixteenth century (no date). For bibliographical description see Henry Bergen, ed., *Lydgate's Fall of Princes.* London, 1927, IV:125 ff. I use the first version of the *De Casibus* because it is the one used by Laurent de Premierfait for his French version and through him by Lydgate for the English. Besides, it was by far the more popular in Europe. See Henri Hauvette, *Recherches sur le «De Casibus Virorum Illustrium» de Boccace,* Paris, 1901, pp. 289 ff. Boccaccio's Latin for the words which I have quoted concerning God and Fortune is as follows: "Et quid deus siue (vt eorum more loquar) fortuna in elatos possit describere." (Fol. i *recto* of the Gourmont-Petit edition.)

[20] "Fortunæ ludibrium." Fol. i *verso.*

[21] Bergen's edition, I:27.

[22] "Set rerum exitus expectandus est." Fol. ix *verso.*

[23] "Si tam grandis cecidit moles: Quid nobis posse contingere arbitramur? Equidem Pompeio compatiendum est: Set longe magis nobis timendum." Fol. lxv *verso.*

[24] Patch, *op. cit.,* p. 69.

[25] *Ibid.,* pp. 69–70.

[26] "Quidquid egit in posterum aut ad percellationem prosperitatis adsumtae aut ad decliuium pertinuit." Fol. lii *verso.*

[27] "Cui ignea vis origo cælestis & gloriæ inexplebilis est cupido." Fol. xxxi *recto.*

[28] "Et si contingat deiici: non vestro crimine factum adpareat: set proteruia potius Fortunæ vertentis." Fol. cxvii *recto.*

[29] See n. 19, above.

[30] See H. R. Patch, *Smith College Studies in Modern Languages,* III(1922): 135 ff.

[31] See Lynn Thorndike, *A History of Magic and Experimental Science during the First Thirteen Centuries of Our Era,* New York, 1923, I:210, 354.

[32] See T. O. Wedel, *The Mediaeval Attitude toward Astrology Particularly in England (Yale Studies in English,* LX), New Haven, Conn., 1920, pp. 57 ff.

[33] See Thorndike, *op. cit.,* I:680 ff.

[34] See a typical rhymed moon book in English of the fourteenth or fifteenth century, which I have edited in *Studies in Philology,* XX(1923):70 ff.

[35] See n. 22, Chap. I, above.

[36] See the two translations, one by Gilbert Murray, *Five Stages of Greek Religion* (ed. 2), New York, 1925, p. 255, and the other by A. D. Nock, *Sallustius concerning the Gods and the Universe,* Cambridge, 1926, p. 21.

[37] See Patch, *Goddess Fortuna,* p. 50, n. 6; p. 61.

[38] *Ibid.,* p. 77, nn.

[39] *The Pricke of Conscience (Stimulus Conscientiae),* ed. Richard Morris, Berlin, 1863, pp. 34–35.

[40] *Ibid.,* p. 36.

[41] See Patch, *Goddess Fortuna,* pp. 58, 63–64.

[42] *Ibid.*, p. 58, n. 1.

[43] *Fortune*, ll. 69–72. Chaucer is following the statements of Boethius, *De Consolatione Philosophiae*, Bk. II, conclusion of pr. 3 and conclusion of pr. 4.

[44] See H. R. Patch, *Smith College Studies in Modern Languages*, III(1922): 180 ff. for a collection of pertinent material from the Church Fathers.

[45] See Wedel, *op. cit.*, pp. 16 ff. For the attitude of the Church toward astrology see also Thorndike, *op. cit.*

[46] For a discussion of this departure from Neo-Platonic thought see Rand, *op. cit.*, pp. 175 ff. See also H. R. Patch, "Fate in Boethius and the Neo-platonists," *Speculum*, IV(1929):62 ff.

[47] *Consolation*, Bk. IV, pr. 6; *Boethius*, ed. and tr. H. F. Stewart and E. K. Rand (Loeb Classical Library), London and New York, 1926, pp. 340 ff.

[48] Bk. II, pr. 2. See Patch, *Goddess Fortuna*, p. 151.

[49] Bk. V, pr. 1, *Boethius*, ed. Stewart and Rand, pp. 366 ff.

[50] Patch, *Goddess Fortuna*, pp. 18 ff., 27 ff.

[51] For a collection of references to passages in Dante's work see Wedel, *op. cit.*, p. 80.

[52] Cary's translation, *Inferno*, VII, 80–83.

[53] *Ibid.*, VII, 93–97.

[54] See Patch, *Goddess Fortuna*, pp. 21–22. See also the same author in *Smith College Studies in Modern Languages*, III(1922):209, 212.

[55] See Wedel, *op. cit.*, pp. 155 ff.

[56] See Henry Bett, *Johannes Scotus Erigena: a Study in Mediaeval Philosophy*, Cambridge, 1925, pp. 51, 57, 64, 102, 176. See also Karl Vossler, *Mediaeval Culture: an Introduction to Dante and His Times*, tr. W. C. Lawton, New York, 1929, I:100 ff.

[57] See Vossler, *op. cit.*, p. 120, and Maurice de Wulf, *Philosophy and Civilization in the Middle Ages*, Princeton, N. J., 1922, pp. 284 ff.

[58] *Summa Theologica*, I, qu. 47, art. 1, tr. Fathers of the English Dominican Province, London, 1921, p. 257.

[59] *Ibid.*, I, qu. 49, art. 2, pp. 280–281.

[60] Vossler, *op. cit.*, I:114.

[61] *Summa Theologica*, I, qu. 48, art. 2, tr. Dominican Fathers, p. 268.

[62] *De Potentia*, 4, 1, quoted by Martin Grabman, *Thomas Aquinas: His Personality and Thought*, tr. Virgil Michel, New York, 1928, pp. 36–37.

[63] See n. 28 above.

[64] Moutier ed., Florence, 1831, I:71–72; II:55–56. Referred to by J. S. P. Tatlock, *The Scene of the Franklin's Tale Visited* (Chaucer Society), London, 1914, p. 24.

[65] For examples see Wedel, *op. cit.*, p. 68; Thorndike, *op. cit.*, II:584; Tatlock, *op. cit.*, pp. 24–26.

[66] See Thorndike, *op. cit.*, I:306.

Notes to Chapter IV

FALLS OF PRINCES: CHAUCER AND LYDGATE

[1] *Inferno*, Canto XXXIII.

[2] See the discussion of the *Monkes Tale* in Chap. II above.

[3] See T. R. Price, "Troilus and Criseyde: a Study in Chaucer's Method of Narrative Construction," *Publ. Mod. Lang. Assoc.*, XI(1896):307 ff.

[4] The extent of such study is indicated, of course, in the Chaucer bibliographies of Eleanor P. Hammond, New York, 1908, and later compilers.

[5] A recent discussion of the *Troilus* as a tragedy, referring to much that has been said before on the subject, is W. C. Curry, "Destiny in Chaucer's *Troilus*," *Publ. Mod. Lang. Assoc.* XLV(1930):129 ff.

[6] See note to the *Troilus* passage in R. K. Root's edition. In *biwayle* is also an echo of Chaucer's translation and interpretation of Boethius' reference to tragedy, *De Consolatione Philosophiae*, Bk. II, pr. 2, 36 ff. For other medieval interpretation of this Boethius passage see Wilhelm Cloetta, *Beiträge zur Litteraturgeschichte des Mittelalters und der Renaissance*, Halle, 1890, I:44 ff.

[7] See B. L. Jefferson, *Chaucer and the Consolation of Philosophy of Boethius*, Princeton, N. J., 1917, p. 125.

[8] See introduction to the *Filostrato*, ed. and tr. N. E. Griffin and A. B. Myrick, Philadelphia, Pa., 1929, pp. 12–13.

[9] Professor G. L. Kittredge has said this memorably in *Chaucer and His Poetry*, Cambridge, Mass., 1920, p. 143.

[10] Translation of Griffin and Myrick as cited above, I, st. 25, p. 145.

[11] *Troilus and Criseyde*, IV, 953–1085; *De Consolatione Philosophiae*, Bk. V, pr. 3, 7–71.

[12] See R. K. Root's note in his edition of the *Troilus*, IV, 953–1085; also his *The Textual Tradition of Chaucer's Troilus* (Chaucer Society), London, 1916, pp. 216–220, 262. See Aage Brusendorff, *The Chaucer Tradition*, London and Copenhagen, 1925, pp. 170 ff.

[13] Edition of the *Troilus*, p. xlviii. See also Kittredge, *Chaucer and his Poetry*, p. 129.

[14] I have discussed this combination of free will and predestination at some length in Chap. III above.

[15] As is argued, upon a somewhat different basis from that which I take, by H. R. Patch, "Troilus on Predestination," *Jour. Eng. and Germ. Philol.*, XVII (1918):399 ff., and "Troilus on Determinism," *Speculum*, VI(1931):225 ff.

[16] See J. S. P. Tatlock, *The Scene of the Franklin's Tale Visited* (Chaucer Society), London, 1914, pp. 23 ff., and B. L. Jefferson, *op. cit.*, pp. 71–80.

[17] *Boethius*, tr. H. F. Stewart and E. K. Rand (Loeb Classical Library), London and New York, 1926, p. 371.

[18] VII, stt. 83 ff.

[19] The significance of this interpolation in the *De Casibus* spirit has been remarked by B. L. Jefferson, *op. cit.*, p. 125.

20 P. 117.

21 *Inferno*, VII, 73 ff.

22 W. C. Curry, "Destiny in Chaucer's *Troilus*," *Publ. Mod. Lang. Assoc.*, XLV (1930):167–168.

23 "The Epilog of Chaucer's *Troilus*," *Mod. Philol.*, XVIII(1921):636. See also Karl Young, "Chaucer's Renunciation of Love in *Troilus*," *Mod. Lang. Notes*, XL(1925):270 ff.

24 I, 232–259. The passage begins:

> For-thy ensample taketh of this man [Troilus],
> Ye wyse, proude, and worthy folkes alle,
> To scornen Love, which that so sone can
> The freedom of your hertes to him thralle.

Root notes for these lines in his edition of the poem that some MSS have *serven* instead of *scornen*. His collation shows that they are not MSS in the best tradition. With *scornen* the text may be paraphrased: "Take example . . . with respect to this matter of scorning love . . . [and do not scorn it]." From what follows it is obvious that Chaucer is not telling us that we *should* scorn love.

25 As Professor H. R. Patch says in "Chaucer and Lady Fortune," *Mod. Lang. Rev.*, XXII(1927):383 ff.

26 *Confessio Amantis*, Prol., 546–555.

27 See Emil Koeppel, *Laurents de Premierfait und John Lydgates Bearbeitungen von Boccaccios De Casibus Virorum Illustrium*, Munich, 1885. For dates see also Henry Bergen's edition of the *Fall of Princes* (Early English Text Society), London, I(1924):ix–xiii. All quotations from Lydgate in this chapter are from Bergen's text.

28 See Koeppel, *op. cit.*, pp. 103 ff.

29 See note in Bergen's edition of the *Fall of Princes* for Bk. VIII, ll. 1464 ff.

30 Bergen's edition, I:272; II:462; III:829, 949, 956, 991.

31 Bk. VIII, ll. 3149–3150.

32 Bergen's edition, IV:196.

33 It is to be noted, however, that the "Envoy to Duke Humphrey," which Bergen prints after this "Chapitle of Fortune," changes tone and speaks of men who fall through demerits and lack of virtue (Bergen, III:1017). This envoy was not always made a part of the book in publication.

34 See Wilhelm Cloetta, *Beiträge zur Litteraturgeschichte des Mittelalters und der Renaissance*, Halle, 1890, I:126–127.

35 *Ibid.*, I:32.

36 Paget Toynbee, *Dante Studies and Researches*, London, 1902, p. 103. Detailed studies of tragic and comic theory in the Middle Ages will be found in the work of Cloetta cited above, and in Wilhelm Creizenach, *Geschichte des neueren Dramas*, Halle, 1893, I:1–46. For a briefer survey see E. K. Chambers, *The Mediaeval Stage*, Oxford, 1903, II:209 ff.

37 See Cloetta, *op. cit.*, I:45–46.

38 See index to Bergen's edition, *Fall of Princes*.

39 See Cloetta, *op. cit.*, I:43–44.

Notes to Chapter V

TRAGEDY AND THE ENGLISH MORAL PLAY: FIFTEENTH CENTURY

[1] See Raymond Lebègue, *La Tragédie religieuse en France: Les Débuts* (1514–1573), Paris, 1929, pp. 169 ff.

[2] E. N. S. Thompson, "The English Moral Plays," *Trans. Connecticut Acad. Arts and Sci.*, XIV(1910):293. See the discussion in G. R. Owst, *Literature and Pulpit in Medieval England*, Cambridge, 1933, pp. 526 ff.

[3] Gustave Cohen, *Mystères et moralités du manuscrit 617 de Chantilly*, Paris, 1920, p. cxlvi.

[4] *Art poétique françoys*, ed. Félix Gaiffe, Paris, 1910, p. 161.

[5] The passage from Sebillet is quoted by Lebègue, *op. cit.*, p. 107, along with passages from other French authors of the time, both for and against Sebillet's view.

[6] *The English Works of Sir Thomas More*, ed. W. E. Campbell *et al.*, London and New York, I(1931):72–73 (facsimile reproduction of the 1557 edition).

[7] Sig. K 4 *verso*.

[8] *Ed. cit.*, p. 77.

[9] *Ibid.*, p. 75.

[10] *Ibid.*, p. 77.

[11] Émile Mâle, *L'Art religieux de la fin du moyen âge en France* (ed. 3), Paris, 1925, p. 363. See also, for illustrated presentation of the Dance of Death in general, Raimond Van Marle, *Iconographie de l'art profane au moyen-âge et à la renaissance ... allégories et symboles*, The Hague, 1932, pp. 372 ff.

[12] *Ibid.*, p. 360. See also Eleanor P. Hammond, *English Verse between Chaucer and Surrey*, Durham, N. C., 1927, p. 124.

[13] Hammond, *op. cit.*, p. 131. See also *The Dance of Death*, ed. Florence Warren (Early English Text Society), London, 1931.

[14] See the catalogue by W. Seelmann, "Die Totentänze des Mittelalters," *Jahrbuch des Vereins für niederdeutsche Sprachforschung*, XVII(1892):41 ff.

[15] Eleanor P. Hammond, "Latin Texts of the Dance of Death," *Mod. Philol.*, VII (1911):399. See Mâle, *op. cit.*, p. 361.

[16] *English Verse between Chaucer and Surrey*, p. 128.

[17] See Mâle, *op. cit.*, pp. 365 ff.

[18] *Ibid.*, pp. 356 ff.

[19] *Ibid.*, p. 362.

[20] *Ibid.*, p. 347. See also Seelmann, *op. cit.*, pp. 57–58.

[21] See especially, for expressions of doubt, Wilhelm Fehse, *Der Ursprung der Totentänze*, Halle, 1907, pp. 7 ff., and Wolfgang Stammler, *Die Totentänze des Mittelalters*, Munich, 1922, p. 59. The latter work has valuable illustrations.

[22] *Op. cit.*, p. 363.

[23] See E. K. Chambers, *The Medieval Stage*, Oxford, 1903, II:153.

[24] See J. P. Wickersham Crawford, *Spanish Drama before Lope de Vega*, Philadelphia, Pa., 1922, p. 149.

[25] Professor Brandl, who finds it probable that the Dance of Death originated in drama, thinks that *The Pride of Life* contains some attempt at classification of various characters in the fashion of the Dance. I cannot feel that it does. See A. Brandl, *Quellen des weltlichen Dramas in England vor Shakespeare*, Strassburg, 1898, pp. xvii–xviii.

[26] *The Non-Cycle Mystery Plays, together with the Croxton Play of the Sacrament and the Pride of Life*, ed. Osborn Waterhouse (Early English Text Society), London, 1909, ll. 305–306.

[27] *Ad Lucilium Epistolae Morales*, ed. and tr. R. M. Gummere (Loeb Classical Library), London and New York, 1920, II:438–443.

[28] F. P. Weber, *Aspects of Death and Correlated Aspects of Life in Art, Epigram, and Poetry*, New York, 1920, p. 726.

[29] See Mâle, *op. cit.*, pp. 347 ff.

[30] See Hope Traver, *The Four Daughters of God*, Philadelphia, Pa., 1907.

[31] *The Macro Plays*, ed. F. J. Furnivall and A. W. Pollard (Early English Text Society), London, 1904, ll. 3572–3574.

[32] *Ibid.*, ll. 3647–3649.

[33] Ed. K. S. Block (Early English Text Society), London, 1922, p. 229.

[34] The ending of the sixteenth-century *Respublica*, though related to the theme of the Four Daughters, is a very worldly affair. See Hope Traver, *op. cit.*, pp. 125 ff.

[35] See W. K. Smart, *Some English and Latin Sources and Parallels for the Morality of Wisdom*, Menasha, Wis., 1912, pp. 78 ff.

[36] *Ibid.*, pp. 26 ff.

[37] *The Macro Plays, ed. cit.*, l. 751.

[38] De Raaf's argument for the priority of the English text is favored by Creizenach, *Cambridge History of English Literature*, V(1910):59.

[39] J. Q. Adams, *Chief Pre-Shakespearean Dramas*, New York, 1924, p. 289, ll. 72–79.

[40] *Ed. cit.,* p. 174.

[41] J. M. Manly, *Specimens of the Pre-Shakespearean Drama*, Boston and London, 1897, I:365.

[42] *Ibid.*, I:370.

[43] See E. K. Chambers, *The Mediaeval Stage*, Oxford, 1903, II:181 ff., and A. W. Pollard, *English Miracle Plays, Moralities, and Interludes* (ed. 7), Oxford, 1923, pp. lii ff.

[44] See conclusion of Chap. I above.

[45] Gilbert Murray, *Five Stages of Greek Religion* (ed. 2), New York, 1925, p. 200.

[46] Friedrich Ueberweg, *A History of Philosophy*, tr. G. S. Morris, New York, 1909, p. 374.

HH

Notes to Chapter VI

TRAGEDY AND THE ENGLISH MORAL PLAY: SIXTEENTH CENTURY

[1] See *Magnyfycence,* ed. R. L. Ramsay (Early English Text Society), London, 1908, pp. clv, clxxxi.

[2] J. M. Manly, *Specimens of the Pre-Shakespearean Drama,* Boston and London, 1897, I:390, ll. 119–120.

[3] Ramsay, *op. cit.,* pp. cvi ff.

[4] *Nicomachean Ethics,* Bk. IV. See Ramsay, *op. cit.,* p. xxxiii.

[5] *Nicomachean Ethics,* I, 8. Translation of F. H. Peters (ed. 14), London, n. d., p. 21.

[6] *Ibid.,* p. 109.

[7] Ramsay, *op. cit.,* p. 6, ll. 152–154.

[8] *Ibid.,* p. 61, l. 1947.

[9] *Ibid.,* p. 79, ll. 2531–2539.

[10] *Ibid.,* p. 2, ll. 14–15.

[11] *The Dramatic Writings of John Bale,* ed. J. S. Farmer, London, 1907, p. 72.

[12] *King Johan,* ed. J. H. P. Pafford and W. W. Greg (Malone Society Reprints), 1931, p. 130, ll. 2557–2563.

[13] *The Poetical Works of Sir David Lyndsay,* ed. David Laing, Edinburgh, 1879, II:34, ll. 573–579.

[14] *Ad Lucilium Epistolae Morales,* ed. and tr. R. M. Gummere (Loeb Classical Library), London and New York, 1920, p. 438.

[15] A. Brandl, *Quellen des weltlichen Dramas in England vor Shakespeare,* Strassburg, 1898, p. 300.

[16] *Ibid.,* p. 301.

[17] Ed. R. A. McKerrow, *Materialien zur Kunde des älteren englischen Dramas,* XXXIII(1911):9, ll. 216–217.

[18] *Ibid.,* p. 10, ll. 235–236.

[19] *Ibid.,* p. 34, ll. 1052–1054.

[20] See E. K. Chambers, *The Mediaeval Stage,* Oxford, 1903, II:214, 223; E. N. S. Thompson, "The English Moral Plays," *Trans. Connecticut Acad. Arts and Sci.,* XIV(1910):381 ff.; R. W. Bond, *Early Plays from the Italian,* Oxford, 1911, pp. xciii ff.

[21] C. F. Tucker Brooke, *The Tudor Drama,* New York, 1911, p. 125.

[22] See the edition of the play by A. Brandl, *Jahrbuch der deutschen Shakespeare-Gesellschaft,* Vol. XXXVI (1900), introduction, p. 2.

[23] *Ibid.,* p. 59, l. 1748.

[24] *Ibid.,* p. 61, ll. 1837–1839.

[25] *Ibid.*, pp. 22, 61. Moros is called a "half-wit" and a "real idiot" by Barbara Swain, *Fools and Folly during the Middle Ages and the Renaissance,* New York, 1932, p. 167. In a discussion of the relationships of sin and folly this, it would seem, is peculiarly to miss the point.

[26] *Enough Is as Good as a Feast,* reprint by Seymour de Ricci (The Henry E. Huntington Facsimile Reprints, II), New York, 1920, sig. B. *recto* and *verso.*

[27] *Ibid.*, sig. B *verso.*

[28] *Ibid.*, sig. E 4 *verso.*

[29] *Ibid.*, sig. F *verso.*

[30] *The Tyde Taryeth No Man,* ed. Ernest Rühl, *Jahrbuch der deutschen Shakespeare-Gesellschaft,* XLIII(1907):27, l. 703.

[31] *All for Money,* ed. Ernest Vogel, *Jahrbuch der deutschen Shakespeare-Gesellschaft,* XL(1904):148, ll. 85–88.

[32] *Ibid.*, p. 148, ll. 91–98.

[33] Raymond Lebègue, *La Tragédie religieuse en France: Les Débuts (1514–1573),* Paris, 1929, p. 104.

[34] *King Johan, ed. cit.,* pp. xxii–xxiii.

[35] *Pacient and Meeke Grissill,* ed. R. B. McKerrow and W. W. Greg (Malone Society Reprints), 1909, ll. 1683–1684.

[36] The relationship of *Apius and Virginia* to Chaucer's *Phisiciens Tale* has been studied in detail by Otto Rumbaur, *Die Geschichte von Appius und Virginia in der englischen Litteratur,* Breslau, 1890, pp. 18 ff. For the background of Webster's *Appius and Virginia* see Rumbaur, pp. 28 ff., and F. L. Lucas, *The Complete Works of John Webster,* London, 1927, III:131 ff.

[37] III:44 ff.

[38] Ll. 6324–6394.

[39] *De Claris Mulieribus,* LVII; *Confessio Amantis,* VII, 5131–5306; *Fall of Princes,* II, 1345–1463, and III, 3011–3115.

[40] *Apius and Virginia,* ed. R. B. McKerrow and W. W. Greg (Malone Society Reprints), 1911, ll. 416–424.

[41] *Ibid.*, ll. 160–161.

[42] *Ibid.*, ll. 501–509.

[43] *Ibid.*, l. 1065.

[44] The relationship has been studied by Friedrich Brie, "*Horestes* von John Pickeryng," *Englische Studien,* XLVI(1912):66 ff.

[45] *The Recuyell of the Historyes of Troye,* ed. Oskar Summer, 1894, p. 684.

[46] *Ibid.*, p. 685.

[47] *The History of Horestes,* ed. J. S. Farmer (Tudor Facsimile Texts), 1910, sig. A 4 *verso.*

[48] *Ed. cit.,* p. 686.

[49] That is, definitely traced as a whole. See C. R. Baskervill, "Taverner's *Garden of Wisdom* and the *Apophthegmata* of Erasmus," *Stud. in Philol.,* XXIX (1932):158. Professor Baskervill's study is not concerned with the relationship between Taverner's work and Preston's play. So far as I know, this relationship has not hitherto been noticed.

[50] Fol. 17 of the first edition, 1539.

[51] Herodotus, III, 30 ff., and V, 25.

[52] It has recently been remarked that Johann Carion, in his *Chronicorum Libri Tres* (edition of 1550), deals with Cambyses in a way quite similar to Preston's. See D. C. Allen, "A Source for *Cambises*," *Mod. Lang. Notes*, XLIX(1934): 384 ff. Obviously there is a close relationship between Carion's and Taverner's accounts, though in Carion the incident of Sisamnes is dealt with last and in Taverner (as in Preston) it is dealt with first. This relationship and what lies behind it I have not had opportunity to investigate. Cambyses was well known in the Middle Ages as a horrible example of vicious life. See Arthur Lincke, "Kambyses in der Sage, Litteratur und Kunst des Mittelalters," *Aegyptiaca, Festschrift für Georg Ebers*, Leipsic, 1897, pp. 41 ff.

[53] *Cambyses King of Persia*, ed. J. S. Farmer (Tudor Facsimile Texts), 1910, sig. D *verso*. See also sig. F 3 *verso*.

[54] Phrasing as quoted for the Praxaspes incident may be found in the 1539 edition of *The Garden of Wisdom*, fols. 18 *verso* and 19 *verso*, and in the Tudor Facsimile Text of the play, sigs. C 3 *verso* and D *recto*.

[55] *Ed. cit.*, sig. F 4 *recto*.

Notes to Chapter VII

THE "MIRROR FOR MAGISTRATES"

[1] A poem of much the same kind as Skelton's is *The Lamentation of King James IV, slain at Flodden* (*ca.* 1513), which may be by Francis Dingley. Like Skelton's poem, it was later included in the *Mirror*. See W. F. Trench, *A Mirror for Magistrates: Its Origin and Influence*, Edinburgh, 1898, pp. 91, 105.

[2] *The Poetical Works of John Skelton, principally according to the Edition of the Rev. Alexander Dyce*, Boston, 1856, I:3 ff.

[3] In this London edition the poem is adapted in language to the uses of English rather than Scottish readers. It was later published in Lyndsay's dialect, once at Paris in 1558.

[4] They were edited with Cavendish's *Life of Cardinal Wolsey* by S. W. Singer, Chiswick, 1825.

[5] See D. A. Stauffer, *English Biography before 1700*, Cambridge, Mass., 1930, pp. 121 ff.

[6] *Ibid.*, p. 122, n.

[7] See Trench, *op. cit.*, pp. 10 ff.; also Lily B. Campbell, "The Suppressed Edition of *A Mirror for Magistrates*," *Huntington Library Bulletin*, VI(1934):6 ff.

[8] See W. A. Jackson, "Wayland's Edition of *The Mirror for Magistrates*," *The Library*, ser. 4, XIII(1933):155 ff. Wayland's folio numbering, which breaks at "Leaf clxiii" and concludes with a series beginning "Fol. i," indicates that he intended to make two volumes, including in the second volume the last two books of Lydgate and the tragedies of the English princes. For further description of the edition see Trench, *op. cit.*, p. 4, and *Lydgate's Fall of Princes*, ed. Henry Bergen (Early English Text Society), London, IV(1927):120–123.

[9] See Eveline I. Feasey, "The Licensing of the *Mirror for Magistrates*," *The Library*, ser. 4, III(1923):177 ff.; also Campbell, *op. cit.*

[10] See his "Epistle to the Reader," edition of 1559.

[11] See the *Mirror*, edition of 1587, fol. 259 *recto*, and Eveline I. Feasey, "William Baldwin," *Mod. Lang. Rev.*, XX(1925):417–418.

[12] Edition of 1559, sig. ¢ 3 *recto* and *verso;* edition of the complete *Mirror* by Joseph Haslewood, London, 1815, II:5–6. This passage and the following passages quoted from the *Mirror* are given in their original printed form. Reference is made to Haslewood for the convenience of the reader. Baldwin's first part of the *Mirror* appears in Haslewood as the text of 1587 collated with the texts of 1559, 1563, 1571, 1575, 1578, and 1610.

A few of the passages quoted from the *Mirror* in this chapter have been dealt with briefly in my study, "The *Mirror for Magistrates* and Elizabethan Tragedy," *Jour. Eng. and Germ. Philol.*, XXV(1926):66 ff.

[13] Edition of 1559, sig. A 2 *recto;* Haslewood, II:7–10.

[14] Edition of 1559, fol. iii *verso;* Haslewood, II:21.

15 For varying judgments concerning the authorship of stories in the *Mirror* of 1559, see Haslewood and Trench, *opp. cit.;* also chapter on the *Mirror* by J. W. Cunliffe, *Cambridge History of English Literature,* Vol. III. For a thorough discussion of the two tragedies listed but not printed, especially with respect to the significance of their temporary suppression, see Lily B. Campbell, "Humphrey Duke of Gloucester and Elianor Cobham His Wife in the *Mirror for Magistrates,*" *Huntington Library Bulletin,* V(1934):119 ff.

16 Edition of 1559, fol. xiiii *verso;* Haslewood, II:50.

17 Edition of 1559, fol. xl *recto;* Haslewood, II:148.

18 Edition of 1559, fol. v *recto;* Haslewood, II:26.

19 Edition of 1559, fol. xxiii *verso;* Haslewood, II:75.

20 See also the tragedies of Cambridge and Salisbury.

21 Edition of 1559, fol. xii *recto;* Haslewood, II:44.

22 Edition of 1559, fol. xliiii *recto;* Haslewood, II:157.

23 Edition of 1559, fol. xlvii *recto;* Haslewood, II:165.

24 Edition of 1559, fol. lxxxii *recto;* Haslewood, II:241.

25 Edition of 1559, fol. lxxxiii *recto;* Haslewood, II:219.

26 See Lily B. Campbell, *Shakespeare's Tragic Heroes: Slaves of Passion,* Cambridge, 1930, pp. 51 ff.

27 Edition of 1563, fol. cxxxviii *verso;* Haslewood, II:362.

28 There is an edition of 1571, which adds no new stories.

29 Edition of 1574, sig. *3 *verso;* Haslewood, I:3. In editing Higgins' *Mirror,* Haslewood collates the edition of 1587 only with those of 1575 and 1610, not with that of 1574. The edition of 1575, however, is a fairly close reprint of that of 1574.

30 For extensive discussion of the "affections" in connection with Elizabethan tragedy see Campbell, *Shakespeare's Tragic Heroes.*

31 Edition of 1574, fol. 17 *recto;* Haslewood, I:51.

32 Edition of 1574, fol. 36 *recto;* Haslewood, I:96.

33 Edition of 1574, fol. 67 *verso;* Haslewood, I:217.

34 This tragedy appears in the edition of 1575. Trench (p. 102) finds that some of the copies of the edition of 1574 have it.

35 Edition of 1575, fol. 77 *recto;* Haslewood, I:248–249.

36 Edition of 1610, p. 769; Haslewood, II:810.

Notes to Chapter VIII

THE PROGENY OF THE "MIRROR"

[1] An informative discussion of such poems is to be found in W. F. Trench, *A Mirror for Magistrates: Its Origin and Influence*, Edinburgh, 1898, pp. 106 ff. See all editions of Thomas Warton's *History of English Poetry*. General Relationships of tragical poetry and biography are discussed by D. A. Stauffer, *English Biography before 1700*, Cambridge, Mass., 1930, and general relationships of tragical poetry and moral philosophy by Lily B. Campbell, *Shakespeare's Tragic Heroes: Slaves of Passion*, Cambridge, 1930.

[2] Richard Johnson's *The Nine Worthies of London* (1592) is a glorification of certain famous London lord mayors, not at all tragic in spirit though apparitions of the worthies tell their stories in verse. John Dickenson's *Speculum Tragicum Regum, Principum, & Magnatum superioris saeculi celebriorum ruinas exitusque calamitosos breviter complectens* (1601; also 1602, 1603, and 1605), is a collection of tragical narratives from later British history written in Latin, almost wholly in prose, and without the moral force of the *Mirror*. Johnson's work is reprinted by Thomas Park, *The Harleian Miscellany*, VIII (London, 1811):437 ff. Dickenson's is described, and an excerpt from it is given, by A. B. Grosart in the introduction to his edition of *John Dickenson's Prose and Verse*. (*Occasional Issues of Unique or Very Rare Books*, V), 1878, pp. ix ff.

[3] See Celeste Turner, *Anthony Mundy: an Elizabethan Man of Letters*, Berkeley, Calif., 1928.

[4] I do not note any mention of Fortune before the complaint of Tryphon in the second book (sig. F 4).

[5] Sig. K 3 *recto*.

[6] Sig. L 2 *verso*.

[7] Trench mentions the *Testament and Tragedy of vmquhile King Henrie Stewart* and says, too, that its author (unnamed) probably did not know the *Mirror* (p. 98). All three of these tragedies are reprinted in *The Sempill Ballates: a Series of Historical, Political, and Satirical Scotish Poems, ascribed to Robert Sempill*, Edinburgh, 1872, pp. 8 ff., 50 ff., 133 ff. The first two had been previously reprinted by J. G. Dalyell, *Scotish Poems of the Sixteenth Century*, Edinburgh and London, 1801, pp. 223 ff. and 257 ff.

[8] *The Bischoppis Lyfe*, Sempill Ballates, p. 133.

[9] *Ane Complaint vpon Fortoun*, Sempill Ballates, p. 189.

[10] *The Harleian Miscellany*, ed. Thomas Park, IX(London, 1812):353.

[11] Title page.

[12] *The Rocke of Regard*, ed. J. Payne Collier, *Illustrations of Early English Poetry*, London, 1866–1870, II:16.

[13] *Ibid.*, p. 34.

[14] *Ibid.*, p. 41.

[15] For an account of this process see H. E. Rollins, "The Troilus-Cressida Story from Chaucer to Shakespeare," *Publ. Mod. Lang. Assoc.*, XXXII(1917):383 ff.

¹⁶ For these three poems see sigg. X 2 *verso*, Aa 4 *recto*, Bb 4 *recto*.

¹⁷ *Licia, ca.* 1593, p. 70.

¹⁸ From the epistle dedicatory of *The Theatre of Gods Judgements*, 1597.

¹⁹ I quote from a copy of this pamphlet which is in the Henry E. Huntington Library.

²⁰ I omit from consideration Richard Johnson's *The Nine Worthies of London* (1592), which, as I have said, is not at all tragic.

²¹ *The Complete Works in Verse and Prose of Samuel Daniel*, ed. A. B. Grosart (Spenser Society), 1885, I:96. The text is that of the quarto of 1623 collated with earlier editions.

²² In the medley of his *Challenge*, Churchyard also prints *The Earle of Murtons Tragedie, Sir Simon Burleis Tragedie* (again), and *A Tragicall Discourse of a dolorous Gentlewoman*, all with more or less inspiration from the *Mirror*. *Murtons Tragedie* is similar in spirit to *Burleis Tragedie*.

²³ See Sir Sidney Lee's introduction to the facsimile reprint of *Lucrece* (1594), Oxford, 1905, pp. 18 ff.

²⁴ Sig. K 4 *recto* of the 1593 edition.

²⁵ A tragedy of a good man in the later sophisticated vein is Christopher Middleton's *The Legend of Humphrey, Duke of Glocester* (1601). This is not autobiographical in form.

²⁶ Though it has a separate title page, *Sheretine and Mariana* is bound with certain songs and sonnets and other poems by the same author, all under the date 1622.

²⁷ P. 70 of the first edition, which is undated on the title page but has an epistle "To the Reader" dated "Septemb 8. 1593."

²⁸ Ed. F. J. Furnivall, *Ballads from Manuscripts. A Poore Mans Pittance, by Richard Williams* (Ballad Society), London, 1868. Samuel Rowlands' *Hell's Broke Loose* (1605) deals with another leader of religious insurrection, the German John Leyden. It begins with a ghostly complaint, but soon falls into narrative in the third person. It is more the story of an uprising than the tragedy of Leyden.

²⁹ Ed. J. Fry, *The Legend of Mary, Queen of Scots, and Other Ancient Poems*, London, 1810.

³⁰ Stanza 120 in the 1596 edition.

³¹ Sig. C *verso*.

³² Sig. I *recto*.

³³ See the dedication of the 1629 edition to the author's brother, Richard Hubert. It is also said there that the 1628 edition was unauthorized by the author and issued in mutilated form.

³⁴ The three stanzas quoted are Nos. 6, 7, and 12 of the 1629 edition.

³⁵ *The Complete Poems of Christopher Brooke*, ed. A. B. Grosart (*Miscellanies of the Fuller Worthies Library*, IV), 1872, p. 62.

³⁶ *Ibid.*, p. 78.

³⁷ *Ibid.*, p. 104.

³⁸ *Ibid.*, p. 105.

³⁹ *Ibid.*, p. 134.

[40] See Grosart's memorial-introduction, p. 31.

[41] See Chap. II above.

[42] The second part of *The French Academie*, 1594 (first part, 1586), p. 327; this passage is quoted by Lily B. Campbell, *op. cit.*, p. 19. See Professor Campbell's discussion of Elizabethan moral philosophy in this connection.

[43] *Il Principe*, Cap. XXV.

[44] No. 32 of the *Second Part*. The *First Part* of Cornwallis' *Essayes* was published in 1600.

[45] Sig. E *recto*.

Notes to Chapter IX

THE ESTABLISHMENT OF TRAGEDY UPON THE ELIZABETHAN STAGE

[1] Throughout this and the following chapter the dates given for plays are not those of printing unless so indicated.

[2] *Elizabethan Critical Essays*, ed. G. Gregory Smith, Oxford, 1904, I:80.

[3] *Ibid.*, I:177, 196.

[4] *Ibid.*, II:35.

[5] Preface, edition of 1560.

[6] Gregory Smith, *op. cit.*, I:19.

[7] Sig. A 6 *verso*.

[8] Fol. 194 *recto*.

[9] P. 231.

[10] Sig. M 4 *recto*.

[11] Edition of 1586, p. 229.

[12] See Lily B. Campbell, "Theories of Revenge in Renaissance England," *Mod. Philol.*, XXVIII(1931):281 ff. Professor Campbell argues well that revenge in Elizabethan tragedy has far more than Senecan significance.

[13] Pp. 153–160.

[14] P. 1.

[15] Reprint for the Spenser Society, 1883, pp. 12–13.

[16] *Ibid.*, p. 29.

[17] The Elizabethan philosophy of the passions in relation to tragedy is studied at length by Lily B. Campbell, *Shakespeare's Tragic Heroes: Slaves of Passion*, Cambridge, 1930; see particularly Chaps. VI, VII, and VIII. See also Hardin Craig, "Shakespeare's Depiction of Passions," *Philol. Quart.*, IV(1925):289 ff.

[18] Edition of 1586, p. 231.

[19] *Epistles, The First Volume*, p. 12.

[20] Fol. 1 *recto*.

[21] Fol. 2 *recto*.

[22] Fol. 2 *recto* and *verso*.

[23] Act III, sc. i.

[24] See *Early English Classical Tragedies*, ed. J. W. Cunliffe, Oxford, 1912, p. 302 (notes by H. A. Watt).

[25] *Ibid.*, p. 21.

[26] *Ibid.*, p. 61.

[27] Edition of Joseph Haslewood, London, 1815, II:223.

[28] Cunliffe, *op. cit.*, p. 64.

[29] *The Poetical Works of Sir William Alexander, Earl of Stirling*, ed. L. E. Kastner and H. B. Charlton, Manchester, 1921, I:clix, n.

[30] *Ibid.*, I:lvii.

[31] *Tragedie*, Venice, 1560, p. 6.

[32] Cunliffe, *op. cit.*, p. 157.

33 *Ibid.*, pp. lxxxiii ff., 307 ff.
34 *Ibid.*, p. 67.
35 *Ibid.*, pp. 314 ff.
36 *Ibid.*, p. 191.
37 J. W. Cunliffe, *The Influence of Seneca on Elizabethan Tragedy*, New York, 1907 (anastatic reprint of 1893 edition), pp. 52 ff., 130 ff.; *Early English Classical Tragedies*, pp. 326 ff.
38 Cunliffe, *Early English Classical Tragedies*, p. 287.
39 *Ibid.*, p. 223.
40 Mention may be made, however, of the sixteenth-century Latin play *Absalon*, extant in manuscript, which makes its Scriptural hero into a bloodthirsty Senecan tyrant. It may not be the *Absalon* by Thomas Watson of St. John's, Cambridge, alluded to by Ascham in *The Scholemaster*. There is no indication of its exact date. See F. S. Boas, *University Drama in the Tudor Age*, Oxford, 1914, pp. 63–64, 352 ff.
41 See G. B. Churchill, "Richard the Third up to Shakespeare," *Palaestra*, X (1900):332 ff. Professor Churchill's discussion of Legge's play is exhaustive.
42 *Ibid.*, pp. 328 ff.

Notes to Chapter X

THE ESTABLISHMENT OF TRAGEDY UPON THE ELIZABETHAN STAGE

(Continued)

[1] *The Works of Christopher Marlowe,* ed. C. F. Tucker Brooke, Oxford, 1925, p. 18, ll. 371–372.

[2] *Ibid.,* p. 21, ll. 487–490.

[3] See Chap. III above for discussion of the defensive attitude taken by Boccaccio when he praises heroic aspiration.

[4] For these works see *Tamburlaine the Great,* ed. U. M. Ellis-Fermor, London, 1930, pp. 17 ff., 305 ff.

[5] Among other places the document is to be found in C. F. Tucker Brooke, *The Life of Marlowe and Dido Queen of Carthage,* London, 1930, p. 98. See pp. 62 ff. for discussion.

[6] *The Plays and Poems of Robert Greene,* ed. J. Churton Collins, Oxford, 1905, I:89, ll. 352–354.

[7] *Selimus,* ed. W. Bang (Malone Society Reprints), 1908, ll. 350–351.

[8] *Caesar's Revenge,* ed. F. S. Boas (Malone Society Reprints), 1911, ll. 1972 ff.

[9] See E. K. Chambers, *The Elizabethan Stage,* Oxford, 1923, IV:22.

[10] *The Battle of Alcazar,* ed. W. W. Greg (Malone Society Reprints), 1907, ll. 1–2.

[11] Dating of *Locrine* involves consideration of its curious relationships with Spenser's *Complaints* (1591), Wilmot's *Tancred and Gismund* (1591), and *Selimus* (1591–1594). See E. K. Chambers, *The Elizabethan Stage,* Oxford, 1923, IV:26–27. The study by F. G. Hubbard there mentioned as in manuscript has been published as "Locrine and Selimus," *Shakespeare Studies,* Madison, Wis., 1916, pp. 16 ff.

[12] See T. Erbe, "Die Locrinesage und die Quellen des pseudo-shakespeareschen Locrine," *Studien zur englischen Philologie,* XVI(1904):70 ff.

[13] See my study, "John Higgins' *Mirror* and *Locrine*," *Mod. Philol.,* XXIII(1926): 307 ff. By permission of the editors of *Modern Philology,* matter from that study is incorporated in this chapter.

[14] *Locrine,* ed. R. B. McKerrow (Malone Society Reprints), 1908, ll. 289–290.

[15] *Ibid.,* ll. 1675–1679.

[16] *Mirror for Magistrates,* ed. Joseph Haslewood, London, 1815, I:51.

[17] For brief discussion of new arguments concerning questions of priority see R. A. Law, "Shakespeare's Earliest Plays," *Stud. in Philol.,* XXVIII(1931):99. See also C. A. Greer, "The York and Lancaster Quarto-Folio Sequence," *Publ. Mod. Lang. Assoc.,* XLVIII(1933):655 ff.

[18] *The Shakespeare Apocrypha,* ed. C. F. Tucker Brooke, Oxford, 1908, p. 189.

[19] See *The Works of Thomas Kyd,* ed. F. S. Boas, Oxford, 1901, p. xxxi.

[20] *Ibid.,* p. 343.

[21] *The Complete Works in Verse and Prose of Samuel Daniel,* ed. A. B. Grosart, 1885–1896, III:24–25.

[22] For still another report of the murder see *The School of Shakespeare,* ed. Richard Simpson, New York, 1878, II:220 ff.

[23] *The Works of Christopher Marlowe,* ed. Tucker Brooke, p. 166, ll. 632–641.

[24] *Ibid.,* p. 194, ll. 1478–1480.

[25] *Shakespeare's Library,* ed. W. C. Hazlitt, London, 1875, V:271.

[26] *Ibid.,* p. 277.

[27] *Ibid.,* p. 315.

[28] *The Works of Christopher Marlowe,* ed. Tucker Brooke, p. 382, ll. 2537–2538.

[29] *Shakespeare's Library,* ed. Hazlitt, V:101.

[30] *Ibid.,* p. 117.

[31] See G. B. Churchill, "Richard the Third up to Shakespeare," *Palaestra,* X (1900):409 ff.

[32] *Ibid.,* pp. 159–160, 404 ff.

[33] See E. K. Chambers, *William Shakespeare,* Oxford, 1930, I:304.

[34] See H. R. Patch, *The Goddess Fortuna in Mediaeval Literature,* Cambridge, Mass., 1927, pp. 53–54.

[35] *Holinshed's Chronicles of England, Scotland and Ireland,* London, 1807 (reprint of 1587 edition), II:855.

Notes to Chapter XI

CONCLUSION

[1] *Shakespearean Tragedy* (ed. 2), London, 1920, p. 7.

[2] By permission of the editors, matter in this and in the following section of the chapter has been taken from my essay, "Tragic Prodigality of Life," *Essays in Criticism, Second Series, Univ. Calif. Publ. Eng.*, IV(1934):185 ff.

[3] *De Republica Anglorum*, ed. L. Alston, Cambridge, 1906, pp. 105–106.

[4] *The Mirror of Minds or, Barclays Icon animorum*, tr. Thomas May, 1633, p. 81.

[5] *Somniorum Synesiorum Omnis Generis Insomnia Explicantes, Libri IIII*, Basel, 1585, pp. 371–372. A part of this passage has been translated by W. B. Rye, *England as Seen by Foreigners in the Days of Elizabeth and James the First*, London, 1865, p. xlix.

[6] Translation as given by W. B. Rye, *op. cit.*, p. 70.

[7] Quotations are from the last two scenes of Act V. The text is that of C. F. Tucker Brooke, *The Shakespeare Apocrypha*, Oxford, 1908, pp. 415 ff.

[8] Here I am indebted to P. H. Frye, *Romance and Tragedy*, Boston, 1922. The curious reader may discover differences as well as agreements in our views, however. The expression "tragic qualm," which I use more than once in this chapter, I borrow gratefully from Professor Frye (pp. 146 ff.).

[9] *Op. cit.*, p. 32.

[10] *Ibid.*, p. 35.

[11] *Ibid.*, p. 37.

[12] *Ibid.*, pp. 36–37.

INDEX

Accius, 12

Adam (or Adam and Eve), 74, 85, 86, 131, 132, 133, 185, 200, 201, 225, 421

Address of the Lost Soul to the Body, 36

Aeschylus, 1, 5, 7, 12, 124, 126, 158, 159, 343, 439, 441, 446; *Agamemnon,* 90–91, 148; Orestean trilogy, 9–10, 261; *Prometheus,* 10, 20, 174, 175, 439

Agamemnon, 10, 90–91, 93, 97, 100, 260, 261

Albumazar, 106

Alcibiades, 97, 98–99, 100–101, 133, 155, 167, 301, 424

Alexander Severus, 26

Alexander the Great, 22, 134, 135, 238, 272, 295, 391, 425

Alphonsus Emperour of Germany, 397

Ambition: in Elizabethan moral philosophy, 343–346, 349–350; on the Elizabethan stage, 355–356, 357–359, 362, 363–366, 368–390. *See also* Contempt of the World; Fortune

Andalò di Negro, 87, 104

Antisthenes, 21

Antony, Mark, 96, 419, 449, 450

Apius and Virginia, 251–258, 259, 270, 340

Aquino, Maria d', 140

Arden of Feversham, 317, 398, 399–400, 434

Arian heresy, the, 175

Aristophanes, *Frogs,* 12, 158

Aristotle, 1, 22, 39, 56, 82, 93, 124, 138, 199, 218, 219, 222, 223; *Nicomachean Ethics,* 217

Arte of English Poesie, by George Puttenham (?), 341–342

Arthur, King, 92, 166, 302, 362, 363

Asceticism: Boccacesque, 70, 83; Buddhistic, 62; Gnostic, 33; Manichean, 35; Monastic, 34; Neo-Platonic, 23. *See also* Contempt of the World

Ascham, Roger, 343

Astrology: the moon, 27, 28, 105–108, 109, 452; the stars, 26–27, 87, 102, 104, 105–106, 107, 108, 109–110, 111, 112, 114, 115, 116, 118, 127, 128, 289, 290, 443

Augustine, St., 33, 34, 110, 111, 119, 120; in Petrarch's *Secretum,* 48–51

Augustus (Octavius Caesar), 26, 75, 80, 445, 449

Aurelius, Marcus, 16, 17, 18

Averroës, 121

Bacon, Francis, 337; *Of Fortune,* 338

Baines, Richard, 372

Baldwin, William, 288, 294–295, 300, 303, 304, 315, 319, 325, 336, 342; *Mirror for Magistrates,* 55, 234, 278–279, 280, 282, 283, 286, 291, 298, 310, 311, 378; *Treatise of Morall Phylosophie,* 55–56, 279. See also *Mirror for Magistrates*

Bale, John, 224; *Chefe Promyses of God,* 225; *Kynge Johan,* 225–226, 248–249; *Thre Lawes of Nature, Moses, and Christ,* 225

Bandello, Matteo, 312

Barclay, John, *Icon Animorum,* 429–430

Barthélemy, Nicolas, *Christus Xylonicus,* 173

Beard, Thomas, 318; *Theatre of Gods Judgements,* 317

Beaton, David Cardinal, 273, 310

Bernard of Morlaix, *De Contemptu Mundi,* 41, 63

Bernard, St., 61, 81–82

Bible, the, 37; *Ecclesiasticus,* 37, 179; *Job,* 37; *Psalms,* 192; *Wisdom of Solomon,* 37

[479]